STRATEGIC MANAGEMENT

A Focus on Process

Second Edition

SAMUEL C. CERTO
Rollins College

J. PAUL PETER
University of Wisconsin-Madison

IRWIN

Burr Ridge, Illinois

This symbol indicates that the paper in this book is made of recycled paper. Its fiber content exceeds the recommended minimum of 50% waste paper fibers as specified by the EPA.

The previous edition of this text was published by McGraw-Hill, Inc. under the title, *Strategic Management: Concepts and Applications.*

Publisher: William Schoof
Project editor: Karen J. Nelson
Production manager: Mary Jo Parke
Cover designer: Mercedes Santos
Compositor: Monotype Composition Company, Inc.
Printer: R. R. Donnelley & Sons Company

Library of Congress Cataloging-in-Publication Data

Certo, Samuel C.
Strategic management : a focus on process / Samuel C. Certo, J. Paul Peter. 2nd ed.
p. cm.
Previously published as part of Strategic management : concepts and applications.
ISBN 0-256-14120-7
1. Strategic planning. I. Peter, J. Paul. II. Title.
HD30.28.C42 1993
658.4'012—dc20 92-36103

Printed in the United States of America

3 4 5 6 7 8 9 0 DOC 9 8 7 6 5 4

PREFACE

We are pleased that the first edition of our text was found by both instructors and students to be a valuable learning tool. Although the second edition of the text includes several improvements, its basic goal remains the same and mirrors the purpose of the capstone course in the business curriculum. This goal is to provide students with an integrative learning experience that helps them develop strategic management knowledge and skills. We believe that for students to become effective strategic managers they first need to learn strategic management concepts and to practice applications of these concepts.

We also believe that a strategic management text should do more than simply discuss theoretical concepts and their applications—leaving students to relate the former to the latter. It is our view that a strategic management text should actually help students bridge the gap between theoretical concepts and how those concepts should be applied. The following sections discuss how *Strategic Management: A Focus on Process* bridges this gap through the combination of a clear, organized, pragmatic presentation of strategic management theory and a unique array of related student learning activities that stress how the theory should be applied.

STRATEGIC MANAGEMENT THEORY: AN EMPHASIS ON CLARITY AND PRAGMATISM

This text includes five sections devoted to concepts of strategic management. These concepts sections and related chapters are organized around the strategic management model shown on page xviii.

Section One: An Overview of Strategic Management

This section provides a survey of strategic management and a framework for the remainder of the textual material. After reading Chapter 1, students should

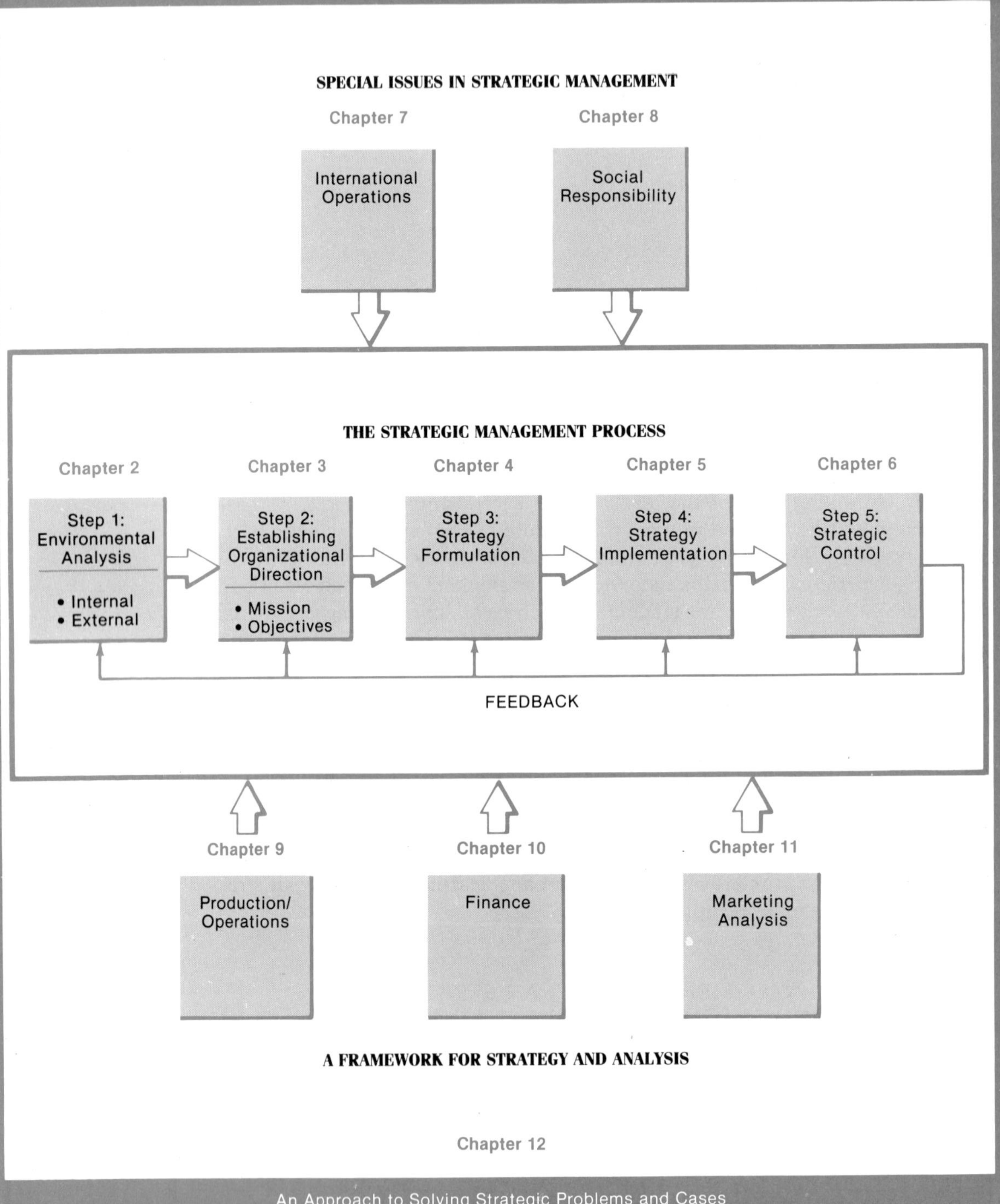

Strategic Management Model Used in This Text.

have a clear understanding of the nature and scope of strategic management and the strategic management process.

Section Two: The Strategic Management Process

In this section we discuss the five major steps in the strategic management process. These steps include environmental analysis (Chapter 2), establishing organizational direction (Chapter 3), strategy formulation (Chapter 4), strategy implementation (Chapter 5), and strategic control (Chapter 6).

Section Three: Special Issues in Strategic Management

Although the previous sections include the major topics commonly discussed in strategic management courses, we believe at least two other areas require special consideration. These areas are international operations (Chapter 7) and social responsibility (Chapter 8). We have devoted an entire chapter to each of these topics because of their important influence on strategic management decision making and the need for specialized knowledge of these topics in a variety of strategic management problems and cases. These topics have also been recommended for special emphasis in modern management education by the American Assembly of Collegiate Schools of Business (AACSB).

Section Four: Foundations for Strategic Management

We have found in teaching upper-level undergraduate and graduate courses that students often forget a good deal of information from previous foundation courses. Since they may have sold their textbooks from these courses or have no readily available source of information on strategic business areas, we have included foundation chapters on the functional areas of operations (Chapter 9), finance (Chapter 10), and marketing (Chapter 11). The chapters should provide students with a refresher course on major topics, issues, and techniques in these areas that can be useful in analyzing strategic management problems and cases. Information on these and other functional areas is also included throughout the text.

Section Five: A Framework for Strategic Analysis

While we recognize that no single approach can be universally applied to all strategic management cases and problems, we are also mindful that students often need a framework for approaching case and problem analysis. A sound framework is particularly important when students first begin analyzing major strategic management cases and problems. For this reason we have included an extended discussion of a general approach to case and problem analysis in Chapter 12. This chapter on the process of case and problem analysis is designed to provide another bridge between concepts and application. Even if students are not asked to analyze cases in a strategic management course, this chapter can be extremely useful in helping them to solve actual strategic management problems.

APPLYING STRATEGIC MANAGEMENT THEORY: SPECIAL LEARNING EXERCISES

Each chapter in our text contains a variety of pedagogical aids to enhance student learning and to facilitate the transfer of concepts to application. Each major pedagogical aid is called a "Highlight," and each text chapter contains one or more of the following types:

- *Illustrative Examples* that extend text material and provide illustrations of the application of strategic management concepts to well-known organizations.
- *Skills Modules* that challenge students to apply strategic management concepts to real organizational situations. These short exercises follow selected topics in the chapters, thus affording students directed activities for increasing their understanding and ability to apply strategic management concepts.
- *Checklists* that itemize major issues to be addressed in analyzing strategic management problems and cases. These checklists are keyed to the topics covered in each chapter and offer students a starting point for applying strategic management concepts to case situations.
- *Applications* (at the end of each theory chapter) that provide a short case focused on one or more topics covered in the chapter. They include specific questions for analysis, thus offering students an opportunity to apply chapter material in a directed way. The Applications help students reach a better understanding of strategic management concepts and their application, and prepares them for longer, more involved strategic management cases.

CHANGES IN THE SECOND EDITION

We have made two important changes in the second edition in an attempt to better meet the needs of strategic management educators and students. These include:

1. Recognizing the importance of small businesses to our economy and that many students' careers will be spent in smaller organizations, we have increased our emphasis on this topic in text material and highlights.
2. Recognizing the importance of timeliness for enhancing student interest in text material, we have provided a variety of new examples, highlights and applications and have provided increased emphasis on such timely topics as the role of a board of directors in organizations.

INSTRUCTOR'S RESOURCE PACKAGE

This text is supported by a comprehensive Instructor's Resource package. Carefully developed to meet the unique demands of strategic management educators, the package consists of the following items:

- *Instructor's Manual.* The instructor's manual for this text has been entirely prepared by the text authors. In essence, the manual was specifically designed to provide exceptional instructional support for anyone using this text to teach a course in strategic management or business policy. The following is a discussion of the major sections of the instructor's manual:

  1. *Suggestions for Teaching Strategic Management.* This introductory section provides insight about how the strategic management (or business policy) course can be taught. Discussion focuses on various teaching tools like cases, lectures, exams, films, speakers, simulations, projects, and readings. A special section on how to use student study teams discusses team assignments, progress reporting, peer group evaluations, presentation evaluations, and suggestions on using team cases or projects. This section ends with discussion of course design and grading.
  2. *Materials Supporting Text Chapters.* The second major section of the instructor's manual presents several ingredients to support each text chapter. These ingredients include an author's overview or summary of a chapter, chapter outline, key concepts and issues for classroom discussion, and detailed suggestions on how to use chapter Highlights (Illustrative Examples, Skills Modules, and Applications at the end of each chapter) within the classroom.
  3. *Transparency Program.* Seventeen transparency masters are available to adopters of *Strategic Management: A Focus on Process.* These masters focus on key theoretical concepts and issues in strategic management. Most are reproductions of selected graphics in the text.
  4. *Test Item File.* Section 4 of the instructor's manual is a comprehensive test bank of about 350 true/false and multiple choice items. It is also available on Irwin's Computerized Testing Software.

- *Strategic Management Casebook Selected Cases in Strategic Management,* second edition, also by Certo and Peter, is available as a set of comprehensive strategic management cases that can be used to supplement this text. The casebook offers an array of cases that are organized by the same major section titles as this text. In essence, the casebook and this theory-oriented text were carefully designed for efficient and effective use within the same course. A comprehensive *Case Enrichment Portfolio* provides exceptional instructional support for professors who use this casebook.

Samuel C. Certo
J. Paul Peter

ACKNOWLEDGMENTS

We have been very pleased with the widespread acceptance and support of the two editions of our text, *Strategic Management: Concepts and Applications*. This is a comprehensive, hardback text designed for strategic management or business policy courses at either the undergraduate or graduate level. In general, this text is comprised of major sections focusing on strategic management theory and strategic management cases.

Publication of this separate paperback text is the result of feedback primarily from colleagues who have reviewed our hardback text with cases and would like to use the strategic management theory section without the case portion. Thus, this paperback, designed to meet the educational needs of these instructors, is the strategic management theory portion of our hardback text.

The positive feedback we have received relating to this project has been extremely satisfying. As with any project of this magnitude, however, such feedback is actually the result of the efforts of several people and not simply due to the work of the authors. At this time we are pleased to recognize the efforts of the many people who have made valuable contributions to this project.

In particular, we would like to recognize the valuable role which our reviewers played in this project. Their dedication to high teaching standards and professionalism provided us with many worthwhile ideas which helped us to make our text a more efficient and effective learning instrument. Our review team is listed below.

Bruce Charnov, *Hofstra University*
V. C. Doherty, *Wayne State University*
James H. Donnelly, Jr., *University of Kentucky*
Bruce Fisher, *Northeastern Illinois University*
Robert Goldberg, *Northeastern University*
James R. Harris, *Florida State University*
Calvin Kellogg, *Illinois State University*
Rose Knotts, *North Texas State University*

Daniel Kopp, *Southwest Missouri State University*
Edwin C. Leonard, Jr., *Indiana University, Purdue University at Fort Wayne*
William Litzinger, *University of Texas at San Antonio*
Martin K. Marsh, *California State University, Bakersfield*
Shiv Sawhney, *Quinnipiac College*
Marilyn Taylor, *University of Kansas*
Robert Vichas, *Old Dominion University*
Wendy Vittori, *Northeastern University*
Stanley Willing, *St. Francis College*

Finally, we extend thanks to our colleagues and students for all they have taught us, as well as the many strategic management educators who responded to our research surveys and provided other inputs into the project. We thank Bill Schoof and his staff at Austen Press for making this edition a reality. And, of course, we thank our families and friends for their encouragement and tolerance during the preparation of this work.

S.C.C.
J.P.P

ABOUT THE AUTHORS

Samuel C. Certo is presently Dean and Professor of Management at the Roy E. Crummer Graduate School of Business, Rollins College, Winter Park, Florida. His current teaching responsibilities include an array of management courses with special emphasis on business strategy as well as a strategy-focused computer simulation course. He has been actively involved in management education at the college and university levels for over fifteen years. Dr. Certo's numerous publications include articles for such journals as the *Academy of Management Review, The Journal of Experiential Learning and Simulation,* and *Training.* He has also written several successful textbooks, including *Principles of Modern Management* and *Introduction to Business.* A past chairman of the Management Education and Development Division of the Academy of Management, he was recently honored by that group with its Excellence of Leadership Award. Dr. Certo has also served as president of the Association for Business Simulation and Experiential Learning, as associate editor for *Simulation and Games,* and as a review board member of the *Academy of Management Review.* His consulting experience has been extensive.

J. Paul Peter is James R. McManus-Bascom Professor in Marketing at the University of Wisconsin—Madison. He taught at Indiana State University, Washington University, and Ohio State University before joining the faculty at Wisconsin in 1980. His articles on consumer behavior, marketing theory, and research methodology are frequently cited in the marketing literature. He was awarded the prestigious William O'Dell Award from the *Journal of Marketing Research* in 1986. Dr. Peter has co-authored several books, including *A Preface to Marketing Management, Marketing Management: Knowledge and Skills,* and *Consumer Behavior: Marketing Strategy Perspectives;* he is co-editor of *Measurement Readings for Marketing Research.* He has served as editor of AMA Professional Publications and as editor of *JMR's* Measurement Section. He has served on the Editorial Review Boards of the *Journal of Marketing Research, Journal of Consumer Research, Journal of Marketing* and *Journal of Business Research* and has been a consultant for a variety of corporations as well as the Federal Trade Commission.

CONTENTS IN BRIEF

CONTENTS

NOTE TO THE INSTRUCTOR:

Austen Press texts are marketed and distributed by Richard D. Irwin, Inc. For assistance in obtaining supplementary material for this and other Austen Press titles, please contact your Irwin sales representative or the customer service division of Richard D. Irwin at (800) 323–4560.

STRATEGIC MANAGEMENT

A Focus on Process

SECTION ONE

An Overview of Strategic Management

This section provides an overview of strategic management and a framework for the remainder of the text. Its major purpose is to acquaint you with the nature and scope of strategic management and its development as a critical area of management education. After careful study of this section, you should develop a fundamental understanding of the strategic management process and an appreciation for the importance of strategic management in running successful organizations.

CHAPTER 1

Introduction to Strategic Management

- Philip Morris Jabs at Its Weakened Rival[1]
- Eastern Air Retreats from Fare Cuts on New Routes[2]
- Japan's Next Push into U.S. Markets[3]
- People Aren't Laughing at U.S. Sprint Anymore[4]

These headlines capture the glamor and excitement of a successful career in the business world. The area of study you are about to explore through this text, strategic management, explains why the decisions behind such headlines are made and helps you prepare for an upper-level management position. You will undoubtedly find strategic management interesting and exciting, and mastery of this area will be both personally and professionally rewarding.

[1] Betsy Morris, "Philip Morris Jabs at Its Weakened Rival," *The Wall Street Journal*, July 21, 1989, p. B1.
[2] Asra Q. Nomani, "Eastern Air Retreats from Fare Cuts on New Routes," *The Wall Street Journal*, July 20, 1989, p. B1.
[3] Brian Dumaine, "Japan's Next Push into U.S. Markets," *Fortune*, September 26, 1988, pp. 135–144.
[4] William C. Symonds, John J. Keller, and Tim Smart, "People Aren't Laughing at U.S. Sprint Anymore," *Business Week*, July 31, 1989, pp. 82–86.

This book focuses on the theoretical concepts used in strategic management in organizations. In addition to explaining theory, however, it emphasizes the application of these concepts to actual strategic management situations.

Chapter 1 offers an overview of the subject of strategic management. First we outline the evolution of strategic management as a field of study. Then we provide a formal definition of the subject and a description of how it is applied and what benefits accrue to organizations that practice it. Next we briefly trace the steps in the process of strategic management, consider several special topics in the field, examine how three major business functions are related to the strategic management process, and review the case analysis approach to learning the subject. Finally, we suggest the phases through which the strategic management process usually develops in an organization.

THE EVOLUTION OF STRATEGIC MANAGEMENT AS AN AREA OF STUDY

The study of strategic management first took shape after the Ford Foundation and the Carnegie Corporation sponsored research into the business school curriculum in the 1950s. A synopsis of this research, called the Gordon–Howell report, recommended that business education be made broader in nature and include a capstone course in an area called business policy.[5]

The proposed business policy course was to have very distinctive characteristics. Instead of presenting students with business problems for analysis in such specific areas as marketing or finance, it would emphasize the development of skill in identifying, analyzing, and solving real-world problems in a wide range of substantive business areas. It would thus give students the opportunity to exercise qualities of judgment that are not explicitly called for in any other course. The report also recommended that the new policy course concentrate on integrating knowledge already acquired in other courses and on developing further the student's skill in using that knowledge.

The Gordon–Howell report gained widespread acceptance. By the early 1970s, most schools of business had a course called business policy within their curriculum. As time passed, however, the initial focus of the course was widened. The business policy course came to include consideration of the total organization and its environment. For example, social responsibility and ethics, as well as the potential impact of political, legislative, and economic factors on the successful operation of an organization, became topics of concern.

This newer, broader emphasis prompted leaders in the field to change the name of the course from business policy to strategic management.[6] This text has been carefully designed to reflect the more current emphasis and to serve as a foundation for students to learn concepts that are both "state of the art"

[5] R. A. Gordon and J. E. Howell, *Higher Education for Business*, New York: Columbia University Press, 1959.

[6] M. Leontiades, "The Confusing Words of Business Policy," *Academy of Management Review*, January 1982, p. 46.

and pragmatic. After completing this text and course, students should have acquired many of the skills listed in Table 1.1.

THE NATURE OF STRATEGIC MANAGEMENT

Strategic management as a concept has evolved over time[7] and will continue to evolve. As a result there is noticeable lack of consensus about precisely what the term means.[8] Despite this disagreement, strategic management is carried on in most organizations today—and most organizations that practice it benefit significantly.

A Definition of Strategic Management

In this text, *strategic management* is defined as a continuous, iterative process aimed at keeping an organization as a whole appropriately matched to its environment. The following excerpt from a message by Cornell Maier, the chairman of the board and chief executive officer of Kaiser, provides a good indication of how seriously strategic management can and should be taken in organizations:

> We have begun implementation of our strategic plan for the decade. Two years in formulation, the plan calls for Kaiser to identify its most promising business and to focus its resources on long-term development and profitability. Increased resources will be allocated to business lines where the company believes it has existing strengths, such as superior technology, low costs, or strong market positions.[9]

Without two years of planning, Kaiser might well have floundered, uncertain of where it should be headed.

The definition of strategic management we have proposed emphasizes that managers engage in a series of steps. These steps, which we will discuss individually in the following pages, are: performing an environmental analysis, establishing organizational direction, formulating organizational strategy, implementing organizational strategy, and exercising strategic control. Additional information on each of these steps will appear throughout this text.

The definition also suggests that the strategic management process is continuous—it never really stops within the organization. Although different strategic management activities may receive more or less emphasis and may be pursued with different intensity at different times, management should virtually always be focusing or reflecting on some aspect of strategic management.

The term "iterative" in the definition of strategic management indicates

[7] Peter M. Ginter and Donald D. White, "A Social Learning Approach to Strategic Management: Toward a Theoretical Foundation," *Academy of Management Review*, April 1982.
[8] H. Igor Ansoff, *Implanting Strategic Management*, Englewood Cliffs, N.J.: Prentice-Hall, 1984.
[9] Kaiser Annual Report, 1982, p. 6.

TABLE 1.1 Skills Emphasized in a Strategic Management Course

STUDENTS WHO COMPLETE THIS COURSE IN STRATEGIC MANAGEMENT SHOULD BE ABLE TO:

1. Size up quickly and accurately the situation presented by identifying the core problems and/or issues and by evaluating management's strategy in relation to the environment, top-management values, societal expectations, the financial position of the organization, and so on.
2. Analyze facts to identify opportunities and threats in the environment and the strengths and weaknesses of the organization so as to be able to appraise managerial behavior and/or prepare a situation audit useful in formulating, evaluating, and implementing policies and strategies.
3. Identify strategies that are appropriate to each situation and evaluate alternatives in terms of all relevant criteria; top-management values; societal expectations; internal financial, production, and technical capabilities; and so on.
4. Recommend specific courses of action by means of (when appropriate) detailed strategies and plans, taking into account organizational changes, financial requirements and implications, timing, personnel relations, and so forth.
5. Sharpen analytical skills acquired in functional areas—production, finance, marketing, operations research, personnel, and so forth—in dealing with problems of the total organization. These skills integrate the knowledge a student has so that he or she can deal with a total enterprise.
6. Link theory and practice by developing an understanding of management tools and their limitations and applying this understanding in particular problem-solving situations. Within the strategic management area, decision makers can use a variety of tools. The student who can choose the most appropriate tools for analysis and accurately determine how far to employ them in a particular situation has a highly valuable and marketable skill.
7. Prepare written analyses of cases and recommendations for action. This presents an opportunity for both the instructor and the student to improve their writing, a skill that has high market value.
8. Improve skills in making presentations—both speech-making and visual aid skills. There is a definite art to doing both well, and the most effective approach to each in the world of business and government differs from those needed in the academic world. Career advancement can be furthered by learning these skills, too.

Source: Based on George A. Steiner, John B. Miner, and Edmund R. Gray, *Management Policy and Strategy* (New York: Macmillan Publishing Company, 1986), pp. 9–10.

that the process of strategic management starts with the first step, ends with the last step—and then begins again with the first step. Strategic management, then, consists of a series of steps that are repeated in cyclical fashion.

The last part of the definition of strategic management states that the purpose of strategic management is to ensure that an organization as a whole is appropriately matched to its environment—that is, to its operational surroundings. Organizational environments are constantly changing, and organizations must be modified accordingly to ensure that organizational goals can be attained. Legislation affecting the organization, changes in the labor supply available to it, and actions taken by its competition are examples of changes within the organization's environment that are normally addressed by management.

Although the definition of strategic management seems clear and simple, actually implementing the process in an organization is usually very complicated. Some of the strategic management responsibilities that contribute to this complexity are outlined in Table 1.2.

WHO IS INVOLVED IN STRATEGIC MANAGEMENT?

Overall, top management, boards of directors, and planning staff tend to be those positions that have the most significant involvement and influence in the strategic management process of organizations.[10] The following sections discuss, in more detail, the relationships of each of these positions to the strategic management process.

Top Management's Involvement in Strategic Management

Traditionally, top management has made strategic decisions for organizations. The term "top management" refers to a relatively small group of people who are at the uppermost levels of the organization. Titles generally considered as top management positions include president, chief executive officer (CEO), vice president, and executive vice president.

The strategic management process of today tends to be dominated by the CEO, the executive who is responsible for and held accountable for the performance of the organization as a whole. Although this dominance is generally apparent in organizations of all sizes, it is especially apparent in smaller organizations where the CEO might also be an owner/entrepreneur. CEO dominance may diminish somewhat in medium-sized companies and somewhat further in large companies because CEOs tend to face broader and more comprehensive job duties proportionate to a greater number of people involved in the strategic management process.

The CEO is usually considered responsible and accountable for the success of the strategic management process. This does not necessarily mean, however, that the CEO carries out the strategic management process independently. Instead, the CEO who is successful in this area generally designs a strategic management process that involves members from many different organizational areas and levels. For example, in addition to the CEO, organizations commonly enlist production specialists, marketing personnel, and divisional managers in making strategic decisions.

According to George Grune, chairman of the board and CEO of Reader's Digest Association, allowing others to participate in the strategic management

[10] Henry Mintzberg, "Strategy-Making in Three Modes," *California Management Review,* Winter 1973, pp. 44–53.

TABLE 1.2 Strategic Management Responsibilities of Managers

1. *Establishing the mission*—deciding on the business or businesses that the company or division should engage in and other fundamentals that will guide and characterize the business, such as continuous growth. A mission is usually enduring and timeless.
2. *Formulating a company philosophy*—establishing the beliefs, values, attitudes, and unwritten guidelines that add up to "the way we do things around here."
3. *Establishing policies*—deciding on plans of action to guide the performance of all major activities in carrying out strategy in accordance with company philosophy.
4. *Setting objectives*—deciding on achievement targets within a defined time range. Objectives are narrower in scope than the mission, and are designed to aid in making operational plans for carrying out strategy.
5. *Developing strategy*—developing concepts, ideas, and plans for achieving objectives successfully and meeting and beating the competition. Strategic planning is part of the total planning process that includes management and operation planning.
6. *Planning the organization structure*—developing the plan of organization and the activities that help people work together to perform activities in accordance with strategy, philosophy, and policies.
7. *Providing personnel*—recruiting, selecting, and developing people to fill the positions in the organization plan.
8. *Establishing procedures*—determining and prescribing how all important and recurrent activities will be carried out.
9. *Providing facilities*—providing the plant, equipment, and other physical facilities required to carry on the business.
10. *Providing capital*—making sure the business has the money and credit needed for working capital and physical facilities.
11. *Setting standards*—establishing measures of performance that will enable the business to best achieve its long-term objectives successfully.
12. *Establishing management programs and operational plans*—developing programs and plans governing activities and the use of resources that, when carried out in accordance with established strategy, policies, procedures, and standards, will enable people to achieve particular objectives. These are phases of the total planning process, which includes strategic planning.
13. *Providing control information*—supplying facts and figures to help people follow the strategy, policies, procedures, and programs; to keep alert to forces at work inside and outside the business; to measure overall company performance against established plans and standards.
14. *Activating people*—commanding and motivating people to act in accordance with philosophy, policies, procedures, and standards in carrying out the plans of the company.

Source: Marvin Bower, *The Will to Manage: Corporate Success Through "Programmed Management"* (New York: McGraw-Hill, 1966), pp. 17–18. Reprinted by permission.

process, even to the extent of involving lower-level line managers, generally results in more realistic goals, objectives, and strategies. In this situation, others suggest to top management how their areas should be integrated within the strategic management of the organization as a whole.[11] Grune maintains

[11] Roy Forman, "Strategic Planning and the Chief Executive," *Long Range Planning* 21, August 1988, pp. 57–64.

that such participation and involvement builds organizational commitment to achieve established goals and to implement those strategies that have been selected.[12]

The Board of Directors' Involvement in Strategic Management

The business which exists in corporate form has a board of directors, elected by stockholders and given ultimate authority and responsibility. The board guides the affairs of the corporation and protects stockholder interests.[13] "Inside board members" are those people who already work for the organization in some other capacity; "outside board members" work for other organizations. Boards typically elect a chairperson who is responsible for overseeing board business, and they form standing committees which meet regularly to conduct their business. A list of standing committees and their responsibilities within a typical board of directors is presented in Table 1.3

In general, the board of directors should be viewed as a scarce resource to be used to perform those activities that it can uniquely and best contribute to organizational goal attainment.[14] As Table 1.3 implies, board duties have historically focused on issues like financial auditing and compensation, with little or no emphasis on the strategic management of an organization. Over the last few years, however, stronger interest has developed in expanding the duties of the board to make it much more active in the strategic management process.[15]

Most authorities on corporate governance argue that greater board involvement in the strategic management process should be used as a means to improve the quality of strategic decision making, enabling them to better discharge their responsibility to represent stockholder interests.[16] One means being used to expand this involvement is the addition of a strategy committee to the board's list of standing committees.[17] A strategy committee is a board committee that works with the CEO to develop corporate goals as well as strategies to be used to reach those goals. As part of its duties, the strategy committee commonly audits various components of an organization's strategic management process in order to make it more effective and efficient. A series of questions that the strategy committee can pursue in conducting such an audit is presented in Table 1.4.

Overall, involvement of boards of directors in the strategic management of organizations seems advisable. One barrier hampering this involvement,

[12] George Grune, "Strategic Planning at the Reader's Digest Association" (Speech given at the annual meeting of the Crummer Graduate School of Business Corporate Council, Rollins College, 1986).

[13] H. Olson, "Why Directors Keep Getting Sued," *Fortune*, March 13, 1989, pp. 143–144.

[14] Ada Demb, Danielle Chouet, Tom Lossius, and Fred Neubauer, "Defining the Role of the Board," *Long Range Planning* 22 (February 1989): 60–68; R. H. Rock and Marv Eisthen, "Implementing Strategic Change," in K. J. Albert, ed., *The Management Handbook* (New York: McGraw-Hill, 1983).

[15] Joseph Rosenstein, "Why Don't U.S. Boards Get More Involved in Strategy?" *Long Range Planning* 20, no. 3 (1987): 30–34.

[16] Kenneth R. Andrews, "Corporate Strategy as a Vital Function of the Board," *Harvard Business Review* 59 (November–December 1981): 174–184.

[17] J. Richard Harrison, "The Strategic Use of Corporate Board Committees," *California Management Review* 30, no. 1 (Fall 1987): 109–125.

TABLE 1.3 Committees and Their Responsibilities within a Typical Board of Directors

EXECUTIVE COMMITTEE

1. To act within specified bounds for the board of directors between board meetings.
2. To serve as a "sounding board" for ideas of the CEO before they are presented to the full board.
3. To monitor extended negotiations.
4. To oversee activities not specifically delegated to other committees.

AUDIT COMMITTEE

1. To assure that company policies and practices are within the bounds of accepted conduct.
2. To select (or recommend) auditors and determine the scope of audits.
3. To review financial reports to gain full insight into the company's current and future financial condition.
4. To review internal accounting procedures.
5. To assure the integrity of the company's operations.

COMPENSATION COMMITTEE

1. To assure that compensation (including stock options, benefits, bonuses, and salaries) will attract, hold, and motivate key personnel.
2. To see that compensation and benefit plans throughout the organization are competitive, equitable, and well executed.
3. To oversee the development and implementation of human resource plans.

FINANCIAL COMMITTEE

1. To review and advise the board on the financial structure and needs of the organization.
2. To recommend to management and the board the timing and types of financing needed (both long- and short-term).
3. To assist top management in establishing good working relationships with the financial community.
4. To provide advice about various investment, expenditure, and funding alternatives.

NOMINATING COMMITTEE

1. To recommend candidates for membership on the board.
2. To recommend candidates for managerial or officer positions in the company.
3. To advise management on human resource planning.

Source: Adapted from J. K. Louden, *The Director* Copyright 1984. Reprinted by permission of the Corporate Director Institute.

however, is the conviction held by some managers and management scholars that the most effective and creative strategies emerge from interaction between the CEO and the CEO's key subordinates.[18] Others indicate that board members are generally not qualified to make strategic decisions.[19] Although for various reasons some boards might be more successful in handling strategic management issues than others, it seems reasonable to conclude that most organiza-

[18] Rosenstein, op cit.

[19] Harold S. Geneen, with Alvin Moscow, *Managing*, New York: Doubleday, 1984.

TABLE 1.4 Questions a Board of Directors Can Ask in Auditing a Strategic Management Process

- Is the company adequately informed about its markets? What further information would be worth the cost of getting? How should it be obtained?
- How well informed is the company about its competition? How well is it able to forecast what competitors will do under various circumstances? Is there a sound basis for such competitive appraisals? Is the company underestimating or overestimating its competitors?
- Has management adequately explored various ways of segmenting its market? To what extent is it addressing market segments in which the company's strengths provide meaningful advantages?
- Are the products and services the company proposes to sell ones that it can provide more effectively than competitors? What is the basis for such a belief?
- Do the various activities proposed in the strategy provide synergistic advantages? Are they compatible?
- Does the proposed strategy adequately address questions of corporate objectives, financial policy, scope of operations, organization, and integration?
- What specific resources (personnel, skills, information, facilities, technology, finances, relationships) will be needed to execute the strategy? Does the company already possess these resources? Has management established programs for building these resources and overall competence which will provide telling competitive advantages over the long run?
- To what extent does the strategy define a unique and appropriate economic role for the company? How different is it from the competitors' strategy?
- Has the issue of growth rate been raised? Are there good reasons to believe that investment in growth will pay off? Does the company's track record support such a conclusion?
- Does the proposed dividend policy reflect the company's growth policy, based on a demonstrated ability or inability to reinvest cash flow advantageously? Or is it just a "safe" compromise, conforming to what others usually do?
- Is management capable of implementing the strategy effectively? What leads to this conclusion?
- How and to what extent is the strategy to be communicated to the organization? Is it to be distributed in written form? If competitors are aware of the company's strategy, will that help or hurt?
- What provision is to be made for employing the strategy as a guide to operating decisions? To what extent is it to be used by the board? How?
- How is it to be kept up to date? Are there to be regular reviews? How often and by whom?
- Has a set of long-range projections of operations following the strategy been prepared? Have the possible results of following alternative strategies been prepared?
- Does the strategy focus on the few really important key issues? Is it too detailed? Does it address genuine business questions (as opposed to "motherhood" statements)?
- In its strategic thinking, has management avoided the lure of simplistic approaches such as:
  Growth for growth's sake?
  Diversification for diversification's sake?

(*Continued*)

TABLE 1.4 (Continued)

Aping the industry leader?
Broadening the scope in order to secure "incremental" earnings?
Assuming it can execute better than competitors without objective evidence that such is the case?

- Are there other issues, trends, or potential events that should have been taken into account?

Source: Milton Lauenstein, "Board of Directors: The Strategy Audit," *Journal of Business Strategy* 4, no. 3 (Winter 1984): 90–91.

tions would benefit by some type of board involvement in the strategic management process. The extent and type of involvement should vary from organization to organization depending upon issues such as the board member experience in handling strategic management issues.

Planning Staff's Involvement in Strategic Management

In many organizations, the job of strategic management can become so overwhelming that the CEO must assign individuals, typically called planning staff personnel, to help with the task. In smaller organizations, the CEO might simply appoint someone to act as a planning assistant. In medium to larger organizations, the CEO might establish a planning committee or even a planning department headed by its own director or vice president for organizational planning. Planning staff positions is generally advisory in nature, with planning personnel gathering and analyzing data and making recommendations to the CEO concerning how various strategic management decisions should be made.

In the past, the strategic management process was heavily influenced by planning departments within organizations. Individuals within these departments were involved with designing and implementing strategic management systems while CEOs generally took a hands-off attitude, basically allowing the departments much freedom in carrying out their duties. More recently, however, CEOs have taken a more active role in strategic management which includes giving planning departments more guidance and direction. As a result of this more active role of the CEOs, planning departments are generally thought to have lost some of their overwhelming influence over the strategic management process.[20]

The roles and the extent of influence and involvement of CEOs, boards of directors, and planning staff in the strategic management process of organizations have changed somewhat. This change will undoubtedly continue into the future. Regardless of the specifics of the roles these three groups play in the future, however, they will have to work together as a team in order to best implement the strategic management process of organizations.

[20] "The New Breed of Corporate Planner," *Business Week*, September 17, 1984, pp. 62–66.

Benefits of Strategic Management

An organization can reap several benefits from appropriately practicing strategic management. Perhaps the most important benefit is the tendency of such organizations to increase their levels of profit. Although studies in the more distant past concluded that increased profitability does not normally accompany the application of strategic management,[21] a significant number of recent investigations suggest that an efficient and effective strategic management system *can* increase profitability.[22]

In addition to benefiting financially, organizations can gain other distinct advantages by implementing a strategic management system. For example, strategic management can boost the commitment of organization members to the attainment of long-term organizational goals. This increased commitment normally comes about when organization members participate in setting organizational goals as well as in setting strategies for reaching those goals. In addition, strategic management's emphasis on assessing the organization's environment makes the organization less likely to be surprised by movement within the marketplace or by actions of competitors that could put the organization at a sudden disadvantage. Table 1.5 lists several additional benefits that strategic management often confers on organizations.

Of course, the benefits we have just noted do not automatically accrue to an organization that employs a strategic management system. They are obtained only if the organization uses such a system in an effective and efficient manner. Employment of an ineffective and inefficient strategic management process could easily lead to such problems as decreasing profitability, lower motivation of members to achieve organizational goals, and surprises within the environment that handicap the organization.

THE STRATEGIC MANAGEMENT PROCESS

We have defined strategic management as a process or series of steps. The basic steps of the strategic management process are shown in Figure 1.1. They include (1) performing an environmental analysis, (2) establishing organizational direction, (3) formulating organizational strategy, (4) implementing organizational strategy, and (5) exerting strategic control. Let's take a look at each of these steps and its relationship to a strategic management system.

The Steps Involved in Strategic Management

Step 1: Environmental Analysis

The strategic management process begins with *environmental analysis,* the process of monitoring the organization's environment to identify both present and future threats and opportunities. In this context, the organizational

[21] As an example of such studies see R. Fulmer and L. Rue, "The Practice and Profitability of Long-Range Planning," *Managerial Planning* 22 (1974): 1.

[22] As an example of such studies see Richard Robinson, Jr., "The Importance of Outsiders in Small Firm Strategic Planning," *Academy of Management Journal* 25, no. 1, March 1982, p. 80.

TABLE 1.5 Additional Potential Benefits of a Strategic Management Emphasis in an Organization

Signals that problems may arise before they happen.
Helps managers become more genuinely interested in an organization.
Alerts the organization to changes and allows for action in response to change.
Identifies any need to redefine the nature of the business.
Improves the channeling of effort toward the attainment of predetermined objectives.
Enables managers to have a clearer understanding of business.
Facilitates the identification and exploitation of future marketing opportunities.
Offers an objective view of management problems.
Provides a framework for reviewing the execution of the plan and for controlling activities.
Minimizes the ill effects of adverse conditions and changes.
Helps managers relate major decisions more effectively to established objectives.
Renders more effective the allocation of time and resources to identified opportunities.
Coordinates the execution of the tactics that make up the plan.
Allows for the integration of all marketing functions into a combined effort.
Minimizes the resources and time that must be devoted to correcting erroneous ad hoc decisions.
Creates a framework for internal communication among personnel.
Allows for the ordering of priorities within the time frame of the plan.
Gives the firm an advantage over competitors.
Helps marshal the behavior of individuals in the organization into a total effort.
Provides a basis for the clarification of individual responsibilities, and thereby contributes to motivation.
Encourages "forward thinking" on the part of personnel.
Stimulates a cooperative, integrated, and enthusiastic approach to tackling problems and opportunities.

Source: Based on Gordon E. Greenley, "Does Strategic Planning Improve Company Performance?" *Long Range Planning* 19, no. 2 (1986): 106.

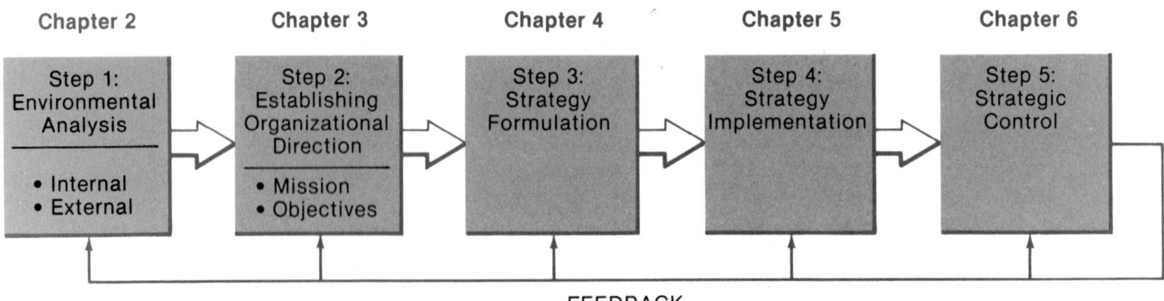

FIGURE 1.1 Major Steps of the Strategic Management Process

environment encompasses all factors both inside and outside the organization that can influence progress toward the attainment of organizational objectives. Examples of environmental variables that are commonly monitored during environmental analysis are presented in Figure 1.2.

One environmental issue receiving much attention recently deals with counterfeit products. Many companies are finding that because counterfeiters are manufacturing and selling their products, millions of dollars in potential sales are being lost annually. Companies facing this issue generally claim that they have established an exclusive legal right to manufacture and sell their products. Such companies normally attempt to eliminate the drain on potential profits caused by counterfeiting by attacking the counterfeiters through the legal system. Highlight 1.1 describes the magnitude of a counterfeiting issue faced by Walt Disney Company and how the company is attempting to deal with it.

Managers must grasp the purpose of environmental analysis, must recognize the various levels of organizational environment that exist, and must understand the recommended guidelines for performing an environmental analysis. These issues, along with others related to environmental analysis, are fully discussed in Chapter 2, "Environmental Analysis."

Step 2: Establishing Organizational Direction

The second step of the strategic management process is *establishing organizational direction,* or determining the thrust of the organization. There are two

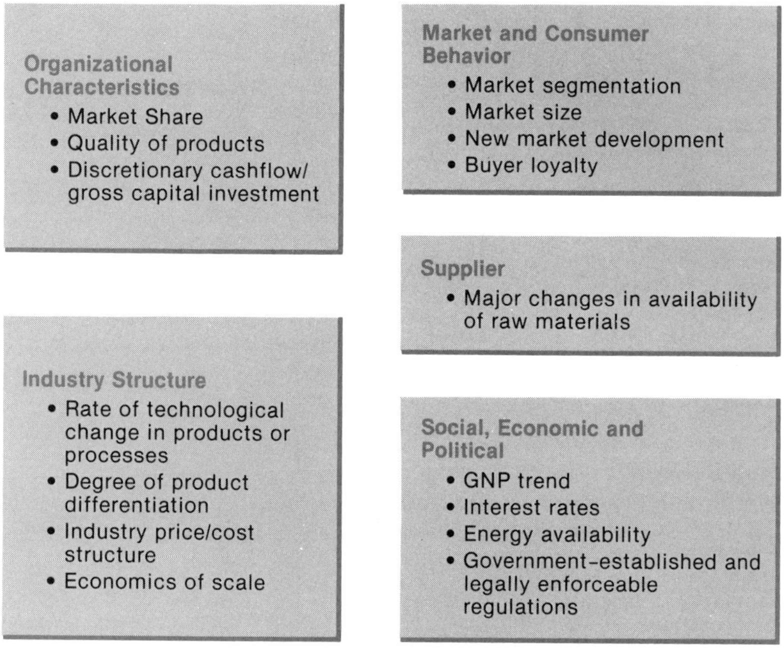

Organizational Characteristics
- Market Share
- Quality of products
- Discretionary cashflow/ gross capital investment

Market and Consumer Behavior
- Market segmentation
- Market size
- New market development
- Buyer loyalty

Supplier
- Major changes in availability of raw materials

Industry Structure
- Rate of technological change in products or processes
- Degree of product differentiation
- Industry price/cost structure
- Economics of scale

Social, Economic and Political
- GNP trend
- Interest rates
- Energy availability
- Government-established and legally enforceable regulations

FIGURE 1.2 Sample Environmental Factors to Be Monitored for Strategic Management

HIGHLIGHT 1.1

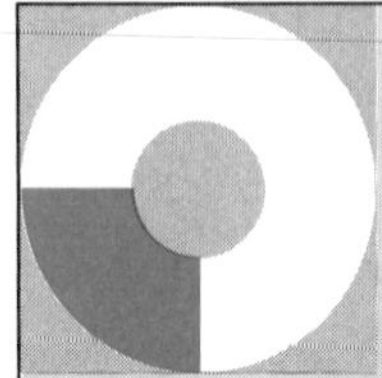

ILLUSTRATIVE EXAMPLE ■ **Disney Goes After Counterfeiters in Its Environment**

Disney goes after counterfeiters

They're burning Donald Duck, Mickey Mouse and Bambi in Bangkok—and Walt Disney Co. executives couldn't be happier.

Torching toys, T-shirts and books emblazoned with the famous cartoon characters is part of an offensive by Disney against rife counterfeiting of its products across Asia.

The American entertainment giant is enjoying a boom in Asia but also loses between $10 million and $20 million annually in royalties because of the pirates, said John J. Feenie, who heads Disney's consumer-products division in Asia. That estimate does not include losses to pirates of Disney videotapes.

Short of erecting their own Disneyland, adroit craftsmen fake virtually all of the company's merchandise: fluffy Mickey Mouse dolls, videotapes of cartoon classics, children's clothing, books, pens, stationery, figurines and watches.

Disney has kept close tabs on its characters in North America, too, moving aggressively to protect the copyrights it holds on its characters.

For example, it sued the Academy of Motion Picture Arts and Sciences in April for using Disney's Snow White character without authorization. A month later, it told a tiny Canadian town that it could not erect a statue of Winnie the Pooh, another character for which Disney holds a copyright.

While many foreign companies are reluctant to become involved in the legal wrangles and costs of tackling Asia's pirates, Feenie said Disney decided to take action after its fortunes surged in Asia about two years ago and local licensees began to complain about rip-offs.

Thailand was picked as the first target. That country affords copyright protection by law but has become a haven for pirates because of lax enforcement, mild penalties, cheap labor costs and a vigorous entrepreneurial spirit. Copies of the world's leading brand-name products can be found on Bangkok's streets.

Feenie said Thailand was also singled out because it is a big exporter of Disney fakes to the Middle East and, perhaps most importantly, is seen as a major future market for and a legitimate manufacturer of the company's consumer line.

Disney already has licensed six companies in the country, including

Srithai Superware Co. Ltd., which Feenie described as "a model for us" because it is following the rules and still making hefty profits. Srithai produces children's dinnerware sets and utensils for Disneyland and Disney World in the United States, Tokyo's Disneyland and other foreign outlets.

"We're not just going to be the big foreigner clubbing the little guy," Feenie said. "We want to help develop local business. And it will be the locals who will fight for us, because they will see their own interests hurt by the pirates."

Following complaints from the Thai licensees, Disney hired an outfit in the anti-counterfeiting field to run a three-month survey of the market.

A "pile of cases" accumulated, he said, and raids were staged with police cooperation beginning in March against the most flagrant violators. Typically, those were sweatshop operators with their own retail outlets.

Confiscated merchandisc worth about $30,000 has been burned in big piles at a city dump. Disney executives hope the bonfires will deter the fakers.

The Disney vice president said similar compaigns to protect copyrights and trademarks will be launched in Taiwan, South Korea and Malaysia, while a "second phase" will focus on the Philippines and Indonesia.

Source: "Disney Goes After Counterfeiters," *The Orlando Sentinel,* June 24, 1989, pp. B1, B6.

main indicators of the direction in which an organization is moving: organizational mission and organizational objectives. *Organizational mission* is the purpose for which, or reason why, an organization exists. *Objectives* are the targets the organization has chosen.

After management has performed an environmental analysis to pinpoint the organization's strengths, weaknesses, opportunities, and threats, it is often better able to establish, reaffirm, or modify its organizational direction. In order to establish organizational direction appropriately, however, management must know what comprises an organizational mission statement, understand the nature of organizational objectives, and adopt an effective and efficient process for establishing organizational direction. These issues are discussed in detail in Chapter 3, "Establishing Organizational Direction."

Step 3: Strategy Formulation

The third step of the strategic management process is strategy formulation. *Strategy* is defined as a course of action aimed at ensuring that the organization will achieve its objectives. *Strategy formulation,* then, is the process of designing and selecting strategies that lead to the attainment of organizational objectives. The central focus of organizational strategy is how to deal better with competition. Once the environment has been analyzed and organizational direction has been stipulated, management is able to chart alternative courses of action in an informed effort to ensure organizational success.

In order to formulate organizational strategy properly, managers must thoroughly understand such various approaches to strategy formulation as Critical Question Analysis, Strength/Weakness/Opportunity/Threat (SWOT) Analysis, the Boston Consulting Group Growth–Sharc Matrix, and General Electric's Multifactor Portfolio Matrix. Chapter 4, "Strategy Formulation," discusses these and other tools in great detail.

Step 4: Implementing Organizational Strategy

The fourth step of the strategic management process is *implementing organizational strategy*. This step involves putting into action the logically developed strategies that emerged from the previous steps of the strategic management process. Without the effective implementation of strategy, organizations are unable to reap the benefits of performing an organizational analysis, establishing organizational direction, and formulating organizational strategy.

In order to implement organizational strategy successfully, managers must have a clear idea of several diverse issues: how much change is necessary within an organization when it implements a new strategy, how it is best to deal with organization "culture" in order to ensure that a strategy will indeed be implemented smoothly, how strategy implementation and various types of organizational structures are related, what different implementation approaches a manager can follow, and what skills are necessary in managers who hope to implement organizational strategy successfully.

A recent survey conducted by Larry D. Alexander investigated the types of strategic decisions commonly made in organizations and the difficulties involved in implementing these decisions. Ninety-three firms participated in the survey. Seventy-two of them appear in the Fortune 500 list of leading industrial firms. Compiled on the basis of the results of this survey, Table 1.6 presents the types of strategic decisions commonly made by organizations, as well as the ten problems that arise most frequently as a result of implementing those decisions. Chapter 5, "Strategy Implementation," focuses on the implementation phase of the strategic management process and on ways to avoid or minimize the impact of strategic implementation problems of this nature.

Step 5: Strategic Control

Strategic control is a special type of organizational control that focuses on monitoring and evaluating the strategic management process in order to improve it and ensure that it is functioning properly.

To successfully perform this strategic control task, managers must understand the process of strategic control and the role that strategic audits (assessments of the organizational environment) normally play in it. In addition, managers must understand the intricacies of management information systems and how such systems can complement the strategic control process. The

TABLE 1.6 Strategic Decisions Commonly Made and Related Implementation Problems

STRATEGIC DECISIONS COMMONLY MADE IN ORGANIZATIONS	RELATED IMPLEMENTATION PROBLEMS COMMONLY FACED
Introducing a new product or service.	Implementation took more time than originally allocated.
Opening and starting up a new plant or facility.	Major problems surfaced during implementation that had not been identified beforehand.
Expanding operations to enter a new market.	Coordination of implementation activities was not effective enough.
Discontinuing a product or withdrawing from a market that was not effective enough.	Competing activities and crises distracted attention from implementing this decision.
Acquiring or merging with another firm.	Capabilities of employees involved were not sufficient.
Changing the strategy in functional departments.	Training and instruction given to lower-level employees were not adequate.
	Uncontrollable factors in the external environment had an adverse impact on implementation.
	Leadership and direction provided by departmental managers were not adequate.
	Key implementation tasks and activities were not defined in enough detail.
	Information systems used to monitor implementation were not adequate.

Source: Reprinted with permission from *Long Range Planning* 18, no. 3, Larry D. Alexander, "Successfully Implementing Strategic Decisions." Copyright © 1985, Pergamon Journals, Ltd.

strategic management process within any organization is only as good as the information on which it is based.[23] These and other important issues are discussed in Chapter 6, "Strategic Control."

Highlight 1.2 gives you an opportunity to consider how the strategic management process could be improved through better strategic control in a situation drawn from a well-known firm's experience.

For purposes of analysis, we have presented the strategic management process as a series of discrete steps. The process is presented in this fashion to facilitate learning about what the process entails and to describe how the steps commonly relate to one another. In practice, however, managers sometimes find that applying strategic management effectively within an organization entails performing several steps simultaneously or performing them in a different order from that suggested here. Managers must be creative in designing

[23] M. D. Skipton, "Helping Managers to Develop Strategies," *Long Range Planning* 18, no. 2, April 1985, pp. 56–68.

HIGHLIGHT 1.2

SKILLS MODULE ■ **Skill in Controlling Robotics Strategy at Westinghouse**

INTRODUCTION

Strategic control is a vital step in the strategic management process. Review the following situation that arose within the Westinghouse Electric Corporation, and then complete the related skill development exercise. Doing so will help you understand the importance of monitoring and evaluating the strategic management process to make sure that planned outcomes occur as expected.

THE SITUATION

The Westinghouse Electric Corporation promotes its efforts to improve quality and productivity with a 14-minute film showing its Unimate robots hard at work welding frames at a Chrysler Corporation assembly line in Windsor, Ontario. The message is clear: Any manufacturer who purchases and uses Westinghouse robots can expect increases in both productivity and product quality at their plants.

What Westinghouse didn't know when it made this film was that its Unimate robots were practically obsolete. When Chrysler opened a second automated plant in Sterling Heights, Michigan, it was "staffed" with robots made by Westinghouse's archrival Cincinnati Milacron, Inc. And Chrysler is considering replacing its Unimates at the Windsor plant.

Westinghouse expects the robot market to soar to almost $2 billion within about the next 5 years from its present level of about $170 million. Competition is stiff, however. There are presently about 60 U.S. robot companies, and more than 200 exist worldwide.

SKILL DEVELOPMENT EXERCISE

You are responsible for the strategic management process at Westinghouse. As part of your strategic control activities, you are considering what specific changes to recommend in the strategic management process. What improvements do you think should be made in the various components of the Westinghouse strategic management process?

Source: Based on Doran P. Levin, "Westinghouse Move into Robotics Shows Pitfalls of High-Tech Field," *The Wall Street Journal*, May 14, 1984, p. 27.

and operating strategic management systems and flexible enough to tailor their use of such systems to the organizational circumstances that confront them.

Special Issues in Strategic Management

The major steps that we have outlined are fundamental to the strategic management process. Two other significant issues have received special attention in the last few years, and managers should consider them carefully in determining how strategic management should be practiced within a particular organization. These issues are international operations and social responsibility.

Strategic Management and International Operations

Over the last several years, businesses have tended to become increasingly involved in international business activities. Since this trend is expected to continue, more and more organizations will have international issues to consider in the future as part of their strategic management process.

Before managers can determine how best to "factor" international issues into the strategic management process, they must be fully aware of those international variables that might significantly affect their organizations. Chapter 7, "Strategic Management and International Operations," elaborates on the fundamentals of international management and of multinational corporations. In addition, this chapter has special sections devoted to possible international implications for each step of the strategic management model.

Strategic Management and Social Responsibility

Social responsibility is the managerial obligation to take action that protects and promotes organizational interests along with the welfare of society as a whole. Recognition that such an obligation exists necessarily has an impact on the strategic management process.

In order to allow social responsibility to influence the strategic management process within an organization appropriately, managers need a thorough understanding of issues such as the following: To what constituencies within society is the organization responsible? In what main areas should management demonstrate a concern for social responsibility? What major influences within society affect business practices? How can "social audits" be used to facilitate the strategic management process? Issues of this nature are discussed in Chapter 8, "Strategic Management and Social Responsibility." Highlight 1.3 offers some practice in dealing with social responsibility issues.

Foundations for Strategic Management

The successful strategic manager must be able to analyze the major business functions within the organization and understand how they affect the strategic management process and should be integrated with it. The importance of the relationship between these business functions and the strategic management process cannot be overestimated.

Traditionally, three major business functions are identified within an organization: operations or production, finance, and marketing. However, there is some debate about exactly how many major business functions are performed in organizations. Some management theorists argue that human resource activities constitute a fourth major business function, whereas others maintain that research and development constitute a fifth. *All* important business

HIGHLIGHT 1.3

SKILLS MODULE ■ Social Responsibility Skill at Gerber

INTRODUCTION

Issues involving social responsibility have a significant impact on the strategic management process. Review the following situation and complete the related skill development exercise. Doing so will give you practice in confronting the kind of dilemma that often troubles managers as they seek to discharge the firm's social responsibilities *responsibly.*

THE SITUATION

The Gerber Products Company keeps teddy bears and cookies in its headquarters lobby in order to welcome its main customers, children. Recently, however, the company image is getting much tougher to uphold as the result of a recent wave of complaints voicing the fear of glass in Gerber baby food jars.

Gerber notes that none of the complaints has been substantiated. Because the Food and Drug Administration has yet to validate any of the complaints, the company feels that a recall is pointless and would simply serve to fuel more complaints. According to James Lovejoy, director of corporate communications at Gerber, "This is a lynch mob. Nobody wants to wait for due process. We're guilty until proven innocent."

Believing that all the complaints will eventually prove groundless, the company is making no recalls and no changes in product packaging. If Gerber, the largest U.S. baby food producer, is correct, it will ride out the crisis with minimal damage. If, on the other hand, glass *is* found in some of the products, lawsuits could result in monumental judgments against the firm.

Gerber's strategy is largely based on a similar problem that the company faced in 1984. At that time, the Department of Agriculture and the Food and Drug Administration claimed that glass had contaminated two separate lots of Gerber products. Gerber's reaction was to recall hundreds of thousands of jars of food. Additional testing revealed that no glass was present in any of Gerber's recalled products.

SKILL DEVELOPMENT EXERCISE

You are the chief executive officer at Gerber. You have recently come under strong attack throughout the country because your failure to order a recall does not seem to be socially responsible. You have decided to hold a press conference to explain why your strategy is indeed *very* socially responsible. What would the main points of your argument be?

Source: Based on John Bussey, "Gerber Takes Risky Stance as Fears Spread About Glass in Baby Food," *The Wall Street Journal,* March 6, 1986, p. 19. For additional related information see P. Strnad, "Gerber to Grow into Adult Market: Food for Adults," *Advertising Age* 59 (August 8, 1988): 12.

functions and their impact on strategic management are discussed in this text. Operations, finance, and marketing are treated in separate chapters; information on human resource activities, research and development, and other functions is integrated throughout the text.

Operations Foundations for Strategic Management

The operations function is performed by those people within a business who are responsible for producing the goods or services that the organization offers for public consumption. Chapter 9, "Operations Foundations for Strategic Management," discusses the essential principles of organizational operations and explains how this function is related to the strategic management process. This section addresses the appropriateness of different strategies for different operations, characterizes operations as a vital element of strategy, presents product design as an important operations and strategy issue, and probes the nature of strategic decision making within the operations area.

Financial Foundations for Strategic Management

Financial analysis is the process of evaluating assets, liabilities, and equity and making decisions on the basis of this evaluation.[24] Chapter 10, "Financial Foundations for Strategic Management," discusses how financial concepts are related to strategic management. These concepts are fundamental to performing a financial analysis that can contribute to the success of the strategic management process. The analytical approaches covered include financial ratio analysis, break-even analysis, and net present value analysis.

Marketing Foundations for Strategic Management

Marketing has recently been defined as "the process of planning and executing conception, pricing, promotion, and distribution of ideas, goods, and services to create exchanges that satisfy individual and organizational objectives."[25] Chapter 11, "Marketing Foundations for Strategic Management," reveals how fundamental marketing principles are related to strategic management and can yield a situational analysis that constructively contributes to the strategic management process. This chapter focuses on the strategic marketing process: analysis of consumer/product relationships, selection of market segmentation strategy, designing of the marketing mix strategy, and implementation and control of marketing strategy.

A Comprehensive Approach to Analyzing Strategic Problems and Cases

Perhaps the most commonly used instructional method for teaching strategic management is case analysis. Cases are descriptions of actual strategic management problems that students must analyze in order to suggest solutions.

This text contains many cases that raise fascinating issues in strategic

[24] Robert Hartl, *Basics of Financial Management* (Dubuque, Iowa: William C. Brown Publishers, 1986), pp. 4–5.

[25] J. Paul Peter and James H. Donnelly, Jr., *Marketing Management Knowledge and Skills*, Plano, Tex.: Business Publications, Inc., 1986, p. 9.

management. Chapter 12, "A Comprehensive Approach to Analyzing Strategic Problems and Cases," outlines in detail a method that students can use to analyze strategic management problems and to make their recommendations. The major steps of this case analysis method are problem definition, formulation of alternative solutions to the problem, evaluation of developed alternatives, and selection and implementation of the chosen alternative. Worksheets are furnished for students to use in their analysis. The analytical method for student use presented in Chapter 12 is just as useful to practicing managers facing strategic management problems in actual organizations.

The Plan of This Book

Figure 1.3 presents the overall plan for this book visually. It depicts all the major topics we have previewed in this chapter and indicates which chapters treat each one in detail. This figure will appear (with appropriate shading to highlight the relevant topic) at the beginning of each chapter in order to place the subject of each chapter in the context of strategic management as a whole. The figure will also serve as a review of how these diverse topics are related to one another, and it will illustrate the progress you are making in your study of strategic management.

THE DEVELOPMENT OF STRATEGIC MANAGEMENT WITHIN ORGANIZATIONS

Although managers may be eager to design and implement a strategic management system in their organization, accomplishing the task takes time. And in most organizations, the strategic management process in use has evolved over a period of several years and has been tailored to meet specific company needs.[26]

The developmental phases that such a strategic management process commonly goes through are shown in Figure 1.4. Strategic management is usually first seen as a fairly simple phase called basic financial planning. During this phase, the primary concern is simply meeting budget constraints through operational control, the annual budgeting process, and a focus on functions like operations, finance, and marketing.

From these humble beginnings there eventually evolves the culminating phase that we know as strategic management. The focus has shifted from meeting the budget, predicting the future, and thinking abstractly to actually trying to *create* a future. This goal of creating a future is pursued by orchestrating all resources to gain a competitive advantage, using a carefully chosen planning framework, building flexibility into the organizational planning process, and fostering a supportive climate within the organization.

[26] Frederick W. Gluck, Stephen P. Kaufman, and A. Steven Walleck, "Strategic Management for Competitive Advantage," *Harvard Business Review*, July–August 1980, pp. 154–161.

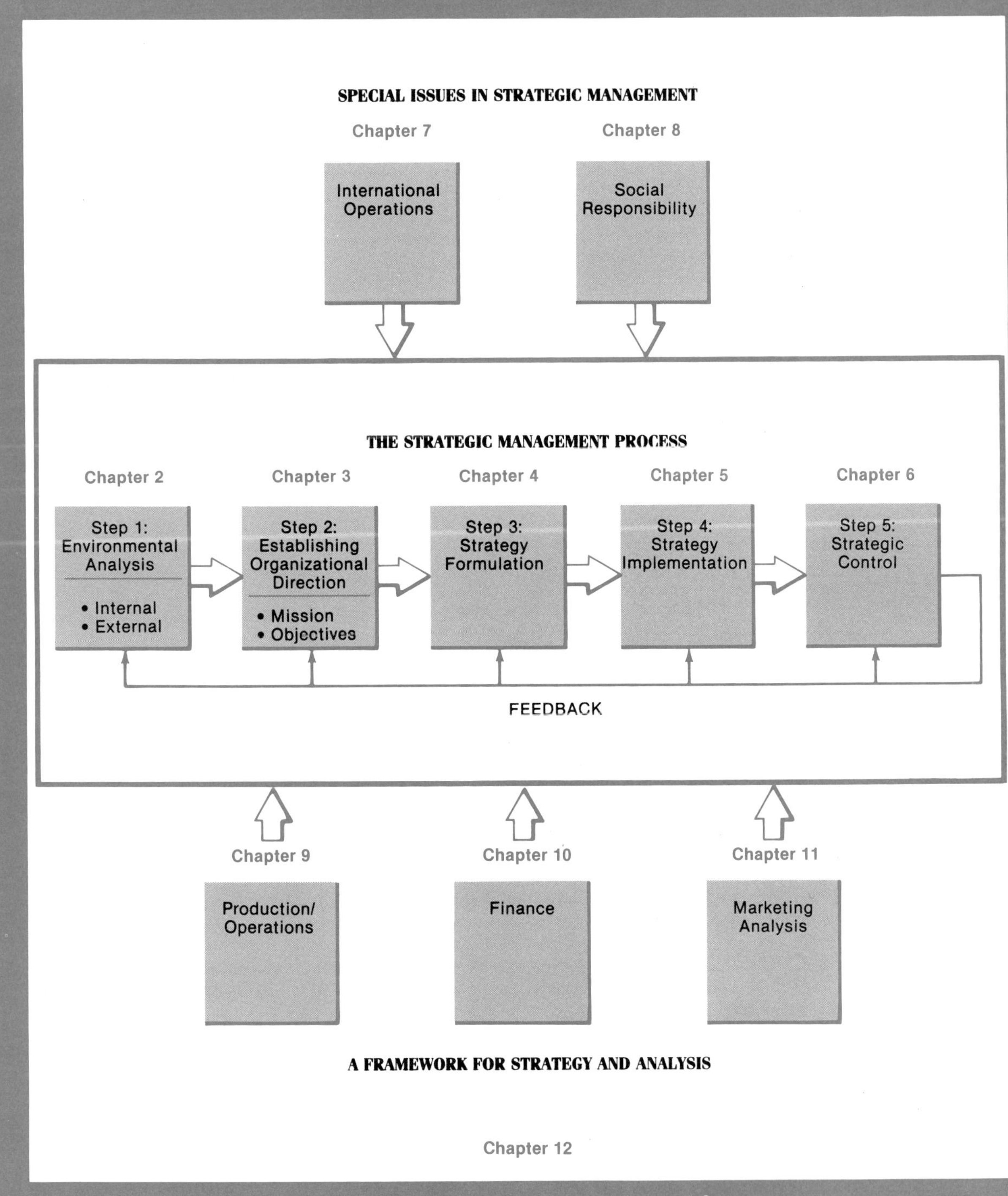

FIGURE 1.3 Major Strategic Management Topics and Related Chapters in This Text.

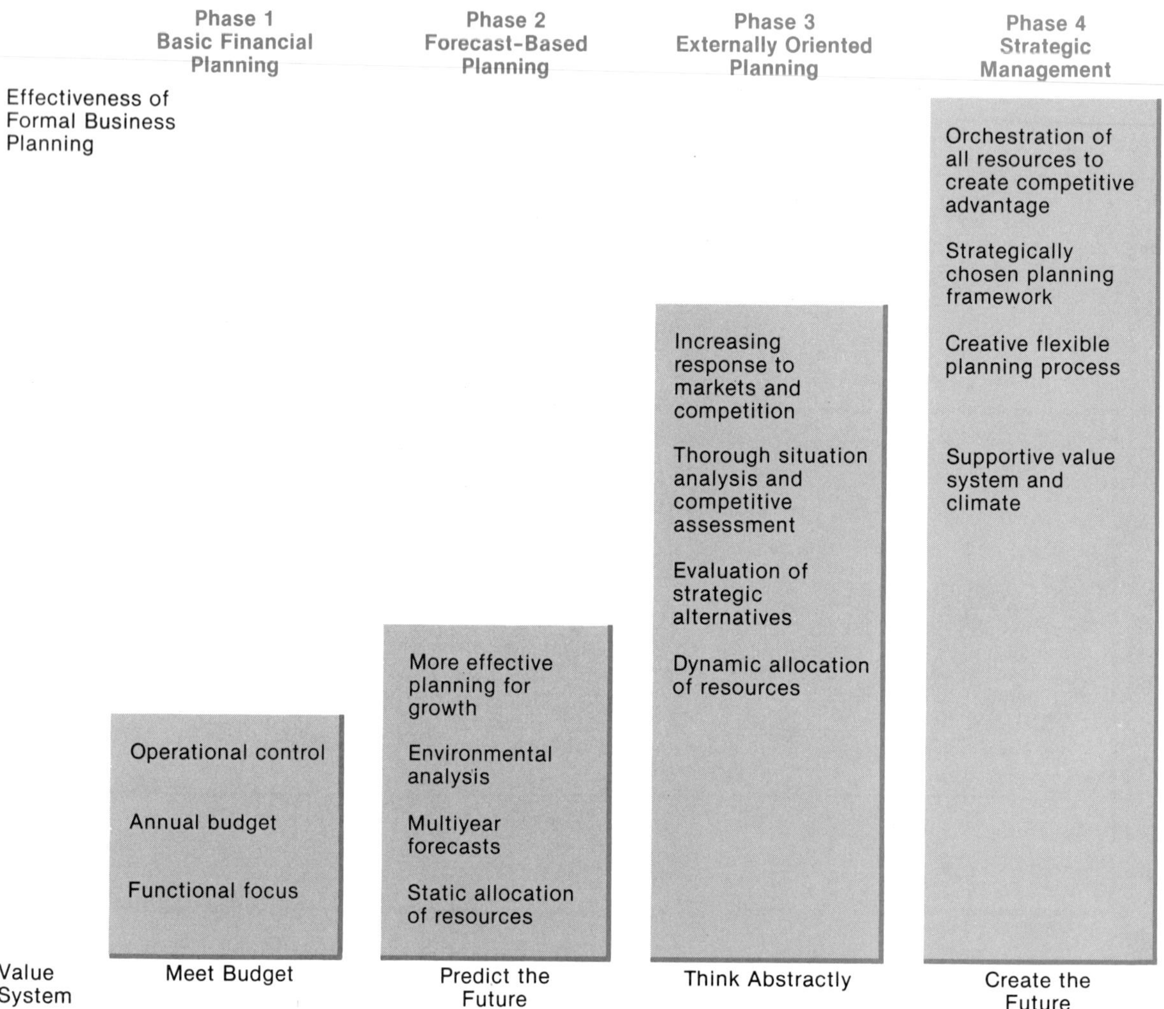

FIGURE 1.4 Phases in the Development of a Strategic Management System

Managers must understand that developing an effective and efficient strategic management system in any organization can be a long and difficult task that requires sustained, concentrated effort and a great deal of patience. Thinking in terms of the evolutionary phases we have outlined can help managers gauge the development of the strategic management system in their own organization, realistically assess the appropriateness of the strategic management process being employed, and consider improvements and alternatives.

SUMMARY

Strategic management is a continuous, iterative process aimed at keeping an organization as a whole appropriately matched to its environment. Typically, the process mostly involves top management, boards of directors, and planning staff. The main steps of the process are: performing an environmental analysis, establishing organizational direction, formulating organizational strategy, implementing that strategy, and exerting strategic control. In addition, international operations and social responsibility may profoundly affect the organizational strategic management process, and it is important that the major business functions within an organization—operations, finance, and marketing—be integrated with the strategic management process. Each of these topics is the subject of a chapter in this text, and Chapter 12 offers guidelines for analyzing strategic management problems through case studies.

Highlight 1.4 contains a summary checklist of questions based on this chapter. Use it when you analyze strategic management problems and cases that focus on fundamental strategic management issues.

ADDITIONAL READINGS

Andrews, Kenneth R. *The Concept of Corporate Strategy.* Homewood, Ill.: Richard D. Irwin, 1987.

Bhide, Amar. "Hustle as Strategy." *Harvard Business Review,* September–October 1986, pp. 59–65.

Fahey, Liam, and V. K. Narayanan. *Macroenvironmental Analysis for Strategic Management.* St. Paul, Minn.: West Publishing Company, 1986.

Frederickson, James W. "The Strategic Decision Process and Organizational Structure." *Academy of Management Review* 11, no. 2 (1986): 280–297.

Hill, Charles W. L., and Gareth R. Jones. *Strategic Management: An Integrated Approach.* Boston: Houghton Mifflin Company, 1989.

Lorsch, Jay W. "The Invisible Barrier to Strategic Change." *California Management Review,* Winter 1986, p. 95.

Meyers, Gerald C., with John Holusha. *When It Hits the Fan: Managing the Nine Crises of Business.* Boston: Houghton Mifflin Company, 1986.

Midas, Michael T., Jr., and William B. Werther, Jr. "Productivity: The Missing Link in Corporate Strategy." *Management Review,* March 1985, pp. 44–47.

HIGHLIGHT 1.4

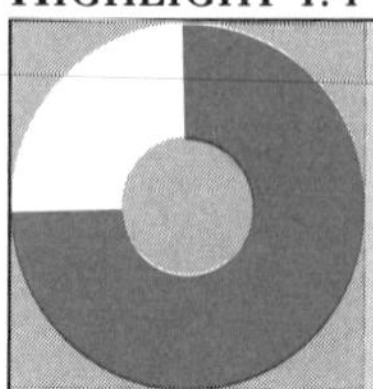

CHECKLIST ■ Analyzing Fundamental Issues in Strategic Management Problems and Cases

- ☐ 1. Does the problem or case involve genuine strategic management issues?
- ☐ 2. Are the board of directors, top management, and planning staff appropriately involved in the strategic management process?
- ☐ 3. Are the major steps of the strategic management process appropriately ordered and integrated?
- ☐ 4. Is organizational direction clear and well expressed through organizational mission and objectives?
- ☐ 5. Is strategy appropriate, given the existing organizational direction and the results of the environmental analysis?
- ☐ 6. Has strategy been appropriately implemented (successfully translated into action)?
- ☐ 7. Is the focus on exerting strategic control in order to improve the strategic management process appropriate?
- ☐ 8. Has the impact of international issues on the strategic management process been assessed and taken into account?
- ☐ 9. Has the impact of social responsibility issues on the strategic management process been assessed and taken into account?
- ☐ 10. Are foundation concepts in operations, finance, and marketing that have special relevance to the strategic management situation properly handled?

Prescott, John E. "Environments as Moderators of the Relationship Between Strategy and Performance." *Academy of Management Journal* 29, no. 2 (June 1986): 329–346.

Schofield, Malcolm, and David Arnold. "Strategies for Mature Businesses." *Long Range Planning* 21/5, no. 3 (October 1988): 69–76.

HIGHLIGHT 1.5 ■ APPLICATION OF CHAPTER MATERIAL

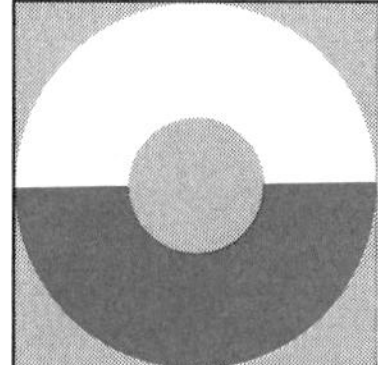

Strategic Analysis for the Mail Order Catalog Business at Sears

As divisional manager in charge of strategic decisions for the catalog division at Sears, you have just opened up your *Wall Street Journal* and see the following article:

Catalog Merchants Try New Strategies As the Field Crowds With Competitors

By WILLIAM M. BULKELEY
Staff Reporter of
THE WALL STREET JOURNAL

For the past five years, the mail-order catalog business has been booming, with overall sales growth surpassing that of retail operations.

But many catalogs are finding that survival has nevertheless become increasingly difficult. Although sales continue to rise, consultants and catalog merchants say that too many companies are fighting for a share of the market. As a result, several retailers have canceled forays into the catalog field, and even established books are disappearing. Last year, Mobil Corp.'s Montgomery Ward & Co. unit ended distribution of its catalog, the nation's oldest, after 113 years of publication.

"The market is certainly growing, but there have been a tremendous number of new entrants," says Charles M. Leighton, chairman of CML Group Inc., a Concord, Mass., retailer and catalog company that has closed down two catalogs in the past two years. Because so many new catalogs have come out, he explains, "there is a saturation of the mailbox."

Segmenting Audiences

To succeed in the face of such mounting competition, marketers are adopting a variety of new tactics. Some are segmenting their audiences more narrowly, keeping better track of customers' buying patterns and reducing their mail volume to cut expenses and build profitability. Others are branching out into retail, advertising in magazines and newspapers or even selling ad space in their catalogs.

"The industry has always had a kneejerk response: Mail more names. At some point that doesn't make sense," says Frederik Wiersema, vice president, marketing, of Persoft, Inc. The Woburn, Mass. company sells a $375,000 computer program designed to cull the best prospects from a company's files.

By combining such information as age and car-purchasing habits obtained from state automobile registries, says Mr. Wiersema, catalog companies can get a fairly precise picture of their customers' tastes.

In their efforts to save money, some companies are producing smaller catalogs that cover a more specific range of items, notes Robert Wyker, president of Allied Graphic Arts, Inc., a New York printer. "I'll put out three 49-page catalogs for a company as opposed to one 128-page or 144-page catalog," he says. "I'm sending out more titles but fewer total pages. They're looking for increased efficiency."

Even Sears, Roebuck & Co., the industry giant with catalog and catalog sales in 1984 of $3.9 billion—out of total merchandise sales of $26.5 billion—is increasingly emphasizing its 22 "specialogues," which focus on such categories as petite clothing, power tools and toys. Oak Brook, Ill.-based Spiegel Inc., which once published a single catalog of low-priced general mer-

(*Continued*)

chandise, now issues more than 30 different upscale catalogs annually and estimates sales topped $700 million last year, up from $615 million in 1984.

Consultants believe that Montgomery Ward's failure to transform its general catalog along these lines contributed to its losses and ultimate demise.

Another successful strategy for catalog marketers is the use of mailing lists from alternative sources. Mr. Leighton of CML Group says that catalog buyers are saturated with catalogs because most companies are renting the same lists of the same customers from each other. He says CML's fastest growing catalog is Nature Co., which sells science-oriented toys for youngsters. The company supplements its lists with names rented from natural-history museums. "The lists they're renting are unique," he says.

Catalog companies are also reaching new customers through retail outlets. Banana Republic, a San Francisco purveyor of natural clothing that was founded in 1978 by Mel and Patricia Ziegler, sold out to Gap Stores Inc., a casual-wear retailer, in 1983 to get enough capital to expand beyond the two stores it operated. It now has 35 and plans to add another 30 this year.

The company, which distributed 12 million catalogs last year and estimates an even higher number for this year still believes that its business is "driven by the catalog."

But, says Mr. Ziegler, the president, "we're a catalog business with two means of distribution—mail and stores. Catalog companies were spending enormous sums on advertising to get an average 2% response. Now customers have stores to go into."

Selling Ad Space

To help its catalog stand out, San Francisco's Sharper Image Inc. started selling ad space in December. The company sells just four pages per issue, at $45,000 a page. Early advertisers include several car manufacturers and this newspaper.

Nancy Ross, executive assistant, says, "It gives our catalog a different look, and it's a great advertising vehicle," as Sharper Image sends out three million catalogs a month. She adds that while some customers have chided the catalog for looking like a magazine, others have called it "a great innovation."

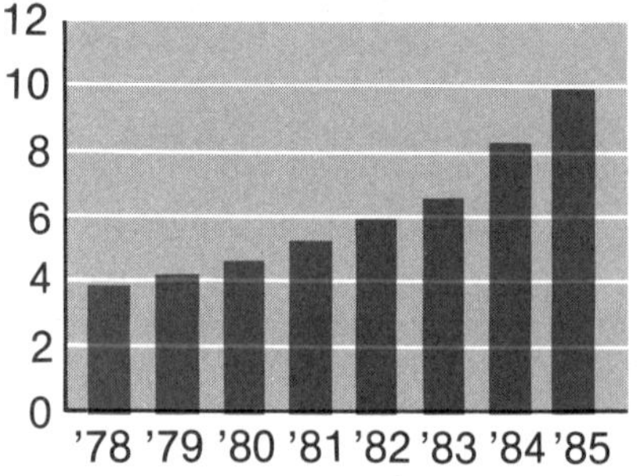

Source: Direct Marketing Association estimates.

Ms. Ross says that Sharper Image is working to "take on more of a magazine format." The January issue opens with a letter from the publisher and includes letters from readers criticizing the company's sale of model guns. (Guns have been dropped from the catalog.) Sharper Image has also added a table of contents—anathema to most catalogs, which usually count on a reader's scanning every page—and feature articles such as one on the best new products of 1985, many of which Sharper Image doesn't sell.

Banana Republic, which has twice won industry awards for best catalog, also features prose pieces—quirky travelogues or inspired testimonials from such writers as humorist Roy Blount Jr.

DISCUSSION QUESTIONS

1. As divisional manager in charge of strategic decisions for the catalog division at Sears, would you find this article useful? Why?
2. What three conclusions that might be drawn from this article would be the most valuable to you at Sears?

3. What impact would each of these three conclusions probably have on the various components of your overall strategic management process at Sears?

Source: William M. Bulkeley, "Catalog Merchants Try New Strategies as the Field Crowds with Competitors," *The Wall Street Journal,* January 20, 1986, p. 17. Reprinted by permission of *The Wall Street Journal.* This module can be further enriched by reading M. Forseter, "Master Plan to Revitalize: Sears Still Under Scrutiny," *Chain Store Age Executive* 65 (January 1989): 38.

SECTION TWO

The Strategic Management Process

Section Two builds upon Section One by providing detailed discussions of the five major steps in the strategic management process. Chapter 2 discusses the importance of environmental analysis in providing data for sound strategic management decisions. Chapter 3 concerns establishing organizational mission and objectives, which shape an organization's direction. Chapter 4 emphasizes strategy formulation—determining appropriate actions for moving the organization in its chosen direction. Chapter 5 discusses strategy implementation, the process of putting formulated strategies into action. Chapter 6 focuses on strategic control to evaluate, monitor, and improve the organization's effectiveness. Careful study of this section should provide a foundation for analyzing many strategic management problems and cases.

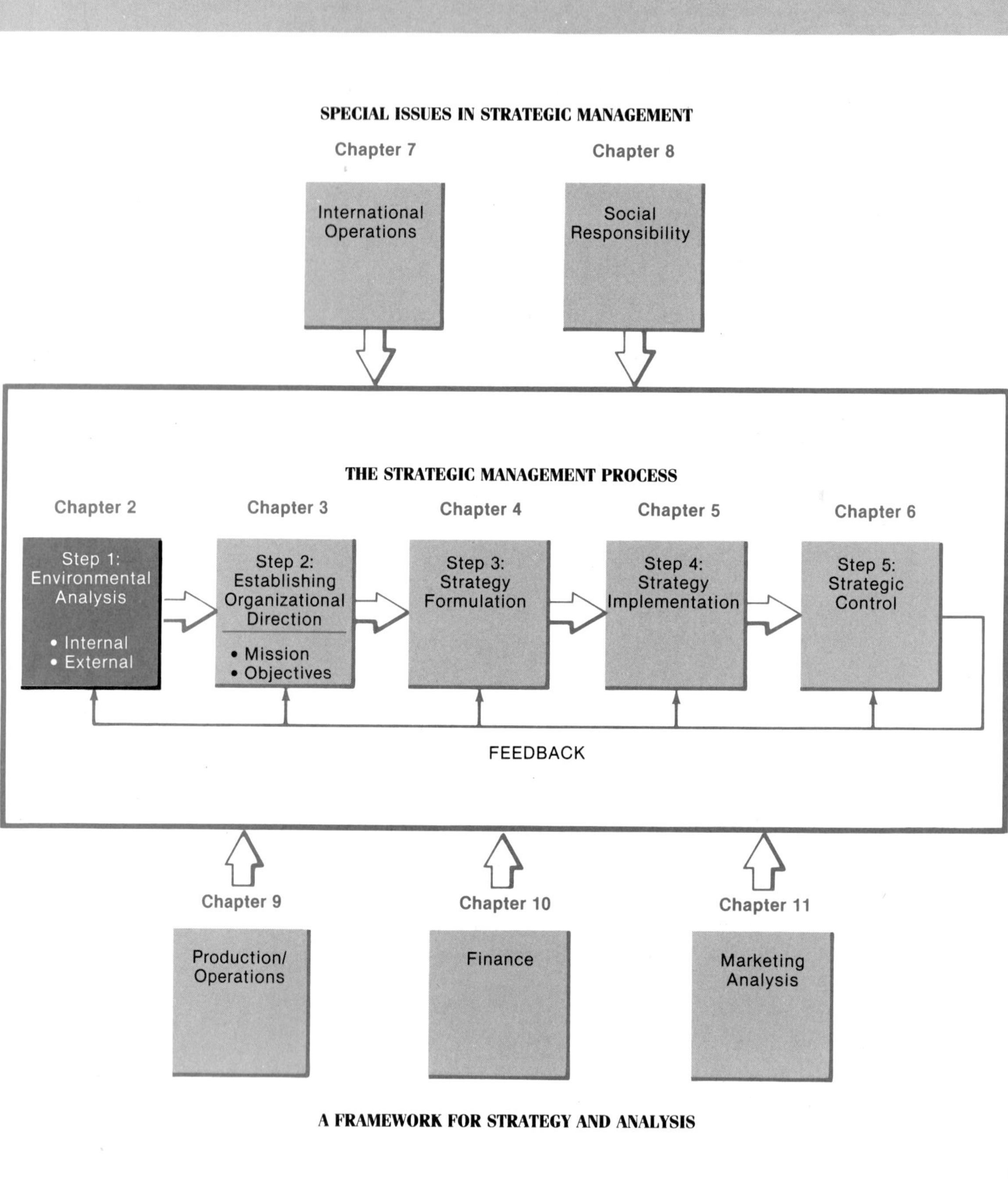
SPECIAL ISSUES IN STRATEGIC MANAGEMENT
Chapter 7
International Operations
Chapter 8
Social Responsibility
THE STRATEGIC MANAGEMENT PROCESS
Chapter 2
Step 1: Environmental Analysis
• Internal
• External
Chapter 3
Step 2: Establishing Organizational Direction
• Mission
• Objectives
Chapter 4
Step 3: Strategy Formulation
Chapter 5
Step 4: Strategy Implementation
Chapter 6
Step 5: Strategic Control
FEEDBACK
Chapter 9
Production/ Operations
Chapter 10
Finance
Chapter 11
Marketing Analysis
A FRAMEWORK FOR STRATEGY AND ANALYSIS
Chapter 12
An Approach to Solving Strategic Problems and Cases

CHAPTER 2

Environmental Analysis

Whereas Chapter 1 described the strategic management process in general terms, Chapter 2 focuses on the initial step of this process, environmental analysis. Environmental analysis is undertaken to ferret out information that will be used mainly in the second step of the strategic management process, establishing organizational direction, and during the later step of strategy formulation.

We begin with the basics: what environmental analysis is, why it is important, for what reasons it is performed, and how it can play various roles in the firm. Next we show how an understanding of environmental structure is vital to effective analysis of the environment. In doing so, we explain environmental structure by defining the general, operating, and internal environments in which firms operate and discussing the key components of each. Then we offer guidelines for performing an environmental analysis, which can be broadly stated as determining what aspects of the environment it is worthwhile to investigate, applying one or more of several environmental analysis techniques, and tirelessly assessing the effectiveness of the environmental analysis process.

FUNDAMENTALS OF ENVIRONMENTAL ANALYSIS

We will first offer a definition of environmental analysis and a rationale for performing it. Then we will discuss further the purpose of environmental analysis and take note of the varying roles that environmental analysis plays in organizations.

Environmental Analysis: Definition and Rationale

As we noted in Chapter 1, *environmental analysis* is the process of monitoring the organizational environment to identify both present and future threats and opportunities that may influence the firm's ability to reach its goals. Here, the *organizational environment* is the set of all factors both outside and inside the organization that can affect its progress toward attaining those goals. According to Michael E. Naylor, the corporate strategic planner for General Motors, awareness of the organizational environment is vital to the organization's success.[1] Accordingly, management should constantly gather and consider the implications of data related to important environmental factors.

The future will probably herald an ever-increasing rate of change in all aspects of organizational environment. Because future organizations will be more complex and more dependent on their environments, performing environmental analyses will almost certainly be even more important to managers of the future than it is to managers today.[2]

One account of why managers should perform an environmental analysis is based on general systems theory. According to general systems theory, modern organizations are *open,* rather than closed, *systems.* That is, modern organizations are influenced by and are constantly interacting with their environments. Because organizations are open systems, environmental factors *inevitably* influence them, and it is up to managers to ensure that this influence is channeled in a positive direction and contributes to organizational success.[3]

Purpose of Environmental Analysis

Although the procedures used to perform an environmental analysis differ widely in different organizations, most firms have the same main reason for performing such an analysis.[4] In general, their purpose is to assess the organizational environment so that management can react to it appropriately and thereby enhance organizational success. Highlight 2.1 demonstrates how environmental analysis fulfilled its purpose at Ryka by helping management to enhance company success. Based upon environmental analysis, Ryka, a

[1] Michael E. Naylor, "Regaining Your Competitive Edge," *Long Range Planning* 18, no. 1 (1985): 30–35.

[2] For a discussion of benefits gained by performing an environmental analysis see John Diffenbach, "Corporate Analysis in Large U.S. Corporations," *Long Range Planning,* June 1983, pp. 107–116.

[3] Samuel C. Certo, *Principles of Modern Management: Functions and Systems,* 4th ed. (Boston: Allyn & Bacon, 1989), pp. 44–47.

[4] This section is based on James K. Brown, *This Business of Issues: Coping with the Company's Environment* (New York: The Conference Board, 1979), p. 54. Note: This work is also available in a 1981 version.

HIGHLIGHT 2.1

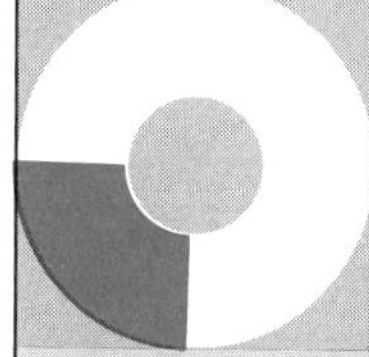

ILLUSTRATIVE EXAMPLE ■ **Ryka: Environmental Analysis Helps a Small Business Take on the Giants**

Ryka, a 25-employee firm led by a husband and wife team, hopes to become the next hot shoe company by using cheap but ingenious "guerrilla" marketing in selling shoes specifically designed for athletic women. Its tactics, other than Mr. Steinfeld, include targeting marketing effects in California.

Treading in the land of consumer product giants is risky business for small companies. **Reebok International** Ltd. may have scored big in the early 1980s when it entered the aerobic shoe market, as well as **L.A. Gear** Inc. when it followed in the mid-1980s by peddling stylish sneakers. But their very success makes it all the harder for Ryka to succeed. Six years ago, for example, athletic-shoe companies spent a total of $20 million on advertising; last year, they spent more than $100 million.

But Ryka is undeterred. "Retailers definitely recognize the need for this category of shoe," said Sheri Poe, Ryka's president. "For many years, major shoemakers designed women's shoes by simply shrinking a man's last (a block of plastic shaped like a foot on which shoes are made) to fit a woman," Ms. Poe said. "But women have different hips and pelvises and their feet strike the ground differently. We developed a special last that takes that into consideration," she said. Industry analysts said they believe Ryka is the only athletic shoemaker that designs strictly for women. It was among the first to use the special last for women in athletic shoes; now competitors like Nike are following suit.

Ryka's problem, like all small companies entering a crowded market, is getting attention. But its budget won't let Ryka go toe-to-toe with the big guys. That's where Jake Steinfeld comes in.

Mr. Steinfeld, a Hollywood body trainer who was given an undisclosed amount of Ryka stock and a small stipend, has all his assistants wearing Ryka shoes on his syndicated TV fitness show, "Body by Jake." The show has a 70 percent female audience.

Advertising isn't Ryka's only problem. Like many small companies, it had quality control problems initially. Specifically, it had diffficulty perfecting its patented technology—a nitrogen molding resembling clear rubber bouncing balls that fit into the foundation of the shoe. Complaints about poor stitching and other quality problems caused one athletic shoe chain to send almost its entire fall shipment back to Ryka. But since then, Ryka's quality problems with the molding have been corrected, Mr. Gillis said.

(*Continued*)

Despite initial setbacks, Ryka's distributors are pleased with the concept behind Ryka. "We think their technology is excellent," said a spokesman for Jordan Marsh, a department store subsidiary of Campbell Corp. of Toronto. "Their styling is definitely contoured for a woman's foot."

Ryka's sales were $1.7 million in the first quarter of 1989 and company officials expect sales of as much as $7 million for the year, compared with $1.4 million in 1988. With 900 accounts and shoes at only 1,500 stores vs. a potential 10,000 stores, retailers like Nordstrom Inc. say it's too early to tell how successful Ryka will be. In 1988, Ryka had a net loss of $1.5 million.

Source: Adapted from Suzanne Alexander, "Tiny Ryka Seeks a Foothold with Sneakers for Women," *The Wall Street Journal*, July 31, 1989, p. B2.

small manufacturer of athletic shoes, decided to develop a new sneaker designed specially for the women's segment of the market.

This general purpose for performing an environmental analysis has been cited by many companies. At the Connecticut General Insurance Company, for example, the overriding purpose of environmental analysis is to provide management with the ability to respond to critical issues in the environment. Connecticut General stipulates that decision makers in the organization *must* take external considerations into account. Similarly, the Sun Exploration and Production Company has stated that the purpose of its environmental analysis is to explore future conditions of the organizational environment and to incorporate what it learns into organizational decision making. Sears, Roebuck has stated that its main purpose in undertaking environmental analysis is to identify current emerging issues that are significant to the company, assign priorities to these issues, and develop a plan for handling each of them.

Roles of Environmental Analysis in Organizations

There is some evidence that, if conscientiously performed, environmental analysis can help ensure organizational success.[5] The specific organizational roles or functions that the environmental analysis system assumes to ensure this success, however, can vary drastically from organization to organization.[6] Three such roles are:

1. The *policy-oriented role:* The main purpose of a policy-oriented environmental analysis is to improve organizational performance by simply keeping top management informed about major trends emerging in the environment. In general, those who perform this kind of environmental

[5] Richard L. Daft, Juhani Sormunen, and Don Parks, "Chief Executive Scanning, Environmental Characteristics, and Company Performance: An Empirical Study," *Strategic Management Journal* 9 (1988): 123–139.

[6] Jack L. Engledow and R. T. Lenz, "Whatever Happened to Environmental Analysis," *Long Range Planning* 18, no. 2 (1985): 93–106.

analysis focus on the corporation as a whole and have direct access to top management. This role emphasizes early detection and appropriate top-management reaction to broad strategic issues such as attitudes, norms, and laws that are likely to affect the organization as a whole. Environmental analysis that is policy oriented is normally unstructured, and the relationship between the environmental analysis process and formal organizational planning is indirect and informal.

2. The *integrated strategic planning role:* The main purpose of this kind of environmental analysis is to improve organizational performance by making top managers and divisional managers aware of issues that arise in the firm's environment, by having a direct impact on planning, and by linking corporate and divisional planning. Those engaged in such environmental analysis operate at either the corporate or the divisional level and report to or operate as part of the organizational planning staff. Normally, an analysis system of this sort has a specific task to perform within the strategic management process. This task usually includes preparing environmental forecasts in order to generate basic assumptions about organizational planning and to provide more detailed information about relevant parts of the environment as specific organizational plans begin to materialize.
3. The *function-oriented role:* The main purpose of a function-oriented environmental analysis is to improve organizational performance by providing environmental information concerning the effective performance of specific organizational functions. This type of environmental analysis is normally undertaken to enhance the performance of a particular function or major organizational activity at either the corporate or the divisional level. Such functions can be very broad (improving organizational recruitment practices) or very specific (complying with a government regulation in a timely fashion). Naturally, those who perform this role focus very narrowly on specific environmental segments related to the organizational function being addressed. The system in which they operate is generally integrated with the normal planning process for that particular organizational function.

As we review these three roles, several facts become clear. First, the policy-oriented role seems the broadest in scope and the most loosely related to formal organizational planning. On the other hand, the function-oriented role seems the most specifically targeted at particular organizational issues. More than the other two roles, the integrated strategic planning role seems to emphasize a close relationship between environmental analysis and formal organizational planning.

These three roles are simply three examples of what an environmental analysis system can be designed to do for an organization. Managers must keep in mind that the role of environmental analysis in any organization must suit the specific needs of that organization. Any one of these roles or any combination of them could be a barrier to organizational success if it does not reflect specific organizational needs.

ENVIRONMENTAL STRUCTURE

In order to perform an environmental analysis efficiently and effectively, a manager must thoroughly understand how organizational environments are structured. In a widely cited article, Thomas divides the environment of an organization into three distinct levels: the general environment, the operating environment, and the internal environment.[7] Figure 2.1 illustrates the relationship of each of these levels to the others, as well as to the organization at large, and outlines the various components that make up each level. Managers must be aware of these three environmental levels, know what factors they include, understand how each factor and the relationships among the factors affect organizational performance, and then manage organizational operations in light of this understanding.

The General Environment

The *general environment* is that level of an organization's external environment made up of components that are normally broad in scope and have little immediate application for managing an organization. What are these components?

The *economic component* of the general environment indicates how resources are distributed and used within the environment. Examples of factors within the economic component are gross national product, corporate profits, inflation rate, productivity, employment rates, balance of payments, interest rates, tax rates, and consumer income, debt, and spending.[8]

The *social component* of the general environment describes characteristics of the society in which the organization exists. Literacy rates, educational levels, customs, beliefs, values, lifestyle, age, geographic distribution, and mobility of a population are part of the social component of the general environment. It is important for managers to remember that although changes in the attributes of a society may come either slowly or quickly, changes will inevitably come.[9]

The *political component* of the general environment comprises those elements that are related to governmental affairs. Examples include the type of government in existence, governmental attitude toward various industries, lobbying efforts by interest groups, progress toward the passage of laws, platforms of political parties, and (sometimes) the predispositions of candidates running for office.

[7] Philip S. Thomas, "Environmental Analysis for Corporate Planning," *Business Horizons,* October 1974, pp. 27–38.

[8] For more information about several of these examples see Abraham Katz, "Evaluating the Environment: Economic and Technological Factors," in William D. Guth, ed., *Handbook of Business Strategy* (Boston: Warren, Gorham & Lamont, 1985), pp. 2–9.

[9] For an illustration of how such changes can have an impact on strategic management see P. D. Cooper and G. Miaoulis, "Altering Corporate Strategic Criteria to Reflect the Changing Environment: The Role of Life Satisfaction and the Growing Senior Market," *California Management Review* 31 (Fall 1988): 87–97.

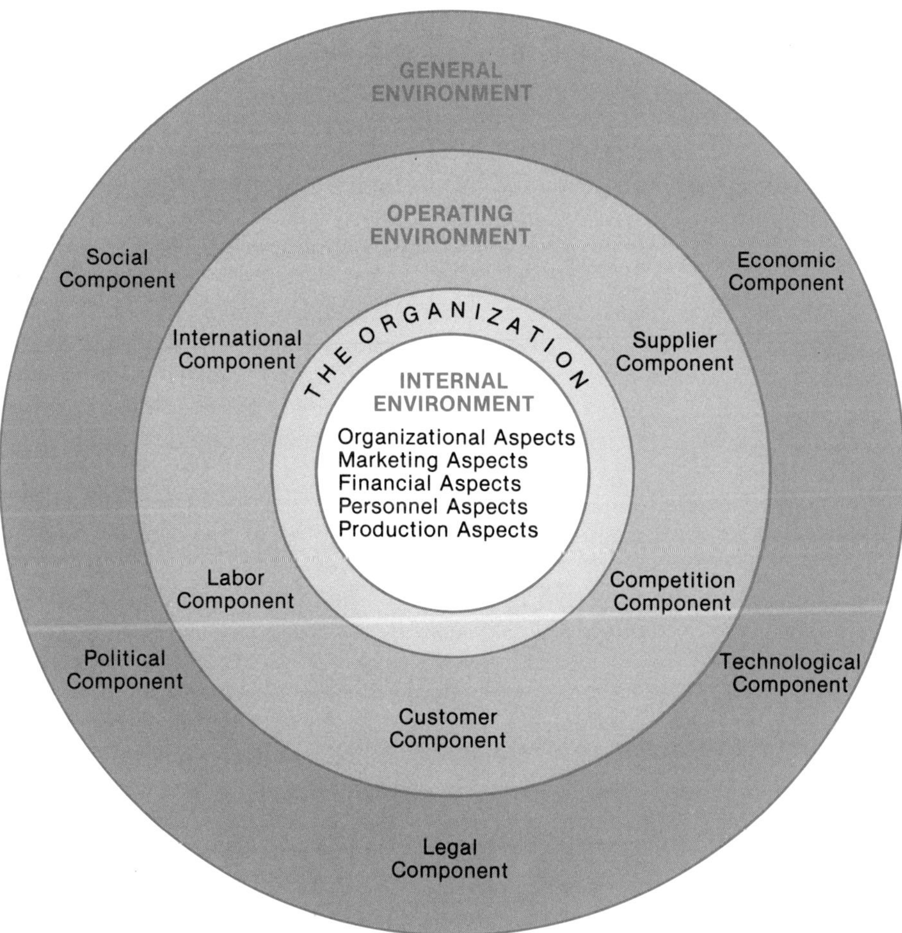

FIGURE 2.1 The Organization, the Levels of Its Environment, and the Components of Those Levels

The *legal component* of the general environment consists of legislation that has been passed. This component prescribes rules or laws that all members of society must follow. Examples of such legislation specifically aimed at the operation of organizations include the Air Quality Act of 1967, the Clean Air Act of 1963, the Occupational Safety and Health Act of 1970, the Consumer Product Safety Act of 1972, and the Energy Policy and Conservation Act of 1975. Naturally, over time new laws are passed and old ones rescinded.

The *technological component* of the general environment includes new approaches to producing goods and services: new procedures as well as new equipment. For example, the contemporary trend toward exploiting robots to improve productivity is closely monitored by many of today's managers. Increasing use of robots in the next decade should vastly improve the efficiency of American industry. Installations of these computer-controlled machines are expected to grow at an annual rate of 35 to 45 percent for the next ten years.[10]

The Operating Environment

The *operating environment* is that level of the organization's external environment made up of components that normally have relatively specific and more immediate implications for managing the organization. As Figure 2.1 indicates, the major components of the operating environment are customers, competition, labor, suppliers, and international issues.

The *customer component* of the operating environment reflects the characteristics and behavior of those who buy goods and services provided by the organization. Decribing in detail those who buy the firm's products is a common business practice. Developing such profiles helps management generate ideas about how to improve customer acceptance of organizational goods and services.

The *competitive component* of the operating environment consists of those with whom an organization must "do battle" in order to obtain resources. Understanding competitors is a key factor in developing effective strategy, so analyzing the competitive environment is a fundamental challenge to management. Basically, the purpose of competitive analysis is to help management appreciate the strengths, weaknesses, and capabilities of existing and potential competitors and predict what strategies they are likely to adopt.[11]

Within any given industry, most of this competition focuses on rivalry among existing firms, the bargaining power of consumers, substitute products being developed, the bargaining power of suppliers, and new entrants into the marketplace. Figure 2.2 illustrates these factors as driving forces of competition within an industry. More extended discussion of these forces is contained in Chapter 4, "Strategy Formulation."

The *labor component* of the operating environment is made up of factors that influence the supply of workers available to perform needed organizational tasks. Issues such as the skill levels, trainability, desired wage rates, and average age of potential workers are important to the operation of the organization. Another important but often overlooked issue is the desirability of working for a particular organization, as perceived by potential workers.

The *supplier component* of the operating environment includes all variables related to those who provide resources for the organization. These resources are purchased and transformed during the production process into final goods and services. How many vendors offer specified resources for sale, the relative quality of materials offered by vendors, the reliability of vendor deliveries, and the credit terms offered by vendors—all such issues are important to consider in managing an organization effectively and efficiently.

The *international component* of the operating environment comprises all factors related to the international implications of organizational operations.

[10] "Robots for Greater Efficiency," *U.S. News & World Report,* September 5, 1983, p. 25.

[11] R. S. Wilson, "Managing in the Competitive Environment," *Long Range Planning* 17, no. 1 (1984): 50–63.

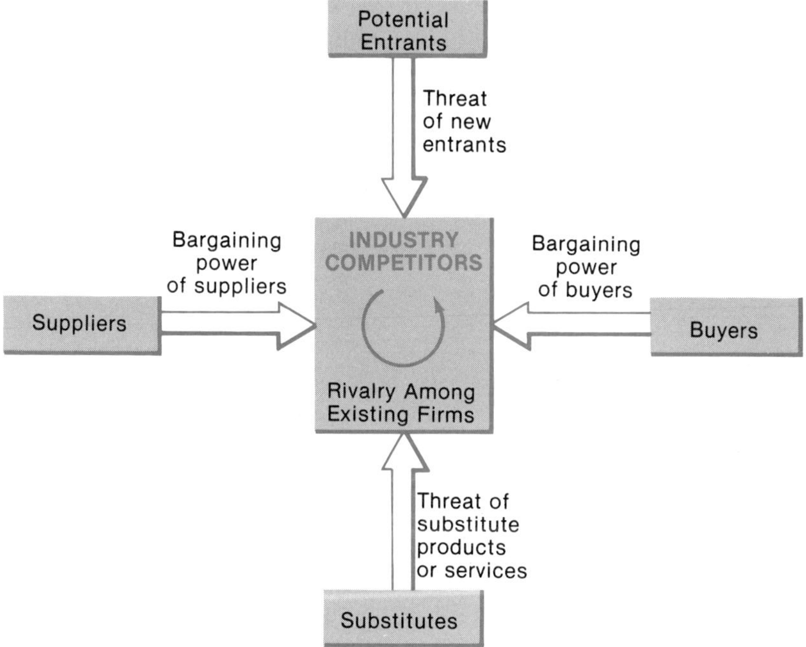

FIGURE 2.2 *Primary Competitive Factors within an Industry (Reprinted with permission of The Free Press, a Division of Macmillan, Inc. from Competitive Strategy: Techniques for Analyzing Industries and Competitors by Michael E. Porter.)*

Though not all organizations must deal with international issues, the number that do is increasing dramatically. Significant aspects of the international component include the laws, political practices, culture, and economic environment that prevail in the foreign countries with which (or in which) the firm does business.[12] Important variables in each of these four categories are presented in Table 2.1. (See Chapter 7, "Strategic Management and International Operations," for further discussion of such international issues.)

The Internal Environment

The *internal environment* is that level of an organization's environment which exists inside the organization and normally has immediate and specific implications for managing the organization. Unlike components of the general and operating environments, which exist outside the organization, components of the internal environment exist within it. Table 2.2 lists a number of factors that are considered important components of the internal environment.

Highlight 2.2 gives you the opportunity to relate discussion of the internal as well as operating and general environments to environmental analysis at the Eastman Kodak Company.

[12] Peter Wright, "MNC—Third World Business Unit Performance: Application of Strategic Elements," *Strategic Management Journal* 5 (1984): 231–240.

TABLE 2.1 Important Aspects of the International Component of an Organization's Operating Environment

LEGAL ENVIRONMENT	CULTURAL ENVIRONMENT
Legal tradition Effectiveness of legal system Treaties with foreign nations Patent trademark laws Laws affecting business firms	Customs, norms, values, beliefs Language Attitudes Motivations Social institutions Status symbols Religious beliefs
ECONOMIC ENVIRONMENT	**POLITICAL SYSTEM**
Level of economic development Population Gross national product Per capita income Literacy level Social infrastructure Natural resources Climate Membership in regional economic blocks (E.E.C.; L.A.F.T.A.; etc.) Monetary and fiscal policies Nature of competition Currency convertibility Inflation Taxation system Interest rates Wage and salary levels	Form of government Political ideology Stability of government Strength of opposition parties and groups Social unrest Political strife and insurgency Governmental attitude toward foreign firms Foreign policy

Source: Arvind V. Phatak, *International Dimensions of Management* (Boston: Kent Publishing Company, 1983), p. 6. Copyright © by Wadsworth, Inc. Reprinted by permission of PWS-KENT Publishing Company, a division of Wadsworth, Inc.

GUIDELINES FOR PERFORMING AN ENVIRONMENTAL ANALYSIS

Keeping in mind the fundamentals of environmental analysis and the dimensions of environmental structure that this chapter has presented, we are ready to propose guidelines that managers can follow when performing an environmental analysis.

There is no one best or standard way to perform an environmental analysis and determine present and future threats to the organization's attainment of its goals. By following the guidelines discussed in this section, however, managers can enhance the quality of their environmental analysis regardless of the specific procedure they use. According to these guidelines, a manager should determine how relevant various environmental levels and strategic

TABLE 2.2 Several Important Aspects of an Organization's Internal Environment

ORGANIZATIONAL ASPECTS	PERSONNEL ASPECTS
Communication network	Labor relations
Organization structure	Recruitment practices
Record of success	Training programs
Hierarchy of objectives	Performance appraisal system
Policies, procedures, rules	Incentive systems
Ability of management team	Turnover and absenteeism
MARKETING ASPECTS	**PRODUCTION ASPECTS**
Market segmentation	Plant facility layout
Product strategy	Research and development
Pricing strategy	Use of technology
Promotion strategy	Purchasing of raw materials
Distribution strategy	Inventory control
	Use of subcontracting
FINANCIAL ASPECTS	
Liquidity	
Profitability	
Activity	
Investment opportunity	

issues are to the organization, implement appropriate environmental analysis techniques, and evaluate the environmental analysis process used.

Determining the Relevance of Environmental Levels: Small vs. Large Business

Just as it is important for managers to know that the success of organizations is influenced by the structure of three distinct levels of organizational environment, they must also realize that all levels do not necessarily affect an organization equally. That is, in different types of organizations, the various environmental levels exhibit different degrees of relevance.

One method that is often used to determine the relevance of environmental levels to organizations is to consider the organization's size and its degree of involvement in international business.[13] As an organization increases in size, the theory goes, and becomes more involved in international business, variables in the general environment become more relevant to successful management of the organization. Conversely, the smaller the organization, the less involved it is likely to be in international business, and factors in the general environment

[13] Paulo De Vasconcellos Filho, "Environmental Analysis for Strategic Planning," *Managerial Planning,* January–February 1985, pp. 23–36.

HIGHLIGHT 2.2

SKILLS MODULE ■ Environmental Analysis Skill at Kodak

INTRODUCTION

We have discussed the structure of the organizational environment at some length. Review the following situation at Kodak and then complete the related skill development exercise. Doing so will help you develop the ability to determine the impact that various environmental factors at different environmental levels can have on organizational success.

THE SITUATION

Eastman Kodak is the world's largest producer of photography products. Kodak manufactures a complete line of film and photographic supplies suitable for both amateur and professional photographers. Not long ago, the company made financial news by reporting higher sales and sharply higher earnings. The company's main business—photography and related chemicals—was largely responsible for this improved performance.

Throughout its history, Kodak has demonstrated its ability to prepare for and capitalize on the future. Acting consistently with this approach, the company has recently made capital investments that should improve the quality of its products and operations, bring about cost reductions, increase productivity, support growth in demand for existing products, and prepare the way for new market entries.

SKILL DEVELOPMENT EXERCISE

Colby H. Chandler is chairman and chief executive officer at Eastman Kodak. He is certainly aware that to capitalize on the future, he must understand and respond appropriately to factors in Kodak's general, operating, and internal environments. In reflecting on our modern business world, list one factor from each of these environmental levels that you think could have a positive impact and one from each level that could have a negative impact on Kodak's future success. Be sure to explain why each factor could have such a positive or negative impact.

Source: Based on *1984 Eastman Kodak Annual Report,* p. 4.

tend to be less relevant to its successful management. Operating and internal environments are generally considered relevant to success regardless of the organization's size or its involvement in international business. Table 2.3 illustrates this relationship between organization size, international business, and the relevance of environmental levels.

TABLE 2.3 Organization Size, International Operations, and the Relevance of Environmental Levels

ORGANIZATIONS \ DEGREE OF RELEVANCE	High	Medium	Reduced
Multinational company	Internal General Operating	—	—
Large national company	Internal General Operating	—	
Medium-sized company	Internal Operating	General	—
Small company	Internal Operating	—	General
Very small company	Internal Operating	—	General

Source: Based on Paulo De Vasconcellos Filho, "Environmental Analysis for Strategic Planning," *Managerial Planning*, January–February 1985, p. 24.

Determining the Relevance of Strategic Issues

A *strategic issue* is an environmental factor, either inside or outside the organization, that is likely to have an impact on the ability of the enterprise to meet its objectives.[14] As is true of environmental levels, not all strategic issues are equally important to all organizations. Some organizations are much more sensitive to certain strategic issues than others are. Table 2.4 shows the degree of sensitivity of a telephone equipment company and a major oil company to six different strategic issues, or environmental factors. This example clearly supports the position that managers must undertake the task of determining which strategic issues have the most significant influence on organizational success.

One way managers can try to determine the sensitivity of their organization to various environmental factors is to design and implement an internal system that gathers and analyzes targeted feedback from key employees. For example, when environmental assessment specialists for the Sun Exploration and Production Company were faced with rating the relative importance of various external environmental factors, they developed just such a system. Various key employees at Sun were asked to respond to the questions listed in Table 2.5, and their answers were analyzed. Sun's specific objective was to guide

[14] H. Igor Ansoff, "Strategic Issue Management," *Strategic Management Journal* 1 (1980): 133.

TABLE 2.4 Differing Sensitivity of Two Companies to the Same Environmental Factors

	A MAJOR MANUFACTURER OF TELEPHONE EQUIPMENT	A MAJOR OIL COMPANY
GNP	Medium	High
Government capital spending	Very high	Low
Technical change	Very high	Medium/Low (except for electric car)
Sociological change	Very high (communication habits)	Very high (private car movements)
Environmental pollution	Low	High
Political risks Middle East	Low	High

Source: Adapted from Basil W. Denning, "Strategic Environmental Appraisal," *Long Range Planning,* March 1973, p. 25. Copyright 1973, Pergamon Journals, Ltd. Reprinted by permission.

TABLE 2.5 Questions to Help Determine the Relevance of Environmental Factors

1. If you could have perfect information about five external factors which impact on our operation, what would they be? (For example, crude oil prices, GNP deflator, etc.)
2. What five external factors do you see as the major threats to our business?
3. What five factors would you like to know about our competitors' future plans?
4. If you were asked to define a company strategic direction, what five external factors would you feel would be the most critical in performing this task?
5. What five external areas would be the most likely to show changes which would be most favorable to the company's future?

Source: Allen H. Mesch, "Developing an Effective Environmental Assessment Function," *Managerial Planning,* March–April 1984, p. 19. Reprinted by permission of the Planning Forum.

management in interpreting and understanding the external environment in which it operated and to gain some perspective on possible future events that might pose threats or offer opportunities.[15] Of course, managers can use modifications of this method to tap other sources of information, such as customers or consultants.

We should also note that information gathered from key employees can be used to help managers interpret and understand the internal environment of the organization as part of an internal environmental analysis. In this situation, the questions are focused on the primary components of the internal environment: organizational aspects, marketing aspects, financial aspects, personnel aspects, and production aspects. Table 2.6 presents several questions

[15] Allen H. Mesch, "Developing an Effective Environmental Assessment Function," *Managerial Planning* 32, no. 5 (March–April 1984): 17–22.

that might be asked in connection with an internal environmental analysis. Section Four of this text, "Foundations for Strategic Management," treats production, finance, and marketing and places special emphasis on how these functions are related to internal environmental analysis.

The foregoing discussion implies that management may want to focus on analyzing one environmental level at a particular time. Keep in mind, however, that in the long run management's ability to understand how all three environmental levels and the relationships among them influence organizational operations is a primary determinant of organizational success.

Implementing Environmental Analysis Techniques

Several techniques are available to help management perform an effective and efficient environmental analysis. We will discuss a few of these techniques here.

TABLE 2.6 Sample Questions for an Internal Environmental Analysis

ORGANIZATIONAL ASPECTS
Does the company delegate authority appropriately?
Is the organizational structure of the company appropriate?
Are jobs and performance goals clearly understood by workers?
MARKETING ASPECTS
Is market research used to best advantage?
Is advertising used efficiently and effectively?
Can the product distribution system of the company be improved?
FINANCIAL ASPECTS
Does an analysis of the income statement for the company pinpoint improvements that can be made?
Does an analysis of the balance sheet for the company pinpoint improvements that can be made?
Can break-even analysis be used to better align costs in relation to profits?
PERSONNEL ASPECTS
Are training programs adequate?
Can procedures for recruitment and selection of employees be improved?
Is our performance appraisal system fair and accurate?
PRODUCTION ASPECTS
Can the organization improve its level of technology?
Can the flow of work within the plant be made more efficient?
Can the organization lower its reject rate?

Environmental Scanning

Environmental scanning is the process of gathering information about events and their relationships within an organization's internal and external environments. In his classic book, Aguilar indicates that the purpose of all this information gathering is to help management determine the future direction of the organization.[16] Although interest in and support for environmental scanning have existed for some time,[17] not all management theorists are certain of its worth.[18]

Basically, scanning simply involves reviewing and evaluating whatever information about internal and external environments can be gleaned from several distinct sources (see Figure 2.3 for a general list of such sources).

Information about more specific sources is also available. For example, a recently reported study by Subhash C. Jain indicated that managers feel daily newspapers such as *The New York Times,* publications of industry groups such as The Conference Board, business magazines such as *Fortune,* consultants, government publications, and seminars are sources of important environmental scanning information. These same businesspeople rated literary magazines such as *The New Yorker,* universities, professional association reports from groups such as the World Future Society, academic journals such as the *Harvard Business Review,* and privately published newsletters such as the *Kiplinger Letter* as relatively unimportant sources of scanning information.[19] Several specific sources of environmental scanning information that are available to managers are cited in the Appendix to Chapter 12.

In organizations, environmental scanning systems exist in many different forms. Perhaps the most widely accepted method for categorizing these forms divides them into the following three types[20]:

1. *Irregular scanning systems:* These consist largely of ad hoc environmental studies. Such systems are normally activated when some environmental crisis (such as an energy shortage) is pending. They focus mainly on the past in an effort to identify some event that has already taken place. Emphasizing intermediate or short-run reaction to crisis, irregular scanning systems pay little attention to future environmental events.
2. *Regular scanning systems:* These systems revolve around a regular review of the environment or significant environmental components. This review is often made annually. Because such a scan is perceived as

[16] Francis Joseph Aguilar, *Scanning the Business Environment* (New York: Macmillan, 1967), p. 1.
[17] W. R. Dill, "Environment as an Influence on Managerial Autonomy," *Administrative Science Quarterly,* 1958; James D. Thompson, *Organizations in Action* (New York: McGraw-Hill, 1967); Philip Kotler, "A Design for the Firm's Marketing Nerve Center," *Business Horizons,* Fall 1966, pp. 63–74.
[18] Charles Stubbart, "Are Environmental Scanning Units Effective?" *Long Range Planning* 15, no. 3 (June 1982): 139–145.
[19] Subhash C. Jain, "Environmental Scanning in U.S. Corporations," *Long Range Planning* 17, no. 2 (1984): 117–128.
[20] Liam Fahley and William R. King, "Environmental Scanning for Corporate Planning," *Business Horizons,* August 1977, pp. 61–71.

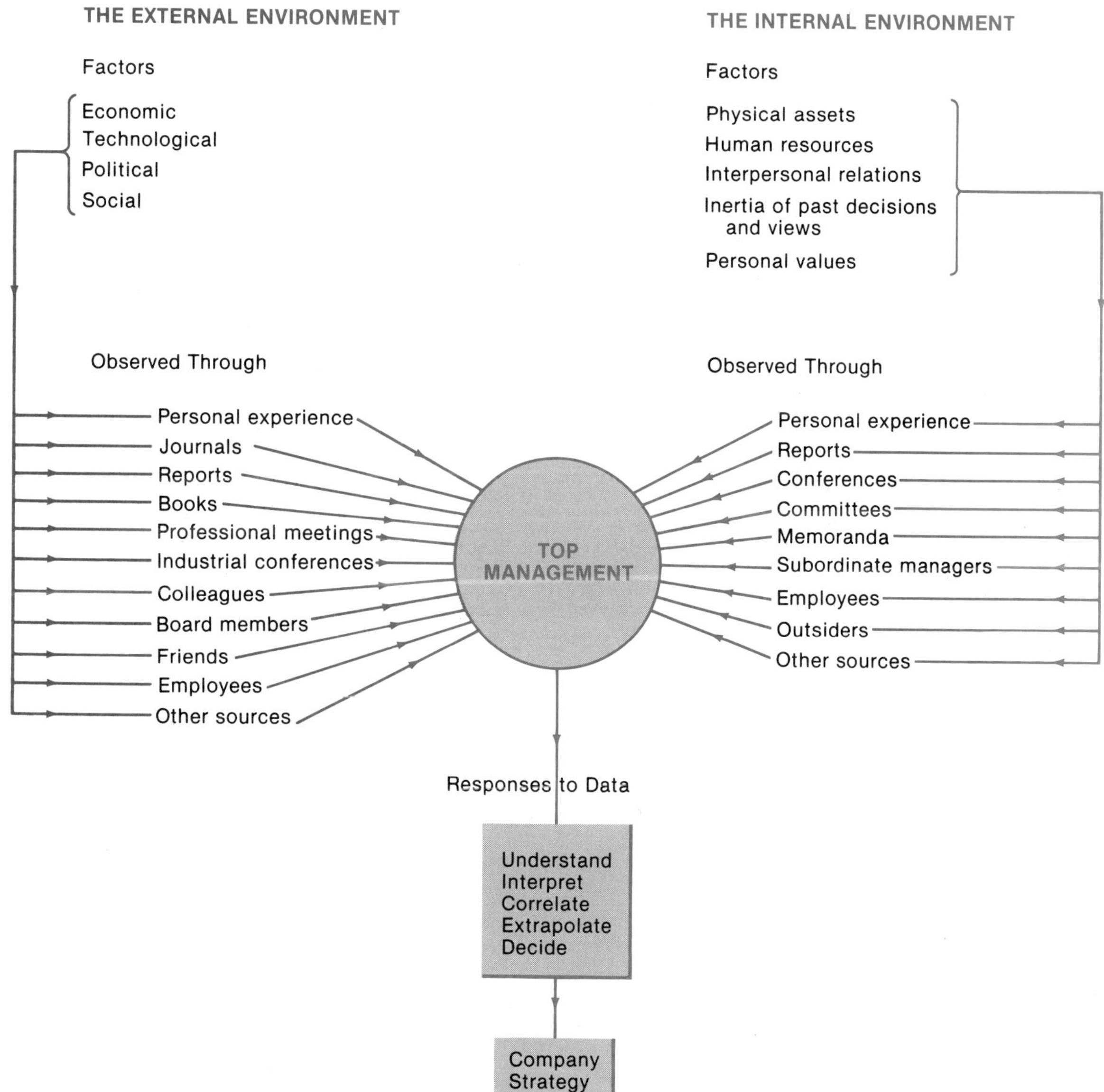

FIGURE 2.3 General Sources of Information for Internal and External Environmental Scanning

decision oriented, management commonly reviews the results during the decision-making process. The focus of this system is primarily retrospective, but some thought is given to future conditions assumed to be evolving within the environment.

3. *Continuous scanning systems:* These systems constantly monitor components of the organizational environment. Such scanning is an ongoing

activity for an established segment of the organization structure and is not performed by a committee set up temporarily for the sole purpose of completing a scan. Continuous scanning systems tend to be more future oriented than either irregular or regular systems.

Table 2.7 compares these three scanning systems along several dimensions. As one moves from the irregular model to the regular model to the continuous model, scanning activities generally become more sophisticated and play a longer-term part in organizational operations. The use of a continuous scanning system generally reflects a serious, sustained commitment to environmental analysis. The first environmental analysis that many organizations conduct takes the form of some type of irregular system. Over time, this irregular scanning system can evolve into a regular and then into a continuous scanning system.

Threats and Opportunities Analysis

Earlier in this chapter, we pointed out that the purpose of performing an environmental analysis is to identify the existence of opportunities and threats that may affect an organization's progress toward attaining its goals. Management must ensure that the information derived from environmental scanning is summarized and analyzed to determine what characterizes these threats and opportunities.

TABLE 2.7 A Comparison of Scanning Models

	SCANNING MODELS		
	Irregular	Regular	Continuous
Media for scanning activity	Ad hoc studies	Periodically updated studies	Structured data collection and processing systems
Scope of scanning	Specific events	Selected events	Broad range of environmental systems
Motivation for activity	Crisis initiated	Decision and issue oriented	Planning process oriented
Temporal nature of activity	Reactive	Proactive	Proactive
Time frame for data	Retrospective	Primarily current and retrospective	Prospective
Time frame for decision impact	Current and near-term future	Near-term	Long-term
Organizational makeup	Various staff agencies	Various staff agencies	Environmental scanning unit

Source: Liam Fahey and William R. King, "Environmental Scanning for Corporate Planning," *Business Horizons*, August 1977, p. 63. Reprinted by permission.

TABLE 2.8 A Sample Threats and Opportunities Analysis for Apple Computer

ENVIRONMENTAL FACTOR	THREAT	OPPORTUNITY
General Environment		
1. Decreasing disposable income of customers	X	
2. Society getting more comfortable using personal computers		X
Operating Environment		
1. IBM introducing new competitive product	X	
2. IBM service on product sold is superior	X	
Internal Environment		
1. Apple hiring more professional managers		X
2. Apple has high worker turnover	X	

Conclusions: This summary of information derived from an environmental analysis suggests that Apple must take steps to deal with IBM's new competitive products, upgrade quality of service on equipment sold, and reduce the rate of worker turnover. New, more professional managers should help the firm make progress in these areas. Because society as a whole is getting more comfortable using personal computers, market size for personal computers is probably growing. Since disposable income of customers is declining, however, future sales of personal computers may be harder to make. Increased profits should be forthcoming if the company is managed appropriately.

One method of performing a threats and opportunities analysis is simply to categorize the environmental factors scanned in terms of environmental level, threat potential, and opportunity potential. Then management should summarize the implications for future organizational direction that emerge. A sample threats and opportunities analysis for Apple Computer is presented in Table 2.8. Chapter 4, "Strategy Formulation," further extends this basic notion of threats and opportunities analysis by discussing the relationships among organizational *s*trengths, *w*eaknesses, *o*pportunities, and *t*hreats (SWOT Analysis).

Environmental Forecasting

Environmental forecasting is the process of determining what conditions will exist within an organization's environment at some future time. One aspect of environmental analysis is gauging the present status of the organization's environment, and for certain companies, determining the present condition of the environment may suffice for effective strategy development. However, most companies find that determining future environmental conditions is critical to ensuring future organizational success.

When they perform environmental forecasts, managers should try to predict the future status of critical environmental components at all environmental levels. Environmental forecasts commonly made for organizations include economic forecasts, social forecasts, political forecasts, and technological forecasts. For example, it is widely believed that technological innovations in microelectronics and telecommunications could shift literally millions of jobs out of the factories and offices into which the industrial revolution swept them and right back where they came from: the home.[21] Managers who judge this technological issue to be important to the future success of their organization should already be busy planning how to cope with this event if and when it materializes.

Naturally, the types of forecasts made by any one organization depend on the unique situation confronting that organization. Several environmental trends, however, are commonly followed and forecast by many organizations. These trends are shown in Table 2.9

Many environmental forecasting techniques are available to managers. Some of these techniques (such as seeking expert opinion) can be fairly simple; others (such as trend extrapolation) can be quite complex. Some organizations may need to hire experts outside the organization to apply these methods properly. Several forecasting techniques are presented and defined in Table 2.10. Highlight 2.3 actually involves you in developing an environmental forecast for Sears, Roebuck.

Evaluating the Environmental Analysis Process

Environmental analysis activities are performed in organizations to help them achieve their goals effectively and efficiently. Naturally, depending on the quality of environmental analysis activities performed, some environmental analyses are more instrumental than others in helping organizations achieve their goals. Hence it is crucial that the environmental analysis process be evaluated like any other organizational activity.

Some of the important characteristics of appropriately implemented environmental analyses are discussed below. These characteristics can be used as a set of standards against which to compare the firm's environmental analysis activities.[22]

A SUCCESSFUL ENVIRONMENTAL ANALYSIS IS LINKED CONCEPTUALLY AND PRACTICALLY TO CURRENT PLANNING OPERATIONS. If the environmental analysis system is not linked to planning, the results of the analysis will be of little use in establishing the direction the organization will take in the long run. One method commonly used to achieve this vital integration is to involve key organizational planners in some facet of environmental analysis. To ensure that this linkage between planning and environmental analysis exists at Atlantic Richfield, for example, management has made the manager of environmental issues directly respon-

[21] Boas Shamir and Ilan Solomon, "Work-at-Home and the Quality of Working Life," *Academy of Management Review* 10, no. 3 (1985): 455–464.

[22] This section is based on Engledow and Lenz, "Whatever Happened to Environmental Analysis"; Eli Segev, "Analysis of the Business Environment," *Management Review,* 1979, p. 59. Also see R. Calori, "Designing a Business Scanning System," *Long Range Planning* 22 (February 1989): 69–82.

TABLE 2.9 Important External and Internal Environmental Trends Followed by Companies

A LIST OF EXTERNAL TRENDS

1. Trends in the global market place (protectionism *vs.* free trade)
2. Growth of government as a customer
3. Development of the Common Market
4. Business with socialist countries
5. Economic and political trends in developing countries
6. Monetary trends
7. Inflationary trends
8. Emergence of the multinational firm
9. Technology as competitive tool
10. Bigness as competitive tool
11. Saturation of growth
12. Emergence of new industries
13. Technological breakthroughs
14. Growth of the service sector
15. Affluent consumers
16. Changes in age distribution of customers
17. Selling to reluctant consumers
18. Social attitudes toward business
19. Government controls
20. Consumer pressures
21. Union pressures
22. Impact of society's concern with ecology
23. Impact of "zero-growth advocates"
24. Shrinking product life cycles
25. Intra-European nationalism
26. Conflict between multinational firms and national interests
27. Public distrust of business
28. Shrinking of forecasting horizons
29. Strategic surprises
30. Competition from developing countries
31. Strategic resource shortages
32. Redistribution of power within the firm
33. Changing work attitudes
34. Pressures for employment maintenance

A LIST OF INTERNAL TRENDS

1. Size
2. Complexity
3. Structure
4. Systems
5. Communications
6. Power structure
7. Role definitions
8. Centralization/decentralization
9. Values and norms
10. Management style
11. Management competence
12. Logistic ("work force") competence
13. Capital intensity
14. Technological intensity
15. Product diversification
16. Market diversification
17. Technology diversification
18. Other

Source: Adapted from H. Igor Anshoff, "Strategic Issues Management," *Strategic Management Journal* 1 (1980): 139. Reprinted by permission of John Wiley & Sons, Ltd.

TABLE 2.10 Methods of Environmental Forecasting

1. *Expert opinion.* Knowledgeable people are selected and asked to assign importance and probability ratings to various possible future developments. The most refined version, the Delphi method, puts experts through several rounds of event assessment, where they keep refining their assumptions and judgments.
2. *Trend extrapolation.* Researchers fit best-fitting curves (linear, quadratic, or S-shaped growth curves) through past-time series to serve as a basis for extrapolation. This method can be very unreliable in that new developments can completely alter the expected direction of movement.
3. *Trend correlation.* Researchers correlate various time series in the hope of identifying leading and lagging relationships that can be used for forecasting.
4. *Dynamic modeling.* Researchers build sets of equations that attempt to describe the underlying system. The coefficients in the equations are fitted through statistical means. Econometric models of more than three hundred equations, for example, are used to forecast changes in the U.S. economy.
5. *Cross-impact analysis.* Researchers identify a set of key trends (those high in importance and/or probability). The question is then put: "If event A occurs, what will be the impact on all other trends?" The results are then used to build sets of "domino chains," with one event triggering others.
6. *Multiple scenarios.* Researchers build pictures of alternative futures, each internally consistent and with a certain probability of happening. The major purpose of the scenarios is to stimulate contingency planning.
7. *Demand/hazard forecasting.* Researchers identify major events that would greatly affect the firm. Each event is rated for its convergence with several major trends taking place in society and for its appeal to each major public group in the society. The higher the event's convergence and appeal, the higher its probability of occurring. The highest-scoring events are then researched further.

Source: Based on James R. Bright and Milton E. F. Schoeman, *A Guide to Practical Technological Forecasting* (Englewood Cliffs, N.J.: Prentice-Hall, 1973).

sible to the director of issues and planning.[23] Figure 2.4 illustrates this relationship at Atlantic Richfield.

A SUCCESSFUL ENVIRONMENTAL ANALYSIS IS RESPONSIVE TO THE INFORMATION NEEDS OF TOP MANAGEMENT WITHIN THE ORGANIZATION. The "client" for whom environmental analysis is performed is top management. Environmental analysts must thoroughly understand and meet the information needs of such managers within their organizations. And they must be aware that these information needs may change over time and be able to adjust the environmental analysis process in accordance with such changes.

A SUCCESSFUL ENVIRONMENTAL ANALYSIS IS CONTINUALLY SUPPORTED BY INTERNAL TOP MANAGEMENT. If any effort is to be successful in an organization, it must be supported and encouraged by top management. Environmental analysis activ-

[23] B. Arrington, Jr., and R. N. Sawaya, "Issues Management in an Uncertain Environment," *Long Range Planning* 17, no. 6 (1984): 17–24.

ities are no exception and will be perceived as important by organization members only to the extent that such support exists and is apparent. Without this support, environmental analysis activities will be wasted.

A SUCCESSFUL ENVIRONMENTAL ANALYSIS IS RUN BY ENVIRONMENTAL ANALYSTS WHO UNDERSTAND WHAT SKILLS ARE NECESSARY TO BE A STRATEGIST. Environmental analysts should focus on identifying existing and potential threats and opportunities suggested by components of the organizational environment. Strategists must interpret the results of environmental analysis in light of their in-depth understanding of company operations. The analyst must share the strategist's skills if he or she is to generate an effective strategy.

HIGHLIGHT 2.3

SKILLS MODULE ■ **Environmental Forecasting Skill at Sears**

INTRODUCTION

Forecasting the future status of critical environmental components is a vital managerial skill. Review the following situation that arose at Sears, and then complete the related skill development exercise. Doing so will help you develop some ability in choosing what trends to forecast for an organization.

THE SITUATION

Sears, Roebuck is the world's largest retailer of general merchandise. The company sells through retail stores, catalogs, telephone sales offices, and independent catalog merchants. Recently the company achieved record annual net income and sales, while continuing to expand its commitment to providing consumers more quality goods and services than any other organization of its kind.

One of the company's strategies for future growth is extending Sears's traditional leadership in merchandising. The vehicle for this growth is known as the "Store of the Future." This concept encompasses strengthened product lines, exciting presentation of merchandise, modernization of existing facilities, and improved customer service at the point of sale.

SKILL DEVELOPMENT EXERCISE

Assume that you are responsible for environmental analysis at Sears. One part of your job is to determine which external trends you should track in order to help Sears's top management make decisions in their effort to ensure that the "Store of the Future" becomes a reality. Brainstorm as many such trends as possible. Why are these trends relevant?

Source: Based on *1984 Sears, Roebuck & Co. Annual Report*, p. 2.

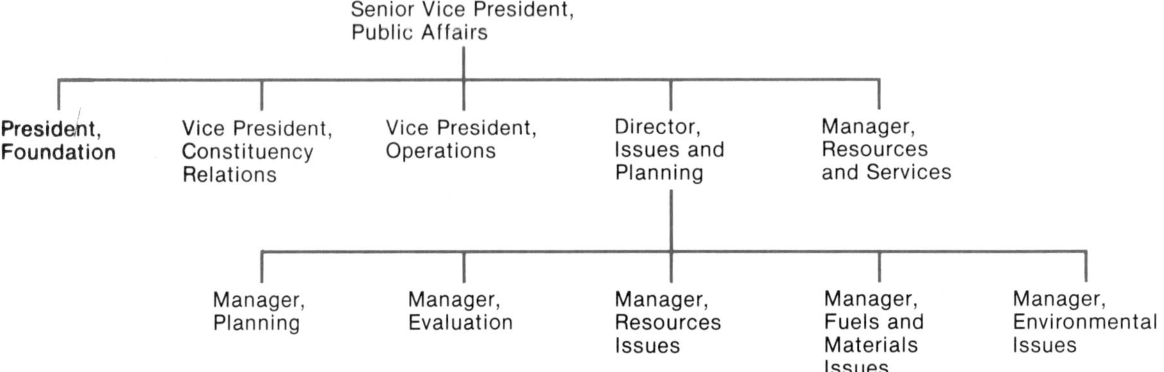

FIGURE 2.4 How Atlantic Richfield Links Planning and Environmental Analysis

SUMMARY

Environmental analysis is the process of monitoring the organizational environment to identify both present and future threats and opportunities that may influence the firm's ability to reach its goals. For purposes of analysis, this environment is divided into three main segments, or levels: the internal environment (consisting of organizational, marketing, financial, personnel, and production aspects), the operating environment (consisting of the supplier, competition, customer, labor, and international components), and the general environment (consisting of the economic, technological, legal, political, and social components).

There is no one best way to perform an environmental analysis. However, determining the relevance to the organization of various environmental levels, as well as various strategic issues, can help improve the quality of environmental analysis regardless of the method used.

Several techniques are available to help management develop a worthwhile environmental analysis. Environmental scanning is a technique whereby the manager reviews information derived from various levels of the organizational environment in order to keep abreast of critical environmental issues and events. Threats and opportunities analysis not only helps managers organize environmental information but also forces them to formulate conclusions based on that information. Environmental forecasting is a technique whereby managers attempt to predict the future characteristics of the organizational environment and hence make decisions today that will help the firm deal with the environment of tomorrow.

Once having implemented the environmental analysis process, management should continually evaluate and strive to improve it. The process should be linked to current planning operations, responsive to the information needs of top management, supported by key managers, and performed by people who understand the difference between being an analyst and being a strategist.

Highlight 2.4 contains a summary checklist of questions based on this chapter. Use it in analyzing strategic management problems and cases that focus on environmental analysis issues.

HIGHLIGHT 2.4

CHECKLIST ■ **Analyzing Environmental Issues in Problems and Cases**

- ☐ 1. Does the strategic management problem or case raise environmental analysis issues?
- ☐ 2. Are factors in the general environment being appropriately considered as part of the environmental analysis?
- ☐ 3. Are factors in the operating environment being appropriately considered as part of the environmental analysis?
- ☐ 4. Are factors in the internal environment being appropriately considered as part of the environmental analysis?
- ☐ 5. Does the organization take into account the varying relevance of different environmental levels in performing its environmental analysis?
- ☐ 6. Does the organization take into account the varying relevance of different strategic issues in performing its environmental analysis?
- ☐ 7. Is there a properly functioning environmental scanning system within the organization?
- ☐ 8. Does the organization thoroughly consider organizational threats and opportunities during the environmental analysis process?
- ☐ 9. Is environmental forecasting properly employed during the environmental analysis process?
- ☐ 10. Does the organization spend enough time evaluating and improving its environmental analysis process?

ADDITIONAL READINGS

Arnold, Danny R., Louis M. Capella, and Gary D. Smith. *Strategic Retail Management.* Reading, Mass.: Addison-Wesley Publishing, 1983.

Bowen, David E., Caren Siehl, and Benjamin Schneider. "A Framework for Analyzing Customer Service Orientation in Manufacturing." *The Academy of Management Review* 14, no. 1 (January 1989): 75–95.

Certo, Samuel C., and J. Paul Peter. *Strategic Management: A Focus on Process.* New York: McGraw-Hill, 1989.

Diffenbach, John. "Corporate Environmental Analysis in Large U.S. Corporations." *Long Range Planning* 16, no. 3 (1983): 107–116.

Glueck, William F., and Lawrence R. Jauch. *Strategic Management and Business Policy.* New York: McGraw-Hill, 1984.

Drucker, Peter F. "Managing for Tomorrow." *Industry Week,* April 14, 1980, pp. 54–64.

————. *Managing in Turbulent Times.* New York: Harper & Row, 1980.

Guth, William D. *Handbook of Business Strategy.* Boston: Warren, Gorham & Lamont, 1985.

Hofstede, Geert. *Culture's Consequences: International Differences in Work Related Values.* Beverly Hills: Sage, 1980.

Steiner, George A., John B. Miner, and Edmund R. Gray. *Management Policy and Strategy.* New York: Macmillan, 1982.

HIGHLIGHT 2.5 ■ APPLICATION OF CHAPTER MATERIAL

Environmental Analysis at Hillerich & Bradsby

Some 70 miles up the road from Hyannis, Boston Red Sox outfielder Mike Greenwell was sorting through his bats. "I ordered mine the second week of spring training and finally got the shipment the first week of June," said Greenwell. "I've used Dwight Evans's bats, Ellis Burks's bats, Jody Reed's. I guess it's just not as simple as saying, 'I need two dozen bats,' and having them delivered a week later."

"Greenwell is a .326 lifetime hitter, the [1988] MVP runner-up," says Toronto Blue Jay assistant general manager Gord Ash. "And he's having trouble getting bats. Imagine what it's like for guys in the A leagues and kids in rookie ball, who are using wood for the first time and breaking a bat a day. The problems are acute in the minors, in terms of cost, availability and quality."

Cost is the biggest reason the wooden bat is an endangered species. Wood bats break; metal bats don't. It's as simple as that. The college game came to grips with this harsh reality in 1974, when the NCAA approved the aluminum bat. "I wish we were all subsidized by the major leagues and could have wood throughout the game," says North Carolina coach Mike Roberts. "But it's economically unfeasible. In college, each player gets an aluminum bat [cost: $70], and most of the players use that one bat the entire season. Over the course of the fall and spring seasons, we'd probably use more than 50 dozen wooden bats." At $14 per bat, that's a difference of about $7,500 a year, a figure no college athletic director can afford to ignore.

Los Angeles Dodger hitting coach Ben Hines is concerned about the availability of wood for bats. "If good wood is getting harder and harder to find for the top major league hitters, then you see what minor league players have to use. College, high school and Little League teams would be getting sawdust glued together if they still used wood. You're going to see aluminum creep farther and farther up the professional pyramid."

"We've been told to prepare for a severe wood shortage over the next few years," says Bill Murray, director of operations for Major League Baseball and chairman of the rules committee. "We may have to start thinking about an alternative to the wood bat."

"I certainly see a time in the not-too-distant future when everyone will be using some alternative bat—aluminum, graphite or some composite," says Jack Hillerich, the third-generation president of Hillerich & Bradsby, which, because of its Louisville Sluggers, has been synonymous with baseball bats for more than 100 years. "A wood bat is a financially obsolete deal. If we were selling them for $40 apiece instead of $14 or $16.50 [the company's prices for minor league and major league bats], then we'd be making a sensible profit. But we aren't. We can't charge that much. The time will come when even the majors will use aluminum or graphite."

Hillerich, whose company's bat production is now more than 50 percent aluminum, says that the availability of wood isn't the primary cause for concern—at least for H & B, which grows its own timber. But other batmakers do experience shortages. And all of them, Hillerich says, have found wood bats to be an increasingly inefficient proposition.

"While once we were making seven million wood bats a year for all levels of baseball, now we're making a million and a half, 185,000 of which go to the major leagues," says Hillerich. "Major leaguers want specific orders, so we make three orders [one dozen bats per order] for one player, then shut down the operation. Then we make three more for

(*Continued*)

another player, and shut it down. That's impractical, and it's highly expensive."

All of the bat companies (H & B, Rawlings-Adirondack, Worth and Cooper) have had trouble filling wood-bat orders this season. "I'm having to stop taking orders," says H & B salesman Paul Shaughnessy, who services several major league teams.

"No one even wants the major league business anymore," adds Chuck Schupp, H & B director of professional bat sales. "We do it but partly because of the 100-year relationship we have had with baseball. When we make a bat, we use 40 percent of the wood, at most. If we sell the billets to other industries, nearly 100 percent is used."

DISCUSSION QUESTIONS

1. Based simply upon the above situation, does environmental analysis at Hillerich & Bradsby seem to assume the policy-oriented role, the integrated strategic planning role, or the function-oriented role?
2. If you were Mr. Hillerich, which environmental level would you give the highest priority for monitoring in your environmental analysis process?
3. If you were Mr. Hillerich, what factors would you forecast as a part of your environmental analysis process? Why?

Source: Adapted from Peter Gammons, "End of an Era," *Sports Illustrated*, July 24, 1989, pp. 16–23.

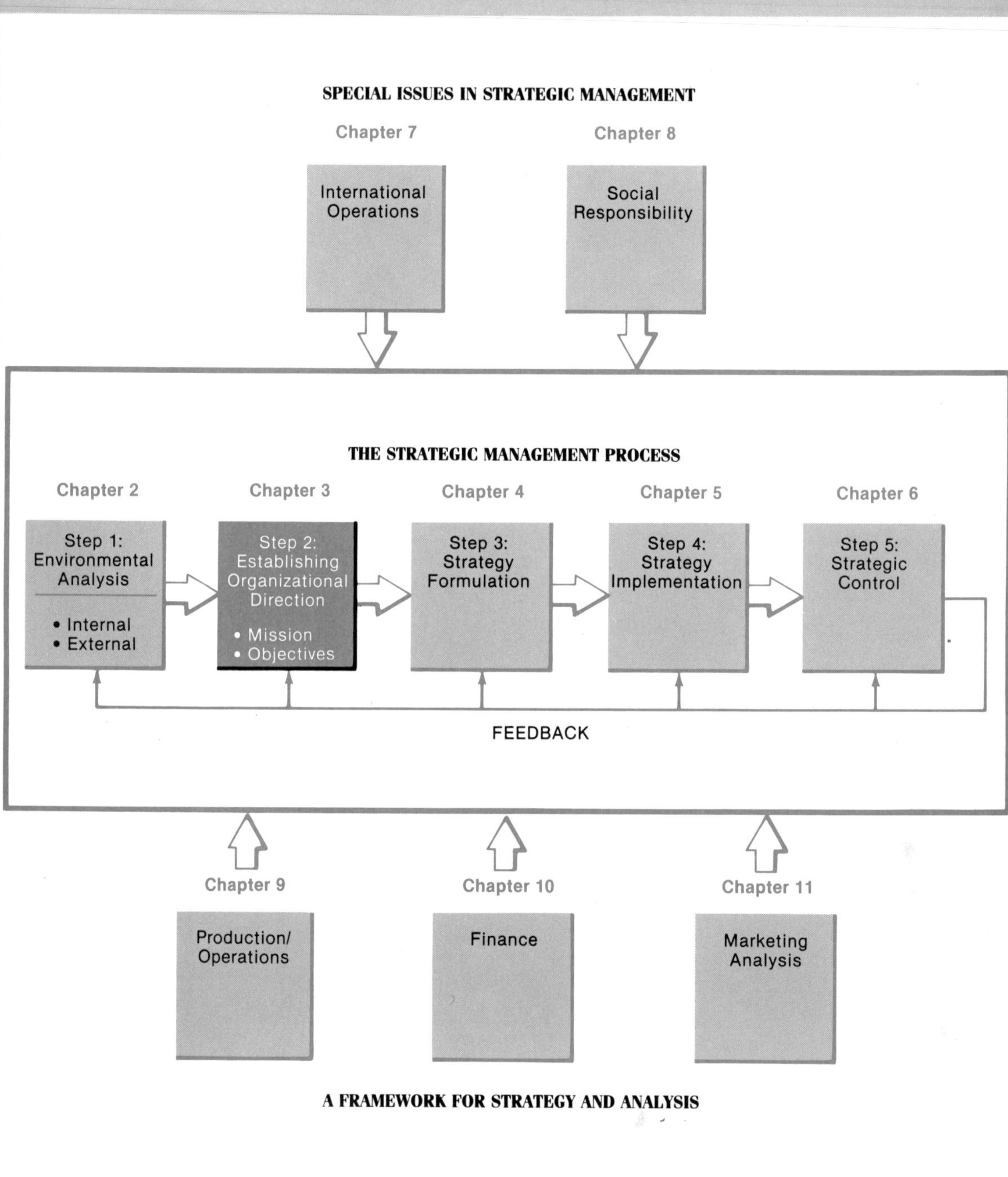

SPECIAL ISSUES IN STRATEGIC MANAGEMENT
Chapter 7
International Operations
Chapter 8
Social Responsibility
THE STRATEGIC MANAGEMENT PROCESS
Chapter 2
Step 1: Environmental Analysis
• Internal
• External
Chapter 3
Step 2: Establishing Organizational Direction
• Mission
• Objectives
Chapter 4
Step 3: Strategy Formulation
Chapter 5
Step 4: Strategy Implementation
Chapter 6
Step 5: Strategic Control
FEEDBACK
Chapter 9
Production/ Operations
Chapter 10
Finance
Chapter 11
Marketing Analysis
A FRAMEWORK FOR STRATEGY AND ANALYSIS
Chapter 12
An Approach to Solving Strategic Problems and Cases

CHAPTER 3

Establishing Organizational Direction: Mission and Objectives

In Chapter 2 we talked about environmental analysis, the first step of the strategic management process. In that chapter, the fundamentals of environmental analysis and environmental structure were discussed, and guidelines for performing an environmental analysis were offered. This chapter focuses on establishing organizational direction, that step of the strategic management process that immediately follows environmental analysis.

Two important considerations commonly used by management to establish and document the direction in which an organization should move are organizational mission and organizational objectives. Essentially, the organizational mission establishes the general direction of the firm, and organizational objectives narrow the focus to more specific targets. Only after pondering the results of a thorough environmental analysis are managers able to formulate an appropriate organizational mission and objectives consistent with it and compatible with each other.

FUNDAMENTALS OF ORGANIZATIONAL MISSION

A critical step in establishing the direction of any organization is developing an organizational mission that reflects the results of an environmental analysis. Here we approach the topic of organizational mission by defining it, explaining its importance, and describing the type of information generally contained in mission statements.

What Is Organizational Mission?

Organizational mission is the purpose for which, or reason why, an organization exists. In general, a firm's organizational mission contains such information as what types of products or services the organization produces, who its customers tend to be, and what important values it holds. Organizational mission is a very broad statement of organizational direction. To develop an appropriate organizational mission, management should thoroughly analyze and consider information generated during the environmental analysis process.

For any given firm, organizational mission is normally summarized and documented in a *mission statement.* Sample mission statements for several different types of organizations appear in Highlight 3.1. The organizations include: Great Scot Supermarkets, a small midwestern grocery store chain in Indiana; International Business Machines (IBM), a giant information technology company; Federal Express, an international shipping company; and The Crummer School, a small graduate school of business at Rollins College in Winter Park, Florida. Further discussion of the contents of organizational mission statements appears later in this chapter.

Why Is Organizational Mission Important?

Establishing an organizational mission is an important part of management's job, because the existence of a formally expressed organizational mission

HIGHLIGHT 3.1

ILLUSTRATIVE EXAMPLE ■ **Organizational Missions: Great Scot Supermarkets, IBM, Federal Express, The Crummer School**

GREAT SCOT SUPERMARKETS

Great Scot Supermarkets is a progressive growth oriented company recognized as a regional leader in retail foods. We will continue to strive to improve our responsiveness to the needs and concerns of our customers, employees, suppliers, and the communities in which we serve. This will be accomplished through the development of our employees, an emphasis on volume, and profitability. We intend to expand within our existing marketing areas to both protect and improve our positions. As personnel and finances are adequate and opportunities arise our growth will continue in other areas.

Source: Mission statement for Great Scot Supermarkets.

IBM

IBM is in the business of applying advanced information technology to solve the problems of business, government, science, space exploration, defense, education, medicine, and other areas of human activity. IBM offers customers solutions that incorporate information processing systems, software, communications systems, and other products and services to address specific needs. These solutions are provided by IBM's worldwide marketing organizations, as well as through the company's Business Partners, including authorized dealers and remarketers.

Source: *IBM 1988 Annual Report*, p. i.

FEDERAL EXPRESS

Federal Express is committed to our People-Service Profit philosophy. We will produce outstanding financial returns by providing totally reliable, competitively superior, global air-ground transportation of high priority goods and documents that require rapid, time-certain delivery. Equally important, positive control of each package will be maintained utilizing real time electronic tracking and tracing systems. A complete record of each shipment and delivery will be presented with our request for payment. We will be helpful, courteous, and professional to each other and the public. We will strive to have a completely satisfied customer at the end of each transaction.

Source: *The Federal Express Manager's Guide.*

THE CRUMMER SCHOOL

The mission of the Crummer School is to improve management through formal education programs stressing an administrative point of view, research and publication involving new knowledge and teaching materials, and relationships with businesses and the community. In fulfilling this mission the School is committed to programs that emphasize high quality, innovation, problem solving, and the application of management theory.

The emphasis of the Crummer School is on the full-time MBA program. The primary target market for this core business is the national pool of applicants, with or without an academic background in business, but including those who have business experience.

Source: *The Roy E. Crummer Graduate School of Business Handbook*, 1989.

generally makes it more likely that the organization will succeed. Having an established and documented organizational mission accomplishes several important things.

- *It helps focus human effort in a common direction.* The mission makes explicit the major targets the organization is trying to reach. By keeping these targets in mind, management can ensure that all organization members work together in a concerted effort to reach them.
- *It helps ensure that the organization will not pursue conflicting purposes.* Purposes that are inconsistent with one another imply that the organization is moving in different, incompatible directions. By developing a sound mission statement, management can make sure that the organization is built on a foundation of clear, compatible purposes and avoids waste and conflict.
- *It serves as a general rationale for allocating organizational resources.* Organizations use various resources to produce goods and services and to make them available to customers. These resources include monetary resources, human resources, raw materials, and equipment. A properly developed mission statement contains general guidelines about what resources an organization should acquire and how it should distribute them.
- *It establishes broad areas of job responsibilities within the organization.* People perform specific jobs within organizations in order to produce goods and services. Broad guidance concerning the types of jobs that should exist within an organization are found in a statement of organizational mission.
- *It acts as a basis for the development of organizational objectives.*[1] When we discussed the strategic management model presented in Chapter 1, we explained that organizational objectives should reflect organizational mission. Because a mission statement outlines the general purpose of the organization, it serves as the point of departure for the more specific organizational objectives. Properly formulated organizational objectives are consistent with organizational mission. Any objectives that are inconsistent with an accurate statement of organizational mission have been improperly formulated and should be abandoned or revised.

What Information Appears in Mission Statements?

The kinds of information contained in mission statements vary somewhat from organization to organization. But even so, most mission statements seem to cover several major topics. These topics may be either addressed within

[1] W. R. King and D. I. Cleland, *Strategic Planning and Policy* (New York: Van Nostrand Reinhold, 1979), p. 124; Lloyd Byars, "The Strategic Management Process: A Model and Terminology," *Managerial Planning* 32, no. 6 (May 1984): 38–44; also in Daniel J. McCarthy, Robert J. Minichiello, and Joseph R. Curran, *Business Policy and Strategy: Concepts and Readings* (Homewood, Ill.: Richard D. Irwin, 1987), pp. 12–23.

the organizational mission statement or contained in materials that accompany it.[2] The topics include:

- *Company product or service:* This information identifies the goods and/or services produced by the organization—that which the company offers to its customers.
- *Market:* This information describes the customers of the organization. Who these customers are and where they are located are common themes.
- *Technology:* This information generally includes such topics as the tools, machines, materials, techniques, and processes used to produce organizational goods and services. Discussion consists largely of a broad description of organizational production techniques. With the advent of such technological innovations as the business computer and robots, technology has come to be emphasized within the strategic planning process of virtually every organization.[3]
- *Company objectives:* Most mission statements make general reference to company objectives. For many firms, these include the intention to survive through continuing growth and profitability. Management must ensure that any more specific and comprehensive organizational objectives are consistent with the general references to organizational objectives that appear in the mission statement.
- *Company philosophy:* Statements of company philosophy (also called company creed) commonly appear as part of the mission statement or in the supplemental material that accompanies it. *Company philosophy* is a statement reflecting the basic beliefs and values that should guide organization members in conducting organizational business. Highlight 3.2 describes the Baxter Travenol Company and summarizes its philosophy or fundamental principles.
- *Company self-concept:* Mission statements inevitably contain or are accompanied by information on the self-concept of the company. *Company self-concept* is the company's own view or impression of itself. In essence, the company arrives at this self-concept by assessing its strengths, weaknesses, competition, and ability to survive in the marketplace.
- *Public image:* Mission statements generally contain some reference, either direct or indirect, to the type of impression the company is attempting to leave with the organization's public. In the end, of course, it is not the image management wants to project that is important, but the image that the public actually forms. Table 3.1 lists several mecha-

[2] This discussion is largely based on John A. Pearce II, "The Company Mission as a Strategic Tool," *Sloan Management Review,* Spring 1982, pp. 15–24.
[3] M. D. Skipton, "Helping Managers to Develop Strategies," *Long Range Planning* 18, no. 2 (1985): 56–68.

HIGHLIGHT 3.2

ILLUSTRATIVE EXAMPLE ■ Baxter Travenol: Description and Philosophy

Baxter Travenol is engaged in the worldwide development, manufacture, and sale of a diversified line of medical care products and related services. These products and services are used principally by hospitals, blood centers, clinical laboratories, dialysis centers, and by patients at home under physician supervision. Baxter Travenol products are manufactured in 17 countries and bring quality therapy to millions of patients in more than 100 countries.

FUNDAMENTAL PRINCIPLES

At Baxter Travenol, we are committed to:

Improving health care for people around the world;

Meeting the highest standards in responsible corporate citizenship;

Attaining a position of leadership in each of the health care markets we serve;

Providing our customers with products and services of consistently high quality and value;

Sustaining a strong spirit of teamwork through mutual commitment, dedication, and loyalty within our employee family; and

Achieving consistent, long-term financial growth and the best possible return to our stockholders.

Source: *1984 Baxter Travenol Annual Report*. Reprinted by permission, Baxter Travenol Laboratories, Inc.

nisms that corporations commonly use to project their chosen image to the public.

Such topics, then, as company product or service, market, technology, and company goals, philosophy, self-concept, and public image are commonly addressed in a statement of organizational mission or in material that accompanies it. Highlight 3.3 consists of a mission statement and supporting information prepared by the Elpaso Electric Company.

THE NATURE OF ORGANIZATIONAL OBJECTIVES

The first part of this chapter outlined the role of organizational mission in establishing the general direction of the firm. This part focuses on establishing progressively *more specific* organizational direction through the use of organi-

TABLE 3.1 Techniques for Projecting Organizational Image

Nomenclature. The names used for the corporation and its divisions, departments, and subsidiary companies as well as the words used to identify the company's industries, markets, offices, services, and the titles of its personnel.
Formal Statements. Statements consistently associated with a company or elements of that company that clarify (to both internal and external audiences) its mission, objectives, philosophy, or unique contribution.
Organization. The communicated "degree of relationship" between divisions, departments, and subsidiaries.
Imagery and Graphics. Logos, other symbols, typestyles, formats, and color—all the forms of visual communication.
Permanent Media. Signs, stationery, business cards and forms, vehicles, facilities—interiors and exteriors.
Promotional Media. Advertising copy, brochures, publications, public relations, articles, events, activities, individuals chosen as representatives and spokesmen, speeches, audiovisual presentations, or any other promotional media.

Source: Edmund R. Gray and Larry R. Smeltzer, "Corporate Image—An Integral Part of Strategy," *Sloan Management Review,* Summer 1985, p. 74. Reprinted by permission of the publisher.

zational objectives. We will define organizational objectives, explain their importance, describe two major types of objectives that exist in organizations, and discuss different areas in which organizational objectives should be formulated.

Definition of Organizational Objectives

An *organizational objective* is a target toward which the organization directs its efforts. For several years a debate has been taking place in the management literature about exactly what term should be used to refer to organizational targets. Some management theorists indicate that the term "objective" should be used[4]; some suggest using either "objectives" or "goals."[5] Still others claim that these two terms mean different things and cannot be used interchangeably.[6] In this text the term *objective* is used to refer to targets that the organization is attempting to reach.

The Importance of Organizational Objectives

The importance of establishing appropriate objectives for an organization cannot be overemphasized. Objectives provide the foundation for planning,

4 Kenneth R. Andrews, *The Concept of Corporate Strategy* (Homewood, Ill.: Richard D. Irwin, 1980).
5 Alfred Chandler, *Strategy and Structure: Chapters in the History of American Industrial Enterprise* (Cambridge, Mass.: M.I.T. Press, 1962).
6 See H. I. Anshoff, *Business Strategy and Policy: An Analytic Approach to Business Policy for Growth and Expansion* (New York: McGraw-Hill, 1965); Charles W. Hofer and Dan Schendel, *Strategy Formulation: Analytical Concepts* (St. Paul, Minn.: West Publishing Company, 1978); and Robert A. Comerford and Dennis W. Callaghan, *Strategic Management: Text, Tools, and Cases for Business Policy* (Boston: Kent Publishing Company, 1985).

HIGHLIGHT 3.3

ILLUSTRATIVE EXAMPLE ■ The Elpaso Electric Company: Mission Statement and Complementary Information

PHILOSOPHY

The El Paso–Las Cruces area is an excellent place to live and to work. The service area of the electric company has provided exceptional opportunities for the company and for its employees. We believe that a value received is worth a value returned. In this regard, we believe that the company must respond to the needs of this community in all areas where economically practical.

MISSION

Elpaso Electric has a threefold mission. The company is dedicated to providing reliable electric service to customers at the most reasonable cost. The company is obligated to protect and enhance the investment of its shareholders, the investment which has created the jobs and the growth opportunity for the company. The company is also obligated to provide an enriching and satisfying place for its employees to work. We believe that the strategic goals and objectives which are presented in this plan provide the necessary direction so that we may successfully accomplish our mission.

AREAS OF FOCUS

To carry out the company's mission as an active organization in the community and one which is dedicated to the betterment of all concerned, we focus on the following general areas of concern:

- Customer service
- Community service
- Shareholder relations
- Employee–management obligations
- Corporate communications

STRATEGIC GOALS AND OBJECTIVES

Each area of focus provides categories for which strategic goals are established as a part of the planning process for individual and departmental action. Proposed projects and activities are formulated to accomplish specific objectives in accord with and in support of one or more of these goals.

Strategic goals and objectives are developed and formalized in order to give general direction to management for the overall corporate planning tasks as well as more specific departmental planning activities. The goals and objectives should not limit the ingenuity and imagination of company management, but rather should provide an overall agreed-upon course of action. It is recognized that the management of the company must remain flexible and innovative in solving the day-to-day operating problems. However, these strategic goals exemplify our philosophy in fulfilling the overall corporate mission.

CUSTOMER SERVICE

- Provide a quality of service to customers at least equal to the highest standards in the industry.
- Maintain reliability of service to customers at a level above 99 percent.
- On a continuing basis, study and implement improved methods and plant betterments for providing electricity to customers at the lowest possible cost.
- Insure that customers are educated on the safety aspects of using electricity.
- Retain all existing customers and seek new customers through system expansion where feasible and consistent with good economics.
- Remain independent in providing power supply and transmission service where possible and consistent with good economics for the customer and shareholder.

COMMUNITY SERVICE

- Promote economic growth and increased development of the company's total service area.
- Protect, enhance, and develop the community's natural resources with particular attention to air, water, and land resources.
- Provide job opportunities and an investment in the service area which promotes a higher standard of living for all citizens.
- Provide to the service area both economic and social support consistent with the level of responsibility expected of the number 1 corporate citizen.
- Promote a high degree of positive involvement in the service area by all employees.
- Cooperate with and serve the educational institutions located in the service area in a manner consistent with other leaders in the industry.
- Maintain leadership positions within and provide appropriate assistance to community service organizations. Continue to support the United Way in a leadership manner.

(*Continued*)

SHAREHOLDER RELATIONS

- Assure that all expenditures are made in such a way as to protect and enhance the shareholders' investment.
- Provide a rate of return to the shareholders which is competitive with other possible investments.
- Maintain the financial integrity of the company in a manner consistent with AA-rated utility companies.
- Earn a rate of return which is above the national average and maintain bond coverages above three times in all financial periods.
- Continue to study the feasibility of new programs and projects which might be undertaken as measures to maintain and improve the financial integrity of the company.
- Base all company involvement in new programs or projects on solid economic principles.

EMPLOYEE–MANAGEMENT OBLIGATIONS

- Monitor and strive to improve the quality of management and supervision.
- Promote a high degree of professionalism throughout the entire company.
- Develop, update, and monitor both long- and short-term plans in a formalized manner.
- Insure the flexibility of corporate plans while establishing performance goals for all levels of employees.
- Undertake research and development consistent with strategic goals, corporate objectives, and sound economics.
- Attract, develop, and retain able and loyal employees.
- Provide equal employment opportunities and a high degree of training along with modern, professional tools.
- Strive to provide employees with compensation levels at or above industry norms.

CORPORATE COMMUNICATIONS

- Make an assertive effort to provide informative communications on relevant company and energy issues.
- Maintain positive communications with all those in contact with the company to specifically include customers, regulators, members of governmental bodies, employees, community and industry leaders, financial community, and regional utilities.
- Keep senior management apprised and educated on current topics of interest, and always maintain an issues management ability.

- Communicate the company's good citizen achievements and future aspirations to support the community.
- Enhance the community image of the company by being receptive to the needs of customers and the community.
- Show and communicate actions by the company which show our concern for the customer.

Source: *1984 Elpaso Electric Company Annual Report.* Reprinted by permission.

organizing, motivating, and controlling. Without objectives and their effective communication, behavior in organizations can stray in almost any direction.[7]

For many years management writers have claimed that organizational objectives should be used much as navigators use the North Star. Such theorists stress that "fixing your objective is like identifying the North Star—you sight it on your compass and then use it as a means of getting back on track when you stray."[8] Other, more specific suggestions about how managers should use objectives to guide their organizations may be more helpful on a day-to-day basis.[9] According to these suggestions:

- *Managers should use organizational objectives as a guide in decision making.* A significant portion of any manager's job involves making decisions. The manager who knows what objectives have been established for the organization finds it easier to make decisions that will ensure that organizational objectives are reached.
- *Managers should use organizational objectives as a guide for increasing organizational efficiency.* An efficient organization is one that wastes little organizational resources in attaining organizational objectives. To develop and maintain an efficient organization, therefore, managers must have organizational objectives clearly in mind.
- *Managers should use organizational objectives as a guide for performance appraisal.* Human effort or work is of critical importance in reaching organizational objectives. Managers should both evaluate and reward worker performance in terms of how instrumental the performance is in helping the organization attain its objectives. By the same token,

[7] Max D. Richards, *Setting Strategic Goals and Objectives* (St. Paul, Minn.: West Publishing Company, 1986), p. 3.

[8] Marshall E. Dimock, *The Executive in Action* (New York: Harper and Brothers, 1945), p. 54. For more recent discussion of this issue see Samuel C. Certo, *Principles of Modern Management: Functions and Systems,* 4th ed. (Boston: Allyn & Bacon, 1989), pp. 59–60.

[9] For a worthwhile discussion on the potential value of establishing objectives in organizations, see Robert C. Ford, Frank S. McLaughlin, and James Nixdorf, "Ten Questions About MBO," *California Management Review,* Spring 1983, pp. 88–94.

worker performance that does not help the organization achieve its objectives is discouraged by virtue of its not being rewarded and perhaps even punished.

Types of Objectives in Organizations

It is usually agreed that organizations have two different types of objectives. *Short-run objectives* are targets that the organization is attempting to reach within about one or two years. *Long-run objectives* are targets that the organization is trying to reach within about three to five years.

These two types of organizational objectives differ in significant ways. The most apparent difference, of course, is the period of time within which the organization is attempting to reach the objective. Another important difference between these objectives is how specifically they are written. In general, short-run objectives tend to be more specific about such issues as who will accomplish them, exactly what is to be accomplished, when it is to be accomplished, and in what organizational area it falls.

Areas in Which Organizational Objectives Are Established

Since the early history of business and industry, most organizations have focused on one primary objective: making a profit. Today, however, many companies do *not* put maximum profit before all else. In practice, no absolute or inviolable financial priorities exist. Rather, these priorities shift as the competitive and economic environments change.[10]

Peter Drucker, perhaps the most influential business writer of modern times, has pointed out in his landmark book *The Practice of Management* that it is a mistake to manage organizations by focusing primarily on one and only one objective.[11] According to Drucker, organizations should aim at achieving several objectives instead of just one. Enough objectives should be set so that all areas important to the operation of the firm are covered. Eight key areas in which organizational objectives should normally be set are:

1. *Market standing:* the position of an organization—where it stands—relative to its competitors. One of the organization's objectives should indicate the position an organization is striving to achieve relative to its competitors.
2. *Innovation:* any change made to improve methods of conducting organizational business. Organizational objectives should indicate targets at which the organization is aiming in the area of innovation.
3. *Productivity:* the level of goods or services produced by an organization relative to the resources used in the production process. Organizations that use fewer resources to produce a specified level of products are

[10] Gordon Donaldson, "Financial Goals and Strategic Consequences," *Harvard Business Review,* May–June 1985, pp. 57–66.

[11] Peter F. Drucker, *The Practice of Management* (New York: Harper & Row, 1954), pp. 62–65, 126–129.

said to be more productive than organizations that require more resources to produce at the same level.

4. *Resource levels:* the relative amounts of various resources held by an organization, such as inventory, equipment, and cash. Most organizations should set objectives indicating the relative amounts of each of these assets that should be held.
5. *Profitability:* the ability of an organization to earn revenue dollars beyond the expenses necessary to generate the revenue. Organizations commonly have objectives indicating the level of profitability they seek.
6. *Manager performance and development:* the quality of managerial performance and the rate at which managers are developing personally. Because both of these areas are critical to the long-term success of an organization, emphasizing them by establishing and striving to reach related organizational objectives is very important.
7. *Worker performance and attitude:* the quality of nonmanagement performance and such employees' feelings about their work. These areas are also crucial to long-term organizational success. The importance of these considerations should be stressed through the establishment of organizational objectives.
8. *Social responsibility:* the obligation of business to help improve the welfare of society while it strives to reach organizational objectives. Only a few short years ago, setting organizational objectives in this area would have been somewhat controversial. Today, however, setting such objectives in organizations is commonplace and is considered very important. Chapter 8, "Strategic Management and Social Responsibility," covers this topic in much more detail.

Highlight 3.4 will give you an opportunity to devise and express one of each of these kinds of objectives.

Characteristics of High-Quality Organizational Objectives

Organizational objectives exist in some form in virtually all modern organizations. The *quality* of objectives, of course, largely determines how useful they actually are. Several guidelines have been developed over time to help managers develop high-quality organizational objectives, including the following:

- *Managers should develop organizational objectives that are specific.* Specific objectives indicate exactly what is to be accomplished, who is to accomplish it, and within what time frame it is to be accomplished. Being specific eliminates confusion about objectives and ensures that all organization members know and understand what is expected of them. Furthermore, the step in the strategic management process that follows establishing organizational direction deals with formulating organizational strategy (see Chapter 4). In general, the more specific an objective, the easier it is for management to develop strategies that will

HIGHLIGHT 3.4

SKILLS MODULE ■ Writing Multiple Objectives for Cracker Barrel

INTRODUCTION

The material you have just read maintains that there are eight key areas in which objectives can be established for organizations. Study the following description of Cracker Barrel Old Country Store, Inc., and then complete the skill development exercise that follows. Doing so will help you develop some skill in writing objectives in each of these areas.

THE SITUATION

Cracker Barrel Old Country Store, Inc., owns and operates 44 Cracker Barrel Old Country Stores. The stores themselves are actually store/restaurants located primarily near interstate interchanges in Tennessee, Kentucky, Georgia, South Carolina, North Carolina, Florida, and Alabama.

Each of the stores sports a rustic "country store" building, a fireplace, and antique restaurant furnishings. The stores are open seven days a week and serve breakfast, lunch, and dinner. They also highlight early American gifts, crafts, toys, and prepackaged food items. Only a few stores sell gasoline, and this part of the business is being phased out entirely.

SKILL DEVELOPMENT EXERCISE

Write one objective for Cracker Barrel Old Country Stores, Inc., for each of the eight areas covered in the text. Which objectives did you find hardest to write? Why? Do you think practicing managers also find writing objectives in these areas difficult? Why?

Source: Based on 1985 *Cracker Barrel Old Country Stores, Inc., Annual Report.*

ensure its accomplishment. Specific, high-quality organizational objectives are actually the foundation that management needs to formulate appropriate organizational strategies.

- *Managers should set organizational objectives that require a desirable level of effort.* Objectives should be set high enough so that employees must extend themselves somewhat to achieve them. On the other hand, the objectives should not be set so high that employees become frustrated and stop trying! Happily, objectives that challenge employees' abilities are generally more interesting and more motivating than easily attained objectives.[12]

[12] For more information about the effect of challenge on motivation of workers, see Frederick Herzberg, "One More Time: How Do You Motivate Employees?" *Harvard Business Review,* January–February 1968, pp. 53–62. Due to its continuing relevance for modern managers, this article has been reprinted: *Harvard Business Review,* September–October 1987, pp. 109–120.

- *Managers should establish organizational objectives that are reachable.* All organization members should perceive organizational objectives as attainable. Workers who view objectives as impossible to reach may utterly ignore the objectives as an indicator of how they should apply their time and effort.
- *Managers should establish organizational objectives that are flexible.* Objectives should be established with the understanding that they might have to be modified. Objectives are commonly changed in organizations as organizational environments change. Managers must be aware that objectives can change. They must continually assess the organizational environment to discover when changes in organizational objectives should be made, and they must encourage all organization members to raise the issue if they think such changes are required.
- *Managers should establish organizational objectives that are measurable.* A *measurable objective,* sometimes called an *operational objective,* is an objective stated in such a way that an attempt to attain it can be compared to the objective itself to determine whether it actually has been attained. Confusion about whether an objective has been attained generally results in poor relations between management and workers, rapidly transforming an organizational objective into a liability rather than an asset. It is well worth taking great care, in designing objectives, to prevent this damaging outcome.
- *Managers should develop organizational objectives that are consistent in the long run and the short run.* Managers should establish organizational objectives that reflect a desirable mix of time frames and are supportive of one another. Long-term objectives must be consistent with organizational mission and should represent targets to be hit within about a three- to five-year period. Short-run objectives must be consistent with long-run objectives and should represent targets to be reached within about one or two years. As a general rule, shorter-run objectives should be derived from, and lead to the attainment of, longer-run objectives. Figure 3.1 continues the example of Great Scot Supermarkets, which we introduced earlier. It illustrates the consistency of possible objectives for that firm with its organizational mission.

THE PROCESS OF ESTABLISHING ORGANIZATIONAL DIRECTION

The first two parts of this chapter discussed the fundamentals of organizational mission and organizational objectives. This section focuses on the process of establishing organizational direction. This process consists of three major steps: (1) reflecting on the results of an environmental analysis, (2) establishing an appropriate organizational mission, and (3) establishing appropriate organizational objectives.

Step 1: Reflecting on the Results of an Environmental Analysis

Environmental analysis should provide managers with adequate information for reflection. Data should be drawn from all organizational environment

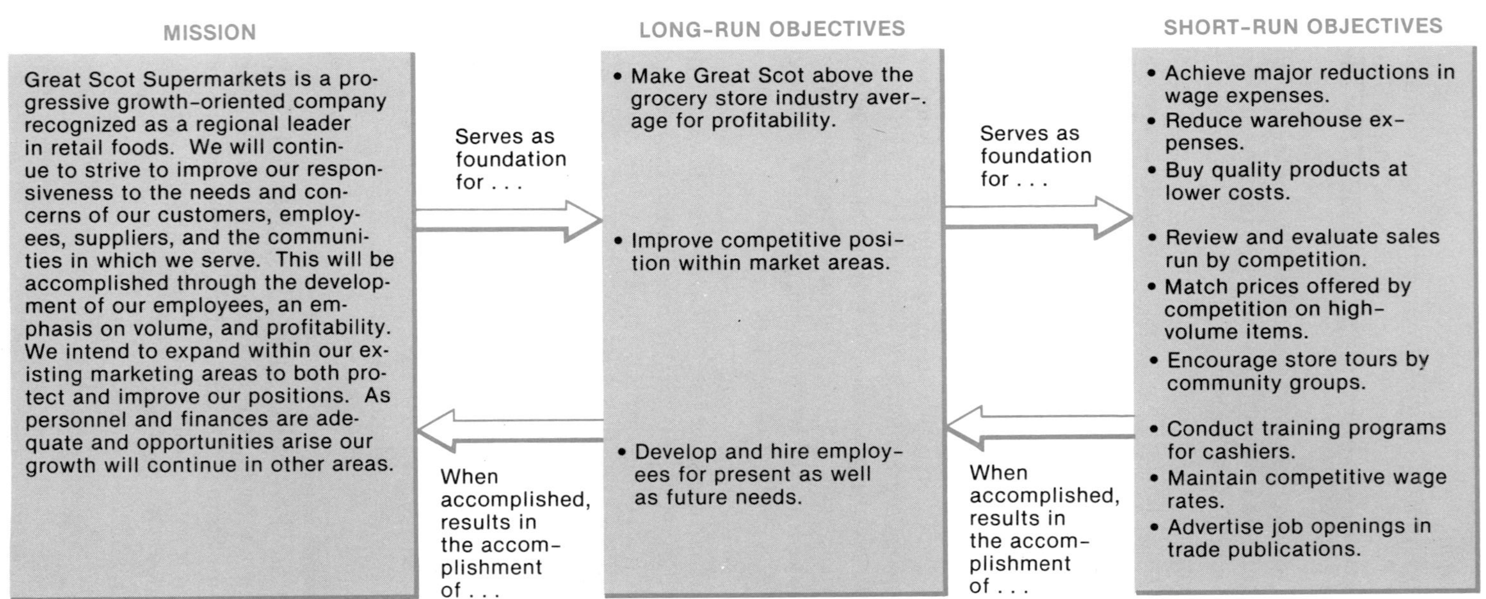

FIGURE 3.1 Consistency of Possible Mission and Objectives for Great Scot Supermarkets

levels—the general, operating, and internal environment. Analysis of this information should establish the relevance of these environmental levels and of various strategic issues to the organization.

Step 2: Developing an Appropriate Organizational Mission

Information derived from the environmental analysis serves as a solid foundation on which the organizational mission can be built. Once managers understand both the internal and external organizational environments, they are better equipped to outline an appropriate purpose or mission for the organization. An *appropriate organizational mission* is one that reflects the organizational environment and thereby increases the probability of the organization's long-term survival.

Step 3: Developing Appropriate Organizational Objectives

After the organizational mission has been developed, *appropriate organizational objectives*—objectives that are consistent with an appropriate organizational mission—must be formulated.

Over time, the process that managers use in systematically developing organizational objectives has evolved into three suggested steps.[13] The first of these steps is analyzing significant trends within the environment, the second is developing objectives for the organization as a whole, and the third is creating a hierarchy of objectives. A fourth step that should be added to this list is developing individual objectives. Each of these steps is discussed in detail below.

Analyzing Environmental Trends

Like organizational mission, organizational objectives should reflect the environment within which the organization operates. As indicated earlier, organizational objectives should change as the organizational environment changes. In addition, those who establish organizational objectives must recognize that environmental trends are then taking shape that will affect the future relevance of the objectives and the odds of accomplishing them.

An example of one such trend followed by many managers is charted by the *index of industrial production.* This index represents the output of industrial concerns throughout the nation and is a general indicator of the health of the nation's economy. Included in this index are outputs of a wide variety of companies involved in such varied activities and businesses as mining, manufacturing, utilities, business equipment, metal products, home goods (furniture and appliances), defense, space equipment, and construction supplies.

[13] Charles H. Granger, "How to Set Company Objectives," *Management Review,* July 1970, pp. 2–8. For human implications of this systematic development see Robert D. Pritchard, Philip L. Roth, Steven D. Jones, Patricia J. Galgay, and Margaret D. Watson, "Designing a Goal-Setting System for Increasing Employee Motivation and Performance," *Organizational Dynamics,* Summer 1988, pp. 69–78.

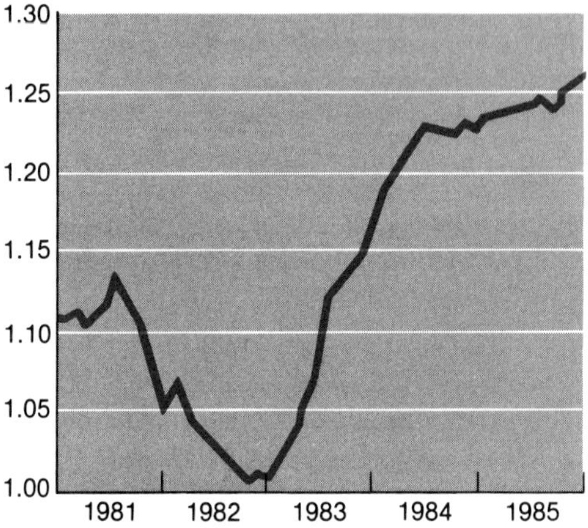

FIGURE 3.2 Index of Industrial Production for 1981–1985

Figure 3.2 shows actual figures for the index of industrial production for 1981 through 1985. A trend like the one reflected in this figure would probably indicate to a manager that industrial production and the economy in general will continue to gain strength well into 1986.[14] Given this favorable indicator for the overall economy, most managers would probably feel justified in establishing a similar upward trend: somewhat higher organizational objectives.

Studying relevant trends over several years can result in a better understanding of factors that influence organizational success. In some cases, however, managers face factors that are relatively new and cannot be substantially evaluated on the basis of past experience. One such factor is at-home shopping, an innovation enabling consumers to purchase goods and/or services by means of an electronic device such as a home computer. In their own homes, customers can see merchandise displayed, identify the seller, place an order, and even pay for their purchase with a credit card.[15] Managers should keep track of such innovations in order to be aware of and react appropriately to any important environmental trends that may emerge.

Developing Objectives for the Organization as a Whole

After identifying significant environmental trends, it is possible to develop objectives for the organization as a whole. Y. K. Shetty examined 193 companies to determine the nature and pattern of organizational objectives as they actually exist within organizations.[16] Four basic industrial groups were surveyed: chemical and drugs, packaging materials, electrical and electronics, and food processing. The types of objectives reported, the number of each type reported, and the percentage of companies having each type of objective are shown in Table 3.2.

[14] "The Value Line View," *Value Line Selection and Opinion,* January 24, 1986, p. 368.

[15] George P. Moschis, Jac L. Goldstucker, and Thomas J. Stanley, "At-Home Shopping: Will Consumers Let Their Computers Do the Walking?" *Business Horizons,* March–April 1985, pp. 22–29.

[16] Y. K. Shetty, "New Look at Corporate Goals," *California Management Review* 22, no. 2 (Winter 1979): 71–79.

TABLE 3.2 Types and Usage Levels of Organizational Objectives

TYPE OF OBJECTIVE	NUMBER OF COMPANIES STUDIED HAVING OBJECTIVE TYPE	PERCENT OF COMPANIES STUDIED HAVING OBJECTIVE TYPE[1]
Profitability	73	89
Growth	67	82
Market share	54	66
Social responsibility	53	65
Employee welfare	51	62
Product quality and service	49	60
Research and Development	44	54
Diversification	42	31
Efficiency	41	50
Financial stability	40	49
Resource conservation	32	39
Management development	29	35
Multinational enterprise	24	29
Consolidation	14	17
Miscellaneous other goals	15	18

[1] Adds to more than 100 percent because most companies have more than one goal.

Source: Adapted from Y. K. Shetty, "New Look at Corporate Goals," *California Management Review* 22, no. 2 (Winter 1979): 73. Copyright © 1979 by the Regents of the University of California. Reprinted by permission of The Regents.

One conclusion we can draw from the Shetty study is that profitability objectives are extremely important to an organization, regardless of its size or industry. First we will extend the Shetty study by elaborating on profitability objectives. Then we will discuss profitability objectives and offer guidelines on how to formulate them.

PROFITABILITY OBJECTIVES. *Profitability objectives* are organizational targets that focus on the ability of an organization to earn revenue dollars beyond the expenses necessary to generate the revenue. Profitability objectives established in organizations commonly include objectives related to return on investment (ROI; also referred to as return on assets), net profit margin, and return on stockholders' equity. Table 3.3 lists these measures of profitability, defines them, and explains how values for them within an organization are actually calculated. Although the basic concept of using such objectives to manage organizations is not new, their use as strategic management tools has received increased attention lately.[17]

GUIDELINES FOR ESTABLISHING PROFITABILITY OBJECTIVES. Profitability objectives are generally established by collecting and analyzing information that compares

[17] John H. Quandt, "Setting Strategy Using Variable ROI Analysis," *The Journal of Business Strategy* 5, no. 1 (Summer 1984): 77–79.

TABLE 3.3 Several Profitability Objectives, Their Descriptions, and How They Are Calculated

PROFITABILITY OBJECTIVES	DESCRIPTION	HOW CALCULATED[1]
Net profit margin	An organizational objective that focuses on the amount of net profit an organization earns in relation to the level of sales attained	$\frac{\text{Net profit}}{\text{Sales}}$
Return on investment (ROI) or Return on assets	An organizational objective that focuses on the amount of net profit earned in relation to total assets owned by the company	$\frac{\text{Net profit}}{\text{Total assets}}$
Return on stockholders' equity	An organizational objective that focuses on the amount of net profit earned by an organization in relation to its level of equity	$\frac{\text{Net profit}}{\text{Stockholders' equity}}$

[1] These ratios are expressed in percentages.

specific organizational data to similar data for other organizations or groups of organizations. Gathering and analyzing this information enables managers to determine not only how an organization is currently performing from a profitability standpoint but also how high profitability objectives *should* be set.

To illustrate how this process might work, let us consider the task of setting 1985 objectives for net profit margin, return on assets, and return on stockholders' equity at the McDonald's Corporation. Managers would normally begin by gathering 1984 information to get a very broad view of how business organizations in general actually performed in these areas. One source of such information would be the industrial composite contained periodically in *Value Line Selection and Opinion.* This particular industrial composite averages such data for over 900 industrial, retail, and transportation companies. These companies account for about 80 percent of the income earned by all U.S. nonfinancial corporations.

In addition to this industrial composite information, McDonald's Corporation management would probably determine how companies more closely related to the fast-food business performed. Information about performance in these areas for the restaurant industry in general, as well as for specific competitors such as Wendy's International, would be very valuable. Information of this sort is also available periodically in *Value Line Selection and Opinion.*

After gathering all this information, McDonald's management is ready to compare it to the data it has compiled for its own company (see Figure 3.3). Upon analyzing all this information, McDonald's management would probably conclude that it is performing competitively in the areas of net profit margin,

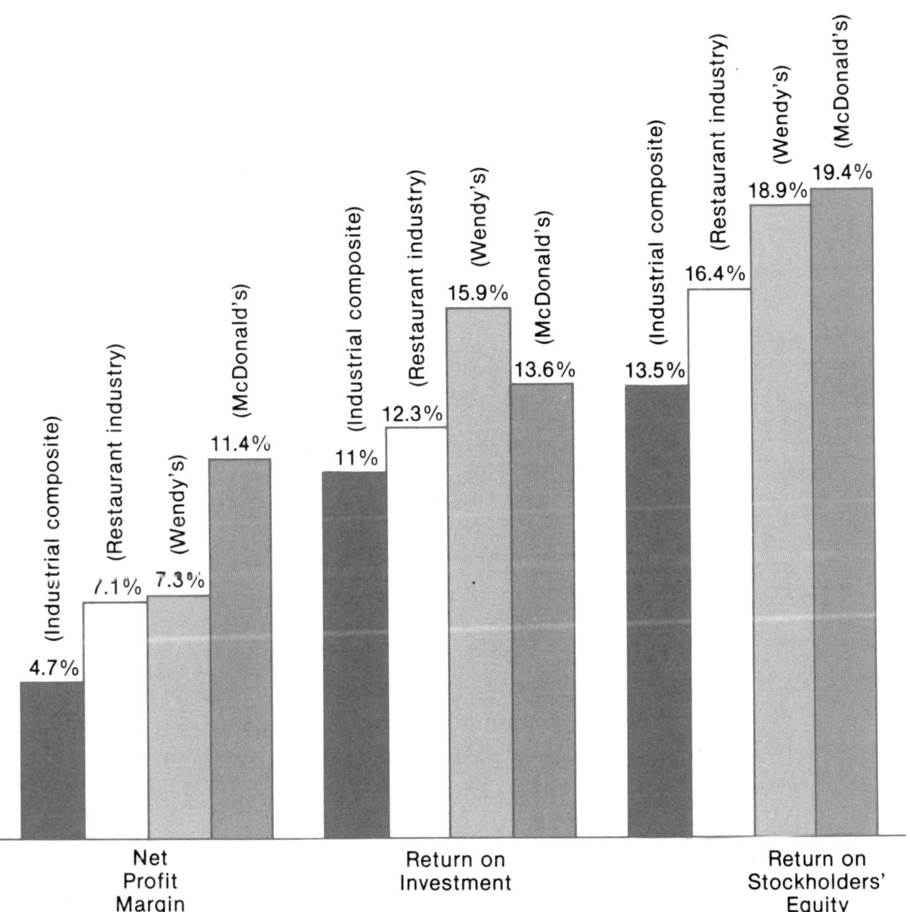

FIGURE 3.3 1984 Comparisons of McDonald Performance on Three Measures of Profitability with the Performance of the Industrial Composite, the Restaurant Industry, and Wendy's

return on investment, and return on stockholders' equity. Significantly unfavorable comparisons in any of these areas would have alerted McDonald's management that improvement was possible and that profitability objectives should be revised upward. As it is, perhaps the same or slightly higher profitability objectives would be appropriate for McDonald's in the 1985 operating period.

McDonald's managers must also consider, however, that the information they gathered reflects 1984 only. Gathering the same information and making the same comparisons for a five-year period might reveal desirable or undesirable trends that management should either encourage or attempt to change through the organizational objectives it establishes.

Highlight 3.5 is designed to give you some experience in spotting issues that may affect the profitability measures that a company establishes for itself.

HIGHLIGHT 3.5

SKILLS MODULE ■ **Profitability Objectives at Gillette Company**

INTRODUCTION

We have discussed various profitability objectives that can exist within organizations. Review the following situation at Gillette Company, and then complete the skill development exercise that follows. Doing so will help you develop some skill in determining what kinds of factors in an organization can affect profitability objectives.

THE SITUATION

Gillette discovered several years ago that only 8 percent of Mexican men who shave use shaving cream. The rest just soften their beards with soapy or plain water. Sensing an opportunity, Gillette recently introduced in Guadalajara plastic tubs of shaving cream that sell for half the price of its aerosol. Within about twelve months, 13 percent of Guadalajaran men were using shaving cream. On the basis of this information, Gillette is planning to sell its new product in the rest of Mexico, in Colombia, and in Brazil.

Tailoring its marketing to foreign budgets and tastes has become important to Gillette. The company has done such things as packaging blades so they can be sold one at a time and educating the unshaven about the joys of a smooth face. As a result, today Gillette draws more than half its sales from foreign countries.

Since the company targeted foreign sales in 1969, the proportion of its sales derived from that source has doubled to 20 percent and the dollar volume that foreign sales generate has risen sevenfold. Gillette's growth in foreign sales over the years is shown in the accompanying chart.

Roderick Mills, an executive vice president for Gillette's international business, recently said that the market for blades is stagnant in developed countries and that new opportunities for growth in this area lie in underde-

Developing a Hierarchy of Objectives

In his now classic *Harvard Business Review* article, Charles Granger defined a *hierarchy of objectives* as a set of organizational objectives that includes objectives for the organization as a whole and corresponding subobjectives for significant segments of the organization.[18] The purpose of establishing a hierarchy of objectives is to ensure that each significant segment of the

[18] Charles H. Granger, "The Hierarchy of Objectives," *Harvard Business Review*, May–June 1963, pp. 63–74.

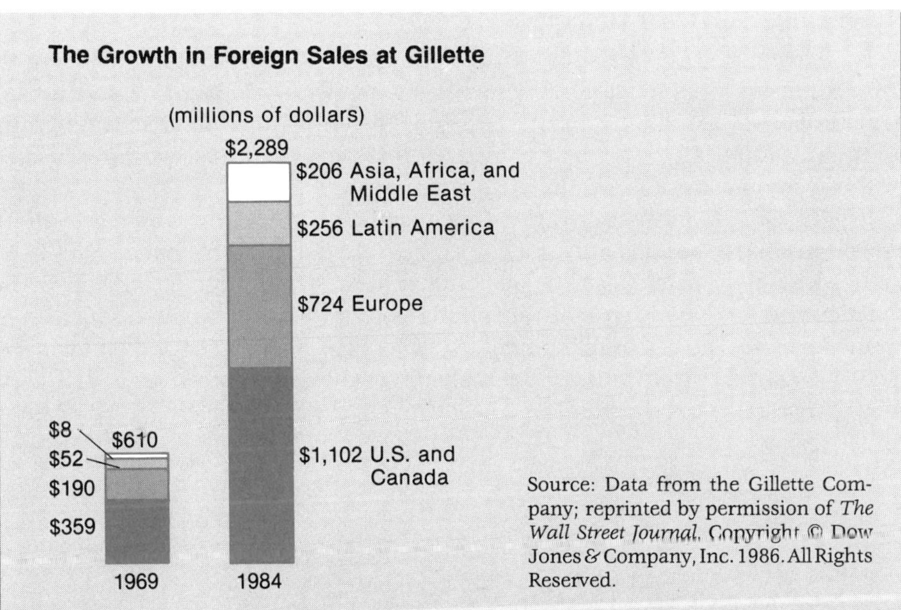

Source: Data from the Gillette Company; reprinted by permission of *The Wall Street Journal*, Copyright © Dow Jones & Company, Inc. 1986. All Rights Reserved.

veloped countries. In these countries, according to Mills, there is a very high proportion of people under 15 years of age who will soon be shaving. This observation seems especially important to Gillette. Despite the fact that the company sells its other products (such as pens and toothbrushes) in foreign countries, razor blades are responsible for one-third of the company's revenue and two-thirds of its pretax profit.

SKILL DEVELOPMENT EXERCISE

What issues outlined here will probably affect the profitability objectives that the company formulates for the future? Be sure to explain *how* each issue is likely to influence the objectives.

Source: Based on David Wessel, "Gillette Keys Sales to Third World Tastes," *The Wall Street Journal,* January 26, 1986, p. 33.

organization knows what role it must play, on both a long-term and a short-term basis, in order for the organization to reach its overall objectives.

Breaking down objectives for the organization as a whole into subobjectives for significant organizational segments is an important part of a manager's job. Subobjectives should be designed so that accomplishing them contributes in some way to the accomplishment of objectives for the organization as a whole. By designing organizational objectives in this fashion, management can help ensure that resources within various parts of the organization are not used on activities that are not directly related to achieving overall organizational objectives.

Developing Individual Objectives

As we have noted, a hierarchy of objectives generally refers to subobjectives for significant organizational segments such as divisions or departments. Another step in developing an effective and efficient pattern of objectives within an organization is to establish objectives for each individual working in one of those significant organizational segments.

Individual objectives are targets that specific people within an organization are attempting to reach. Individual objectives are designed so that accomplishing each one contributes to the accomplishment of the broader objectives of the department. In turn, the accomplishment of departmental objectives contributes to the accomplishment of objectives for the organization as a whole. The primary advantage of establishing individual objectives is that they help individual workers understand exactly what they are expected to contribute to the department.

SUMMARY

Two main organizational ingredients are commonly used to establish organizational direction: organizational mission and organizational objectives. Organizational mission is the purpose for which, or reason why, the organization exists. An organizational mission should help focus human effort, ensure compatibility of organizational purposes, provide a rationale for resource allocation, indicate broad areas of job responsibility, and provide the foundation for organizational objectives. Missions commonly address the topics of company products or services, market, technology, and company objectives, philosophy, self-concept, and image.

Organizational objectives are targets toward which the organization is directed. Objectives reflect organizational mission and are important because managers can use them as decision-making aids and as guides for increasing organizational efficiency and conducting performance appraisals. Objectives, which can be either short-run or long-run, focus on such areas as market standing, innovation, resource levels, profitability, manager performance and development, worker performance and attitude, and social responsibility.

To establish organizational direction, managers should rely on a consistent combination of organizational mission and objectives. Managers can establish this direction by reflecting on the results of an environmental analysis, developing an appropriate organizational mission, and formulating appropriate organizational objectives. In molding organizational objectives, managers should analyze trends, develop objectives for the organization as a whole, create a hierarchy of objectives, and specify individual objectives.

Highlight 3.6 is a checklist of questions based on this chapter. Use it in analyzing strategic management problems and cases that focus on issues in organizational direction.

HIGHLIGHT 3.6

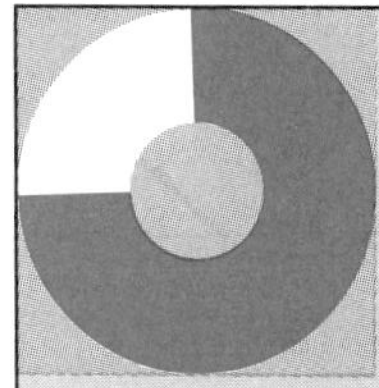

CHECKLIST ■ **Analyzing Organizational Direction in Problems and Cases**

- ☐ 1. Does the strategic problem or case involve issues related to organizational direction?
- ☐ 2. Is there a clear and complete organizational mission?
- ☐ 3. Does the organizational mission appropriately reflect the organizational environment?
- ☐ 4. Does the situation involve organizational objectives that appropriately reflect the organizational mission?
- ☐ 5. Are suitable types of objectives employed?
- ☐ 6. Have objectives been established in all areas critical to organizational success?
- ☐ 7. Are the objectives that are apparent in the case or situation high-quality objectives?
- ☐ 8. Are organizational objectives appropriately arranged in a hierarchy?
- ☐ 9. Are individual objectives sufficiently emphasized?
- ☐ 10. Is an acceptable process for establishing organizational direction apparent in the situation or case?

ADDITIONAL READINGS

Daniels, John D., Robert A. Pitts, and Marietta J. Tretter. "Strategy and Structure of U.S. Multinationals: An Exploratory Study." *Academy of Management Journal* 27, no. 2 (1984): 292–307.

Harvey, Don. *Business Policy and Strategic Management.* Columbus, Ohio: Merrill Publishing Company, 1982.

Hayes, James L. *Memos for Management—The Manager's Job.* New York: American Management Association, 1983.

MacMillan, Ian C., and Patricia E. Jones. *Strategy Formulation: Power and Politics.* St. Paul, Minn.: West Publishing Company, 1986.

Mitroff, Ian I. *Stakeholders of the Organizational Mind.* San Francisco: Jossey-Bass, 1983.

Newman, William H., James P. Logan, and W. Harvey Hegarty. *Strategy: A Multi-Level, Integrative Approach.* Cincinnati: Southwestern, 1989.

Porter, Michael E. *The Competitive Advantage of Nations.* New York: The Free Press, 1989.

Ruch, Richard S., and Ronald Goodman. *Image at the Top.* New York: The Free Press, 1983.

Yavitz, Boris, and William H. Newman. *Strategy in Action.* New York: The Free Press, 1982.

Yip, George S. "Who Needs Strategic Planning?" *Journal of Business Strategy,* Fall 1985, pp. 30–42.

HIGHLIGHT 3.7 ■ APPLICATION OF CHAPTER MATERIAL

The Direction of Domino's Pizza

Bob Popiolek remembers how Tom Monaghan used to drag himself home from his pizza shop about 3 a.m., carrying the night's receipts in a brown paper bag. He would finally get around to counting the cash the next afternoon at the kitchen table in his trailer home.

"Funny, but it seemed like a burden to him, like the fun was in the work, not the money," says Popiolek, who lived in the same Ypsilanti, Mich., trailer park and swapped friendly wagers with Monaghan about who would build the tallest building, make the most money, win the most fame.

They have not seen each other in almost 20 years, but Popiolek is willing to concede that Thomas S. Monaghan, 48, founder of Domino's Pizza, the world's largest privately held restaurant chain, won each bet.

From near-bankruptcy in 1970, the chain fought its way back to solvency—and more. Revenues were $98 million in 1980. The slogan at Domino's in the past year was "One-point-five in '85." That is $1.5 billion in sales and franchise royalties, more than double the 1984 figure. The company's 1985 report, due out in March, will reveal that Domino's met its goal. (Although closely held, Domino's is very public about its finances, in a "we-have-nothing-to-hide" spirit that Monaghan promotes. It publishes annual reports, distributed to each employee, corporate friends, and bankers. The 1984 report came in a polished walnut box that also contained real dominoes.)

In 1984 Monaghan had an estimated worth of $200 million; in 1985 he was worth $50 million more. Domino's is expanding at the rate of 21 stores each week. The days of cash in brown paper bags are over, as evidenced by these Monaghan milestones:

- Having aspired to be a Detroit Tiger shortstop as a kid, he instead bought the team in October, 1983, for $53 million after a 92–70 season in which it placed second in the American League East. The team won the World Series in 1984 and netted just under $4 million, a probable season record for major league baseball teams. National awareness of the company, say Domino's executives, has since grown from 41 percent to 78 percent, in part because of the Tigers but also because of network TV advertising, begun late in 1984.
- In December, in time for the company's 25th anniversary gala, the first phase of a $300 million office complex called Domino's Farms opened in Ann Arbor, Mich., Monaghan's birthplace. The complex is intended as a tribute to architect Frank Lloyd Wright, who tops Monaghan's long list of heroes. It will include a 30-story tower based on Wright's unbuilt Golden Beacon design. "It's going to be a loser, economically," Monaghan admits, "but I won't compromise on the design. No public com-

(*Continued*)

pany would ever build anything like this. My theory is that because no one else will do it, it's going to be unique, and it's going to endure."

The complex will eventually house not only Domino's world headquarters but also a sports medicine center, an employee fitness center, a man-made lake, jogging trails (ski trails in winter), and a 150-acre working farm that will include a pumpkin patch open to locals each fall. A team of Polish monks is being recruited to run the farm. Monaghan would also like to open a small orphanage on the property, staffed by senior citizens.

Friends and competitors of Tom Monaghan agree his success is attributable to a few key traits:

- He is undeterred by failure. In 1970, after trying to expand too fast and go public, he was $1.5 million in debt. Refusing to file for bankruptcy, he instead fired everyone except his wife and his bookkeeper. He paid off the Internal Revenue Service and about 1,500 creditors, writing checks stamped with a personally designed logo of a man wearing only a rain barrel.
- He has kept his concept simple. For most of its 25 years, Domino's menu has included only pizza (two or three sizes, 11 toppings) and cola. No sit-down, only takeout and delivery, guaranteed in 30 minutes or less. Ninety percent of deliveries meet the guarantee, and drivers who make the most deliveries on time win trips to the Indy 500.
- Monaghan rewards his own. His top executives drive $38,000 BMWs or other expensive cars of their choice. The company owns a million-dollar, 64-foot yacht called the *Tigress II,* on which particularly successful store managers spend weekend cruises. In 1984, 68 store managers who increased their sales 50 percent won $3,800 trips for two to Hawaii. On Monaghan's wrist is a $12,000 Patek Philippe gold watch, Swiss-made, which he will give to any store manager whose weekly sales top the company record (the current record, $62,087, is held by a store in Myrtle Beach, S.C.). He has given away half a dozen.

  Last fall, Monaghan bought a 280-acre waterfront estate on an island near Michigan's Upper Peninsula for $350,000, to serve as a corporate retreat where key executives and successful store managers go as a reward for work well done. Once, he removed his Hermes silk tie and gave it to a particularly successful manager. That gesture has been institutionalized, and hundreds of $70 ties are bestowed each year.
- And he tries to be good. Last spring he hired a corporate chaplain, a Catholic priest who says mass each morning in a conference room off the Domino's headquarters cafeteria. Monaghan attends daily. When he is on the road, he goes to a local church.

> "If not for religion," he says, "I'd be the worst guy that ever lived. Once I realize something is wrong, I'll avoid it. I'll cheat and fight and everything until someone points out to me that it's wrong. There's something in me that says, 'Don't break the rules.'"
>
> Says George Griffith, a close friend and a member of the Ann Arbor country club to which Monaghan belongs: "A number of members look down their noses at him, as if God got things screwed up and gave the money to the wrong person. He does not fit what a big, important person should be. Some consider him to be a guy who just lucked out."

Domino's, as a corporation, also continues to dream. BakeUps, a breakfast pizza of cheese with toppings like ham and bacon, is being test-marketed. A low-cal pizza with one-third the calories is in the works. Prototype delivery cars of the future have been built, low to the ground, resembling jets without wings. They get 85 miles per gallon. A dial-a-pizza plan under development would allow customers to punch in their exact orders on a push-button phone.

Within five years, Monaghan wants Domino's to have 10,000 outlets, generating an average of $1 million annually each, for total yearly revenues of $10 billion. Monaghan says he never has enough money to do all he wants to do. But he has a personal five-year plan based on what he expects to have, which is more money.

"I'm working my way down that field toward a touchdown." What's the touchdown? "It's an endless field!" he says, his eyes wide with the exciting possibilities.

DISCUSSION QUESTIONS

1. On the basis of the information given here, write a mission statement for Domino's Pizza that represents the direction the company has taken.
2. Frame three long-run and three short-run objectives that you think reflect this mission. Are the objectives you have written compatible with one another? Explain.
3. List as many areas as you can in which Domino's seems to have objectives. From what we can tell here, what areas might Domino's management be overlooking? Could this hurt the company? Why?

Source: Susan Ager, "An Appetite for More Than Pizza." Reprinted by permission, *Nation's Business,* February 1986.

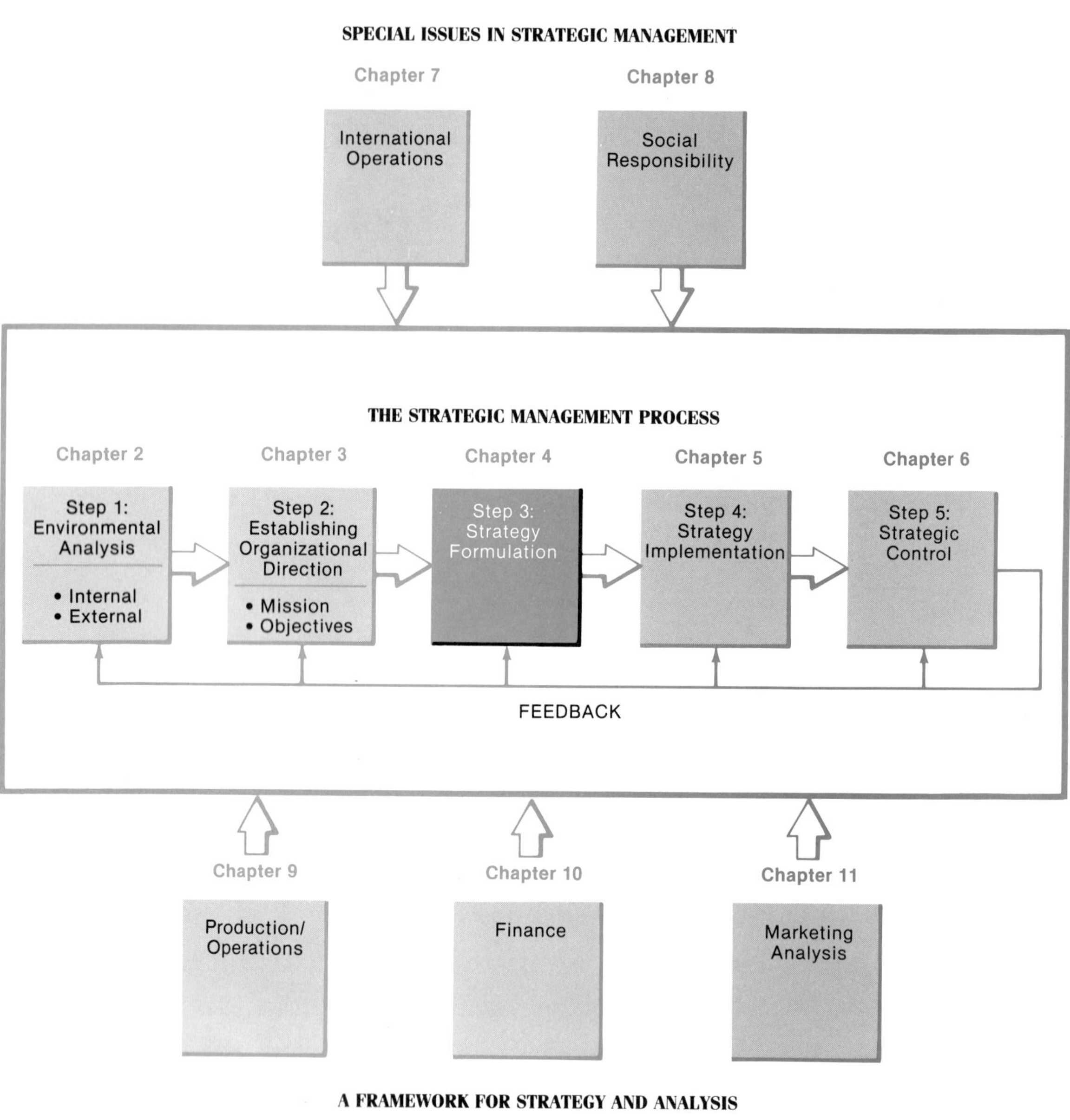
SPECIAL ISSUES IN STRATEGIC MANAGEMENT
Chapter 7
International Operations
Chapter 8
Social Responsibility
THE STRATEGIC MANAGEMENT PROCESS
Chapter 2
Step 1: Environmental Analysis
• Internal
• External
Chapter 3
Step 2: Establishing Organizational Direction
• Mission
• Objectives
Chapter 4
Step 3: Strategy Formulation
Chapter 5
Step 4: Strategy Implementation
Chapter 6
Step 5: Strategic Control
FEEDBACK
Chapter 9
Production/ Operations
Chapter 10
Finance
Chapter 11
Marketing Analysis
A FRAMEWORK FOR STRATEGY AND ANALYSIS
Chapter 12
An Approach to Solving Strategic Problems and Cases

CHAPTER 4

Strategy Formulation

Formulating strategies involves determining appropriate courses of action for achieving objectives. It includes such activities as analysis, planning, and selecting strategies that increase the chances that an organization's objectives will be achieved.

In this chapter we discuss the process of strategy formulation. In the first section we briefly review two techniques used in environmental analysis, because such analysis is the foundation for designing successful strategies. Both of these tools provide information that is useful in strategy formulation at the organizational, business, and functional levels.

In the following sections we discuss each of these levels: organizational strategies geared to achievement of the firm's overall objectives; business strategies designed to help each division or business unit of the firm contribute as effectively as possible to the company of which it is a subsidiary; and functional strategies devised by specialists in the various functional areas, such as finance, marketing, and human resources. Although discussed separately, strategies at all three levels must be synchronized and coordinated to be maximally effective.

In the final section we discuss strategy formulation in terms of the constraints that financial restrictions, the firm's capabilities and attitude toward risk, and conditions in the external environment may impose. And we suggest several criteria to apply in the process of choosing among strategic alternatives.

STRATEGY FORMULATION: INPUTS FROM ENVIRONMENTAL ANALYSIS

Managers rely on environmental analysis to provide the information they need to begin the strategy formulation process. In this section we outline two approaches that focus environmental analysis on strategy formulation: critical question analysis and SWOT analysis.

Critical Question Analysis

Critical question analysis provides a general framework for analyzing an organization's current situation and formulating appropriate strategies. It involves answering the following four basic questions.[1]

1. *What are the purpose(s) and objective(s) of the organization?* The answer to this question tells managers where the organization wants to go. As we stated earlier, appropriate strategies reflect the organization's mission and objectives. Managers who consider this question during strategy formulation are more likely than others to avoid inconsistencies among mission, objectives, and strategies.
2. *Where is the organization presently going?* The answer to this question reveals whether an organization is achieving its goals or at least making satisfactory progress. The first question focuses on where the organization wants to go; this one focuses on where the organization is actually going.
3. *What critical environmental factors does the organization currently face?* This question addresses both internal and external environments—factors both inside and outside the organization. For example, if a poorly trained middle-management team (internal environment) and an increase in competitive pressure (external environment) are critical strategic concerns, then any strategy formulated should deal with these issues.
4. *What can be done to achieve organizational objectives more effectively in the future?* The answer to this question actually results in the formulation of a strategy for the organization. Thus it goes beyond environmental analysis and includes the stages of planning and selection. This question should be answered only after managers have had plenty of opportunity to reflect on the answers to the previous questions. In other words, managers can formulate appropriate organizational strategies only when they have a clear understanding of where the organization wants to go,

[1] This discussion is based on Samuel C. Certo, *Principles of Modern Management: Functions and Systems*, 4th ed. (Boston: Allyn & Bacon, 1989), p. 143.

where the organization is going, and what the environment in which the organization operates is and is likely to be.

SWOT Analysis

SWOT analysis is a useful tool for analyzing an organization's overall situation. (SWOT stands for *s*trengths, *w*eaknesses, *o*pportunities, and *t*hreats.) This approach attempts to balance the internal strengths and weaknesses of an organization with the opportunities and threats that the external environment presents. This approach suggests that the major issues facing an organization can be isolated through careful analysis of each of these four elements. Strategies can then be formulated to address these issues. Table 4.1 lists several key questions in each area that managers should address when performing a SWOT analysis.

Although the questions listed in Table 4.1 may help direct a SWOT analysis, a good deal of work is required to answer them properly. For example, the relative importance of each of these issues needs to be determined, and their potential impact on strategy formulation needs to be evaluated. Furthermore, the relative importance of each issue may vary depending on whether strategy is being formulated at the organizational, business, or functional level. We will distinguish among these levels of strategy formulation in the next three sections.

Highlight 4.1 offers you an opportunity to try your hand at SWOT analysis and to learn something about a very successful company, Pepperidge Farm.

FORMULATING ORGANIZATIONAL STRATEGIES

Organizational strategies are formulated by top management and are designed to achieve the firm's overall objectives. This process includes two related tasks. First, general strategies must be selected and developed. Second, specific decisions must be made about what role various lines of business in the organization will play and how resources will be allocated among them. In this section, we first review a number of the general strategies a firm may adopt and then discuss various analytic approaches to managing a set of different businesses within an organization. These approaches are called business portfolio models.

General Strategy Alternatives

An organization can choose from a wide variety of general strategies. We will discuss a number of them and the conditions under which they are likely to be used.

Concentration Strategy

A *concentration strategy* is one in which an organization focuses on a single line of business. For example, McDonald's concentrates on the fast-food industry and Holiday Inns concentrates on the lodging industry. This strategy is used by firms seeking to gain a competitive advantage through specialized knowledge

HIGHLIGHT 4.1

SKILLS MODULE ■ **SWOT Analysis Skills for Pepperidge Farm**

INTRODUCTION

SWOT analysis is a useful tool for performing environmental analysis, the foundation for the strategic planning stage of strategy formulation. Review the following situation, and then complete the related skill development exercise. Doing so will give you a sense of what SWOT analysis entails.

THE SITUATION

Pepperidge Farm, a subsidiary of Campbell Soup, produces a wide variety of fresh and frozen food products. In 1985, Pepperidge Farm accounted for 10.4 percent of Campbell's sales and increased its parent company's operating earnings 33 percent to $51.1 million on sales of $455 million, even with heavy outlays for new products. The Pepperidge Farm name stands for quality, and it is particularly appealing to the upscale market.

One of Pepperidge Farm's major products is cookies (called biscuits in the industry). The packaged ready-to-eat cookie business is a $3-billion-a-year industry, and in a recent year, Pepperidge Farm increased its market share from 3.5 to 4.5 percent. The gain was brought about in part by the introduction of the American Collection—"lumpy bumpy" cookies so full of goodies that the manufacturing engineers had a hard time getting the cookies to stick together! The demand for these cookies is so high that Pepperidge Farm claims it cannot produce enough. On average, the company's plants operate at a respectable 85 percent of capacity, though one frozen food operation ran at only 14 percent of capacity for some time.

Major competitors offer a variety of cookies and scored a big success a few years earlier with crunchy-chewy cookies that taste homemade. These competitors include Frito-Lay's Grandma's, Procter & Gamble's Duncan Hines, the market leader RJR Nabisco, and Keebler. In a two-year period, these four companies together spent $100 million on advertising, an unprecedented—and unsustainable—amount. However, sales of crunchy-chewy cookies fell 50 percent in 1985 and recovered only modestly in 1986. Although Pepperidge Farm historically has spent relatively little on advertising, in the last quarter of 1986 it spent $14 million, making it the fifth-largest advertiser among all food companies.

Generally, national cookie makers deliver products to stores from inventory that is five to ten days old. Pepperidge Farm has cut its delivery time to less than five days and has a goal of getting cookies from the ovens to the stores in 72 hours to compete with local cookie stores and cookie companies.

SKILL DEVELOPMENT EXERCISE

Pepperidge Farm is doing quite well in the cookie business at this time. Analyze the company's strengths, weaknesses, opportunities, and threats.

Source: Based on Bill Saporito, "A Smart Cookie at Pepperidge," *Fortune,* December 22, 1986, pp. 67–74.

TABLE 4.1 Important Considerations for SWOT Analysis

INTERNAL ANALYSIS	
Strengths	Weaknesses
A distinctive competence?	No clear strategic direction?
Adequate financial resources?	A deteriorating competitive position?
Good competitive skills?	Obsolete facilities?
Well thought of by buyers?	Subpar profitability because . . . ?
An acknowledged market leader?	Lack of managerial depth and talent?
Well-conceived functional area strategies?	Missing any key skills or competences?
Access to economies of scale?	Poor track record in implementing strategy?
Insulated (at least somewhat) from strong competitive pressures?	Plagued with internal operating problems?
Proprietary technology?	Vulnerable to competitive pressures?
Cost advantages?	Falling behind in R&D?
Competitive advantages?	Too narrow a product line?
Product innovation abilities?	Weak market image?
Proven management?	Competitive disadvantages?
Other?	Below-average marketing skills?
	Unable to finance needed changes in strategy?
	Other?
EXTERNAL ANALYSIS	
Opportunities	Threats
Enter new markets or segments?	Likely entry of new competitors?
Add to product line?	Rising sales of substitute products?
Diversity into related products?	Slower market growth?
Add complementary products?	Adverse government policies?
Vertical integration?	Growing competitive pressures?
Ability to move to better strategic group?	Vulnerability to recession and business cycle?
Complacency among rival firms?	Growing bargaining power of customers or suppliers?
Faster market growth?	Changing buyer needs and tastes?
Other?	Adverse demographic changes?
	Other?

Source: Adapted from Arthur A. Thompson, Jr., and A. J. Strickland III, *Strategic Management: Concepts and Cases* (Plano, Tex.: Business Publications, 1987), p. 98. Reprinted by permission.

and efficiency and to avoid the problems involved in managing too many businesses. However, if the industry is shrinking or aggressive competitors dominate the market, a concentrated firm may be wiped out. It has no other lines of business to fall back on.

Stability Strategy

The organization that adopts a *stability strategy* focuses on its existing line or lines of business and attempts to maintain them. This is a useful strategy in several situations. An organization that is large and dominates its market(s) may choose a stability strategy in an effort to avoid government controls or penalties for monopolizing the industry. Another organization may find that further growth is too costly and could have detrimental effects on profitability. Finally, an organization in a low-growth or no-growth industry that has no other viable options may be forced to select a stability strategy.

Growth Strategies

Organizations usually seek growth in sales, profits, market share, or some other measure as a primary objective. *Growth strategies* may be pursued by means of vertical integration, horizontal integration, diversification, and mergers and joint ventures.

VERTICAL INTEGRATION. This strategy involves growth through acquisition of other organizations in a channel of distribution. When an organization purchases other companies that supply it, it engages in *backward integration*. The organization that purchases other firms that are closer to the end users of the product (such as wholesalers and retailers) engages in *forward integration*. Vertical integration is used to obtain greater control over a line of business and to increase profits through greater efficiency or better selling efforts.[2]

HORIZONTAL INTEGRATION. This strategy involves growth through the acquisition of competing firms in the same line of business. It is adopted in an effort to increase the size, sales, profits, and potential market share of an organization. This strategy is sometimes used by smaller firms in an industry dominated by one or a few large competitors, such as the soft drink and computer industries.

DIVERSIFICATION. This strategy involves growth through the acquisition of firms in other industries or lines of business. When the acquired firm has production technology, products, channels of distribution, and/or markets similar to those of the firm purchasing it, the strategy is called *related* or *concentric diversification*. This strategy is useful when the organization can acquire greater efficiency or market impact through the use of shared resources.

[2] See Ted Kumpe and Piet T. Bolwijn, "Manufacturing: The New Case for Vertical Integration," *Harvard Business Review*, March–April 1988, pp. 75–81.

When the acquired firm is in a completely different line of business, the strategy is called *unrelated* or *conglomerate diversification*. This strategy is used for one or more of the following reasons:

1. Organizations in slow-growth industries may purchase firms in faster-growing industries to increase their overall growth rate.
2. Organizations with excess cash often find investment in another industry (particularly a fast-growing one) a profitable strategy.
3. Organizations may diversify in order to spread their risks across several industries.
4. The acquiring organization may have management talent, financial and technical resources, or marketing skills that it can apply to a weak firm in another industry in the hope of making it highly profitable.

MERGERS AND JOINT VENTURES. In the foregoing discussion we spoke of diversification in terms of acquisition—that is, one firm purchasing another with cash or stock. An organization can also grow through mergers and joint ventures. In a *merger*, a company joins with another company to form a new organization. In a *joint venture*, an organization works with another company on a project too large to handle by itself, such as some elements of the space program. Similarly, organizations in different countries may work together to overcome trade barriers in the international market or to share resources more efficiently. For example, GMF Robotics is a joint venture between General Motors Corporation and Japan's Fanuc Ltd. to produce industrial robots.

LEVERAGED BUYOUTS. Another strategy designed to increase the value of organizations involves leveraged buyouts. In a leveraged buyout, the stockholders of a public firm are offered a premium for their shares over the going market price. Often, the buyers of the firm use little cash in the transaction. Rather, they may finance the purchase by selling junk bonds (bonds with low quality ratings) that load the firm up with debt. The firm is then commonly resold for a profit. For example, Gibson Greeting Cards was purchased from RCA by a group of investors for $80 million—$1 million in cash and $79 million borrowed against Gibson's assets. Gibson was turned into a private firm and reorganized. After 18 months, the investors sold $290 million of Gibson stock to the general public, reaping a huge profit.[3]

Retrenchment Strategies

When an organization's survival is threatened and it is not competing effectively, retrenchment strategies are often needed. The three basic types of retrenchment are turnaround, divestment, and liquidation.

[3] This discussion is based on Michael L. McManus and Michael L. Hergert, *Surviving Mergers and Acquisitions* (Glenview, Ill.: Scott, Foresman and Company, 1988), pp. 103–104.

TURNAROUND STRATEGY. This strategy is used when an organization is performing poorly but has not yet reached a critical stage. It usually involves getting rid of unprofitable products, pruning the work force, trimming distribution outlets, and seeking other methods of making the organization more efficient. If the turnaround is successful, the organization may then focus on growth strategies.

DIVESTMENT STRATEGY. This strategy involves selling the business or setting it up as a separate corporation. Divestment is used when a particular business doesn't fit well in the organization or consistently fails to reach the objectives set for it. Divestment can also be used to improve the financial position of the divesting organization.

LIQUIDATION STRATEGY. In this strategy, a business is terminated and its assets sold off. Liquidation is the least desirable retrenchment strategy, because it usually involves losses for both stockholders and employees. However, in a multibusiness organization, the loss of one business typically has less negative impact than it has in a single-business organization.

Highlight 4.2 illustrates the very different strategies with which two industry leaders have responded to the same changes in their external environment.

Combinations Strategies

Large, diversified organizations commonly use a number of these strategies in combination. For example, an organization may simultaneously seek growth through the acquisition of new businesses, employ a stability strategy for some of its existing businesses, and divest itself of other businesses. Clearly, formulating a consistent organizational strategy in large, diversified companies is very complicated, because a number of different business-level strategies need to be coordinated to achieve overall organizational objectives. Business portfolio models are designed to help managers deal with this problem.

Business Portfolio Models

Business portfolio models are tools for analyzing (1) the relative position of each of an organization's businesses in its industry and (2) the relationships among all of the organization's businesses. Two approaches to developing business portfolios include the Boston Consulting Group (BCG) growth–share matrix and General Electric's (GE's) multifactor portfolio matrix.

BCG's Growth–Share Matrix

The Boston Consulting Group, a leading management consulting firm, developed and popularized a strategy formulation approach called the growth–share matrix, which is shown in Figure 4.1. The basic idea underlying this approach is that a firm should have a balanced portfolio of businesses such that some generate more cash than they use and can thus support other businesses that need cash to develop and become profitable. The role of each business is determined on the basis of two factors: the growth rate of its market and the share of that market that it enjoys.

HIGHLIGHT 4.2

ILLUSTRATIVE EXAMPLE ■ **Divergent Organizational Strategies in the Machine-Tool Industry**

Machine tools are power-driven machines that cut, form, and shape metal. They are used to make products ranging from airplane parts and automobile engines to vacuum cleaners. About 20 percent of the machine-tool output in this country is used in the military industry. The automobile industry accounts for an even larger market share: Some machine-tool companies do 50 percent of their business with the automakers.

The machine-tool industry has many problems, including low growth, weakening prices, and intensifying foreign competition. Since 1982 a quarter of the American companies that make machine tools have folded, and a third of the industry's 110,000 jobs have vanished. In this turbulent environment, two machine-tool giants, Cincinnati Milacron and Cross & Trecker, have followed different organizational strategies.

Cincinnati Milacron, following a related diversification strategy, has reduced the percentage of company sales in traditional machine tools from 67 to 40 percent and plans to reduce it even further in the future. It has moved into newer areas such as industrial robots, computer-controlled machines that produce aircraft parts, laser equipment, and plastic-processing machines. The company is moving away from machine tools and into computers and plastics. This change has resulted in over 4,000 employee layoffs as well-educated computer programmers and laser engineers have replaced a larger group of blue-collar assemblers and machine operators.

Cross & Trecker, on the other hand, has committed itself to a concentration strategy in the machine-tool industry and has attempted to grow in several ways. The company was formed by a merger between the Cross Company and Kearney & Trecker in 1979. It has since horizontally integrated by acquiring several other machine-tool companies, including Bendix Automation Group in 1984 and LaSalle Machine Tool in 1985. The company has engaged in extensive cost cutting and has increased spending on new machine-tool products by 50 percent. However, the loss of an order for an engine-machine line for General Motor's Saturn plant resulted in retrenchment; several plants were closed, and the company work force was sharply reduced.

Overall, both companies have experienced losses in profits and face serious environmental threats. Only time will tell which organizational strategy will be more successful.

Source: Based on "Machine-Tool Giants Diverge," *The New York Times*, February 9, 1987, pp. D1, D5, D7.

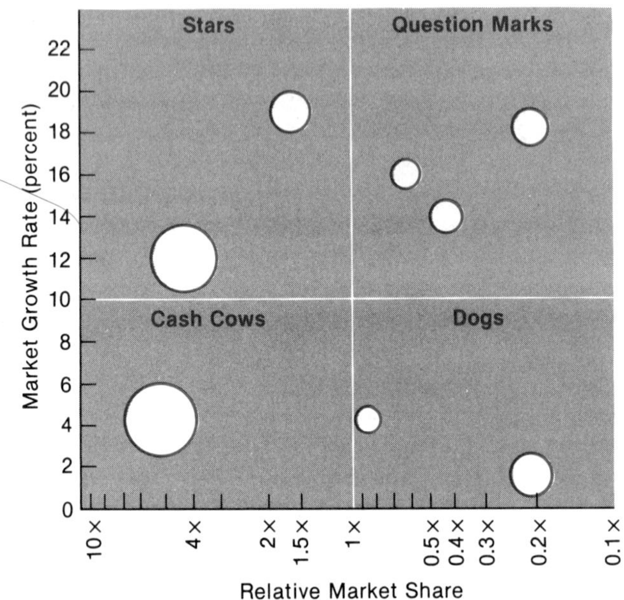

FIGURE 4.1 BCG's Growth–Share Matrix (Source: Adapted from B. Hedley, "Strategy and the Business Portfolio," Long Range Planning, February 1977, p. 12. Copyright © 1977, Pergamon Journals, Ltd.)

The vertical axis indicates the *market growth rate,* which is the annual growth percentage of the market (current or forecasted) in which the business operates. Anything under 10 percent is typically considered a low-growth rate and anything above 10 percent a high-growth rate.

The horizontal axis indicates market share dominance or *relative market share.* It is computed by dividing the firm's market share (in units) by the market share of the largest competitor. For example, a relative market share of 0.2 means that the sales volume of the business is only 20 percent of the market leader's sales volume; a relative market share of 2.0 means that the business has a sales volume twice that of the next largest competitor. A relative market share of 1.0 is set as the dividing line between high and low share. Each of the circles in Figure 4.1 represents the relative revenue of a single business; that is, a larger circle represents more sales than a smaller circle.

The growth–share matrix has four cells, which reflect the four possible combinations of high and low growth with high and low market share. These cells represent particular types of businesses, each of which has a particular role to play in the overall business portfolio. The cells are labeled:

1. *Question marks* (sometimes called problem children): company businesses that operate in a high-growth market but have low relative market share. Most businesses start off as question marks, in that they enter a high-growth market in which there is already a market leader.

A question mark generally requires the infusion of a lot of funds: It has to keep adding plant, equipment, and personnel to keep up with the fast-growing market, and it wants to overtake the leader. The term *question mark* is well chosen, because the organization has to think hard about whether to keep investing funds in the business or to get out.

2. *Stars:* question-mark businesses that have become successful. A star is the market leader in a high-growth market, but it does not necessarily provide much cash. The organization has to spend a great deal of money keeping up with the market's rate of growth and fighting off competitors' attacks. Stars are often cash-using rather than cash-generating. Even so, they are usually profitable in time.
3. *Cash cows:* businesses in markets whose annual growth rate is less than 10 percent but that still have the largest relative market share. A cash cow is so called because it produces a lot of cash for the organization. The organization does not have to finance a great deal of expansion because the market's growth rate is low. And the business is a market leader, so it enjoys economies of scale and higher profit margins. The organization uses its cash-cow businesses to pay its bills and support its other struggling businesses.
4. *Dogs:* businesses that have weak market shares in low-growth markets. They typically generate low profits or losses, although they may bring in some cash. Such businesses frequently consume more management time than they are worth and need to be phased out. However, an organization may have good reasons to hold onto a dog, such as an expected turnaround in the market growth rate or a new chance at market leadership.[4]

STRATEGIC ALTERNATIVES. After each of an organization's businesses is plotted on the growth–share matrix, the next step is to evaluate whether the portfolio is healthy and well balanced. A balanced portfolio has a number of stars and cash cows and not too many question marks or dogs. This balance is important because the organization needs cash not only to maintain existing businesses but also to develop new businesses. Depending on the position of each business, four basic strategies can be formulated:

1. *Build market share:* This strategy is appropriate for question marks that must increase their share in order to become stars. For some businesses, short-term profits may have to be forgone to gain market share and future long-term profits.
2. *Hold market share:* This strategy is appropriate for cash cows with strong share positions. The cash generated by mature cash cows is critical for supporting other businesses and financing innovations.

[4] These descriptions are based on a discussion in Philip Kotler, *Marketing Management: Analysis, Planning, and Control*, 6th ed. (Englewood Cliffs, N.J.: Prentice-Hall, 1988), pp. 41–42.

However, the cost of building share for cash cows is likely to be too high to be a profitable strategy.

3. *Harvest:* Harvesting involves milking as much short-term cash from a business as possible, even allowing market share to decline if necessary. Weak cash cows that do not appear to have a promising future are candidates for harvesting, as are question marks and dogs.
4. *Divest:* Divesting involves selling or liquidating a business because the resources devoted to it can be invested more profitably in other businesses. This strategy is appropriate for those dogs and question marks that are not worth investing in to improve their positions.

EVALUATION OF THE GROWTH–SHARE MATRIX. As one of the earliest approaches to investigating relationships among an organization's businesses, the growth–share matrix helped stimulate interest in this area of strategic concern. Perhaps its main contribution is that it encourages managers to view the formulation of organizational strategy in terms of joint relationships among businesses and to take a long-range view. Indeed, the growth–share matrix acknowledges that businesses in different stages have different cash requirements and make different contributions to achieving organizational objectives. The growth–share matrix is also a simple approach that provides an appealing visual overview of an organization's business portfolio.

However, a variety of problems that arise with this approach suggest that it must be used cautiously in strategy formulation. Among these problems:

- The growth–share matrix focuses on balancing cash flows, whereas organizations are more likely to be interested in the return on investment that various businesses yield.
- It is not always clear what share of what market is relevant in the analysis. For example, much different results would be obtained if Cadillac's market share were determined on the basis of the overall car market rather than just the market for luxury cars.
- The growth–share matrix is based on the idea that there is a strong relationship between market share and return on investment. In fact, it is commonly believed that a 10 percent difference in market share is accompanied by a 5 percent difference in return on investment. However, recent research found a much weaker relationship—a 10 percent change in market share is associated with only a 1 percent change in return on investment.[5]
- Many other factors besides market share and growth rate are critical in strategy formulation. For example, the size and growth profile of the market and the distinctive competencies of the firm and of its competitors are important influences.

[5] See Robert Jacobson and David A. Aaker, "Is Market Share All That It's Cracked Up to Be?" *Journal of Marketing*, Fall 1985, pp. 11–22.

- The growth–share matrix does not provide direct assistance in comparing different businesses in terms of investment opportunities. For example, it is not clear how to compare two question marks to decide which should be developed into a star and which should be allowed to decline.
- The approach offers only general strategy recommendations without specifying how such strategies can be implemented.

Thus, although the growth–share matrix may provide a useful overview of a business portfolio and may point out some important relationships among an organization's businesses, it does not provide a complete framework for strategy formulation. Several other portfolio models have been developed that overcome some of the problems inherent in the growth–share matrix. We will discuss one of them: General Electric's multifactor portfolio matrix.

GE's Multifactor Portfolio Matrix

This approach has a variety of names, including the nine cell GE matrix, GE's nine-cell business portfolio matrix, and the market attractiveness–business strengths matrix. It was developed at General Electric with the help of McKinsey and Company, a leading consulting firm. The basic approach is shown in Figure 4.2.[6] Each circle in this matrix represents the entire market, and the shaded portion represents the organization's business market share.

Each of an organization's businesses is plotted in the matrix on two dimensions, industry attractiveness and business strength. Each of these two major dimensions is a composite measure of a variety of factors. The two dimensions make good sense for strategy formulation, because a successful business is typically one that is in an attractive industry and has the particular business strengths required to succeed in it. Both are needed to produce outstanding performance.

To use this approach, an organization must determine what factors are most critical for defining industry attractiveness and business strength. Table 4.2 lists some of the factors that are commonly used to locate businesses on these dimensions.

The next step in developing this matrix is to weight each variable on the basis of its perceived importance relative to the other factors (hence the total of the weights must be 1.0). Then managers must indicate, on a scale of 1 to 5, how low or high their business scores on that factor. Table 4.3 presents this analysis for one business. These calculations show that the business rates 3.45 in industry attractiveness and 4.30 in business strength. Thus, this business would be rated close to the high–high cell of the matrix.

STRATEGIC ALTERNATIVES. Depending on where businesses are plotted on the matrix, three basic strategies are formulated: invest/grow, selective investment, and harvest/divest. Businesses falling in the cells that form a diagonal from

[6] This discussion is based on Kotler, *Marketing Management*, pp. 43–46.

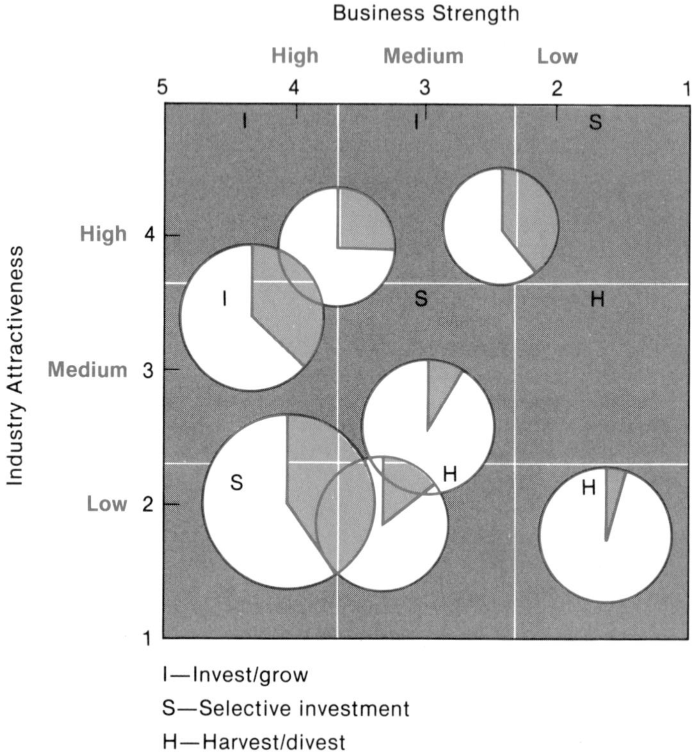

FIGURE 4.2 GE's Multifactor Portfolio Matrix (Source: Reprinted by permission from Strategy Formulation: Analytic Concepts by Charles W. Hofer and Dan Schendel: Copyright © 1978 by West Publishing Company. All rights reserved.)

lower left to upper right are medium-strength businesses that should be invested in only selectively. Businesses in the cells above and to the left of this diagonal are the strongest; they are the ones for which the company should employ an invest/grow strategy. Businesses in the cells below and to the right of the diagonal are low in overall strength and are serious candidates for a harvest/divest strategy.

EVALUATION OF THE MULTIFACTOR PORTFOLIO MATRIX. This approach has several advantages over the growth–share matrix. First, it provides a mechanism for including a host of relevant variables in the process of formulating strategy. Second, as we have noted, the two dimensions of industry attractiveness and business strength are excellent criteria for rating potential business success. Third, the approach forces managers to be specific about their evaluations of the impact of particular variables on overall business success.

However, the multifactor portfolio matrix also suffers some of the same limitations as the growth–share matrix. For example, it does not solve the problem of determining the appropriate market, and it does not offer anything more than general strategy recommendations. In addition, the measures are

TABLE 4.2 Factors Contributing to Industry Attractiveness and Business Strength

INDUSTRY ATTRACTIVENESS	BUSINESS STRENGTH
Market Factors	
Size (dollars, units or both)	Your share (in equivalent terms)
Size of key segments	Your share of key segments
Growth rate per year:	Your annual growth rate:
Total	Total
Segments	Segments
Diversity of market	Diversity of your participation
Sensitivity to price, service features, and external factors	Your influence on the market
Cyclicality	Lags or leads in your sales
Seasonality	
Bargaining Power of Upstream Suppliers	Bargaining power of your suppliers
Bargaining Power of Downstream Suppliers	Bargaining power of your customers
Competition	
Types of competitors	Where you fit, how you compare in terms of products, marketing capability, service, production strength, financial strength, management
Degree of concentration	
Changes in type and mix	
Entries and exits	Segments you have entered or left
Changes in share	Your relative share change
Substitution by new technology	Your vulnerability to new technology
Degrees and types of integration	Your own level of integration
Financial and Economic Factors	
Contribution margins	Your margins
Leveraging factors, such as economies of scale and experience	Your scale and experience
Barriers to entry or exit (both financial and nonfinancial)	Barriers to your entry or exit (both financial and nonfinancial)
Capacity utilization	Your capacity utilization
Technological Factors	
Maturity and volatility	Your ability to cope with change
Complexity	Depths of your skills
Differentiation	Types of your technological skills
Patents and copyrights	Your patent protection
Manufacturing process technology required	Your manufacturing technology
Sociopolitical Factors in Your Environment	
Social attitudes and trends	Your company's responsiveness and flexibility
Laws and government agency regulations	Your company's ability to cope
Influence with pressure groups and government representatives	Your company's aggressiveness
Human factors, such as unionization and community acceptance	Your company's relationships

Source: Derek F. Abell and John S. Hammond, *Strategic Market Planning: Problems & Analytical Approaches.* Copyright © 1979, p. 214. Reprinted by permission of Prentice-Hall, Inc., Englewood Cliffs, New Jersey.

TABLE 4.3 Illustration of Industry Attractiveness and Business Strength Computations

INDUSTRY ATTRACTIVENESS	WEIGHT	RATING (1–5)	VALUE
Overall market size	0.20	4.00	0.80
Annual market growth rate	0.20	5.00	1.00
Historical profit margin	0.15	4.00	0.60
Competitive intensity	0.15	2.00	0.30
Technological requirements	0.15	3.00	0.45
Inflationary vulnerability	0.05	3.00	0.15
Energy requirements	0.05	2.00	0.10
Environmental impact	0.05	1.00	0.05
Social/political/legal	Must be acceptable		
	1.00		3.45

BUSINESS STRENGTH	WEIGHT	RATING (1–5)	VALUE
Market share	0.10	4.00	0.40
Share growth	0.15	4.00	0.60
Product quality	0.10	4.00	0.40
Brand reputation	0.10	5.00	0.50
Distribution network	0.05	4.00	0.20
Promotional effectiveness	0.05	5.00	0.25
Productive capacity	0.05	3.00	0.15
Productive efficiency	0.05	2.00	0.10
Unit costs	0.15	3.00	0.45
Material supplies	0.05	5.00	0.25
R&D performance	0.10	4.00	0.80
Managerial personnel	0.05	4.00	0.20
	1.00		4.30

Source: Philip Kotler, *Marketing Management: Analysis, Planning, and Control*, 6th ed. Copyright © 1988, p. 45. Reprinted by permission of Prentice-Hall, Inc., Englewood Cliffs, New Jersey. Slightly modified from La Rue T. Hormer, *Strategic Management* (Englewood Cliffs, N.J.: Prentice-Hall, Inc., 1982), p. 310.

subjective and can be very ambiguous, particularly when one is considering different businesses.[7]

Portfolio models provide graphical frameworks for analyzing relationships among the businesses of large, diversified organizations, and they can yield useful strategy recommendations. However, no such model yet devised provides a universally accepted approach to dealing with these issues. Portfolio models should never be applied in a mechanical fashion, and any conclusions they suggest must be carefully considered in the light of sound managerial judgment and experience.

[7] David A. Aaker, *Developing Business Strategies* (New York: John Wiley & Sons, 1984), p. 237.

FORMULATING BUSINESS STRATEGIES

Formulating business strategies involves decision making at the division level or the business-unit level. Of course, these strategies must be consistent with the overall organizational strategies for that specific line of business. A useful approach to formulating business strategies is based on Michael Porter's "competitive analysis." In this section, we investigate Porter's approach and three general alternative business strategies that are derived from it.

Structural Analysis of Competitive Forces

Porter's approach is based on the analysis of five competitive forces. These forces (see Figure 4.3) include the threat of new entrants, the bargaining power of suppliers, the bargaining power of buyers, the threat of substitute products, and rivalry among existing firms.[8]

Threat of New Entrants

Firms entering an industry bring new capacity and a desire to gain market share and profits, but whether new firms enter an industry depends on the barriers to entry. (A number of these are shown in Figure 4.3.) In addition, established firms in an industry may benefit from "experience curve" effects. That is, their cumulative experience in producing and marketing a product often reduces their per-unit costs below those of inexperienced firms. In general, the higher the entry barriers, the less likely outside firms are to enter the industry.

Bargaining Power of Suppliers

Suppliers can be a competitive threat in an industry because they can raise the price of raw materials or reduce their quality. Powerful suppliers can reduce the profitability of an industry if companies in the industry cannot pay higher prices to cover price increases that the supplier imposes. Some determinants of supplier power are listed in Figure 4.3.

Bargaining Power of Buyers

Buyers compete with the industry by forcing prices down, bargaining for higher quality or more services, and playing competitors off against each other—all at the expense of industry profitability. Some determinants of buyer power are shown in Figure 4.3.

Threat of Substitute Products

In a broad sense, all firms in an industry are competing with industries producing substitute products. Substitutes limit the potential return in an

[8] This section is based on Michael E. Porter, *Competitive Strategy* (New York: The Free Press, 1980), chapters 1 and 2; and Michael E. Porter, *Competitive Advantage* (New York: The Free Press, 1985), chapter 1.

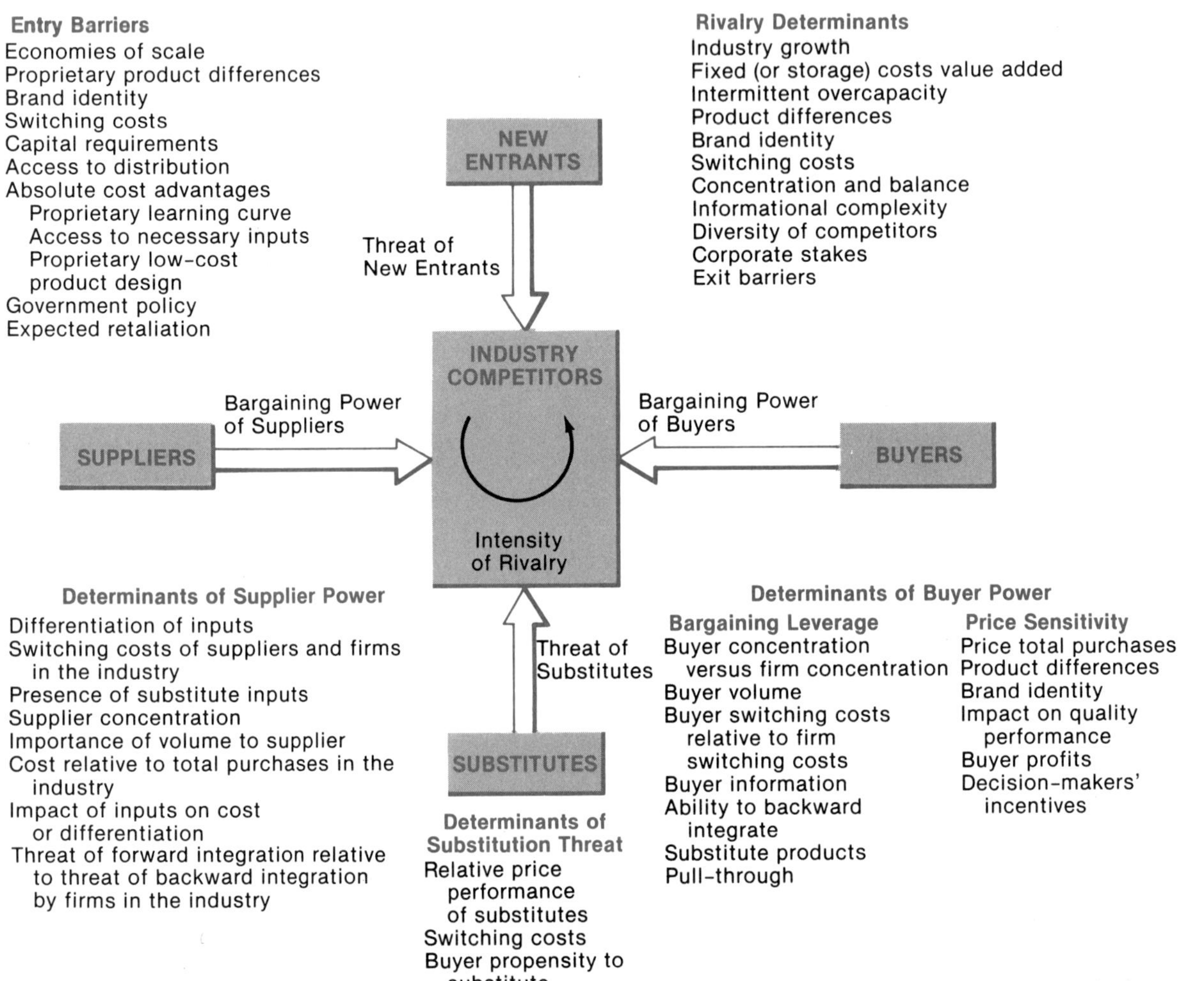

FIGURE 4.3 Elements of Industry Structure *(Source: Adapted from Michael E. Porter,* Competitive Advantage: Creating and Sustaining Superior Performance, *p. 6. Copyright © 1985 by Michael E. Porter. Reprinted with permission of The Free Press, a Division of Macmillan, Inc.)*

industry by placing a ceiling on the prices that firms in the industry can profitably charge. The more attractive the price–performance alternative offered by substitutes, the tighter the lid on industry profits. For example, the price of candy, such as Raisinettes chocolate-covered raisins, may limit the price Del Monte can charge for "healthy snacks," such as Strawberry Yogurt Raisins. Some determinants of the degree of substitution threat are shown in Figure 4.3.

Rivalry Among Existing Competitors

This is the conventional type of competition in which firms try to take customers from one another. Strategies such as price competition, advertising battles, new product introductions, and increased customer service are commonly used to attract customers from competitors. Some of these "rivalry determinants" are shown in Figure 4.3.

Strategic Alternatives

In Porter's scheme, the analysis of these five factors should shape the development of business strategy. For example, a firm has the best chance of high profitability in industries characterized by high barriers to entry and by weak competitors, weak substitutes, weak buyers, and weak suppliers. Although few industries have all of these characteristics, the key to strategy formulation is to focus on the particular opportunities and constraints in the industry. For example, if an industry has high entry barriers, competition from new entrants may be a minor concern in strategy formulation. Efforts may focus instead on changing the structure of the industry via backward integration (buying out suppliers), forward integration (buying out channel members), or horizontal integration (buying out existing competitors).

Typically, however, competitive analysis focuses on rivalry among existing competitors and on the formulation of strategies to outperform other firms in the industry. Porter suggests that three generic strategies should be considered: overall cost leadership, differentiation, and focus. The skills and resources called for and the organizational requirements of each of these strategies are shown in Table 4.4.

Overall cost leadership yields a firm above-average returns in its industry despite the presence of strong competitive forces. However, this strategy often requires high relative market share or other advantages, such as favorable access to raw materials or the ready availability of cash to finance the purchase of the most efficient equipment. National Can Company, for example, is in a no-growth industry but depends on being the low-cost producer of cans and bottles to increase its profits.

Differentiation involves creating and marketing unique products for the mass market. Approaches to differentiation include developing unique brand images (Levi's jeans), unique technology (Macintosh stereo components), unique features (Jenn-Air electric ranges), unique channels (Tupperware), unique customer service (IBM), or the like. In other words, the key to differentiation is obtaining a differential advantage that is readily perceived by the consumer. Differentiation is a viable strategy for earning above-average returns in an industry, because it creates a defensible position for coping with the five competitive forces.

Focus is essentially a strategy of segmenting markets and appealing to only one or a few groups of consumers or industrial buyers. The logic of this approach is that a firm that limits its attention to one or a few market segments

TABLE 4.4 Porter's Three Generic Strategies and Their Requirements

GENERIC STRATEGY	COMMONLY REQUIRED SKILLS AND RESOURCES	COMMON ORGANIZATIONAL REQUIREMENTS
Overall cost leadership	Substained capital investment and access to capital Process engineering skills Intense supervision of labor Products designed for ease in manufacture Low-cost distribution system	Tight cost control Frequent, detailed control reports Structured organization and responsibilities Incentives based on meeting strict quantitative targets
Differentiation	Strong marketing abilities Product engineering Creative flair Strong capability in basic research Corporate reputation for quality or technological leadership Long tradition in the industry or unique combination of skills drawn from other businesses Strong cooperation from channels	Strong coordination among functions in R&D, product development, and marketing Subjective measurement and incentives instead of quantitative measures Amenities to attract highly skilled labor, scientists, or creative people
Focus	Combination of the above policies directed at the particular strategic target	Combination of the above policies directed at the particular strategic target

Source: Michael E. Porter, *Competitive Strategy: Techniques for Analyzing Industries and Competitors.* Copyright © 1980 by The Free Press. Reprinted with permission of The Free Press, a Division of Macmillan, Inc.

can serve those segments better than firms that seek to influence the entire market. For example, products such as Rolls-Royce automobiles, Cross pens, and Hartmann luggage are designed to appeal to the upscale market and serve it well rather than trying to compete in the mass market.

Each of these strategies is designed to give a firm a competitive advantage, but each has several risks associated with it. These are listed in Table 4.5.

Porter's approach offers a useful framework for analyzing competitive forces and formulating generic business strategies. Of course, the specific strategies that it is best to use depend on the characteristics of, and opportunities and constraints in, the industry. A business's relative position in the industry also has important implications for formulating strategies, as illustrated in Highlight 4.3.[9]

[9] For additional discussion of Porter's views and business-level strategies, see Gareth R. Jones and John E. Butler, "Costs, Revenue, and Business-Level Strategy," *Academy of Management Review* 13, no. 2 (1988): 202–213; Alan I. Murray, "A Contingency View of Porter's 'Generic Strategies,' " *Academy of Management Review* 13, no. 3 (1988): 390–400; Charles W. L. Hill, "Differentiation versus Low Cost or Differentiation and Low Cost: A Contingency Framework," *Academy of Management Review* 13, no. 3 (1988): 401–412; James J. Chrisman, Charles W. Hofer, and William R. Boulton, "Toward a System for Classifying Business Strategies," *Academy of Management Review* 13, no. 3 (1988): 413–428; Danny Miller, "Relating Porter's Business Strategies to Environment and Structure: Analysis and Performance Implications," *Academy of Management Journal* 31, no. 2 (1988): 280–308.

TABLE 4.5 Risks of the Generic Strategies

RISKS OF COST LEADERSHIP	RISKS OF DIFFERENTIATION	RISKS OF FOCUS
Cost leadership is not sustained • competitors imitate • technology changes • other bases for cost leadership erode	Differentiation is not sustained • competitors imitate • bases for differentiation become less important to buyers	The focus strategy is imitated The target segment becomes structurally unattractive • structure erodes • demand disappears
Proximity in differentiation is lost	Cost proximity is lost	Broadly targeted competitors overwhelm the segment • the segment's differences from other segments narrow • the advantages of a broad line increase
Cost focusers achieve even lower cost in segments	Differentiation focusers achieve even greater differentiation in segments	New focusers subsegment the industry

Source: Michael E. Porter, *Competitive Advantage: Creating and Sustaining Superior Performance.* Copyright © 1985 by Michael E. Porter. Reprinted with permission of The Free Press, a Division of Macmillan, Inc.

FORMULATING FUNCTIONAL STRATEGIES

Functional strategies are devised by specialists in each functional area of a business. Collectively, functional strategies spell out the specific tasks that must be performed to implement the business strategy. Business-level and functional-area managers must coordinate their activities to ensure that the strategies all are pursuing are consistent. Companies vary in the organization and responsibilities of their functional areas, but the major functional areas are research and development, operations, finance, marketing, and human resources.

Research and Development Strategy

In many industries, organizations cannot grow or even survive without new products. It is the role of research and development (R&D) specialists to come up with new products for the business and organization. R&D finds new product ideas and develops them until the products go into full production and enter the market. This process involves concept generation and screening, product planning and development, and perhaps even actual test marketing, as discussed in Chapter 11.

R&D is very important and new products can be highly profitable for an organization, but R&D can also be time consuming, expensive, and risky. For

HIGHLIGHT 4.3

ILLUSTRATIVE EXAMPLE ■ Military Strategies for Industrial Warfare

Al Ries and Jack Trout argue that military strategy provides a useful perspective on competing in an industry. They suggest that there are four kinds of warfare and that each is appropriate for particular competitors in an industry.

DEFENSIVE WARFARE

Defensive strategies should be used only by market leaders such as General Motors and IBM. Defensive warfare involves protecting market share against competitors by introducing new products and services that render existing ones obsolete. Market leaders should block competitors' attempts at innovation by quickly copying any promising new products that they introduced.

OFFENSIVE WARFARE

Offensive strategies should be used by the number-2 and number-3 firms in the industry, firms that are large enough to mount a sustained attack on the market leader. Offensive warfare focuses on dissecting a leader's strength and finding a weakness where the leader is vulnerable to attack. The attack should be mounted on as narrow a front as possible, usually with a single product. For example, Federal Express became the market leader over Emory and Airborne by emphasizing Priority One service and its high reliability.

FLANKING WARFARE

Flanking strategies involve moving into uncontested areas (no existing market), surprising competitors, and following up one's innovation relentlessly. This strategy is also for market followers rather than market leaders. For example, Miller flanked the industry with Lite beer and now dominates the light-beer market. Flanking is often a high-risk strategy, but successful flanking can be highly profitable.

GUERRILLA WARFARE

Guerrilla strategies entail finding a niche in the market small enough to defend but being ready to withdraw nimbly if necessary. This strategy is for companies with small market share.

Source: Based on Al Ries and Jack Trout, *Marketing Warfare* (New York: McGraw-Hill, 1986).

example, it is estimated that only one out of seven new product ideas ever makes it to the market. Clearly, the time and money allocated to researching and developing the other six ideas greatly increase R&D costs. Furthermore, an average of 30 to 35 percent of new products fail after being put on the market, so *innovation strategies*—those that focus heavily on developing new products—can be very risky.[10] For this reason many organizations use *imitation strategies;* that is, they rapidly copy new competitive products that are doing well. A number of Japanese electronics companies were quite successful in copying American technology and, by avoiding many R&D costs, improved their competitive positions significantly.

Operations Strategy

Specialists in this area focus on making decisions about required plant capacity, plant layout, manufacturing and production processes, and inventory requirements. Two important aspects of operations strategy are controlling costs and improving the efficiency of plant operations. Chapter 9 of this text offers a detailed discussion of operations strategy.

Financial Strategy

Financial specialists are responsible for forecasting and financial planning, evaluating investment proposals, securing financing for various investments, and controlling financial resources. Financial specialists contribute to strategy formulation by assessing the potential profit impact of various strategic alternatives and evaluating the financial condition of the business. Chapter 10 of this text discusses financial strategy further.

Marketing Strategy

Marketing specialists focus on determining the appropriate markets for business offerings and on developing effective marketing mixes. (The marketing mix includes four strategic elements: price, product, promotion, and channels of distribution.) Chapter 11 of this text treats marketing strategy in detail.

Human Resource Strategy

In general, the human resource function is concerned with attracting, assessing, motivating, and retaining the number and types of employees required to run the business effectively. This function is also responsible for affirmative action planning and evaluating the safety of the work environment. Taken collectively, the set of decisions concerning these issues is the human resource strategy for the business.

Like other strategies, human resource strategies are based on both external and internal analysis. External analysis includes such activities as tracking developments in laws and regulations affecting employment (such as those in the equal employment opportunity area), studying changes in labor unions

[10] C. Merle Crawford, *New Product Management*, 2d ed. (Homewood, Ill.: Richard D. Irwin, 1987), p. 21.

TABLE 4.6 Characteristics of Companies That Manage Their Employees Well and of Companies That Do Not

CHARACTERISTICS OF EFFECTIVE COMPANIES	CHARACTERISTICS OF INEFFECTIVE COMPANIES
Genuine concern for people; a positive view of employees as assets.	Do not view employees as important assets; show little concern for work force.
Good training, development, and advancement opportunities.	Managed in an autocratic or bureaucratic manner; rigid and inflexible.
Pay well; good compensation programs.	Little or no employee development; an ineffective internal advancement process.
Able to retain employees; low turnover.	Poor internal communication.
Good internal communication; open communication.	Unclear or outdated policies, inconsistently administered and altered in difficult times.
Top management committed to and supportive of HR [human resources].	High turnover.
Encourage employee participation.	

Source: Adapted from S. W. Alper and R. E. Mandel, "What Policies and Practices Characterize the Most Effective HR Departments." Reprinted from the vol. 29, no. 11, 1984 issue of *Personnel Administrator.*

and labor union negotiations, and analyzing changes in the labor market. Internal analysis includes investigating specific problem areas such as low productivity, excessive turnover, and high on-the-job accident rates. In addition, human resource strategies may involve analyzing and proposing changes in organizational structure and climate. These latter topics are discussed in Chapter 5 of this text. Table 4.6 lists several considerations that the human resource managers should take into account in analyzing organizations.

A complete discussion of the development of human resource strategies is beyond the scope of this text.[11] Highlight 4.4, however, presents a portion of the human resource strategy for Merck and Company. As is appropriate for all functional-area strategies, this strategy is stated at an operational level and specifies the tasks that must be performed to implement it.

STRATEGY FORMULATION CONSTRAINTS AND SELECTION CRITERIA

In order for managers to formulate useful strategies, they must be aware of certain organizational constraints. In addition, managers need a set of general criteria to judge the quality of proposed strategies. In this final section, we discuss some common constraints on strategy formulation and some strategy selection criteria.

[11] For a complete discussion of human resource management and strategy see Herbert G. Henneman III, Donald P. Schwab, John A. Fossum, and Lee Dyer, *Personnel/Human Resource Management,* 4th ed. (Homewood, Ill.: Richard D. Irwin, 1989). Also see Cynthia A. Lengnick-Hall and Mark L. Lengnick-Hall, "Strategic Human Resources Management: A Review of the Literature and Proposed Typology," *Academy of Management Review* 13, no. 3 (1988): 454–470.

HIGHLIGHT 4.4

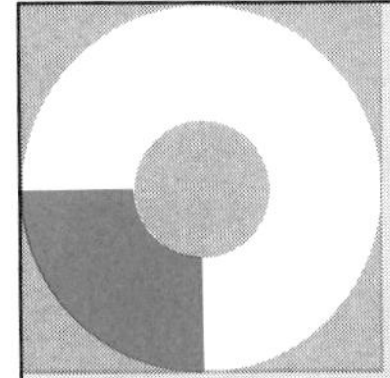

ILLUSTRATIVE EXAMPLE ■ **Excerpts from Merck and Company's Human Resource Strategy**

PRIORITY 6

Develop new and more effective ways to accommodate employee participation in joint problem-solving areas and in appropriate policy/practice development:

Opinion surveys, face-to-face-meetings, focus groups, quality circle groups, and labor–management committees have added channels for employees to express their concerns and suggestions. These are just the start of many avenues which will be explored to improve participation and two-way communications between employees and supervisors.

There continues to be room for and need for expanding and improving employee participation. This will be achieved through improved two-way communication between employees and supervisors. Managers and supervisors need to fully understand and to put into practice the belief that the commitment of people is better assured when they are involved in the decision-making process.

Summary of Action Plans

- Application of "focus group" techniques to develop or revise policies and procedures (successfully tested in 1980 with the Performance Appraisal Program and the Salary Administration Program).
- Continue to measure the effectiveness of management policies, practices, and programs.

PRIORITY 10

Develop innovative approaches to organization design, job design and scheduling, and advanced office systems to improve productivity.

Strengthen our capabilities for more effective organization planning to ensure capability of supporting business plans and objectives. It is critical that skills be broadened in long-term organization planning and in the redesign of jobs and work.

Attract talented professionals who want more flexibility in the workplace.

We will continue our investigation into advanced office systems and the expansion of office automation, which have significant human implications. There is a need to coordinate a stronger planning effort—on a corporatewide basis—between the three elements that are essential to make advanced office systems work effectively. These three elements include the technical (MIS), the physical office design (Engineering), and the behavioral (Human Resources). Given that Merck is office-worker

(*Continued*)

intensive and will become more so in the future, this planning effort has significant implications for the Company's productivity efforts.

Summary of Action Plans

- Continue to develop skills for effective organization planning and implementation of Advanced Office Systems.
- Expand flexible working hours and test new scheduling and work pattern approaches.
- Continue to improve consulting skills of H.R. professionals.

Source: G. T. Milkovich and J. D. Phillips, "Human Resource Planning at Merck & Co.," in L. Dyer, ed., *Human Resource Planning: A Case Study Reference Guide to the Tested Practices of Five Major U.S. and Canadian Companies* (New York: Random House, 1985). Reprinted by permission.

Strategy Formulation Constraints

Ideally, managers select those strategies that optimize the chances of achieving their organization's objectives. However, a number of constraints often need to be considered when planning and selecting organizational, business, or functional strategies. Some of the major ones are:

1. *Availability of financial resources:* Even when a particular strategy appears optimal for an organization, serious consideration must be given to where the money to finance the strategy is going to come from. Some firms may be in such poor financial condition that borrowing large sums to finance expensive strategies may be out of the question: No lending agency would consider the firm an acceptable risk. Similarly, some firms are averse to borrowing per se or to increasing their debt levels beyond a certain point. In addition, stockholders may expect and demand dividends on an annual basis, which may limit the profits available for financing new, expensive strategies.
2. *Attitude toward risk:* Some firms are willing to accept only minimal levels of risk, regardless of the level of potential return. In these cases, acceptable strategies may be limited to those that expose the company to little risk.
3. *Organizational capabilities:* Some otherwise excellent strategies may require capabilities beyond those an organization currently possesses. For example, a firm that has excellent production skills but weak marketing skills may not be able to execute a strategy requiring superior marketing efforts. Of course, a firm could develop these skills or hire this expertise, but such a move might violate corporate norms and create dysfunctional conflict. Similarly, organizational skills are not always transferable from one market to another, as IBM found when it opened its own retail stores. (Highlight 4.7 at the end of this chapter

discusses IBM's problem.) Also, some excellent strategies require very rapid implementation to succeed; a firm without the ability to move quickly, or one with serious internal political problems, may have to forgo such strategies.

4. *Channel relationships:* Strategies that call for the development of new channels of distribution or that involve new suppliers require careful consideration of the availability of these other organizations and their willingness to work with the firm. Some strategies may have to be forgone because the firm cannot establish its own channel and other firms are not available to perform distribution tasks.
5. *Competitive retaliation:* Some strategies may have the unintended effect of dramatically increasing competitors' efforts in the marketplace. For example, a strategy of reducing prices may effectively stimulate short-term demand for a product—but also result in costly price wars.

Strategy Selection Criteria

Although obtaining or surpassing a specific return on investment is a commonly stated organizational objective, it is often difficult to forecast accurately what the ROI for an alternative will be or to adjust it appropriately for risk. According to David Aaker, strategic alternatives should be accepted to the degree that they meet the following six criteria:[12]

1. They are responsive to the external environment.
2. They involve a sustainable competitive advantage.
3. They are consistent with other strategies in the organization.
4. They provide adequate flexibility for the business and the organization.
5. They conform to the organization's mission and long-term objectives.
6. They are organizationally feasible.

In a sense, these criteria are a useful summary of many of the issues discussed in this and the two preceding chapters. Highlight 4.5 offers several recommendations for formulating successful strategies in a small business.

SUMMARY

Strategy formulation cannot begin until the managers responsible for shaping strategy understand the context in which their strategies will unfold. Thus, they rely on environmental analysis to supply the information they need. In

[12] David A. Aaker, "How to Select a Business Strategy," *California Management Review,* Spring 1984, pp. 167–175.

HIGHLIGHT 4.5

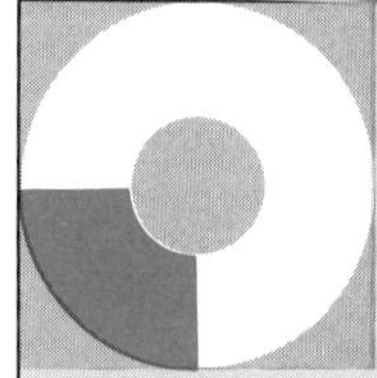

ILLUSTRATIVE EXAMPLE ■ **Formulating Strategy in a Small Business: Ten Suggestions for Survival and Success**

Below is a list of ten suggestions for small business strategy formulation that are designed to enhance the chances of survival and success.

1. *Be objective.* Self-delusion has no place in building a business. An honest, dispassionate assessment of the strengths and weaknesses of the company and its business and management skills is essential.
2. *Keep it simple and focused.* In small business, simple is effective. Efforts and resources should be concentrated where the impact and profits are the greatest.
3. *Focus on profitable markets.* Small businesses survive and prosper by providing distinctive goods and services that meet the wants and needs of select groups of consumers.
4. *Develop sound marketing plans.* Small businesses must determine how to reach and sell customers.
5. *Manage employees effectively.* Small business success depends on building, managing, and motivating a winning team.
6. *Keep clear accounting records.* Small businesses need to keep track of assets, liabilities, sales, costs, and other accounting information in order to survive and prosper.
7. *Never run out of cash.* Cash is king in the small business world.
8. *Avoid the recurring pitfalls of rapid growth.* Small businesses must carefully manage expansion.
9. *Understand all phases of the business.* Control of a small business and improvement of small business profits depends on a complete understanding of all business functions.
10. *Plan ahead.* Small businesses must formulate critical and challenging, yet achievable, goals and convert them into productive activities.

Source: Adapted from Paul Resnik, *The Small Business Bible* (New York: John Wiley & Sons, 1988), pp. 3–4.

this chapter, we surveyed two approaches for focusing environmental analysis on strategy formulation. The manager who has reliable answers to the four questions posed in critical question analysis can be more confident that she or he knows where the organization is, where it is going, and what conditions it is likely to encounter along the way. Similarly, SWOT analysis provides a means of balancing an organization's strengths and weaknesses with the opportunities and threats anticipated or known to exist in the external environment.

Strategy is formulated at three distinct levels: the organizational, business, and functional levels. Devised by top management, organizational strategies are designed to ensure that the firm at large achieves its overall objectives. Such general issues as whether to concentrate on a single line of business or diversify, whether to seek stability or opportunities to grow, and how to respond if the organization's survival is threatened fall in the province of organizational strategy.

We also explored two business portfolio models created to help top management decide how to deploy the various businesses that make up the firm and how to allocate resources among them. The growth–share matrix enables managers to classify every business as a question mark, a star, a cash cow, or a dog; to ascertain whether the firm's roster of businesses is well balanced among the four; and to determine what strategy is appropriate for each. The multifactor portfolio matrix attempts to quantify the strength of a business and the attractiveness of the industry it operates in. The sum of these two numbers is taken as an indication of whether investing aggressively, investing selectively, or refraining from further investment is the best strategy. Both models offer useful information in an interesting graphical format, but it is important to remember that they do not dictate the course to take and that they are no substitute for sound managerial judgment and experience.

We approached the formulation of strategy at the business-unit or division level from the perspective of Michael Porter's analysis of five competitive forces: the threat of new entrants, the bargaining power of suppliers, the bargaining power of buyers, the threat of substitute products, and rivalry among competitors. We also discussed the conditions under which the strategies of overall cost leadership, differentiation, and focus are appropriate and the risks associated with each.

Just as business strategies must dovetail smoothly with organizational strategies, the strategies that each functional unit adopts must be consistent with the business of which it is a part. We touched on such issues as innovation versus imitation in the research and development function, controlling costs and boosting efficiency in the operations function, the planning and controlling tasks of the financial specialists, the marketing function's responsibility for selecting markets and developing effective marketing mixes, and the need for the human resource function to manage employees effectively.

Strategic decisions at all levels are subject to certain constraints, including the availability of financial resources, the firm's attitude toward risk, its relationship with suppliers and distributors, and the probable responses of competitors to its actions. All must be pondered in order to make the best-informed choice among strategic alternatives. The chapter concludes with the criteria that David Aaker suggests be applied in selecting among strategic alternatives and with a reminder that it is important to evaluate every proposed strategy in terms of its probable effect on profit, total revenue, and total cost.

Highlight 4.6 is a checklist of questions based on this chapter. Use it in analyzing strategic management problems and cases that focus on the formulation of organizational, business, or functional strategies.

HIGHLIGHT 4.6

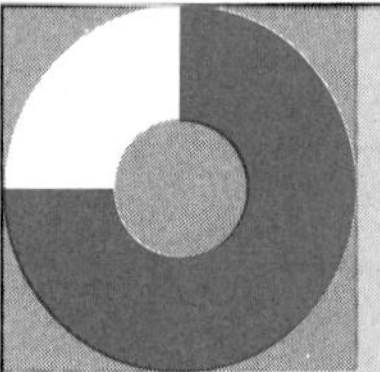

CHECKLIST ■ **Analyzing Strategy Formulation in Problems and Cases**

- ☐ 1. Is strategy formulation the major focus of this problem or case?
- ☐ 2. Has the organization carefully analyzed its environmental situation, or would a critical question or SWOT analysis help focus strategy formulation?
- ☐ 3. What general strategy is the organization following, and would other strategies be more likely to achieve organizational objectives?
- ☐ 4. Is this a large, diversified organization for which a business portfolio analysis would be useful?
- ☐ 5. Is enough information available for management to develop and analyze a growth–share matrix or a multifactor portfolio matrix?
- ☐ 6. What business strategies does the problem or case involve?
- ☐ 7. Would an analysis of the five competitive forces help managers formulate a more effective business strategy?
- ☐ 8. What functional strategies are at issue in the problem or case?
- ☐ 9. What constraints on strategy formulation exist?
- ☐ 10. How does the current or proposed strategy measure up on the six strategy selection criteria?

ADDITIONAL READINGS

Fredericks, Peter, and N. Venkatraman. "The Rise of Strategy Support Systems," *Sloan Management Review,* Spring 1988, pp. 47–54.

Gray, Daniel H. "Uses and Misuses of Strategic Planning." *Harvard Business Review,* January–February 1986, pp. 89–97.

Hax, Arnoldo C., and Nicholas S. Majluf. *Strategic Management: An Integrative Perspective.* Englewood Cliffs, N.J.: Prentice-Hall, 1984.

Lamb, Robert Boyden (ed.). *Competitive Strategic Management.* Englewood Cliffs, N.J.: Prentice-Hall, 1984.

Pfeiffer, William J., Leonard D. Goodstein, and Timothy M. Nolan. *Shaping Strategic Planning.* Glenview, Ill.: Scott, Foresman and Company, 1989.

Prescott, John E., and Daniel C. Smith. "A Project-Based Approach to Competitive Analysis." *Strategic Management Journal* 8 (1987): 411–423.

Yavitz, Boris, and William H. Newman. *Strategy in Action.* New York: The Free Press, 1982.

HIGHLIGHT 4.7 ■ APPLICATION OF CHAPTER MATERIAL

Strategy Formulation for IBM

A bear when it sells big computers to corporations, IBM is a Bambi of a storefront retailer. In the early 1980s the company began opening grandly decorated computer stores called IBM Product Centers in high-rent business districts all over America. While the first 81 stores had sales estimated at $100 million in 1983, IBM shelved plans to expand the chain to 100 stores.

The centers sell IBM's Personal Computer (PC) and typewriters, along with add-on gear and software made by IBM and others. Burdened with start-up costs and high overhead, the stores made far less than the 20 percent per year IBM is accustomed to earning on invested capital.

Glimpsing the chance to sell typewriters to small businesses and branch offices of big companies without costly door-to-door calls, IBM had opened three Product Centers by mid-1981. Then, when the PC burst on the scene, the company decided to plunk stores down in every metropolitan area. However, most of the 1,600-odd independent stores that carry the firm's PC and competing makes have done a better job of selling the target clientele. The rival stores belong mostly to big chains such as ComputerLand, Entré Computer Centers, and Sears Business Systems Centers.

(*Continued*)

IBM made mistakes right off the bat. Although it is a major producer of sophisticated point-of-sale computer systems to centralize billing, inventory, and sales audits—with 1983 sales estimated at $125 million—the company forced its own salespeople to record transactions on Stone Age carbon-paper invoices. At the end of each day, clerks typed the information into a computer in the back room. Result: mistakes galore in record-keeping and billing.

In choosing the Product Centers' decor, IBM revealed retailing naiveté. Anxious not to appear cold and remote, it abandoned its traditional icy blue and decorated the centers bright red. "Red doesn't just irritate bulls," remarked Warren Winger, chairman of CompuShop, a Dallas-based chain, "it makes salesmen hostile and alarms customers." To keep its stores classy, IBM eschewed the usual tacky trappings of computer retailing—flashy in-store displays, brochures, and racks of impulse items near the cash registers. "The in-store merchandising—we never realized how important it was," confessed Jim Turner, the IBM vice president in charge of the centers. IBM also staffed the stores entirely with its own career salespeople, few of whom had retailing experience. Consumer research by a large New York ad agency showed that the staff intimidated first-time customers. In interviews the customers revealed that they expected more of IBM Product Centers than of other computer stores, but came away disillusioned.

Product Center chief Turner hints that in the future the centers may concentrate on selling full-blown office automation systems. While he insists that IBM has no plans to close up shop, there's some question whether the company ought to be in the retail jungle at all. The margins are low, competition is fierce, and the other animals are quick and crafty and know the terrain.

DISCUSSION QUESTIONS

1. IBM clearly failed to analyze consumer/product relationships when it opened its own retail stores. List all of the mistakes it made because of this failure.
2. Why didn't IBM analyze consumer/product relationships?
3. What do you think consumers expected when they went to an IBM Product Center?

Source: Based on Peter Petre, "IBM's Misadventures in the Retail Jungle," *Fortune,* July 23, 1984, p. 80. from J. Paul Peter and Jerry C. Olson, *Consumer Behavior and Marketing Strategy* (Homewood, Ill.: Richard D. Irwin, 1990). Reprinted by permission.

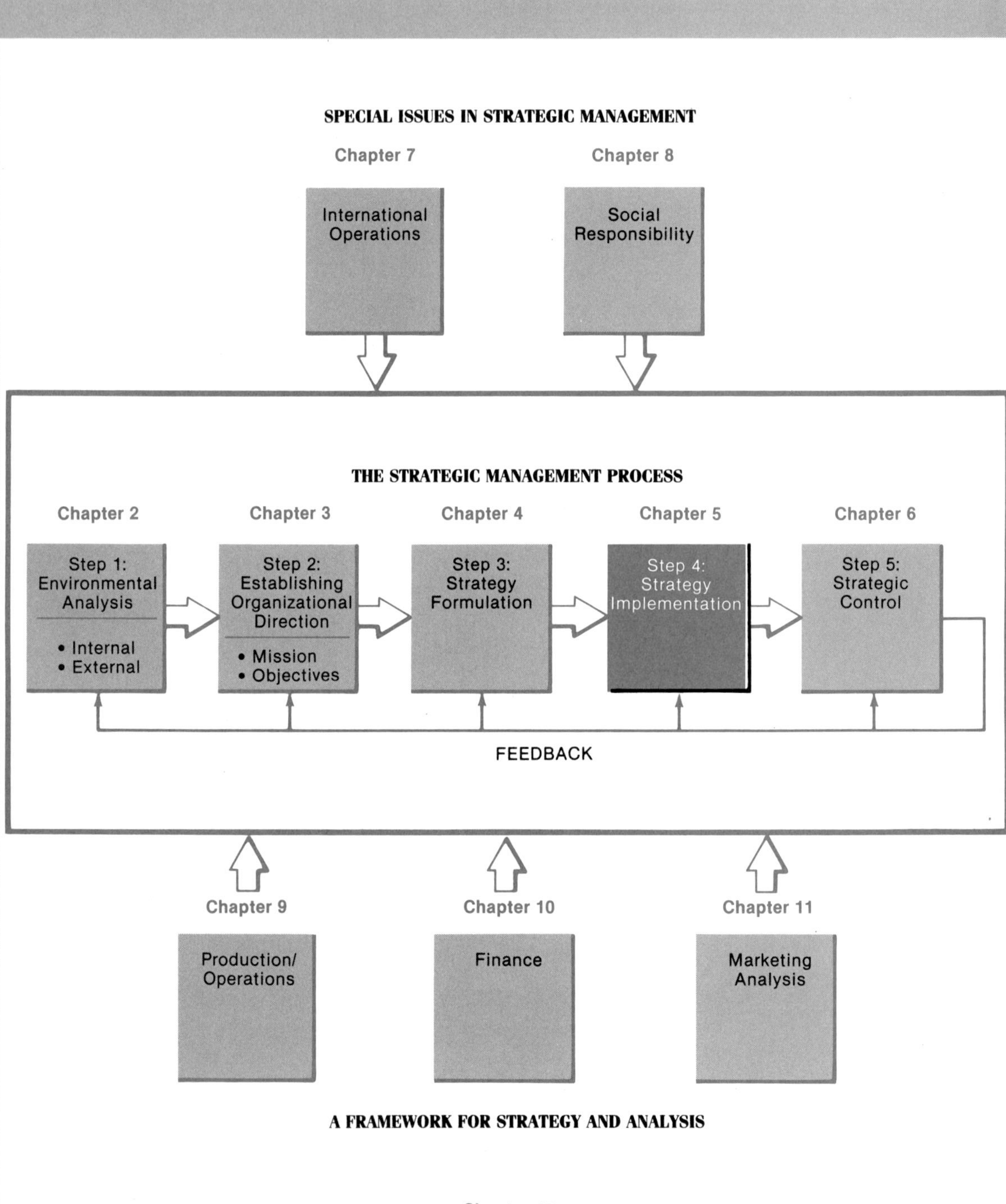

SPECIAL ISSUES IN STRATEGIC MANAGEMENT
Chapter 7
International Operations
Chapter 8
Social Responsibility
THE STRATEGIC MANAGEMENT PROCESS
Chapter 2
Step 1: Environmental Analysis
• Internal
• External
Chapter 3
Step 2: Establishing Organizational Direction
• Mission
• Objectives
Chapter 4
Step 3: Strategy Formulation
Chapter 5
Step 4: Strategy Implementation
Chapter 6
Step 5: Strategic Control
FEEDBACK
Chapter 9
Production/ Operations
Chapter 10
Finance
Chapter 11
Marketing Analysis
A FRAMEWORK FOR STRATEGY AND ANALYSIS
Chapter 12
An Approach to Solving Strategic Problems and Cases

CHAPTER 5

Strategy Implementation

In the previous chapter we discussed a number of important issues that arise as managers formulate strategies. In this chapter we focus on implementing strategies—that is, putting strategies into action. Although the literature on strategy implementation is growing, it is not so well developed as the literature on strategy formulation. However, the success of organizations depends on the effective implementation of strategies. In fact, the first attribute listed by Thomas Peters and Robert Waterman as distinctive of excellent, innovative companies is related to the corporate view of implementation. They suggest that excellent companies have a bias for action—for getting on with it:

> Even though these companies may be analytical in their approach to decision making, they are not paralyzed by that fact (as so many others seem to be). In many of these companies the standard operating procedure is "Do it, fix it, try it." Says a Digital Equipment Corporation senior executive, for example, "When we've got a big problem here, we grab ten senior guys and stick them in a room for a week. They come up with an answer *and* implement it." Moreover, the companies are experimenters supreme. Instead of allowing 250 engineers and mar-

> keters to work on a new product in isolation for fifteen months, they form bands of 5 to 25 and test ideas out on a customer, often with inexpensive prototypes, within a matter of weeks. What is striking is the host of practical devices the excellent companies employ, to maintain corporate fleetness of foot and counter the stultification that almost inevitably comes with size.[1]

As this quote suggests, effective managers often work back and forth between strategy formulation and strategy implementation. In many successful organizations, not every aspect of a strategy is planned in detail and then implemented according to the predefined schedule. Rather, strategies are often partially formulated, implemented, reformulated, and extended to rapidly capitalize on strategic opportunities. Thus, although our focus in this chapter is on implementation, it should be clear that formulation and implementation influence each other and often evolve together.

In the first part of this chapter we investigate the relationship between strategy formulation and strategy implementation, which, it should come as no surprise to discover, must *both* be done well in order to yield the best odds that the strategy will unfold successfully. Then we propose a five-stage model of the strategy implementation process. It is useful, we find, to dissect this crucial process into the discrete steps of (1) determining how much the organization will have to change in order to implement the strategy under consideration, (2) analyzing the formal and informal structures of the organization, (3) analyzing the "culture" of the organization, (4) selecting an appropriate approach to implementing the strategy, and (5) implementing the strategy and evaluating the results.

ISSUES IN STRATEGY FORMULATION AND IMPLEMENTATION

In order for an organization to achieve its objectives, it must not only formulate but also implement its strategies effectively. If either of these tasks is poorly done, the result is likely to be failure of the overall strategy. Figure 5.1 represents the importance of both tasks in matrix form and suggests the probable outcomes of the four possible combinations of these variables: success, roulette, trouble, and failure.[2]

Success is the most likely outcome when an organization has a good strategy and implements it well. In this case, all that can be done to ensure success *has* been done. Environmental factors outside the company's control, such as competitive reactions or customer changes, may still make a strategy unsuccessful. However, organizational objectives have the best chance of being achieved in this cell.

Roulette involves situations wherein a poorly formulated strategy is implemented well. Two basic outcomes may ensue. The good execution may overcome the poor strategy or at least give management an early warning of impending

[1] Thomas J. Peters and Robert H. Waterman, Jr., *In Search of Excellence* (New York: Harper & Row Publishers, 1982), pp. 13–14.

[2] This discussion is based on Thomas V. Bonoma, *The Marketing Edge: Making Strategies Work* (New York: The Free Press, 1985), pp. 12–14.

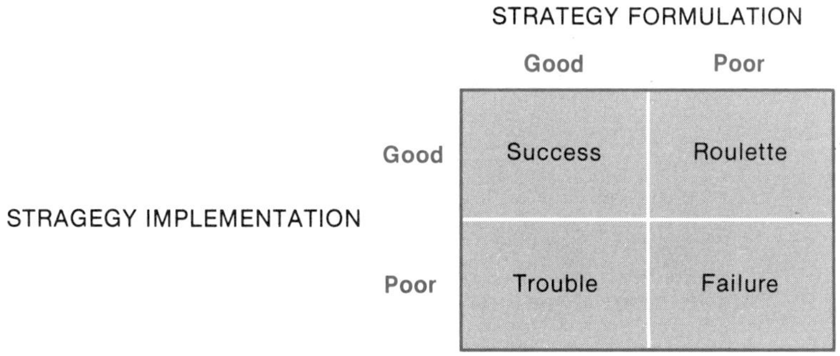

STRAGEGY IMPLEMENTATION		STRATEGY FORMULATION: Good	STRATEGY FORMULATION: Poor
	Good	Success	Roulette
	Poor	Trouble	Failure

FIGURE 5.1 *Diagnosing Strategic Problems (Reprinted with permission of The Free Press, a division of Macmillan, Inc. from The Marketing Edge: Making Strategies Work by Thomas V. Bonoma. Copyright 1985 by The Free Press.)*

failure. Perhaps the field sales force recognizes a problem in the strategy and changes its selling approach to a more successful one. Alternatively, the same good execution can hasten the failure of the poor strategy. For example, rapid production and effective marketing of a faulty new product causes the strategy to fail sooner. Thus, it is impossible to predict exactly what will happen to strategies in the roulette cell, and that's where it gets its name.

The *trouble* cell is characterized by situations wherein a well-formulated strategy is poorly implemented. Because managers are more accustomed to focusing on strategy formulation, the real problem with the strategy—faulty implementation—is often not diagnosed. When things go wrong, managers are likely to reformulate the strategy rather than question whether the implementation was effective. The new (and often *less* appropriate) strategy is then reimplemented and continues to fail.

Failure is the most likely to occur when a poorly formulated strategy is poorly implemented. In these situations, management has great difficulty getting back on the right track. If the same strategy is retained and implemented in a different way, it is still likely to fail. If the strategy is reformulated and implemented the same way, failure remains the probable result. Strategic problems in this cell of the matrix are very difficult to diagnose and remedy.

This discussion should make two things clear. First, strategy implementation is at least as important as strategy formulation. Unfortunately, when formulating strategies, managers are inclined simply to assume that effective implementation will occur. Yet it should be obvious that *what organizations actually do* is at least as important as *what they plan to do*. Second, the quality of a formulated strategy is difficult if not impossible to assess in the absence of effective implementation. Diagnosing why a strategy failed in the roulette, trouble, and failure cells in order to find a remedy requires the analysis of *both* formulation and implementation.

Although, as we noted, the strategic management literature on effective implementation is not fully developed, Figure 5.2 offers a model of the major tasks involved in implementing strategies. In the remainder of the chapter, we will discuss each of these tasks in detail.

FIGURE 5.2 Strategic Implementation Tasks

ANALYZING STRATEGIC CHANGE

A useful first step in implementing a strategy is to get a clear idea how much the organization will have to change in order to implement it successfully. Some strategies require only minimal changes in the way a firm currently conducts its business; others require sweeping changes in the conduct of operations. For example, implementing a new pricing strategy may affect only a few people within the organization and cause very little change in day-to-day operations. However, creating, producing, and marketing product lines different from those previously handled by the firm may require a radical change in every phase of the business.

Strategic change can be viewed as a continuum running from *no* variation in strategy to a *complete* change in an organization's mission. For analytic purposes, it is useful to divide strategic change into the five discrete stages shown in Table 5.1. The value of determining the level of strategic change is that knowing it gives managers a better idea of the problems likely to arise in implementing a particular strategy. Typically, implementation becomes more complex as one moves from a continuation strategy to organizational redirection, because the number of organizational units, people, and tasks increases greatly. In addition, the problems involved in organizational redirection are more likely to be unique or unfamiliar. The five levels of strategic change and the implications of each for strategy implementation are discussed below.

TABLE 5.1 Levels of Strategic Change

	INDUSTRY	ORGANIZATION	PRODUCTS	MARKET APPEAL
Continuation strategy	same	same	same	same
Routine strategy change	same	same	same	new
Limited strategy change	same	same	new	new
Radical strategy change	same	new	new	new
Organizational redirection	new	new	new	new

Continuation Strategy

A continuation strategy is one in which the same strategy that was used in the previous planning period is repeated. Because new skills and unfamiliar tasks are not required at this level, successful implementation is largely a matter of monitoring activities to ensure that they are performed on schedule. At this level, experience curve effects (learning from previous experience) can help to make implementation more cost-effective and efficient. A continuation strategy is typically the simplest to execute. Of course, whether it is the appropriate approach depends on the results of the environmental analysis and on the previous track record of the strategy.

Routine Strategy Change

A routine strategy change involves normal changes in the appeals used to attract customers. Firms alter their advertising appeals, update packaging, use different pricing tactics, and may change distributors or distribution methods in the normal course of operations. Campbell Soup, for example, changes its radio ads with the weather. When a storm is forecast, the commercials encourage consumers to stock up on soup before the weather worsens; after the storm has hit, the message encourages consumers to stay home and enjoy good hot soup. Implementing such strategies requires managers to schedule and coordinate activities with ad agencies and middlemen. In some cases, such as when the firm offers a significant price deal to middlemen or consumers, managers must also coordinate their activities with those of production to ensure that enough inventory is available to handle increased demand.

An important type of routine strategy change involves positioning or repositioning a product in the minds of consumers. A classic example of this involved 7 Up, which for many years had difficulty convincing consumers that it was a soft drink and not just a mixer. By promoting 7 Up as the Uncola, the company positioned it both as a soft drink that could be consumed in the same situations as colas and as an alternative to colas. This strategy was very successful but did not require a major change in the organization. (Table 5.2 lists the steps involved in one approach to product positioning.)

TABLE 5.2 An Operational Approach to Product Positioning

1. *Identify the Competitors.* This step involves defining the relevant market for the firm's offering. For example, Diet Coke might define its competition as (a) other diet cola drinks, (b) other cola drinks, (c) other soft drinks, (d) other nonalcoholic beverages, (e) other beverages. Usually, there will be a primary group of competitors (other diet colas) and a secondary group (other colas and soft drinks). Research identifying consumer product-use situations is useful here.
2. *Determine How Competitors are Perceived and Evaluated.* This step involves identifying product attributes and associations made by consumers so that competitive brand images can be defined.
3. *Determine the Competitor's Position.* This step involves determining how competitors (including the firm's own entry) are positioned with respect to the relevant product associations. Multidimensional scaling and other multivariate approaches are useful at this stage.
4. *Analyze the Customers.* This step involves developing a thorough knowledge of the behavior of various market segments, including the role of the product class in the customer's lifestyle and consumer motivations, habits, and behavior patterns.
5. *Select the Position.* While there is no cookbook solution for selecting an optimal position, key decision criteria include (a) the nature of the market segments, (b) economic criteria, especially market potential and penetration probability, (c) a consistent image across time, and (d) not positioning the product to be better than it is.
6. *Monitoring the Position.* A positioning strategy should be monitored across time to evaluate it and to generate diagnostic information about future positioning strategies. This involves ongoing research and may include one or more techniques such as multidimensional scaling.

Source: Condensed from David A. Aaker and Gary Shandy, "Positioning Your Product," *Business Horizons*, May–June 1982, pp. 56–62. Found in J. Paul Peter and Jerry C. Olson, *Consumer Behavior and Marketing Strategy*, 2nd ed. (Homewood, Ill.: Richard D. Irwin, 1990).

Limited Strategy Change

A limited strategy change involves offering new products to new markets within the same general product class. There are many variations at this level of strategic change, because products can be new in a variety of ways. For example, Extra-Strength Tylenol was a new product formulation that did not require radically different methods of production or marketing, so implementing a strategy to sell this product did not require any major change on Johnson & Johnson's part. On the other hand, the creation, production, and marketing of products such as stereos, televisions, home computers, videocassette recorders, and still-video cameras often involve new and more complex implementation problems.

Radical Strategy Change

A radical strategy change involves a major reorganization within the firm. This type of change is common when mergers and acquisitions occur between firms in the same basic industry. For example, Nestlé acquired Carnation (both of which were in the food industry), and Procter & Gamble acquired Richardson-Vicks (both in consumer products). Such acquisitions can be particularly complex when attempts are made to integrate the two firms completely. The acquiring firm not only obtains new products and markets but also confronts legal problems, the complexities of developing a new organizational structure, and (quite often) the need to reconcile conflicting organizational values and beliefs.

Radical strategy changes can also involve numerous changes in the organizational structure and multiple acquisitions and sales of subsidiaries. For example, when John F. Welch, Jr., became chairman of General Electric, the company was regarded as a "GNP company" whose growth and prosperity could never outpace the overall economy. Welch set out to create a company that *could* outpace the economy and could prosper even in difficult economic times. He stripped entire levels from the corporate hierarchy and shifted resources from manufacturing businesses to fast-growing services and high technology. He greatly automated production facilities and eliminated 100,000 employees, more than one-fourth of the work force. In his first five years as chairman, he sold 190 subsidiaries worth nearly $6 billion and spent $10 billion on 70 acquisitions. Clearly, this is a strategy of radical change, which may eventually develop into a total organizational redirection.[3]

Organizational Redirection

One form of organizational redirection involves mergers and acquisitions of firms in different industries. The degree of strategic change depends on how different the industries are and on how centralized management of the new firm is to be. For example, when Philip Morris, a manufacturer of cigarettes and beverages, acquired General Foods, a food products manufacturer, the redirection consisted primarily of becoming a more diversified organization operating in two similar industries. When General Motors acquired Electronic Data Systems (EDS), however, considerable differences existed between the industries and between the two companies' views of appropriate business conduct. EDS personnel codes forbade employees to drink alcohol at lunchtime or to wear tasseled shoes. GM employees who transferred to EDS were deeply dissatisfied with such EDS rules, and over 600 of them resigned. GM Chairman Roger B. Smith had a near revolt on his hands as he attempted to reconcile the two different "corporate cultures."[4]

[3] See Peter Petre, "What Welch Has Wrought at GE," *Fortune,* July 7, 1986, pp. 43–47; Marilyn A. Harris, Zachary Schiller, Russell Mitchell, and Christopher Power, "Can Jack Welch Reinvent GE?" *Business Week,* June 30, 1986, pp. 62–67; and Stratford P. Sherman, "Inside the Mind of Jack Welch," *Fortune,* March 27, 1989, pp. 38–53.

[4] David E. Whiteside, "Roger Smith's Campaign to Change the GM Culture," *Business Week,* April 7, 1986, pp. 84–85; and Alex Taylor III, "The Tasks Facing General Motors," *Fortune,* March 13, 1989, pp. 52–60.

Another form of organizational redirection occurs when a firm leaves one industry and enters a new one. For example, when one small brewery could no longer compete in the beer industry, it redirected its efforts to the trucking and packaging industries. Similarly, American Can Company redirected its business from packaging to financial services and retailing during the mid-1980s.[5] This type of organizational redirection is the most complex strategy to implement. It involves changes in the firm's mission and may require an entirely new set of skills and technologies to be developed.

ANALYZING ORGANIZATIONAL STRUCTURE

Two basic kinds of organizational structures exist. There is the *formal* organizational structure, which represents the relationships between resources as designed by management. The formal organizational structure is conveyed in the organization chart. Then there is the *informal* organizational structure, which represents the social relationships based on friendships or interests shared among various members of an organization. The informal organizational structure is evidenced in the patterns of communication commonly called the "grapevine."

When implementing a strategy, managers must take both the formal and the informal organizational structure into consideration for three reasons. First, there is the question of whether the existing organizational structure will promote or impede successful implementation. If the organization has so many levels of management that a strategy cannot be implemented effectively or changed rapidly to accommodate changing conditions, then successful implementation may become difficult. In some cases, the formal organizational structure may have to be changed. For example, several echelons of GE's organizational structure were deleted and its 15 businesses were regrouped into three areas to make the company more cost-effective and responsive to change.

Second, there is the question of what management levels and personnel within the organization will be responsible for various implementation tasks. Radical strategy changes or organizational redirections are typically spearheaded by the chief executive officer, whereas routine strategy changes may be under the direction of middle management.

Third, the informal organization can be used to facilitate successful implementation. For example, if several regional managers commonly consult with each other about implementation issues, this informal network can be used to encourage rapid execution of strategies.

The five types of organizational structures that are commonly seen are the simple, functional, divisional, strategic business unit (SBU), and matrix structures.[6] A schematic diagram of each of these structures is shown in Figure 5.3.

[5] See Anthony Bianco, "Jerry Tsai: The Comeback Kid," *Business Week,* August 18, 1986, pp. 72–80.

[6] John A. Pearce II and Richard B. Robinson, Jr., *Strategic Management,* 3rd ed. (Homewood, Ill.: Richard D. Irwin, 1988), p. 358.

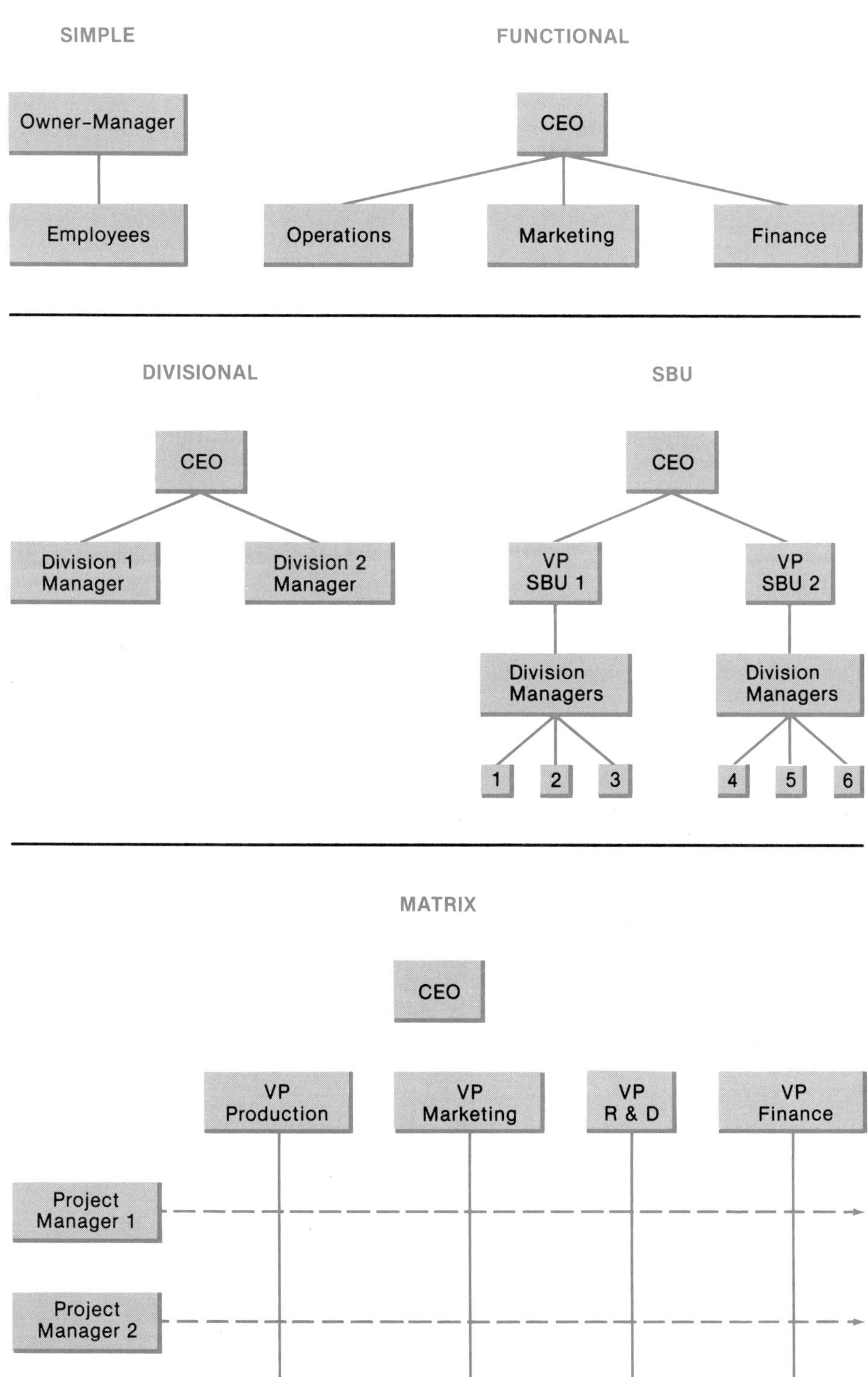

FIGURE 5.3 Five Types of Organizational Structures

Simple Organizational Structure

A simple organizational structure has only two levels, the owner–manager and the employees. Small firms with one product or only a few related ones usually exhibit this structure. A major advantage of this structure is that it allows rapid, flexible implementation of strategies. This advantage is a primary reason why small firms can sometimes compete very effectively with industry giants. However, because success depends so heavily on the skills of a single person (the owner–manager) in formulating and implementing strategies, many such organizations do not survive in the long run.

Functional Organizational Structure

As organizations grow and develop a number of related products and markets, their structures frequently change to reflect greater specialization in functional business areas. Such line functions as production and operations, marketing, and research and development (R&D) may be organized in departments. Functional organizational structures may also include a number of staff departments, such as finance and accounting or personnel and administration, that report to the CEO. Specialization is one of the chief advantages of a functional structure; it promotes the development of greater expertise in each area. However, this structure may lead to coordination problems among departments that may impede efficient implementation.

Divisional Organizational Structure

As firms acquire or develop new products in different industries and markets, they may evolve a divisional organizational structure. Each division may operate autonomously under the direction of a division manager, who reports directly to the CEO. Divisions may be formed on the basis of product lines (automotive, aircraft), markets (consumer, industrial buyers), geographic areas (north, south, international), or channels of distribution (retail store, catalog sales). Each division not only has its own line and staff functions to manage but also formulates and implements strategies on its own with the approval of the CEO. The overall organization has staff positions (such as vice presidents of administration and operations) to assist in coordinating activities and allocating resources. The divisional organizational structure offers large companies a way of remaining close to their markets, but because the different divisions must compete for resources, conflict can also result.

Strategic Business Unit Structure

When a divisional structure becomes unwieldy because a CEO has too many divisions to manage effectively, organizations may reorganize in the form of strategic business units (SBUs) or strategic groups. This structure groups a number of divisions together on the basis of such things as the similarity of product lines or markets. Vice presidents are appointed to oversee the operations of the newly formed strategic business units, and these executives report directly to the CEO. The SBU structure may be useful for coordinating divisions with similar strategic problems and opportunities and may thus facilitate strategy implementation. However, because it imposes another layer of management on the structure, it can also slow down decision making and retard the implementation process unless authority is decentralized.

Matrix Organizational Structure

A matrix organizational structure is used to facilitate the development and execution of various programs or projects. As shown in Figure 5.3, each of the department vice presidents listed at the top has *functional* responsibility for all the projects, whereas each of the project managers listed down the side has *project* responsibility for completing and implementing the strategy. This approach allows project managers to cut across departmental lines and can promote efficient implementation of strategies. However, it does have an important disadvantage: Employees often become confused about their work responsibilities and about whether they are accountable to the project manager or to their functional group manager. In their study of excellent corporations, Peters and Waterman made the following observation about matrix organization structures.

> Virtually none of the excellent companies spoke of itself as having formal matrix structures, except for project management companies like Boeing. But in a company like Boeing, where many of the matrix ideas originated, something very different is meant by matrix management. People operate in a binary way: they are *either* a part of a project team and responsible to that team for getting some task accomplished (most of the time), *or* they are part of a technical discipline, in which they spend some time making sure their technical department is keeping up with the state of the art. When they are on a project, there is no day-in, day-out confusion about whether they are really responsible to the project or not. They are.[7]

Unfortunately, there are no hard and fast rules for determining which organizational structure is best for a particular company. As Table 5.3 suggests, each structural approach has both advantages and disadvantages that managers must consider when designing organizational structure or changing from one structure to another. However, remember that changing an organization's structure is usually a radical strategy change that has a long-term impact on the way strategies are formulated and implemented. Major changes in organizational structure are not usually made to solve problems that arise in implementing routine or limited strategies, although temporary changes in structure can be made to overcome particular implementation problems.

In sum, analyzing organizational structure is a useful step in strategy implementation, because it forces managers to consider the effect of the structure on the tasks that must be performed. In many cases, the structure and the personnel involved are adequate for successful implementation. In some cases, a temporary change in structure may facilitate implementation

[7] Peters and Waterman, *In Search of Excellence,* p. 307.

TABLE 5.3 Advantages and Disadvantages of Five Types of Organizational Structures

SIMPLE

Advantages	Disadvantages
1. Facilitates control of all the business's activities. 2. Makes possible rapid decision making and ability to change with market signals. 3. Offers simple and informal motivation/reward/control systems.	1. Is very demanding on the owner–manager. 2. Grows increasingly inadequate as volume expands. 3. Does not facilitate development of future managers. 4. Tends to focus owner–manager on day-to-day matters and not on future strategy.

FUNCTIONAL

Advantages	Disadvantages
1. Boosts efficiency through specialization. 2. Fosters improved development of functional expertise. 3. Differentiates and delegates day-to-day operating decisions. 4. Retains centralized control of strategic decisions.	1. Promotes narrow specialization and potential functional rivalry or conflict. 2. Fosters difficulty in functional coordination and interfunctional decision making. 3. Can occasion staff–line conflict. 4. Limits internal development of general managers.

DIVISIONAL

Advantages	Disadvantages
1. Forces coordination and necessary authority down to the appropriate level for rapid response. 2. Places strategy development and implementation in closer proximity to the divisions' unique environment. 3. Frees chief executive officer for broader strategic decision making. 4. Sharply focuses accountability for performance. 5. Retains functional specialization within each division. 6. Serves as good training ground for strategic managers.	1. Fosters potentially dysfunctional competition for corporate-level resources. 2. Creates a problem with the extent of authority given to division managers. 3. Fosters the potential for policy inconsistencies between divisions. 4. Raises the problem of arriving at a method to distribute corporate overhead costs that is acceptable to different division managers with profit responsibility.

STRATEGIC BUSINESS UNITS

Advantages	Disadvantages
1. Improves coordination between divisions with similar strategic concerns and product/market environments.	1. Places another layer of management between the divisions and corporate management.

TABLE 5.3 (Continued)

STRATEGIC BUSINESS UNITS	
Advantages	**Disadvantages**
2. Tightens the strategic management and control of large, diverse business enterprises. 3. Facilitates distinct and in-depth business planning at the corporate and business levels. 4. Channels accountability to distinct business units.	2. May increase dysfunctional competition for corporate resources. 3. May make defining the role of the group vice president difficult. 4. May increase difficulty in defining the degree of autonomy for the group vice presidents and division managers.

MATRIX	
Advantages	**Disadvantages**
1. Accommodates a wide variety of project-oriented business activity. 2. Serves as good training ground for strategic managers. 3. Maximizes efficient use of functional managers. 4. Fosters creativity and multiple sources of diversity. 5. Provides broader middle-management exposure to strategic issues for the business.	1. Can create confusion and contradictory policies by allowing dual accountability. 2. Necessitates tremendous horizontal and vertical coordination.

Source: Adapted from John A. Pearce II and Richard B. Robinson, Jr., *Strategic Management*, 3rd ed. (Homewood, Ill.: Richard D. Irwin, 1988), pp. 360–369. Reprinted by permission.

without creating undue problems. In a few cases, when a particular organizational structure is so cumbersome and inefficient that a good strategy cannot be implemented effectively, the structure may need to be overhauled. However, other factors must be considered before management concludes that an organization's structure must be revamped. One of the most important of these factors is the organization's culture.

ANALYZING ORGANIZATIONAL CULTURE

There are many definitions of organizational or corporate culture. For the purposes of this text, we will take *organizational culture* to mean a set of shared values and beliefs that influences the effectiveness of strategy formulation and implementation. The significance of organizational culture for implementing strategies is that it influences the behavior of employees and, it is hoped, motivates them to achieve or surpass organizational objectives. Typically, the

CEO and other present or past leaders in an organization are the key agents influencing the culture. In addition, organizations often exhibit various subcultures in particular divisions or departments that are influenced by leaders at these levels.

Organizational cultures are developed and reinforced in a variety of ways. One authority suggests that there are five primary and five secondary cultural development mechanisms.[8] The five primary mechanisms are:

1. *What leaders pay attention to, measure, and control:* Leaders can communicate very effectively what their vision of the organization is and what they want done by consistently emphasizing the same issues in meetings, in casual remarks and questions, and in strategy discussions. For example, if product quality is the dominant value to be inculcated in employees, leaders may consistently inquire about the effect of any proposed changes on product quality.
2. *Leaders' reactions to critical incidents and organizational crises:* The manner in which leaders deal with crises can create new beliefs and values and reveal underlying organizational assumptions. For example, when a firm faces a financial crisis but does not lay off any employees, the message may be that the organization sees itself as a "family" that looks out for its members.
3. *Deliberate role modeling, teaching, and coaching:* The behaviors that leaders perform in both formal and informal settings have an important effect on employee beliefs, values, and behaviors. For example, if the CEO regularly works very long hours and on weekends, other managers may respond by spending more of their time at work too.
4. *Criteria for allocation of rewards and status:* Leaders can quickly communicate their priorities and values by consistently linking rewards and punishments to the behaviors they are concerned with. For example, if a weekly bonus is given for exceeding production or sales quotas, employees may recognize the value placed on these activities and focus their efforts on them.
5. *Criteria for recruitment, selection, promotion, and retirement of employees:* The types of people who are hired and who succeed in an organization are those who accept the organization's values and behave accordingly. For example, if managers who are action oriented and who implement strategies effectively consistently move up the organizational ladder, the organization's priorities should come through loud and clear to other managers.

Highlight 5.1 asks you to apply some of your insight into organizational culture to one of the divisions of AT&T.

[8] Edgar H. Schein, *Organizational Culture and Leadership* (San Francisco: Jossey-Bass Publishers, 1985), pp. 223–243. The discussion that follows is based on this work. Also see Guy S. Saffold III, "Culture Traits, Strength, and Organizational Performance: Moving Beyond 'Strong' Culture," *Academy of Management Review* 13, no. 4 (1988): 546–558; and Bernard C. Reimann and Yoash Weiner, "Corporate Culture: Avoiding the Elitist Trap," *Business Horizons*, March–April 1988, pp. 36–44.

HIGHLIGHT 5.1

SKILLS MODULE ■ Cultural Development Skills at AT&T

INTRODUCTION

The text outlines five primary cultural development mechanisms. Review the following situation, and then complete the related skill development exercise. Doing so will give you an opportunity to consider some of the issues involved in creating an effective organizational culture.

THE SITUATION

Some analysts claim that AT&T's Information Systems Division is bogged down by bureaucracy. "Trying to negotiate a contract with these people is impossible," complains Jeffrey S. Lipton, director of telecommunications services for the University of Colorado. "It took seven months to get a signed contract, even though we had agreement on major issues within three months. It all has to be reviewed and approved (at headquarters) in New Jersey." One disgusted sales manager, who joined the company from a competitor, calls AT&T's problem "paralysis by analysis." He complains that there are too many task forces and committees. "That's how they put off making decisions—they study them to death." An AT&T executive conceded that there were big problems: "This is still very much a business in transition. It'll probably be another three years before we feel better about our direction and successes."

SKILL DEVELOPMENT EXERCISE

The leaders of AT&T's Information Systems Division clearly recognize that they have a serious problem. For each of the five primary cultural development mechanisms, suggest one thing the leaders of this division should do to develop a more effective organizational culture.

Source: Based on Mark Maremont, Randy Welch, John Wilke, and Michael Pollack, "Why AT&T Isn't Clicking," *Business Week,* May 19, 1986, pp. 88–95.

In addition to the five primary mechanisms we've just mentioned, there are five secondary mechanisms by which organizational culture develops. They are:

1. *The organization's design and structure:* The designing of their organization's structure offers leaders a chance to express their deeply held assumptions about the tasks facing the firm, the best means of accomplishing them, human nature, and the right kinds of relationships among

HIGHLIGHT 5.2

ILLUSTRATIVE EXAMPLE ■ **Stories That Influence Organizational Culture**

Stories can be an effective way to influence an organization's culture. Good stories are memorable and teach employees basic company values. It doesn't matter whether the stories are factually true as long as they communicate values and are retold to other employees. The examples below illustrate stories that are effective in communicating specific corporate values.

- Remember when Ray Kroc (founder of McDonald's Restaurants) visited a McDonald's franchise in Winnipeg? He found a single fly. Even one fly didn't fit with QSC&V (Quality, Service, Cleanliness, and Value—the McDonald's creed). Two weeks later the Winnipeg franchisee lost his franchise. You'd better believe that after this story made the rounds, a whole lot of McDonald's people found nearly mystical ways to eliminate flies—every fly—from their shops. Is the story apocryphal? It doesn't really matter. Mr. Kroc *did* do things *like* that.
- Forrest Mars (of Mars, Inc.) has done things *like* throwing candy bars at his officers after finding a single miswrapped one on a candy counter. A former Mars manager recounts the tale of Mr. Mars visiting a chocolate factory in mid-summer. He went up to the third floor, where the biggest chocolate machines were placed. It was hotter than the hinges of hell. He asked the factory manager, "How come you don't have air conditioning up here?" The factory manager replied that it wasn't in his budget, and he darn well had to make budget. While Mr. Mars allowed as how that was a fact (the fellow had to make budget), he nonetheless went over to a nearby phone and dialed the maintenance people downstairs and asked them to come up immediately. He said, "While we [he and the factory manager] stand here, would you please go downstairs and get all the [factory manager's] furniture and other things from his office and bring them up here? Sit them down next to the big chocolate machine up here, if you don't mind." Said our Mars colleague: "The guy figured out that it was probably a pretty good idea to air-condition the factory, sooner rather than later. Mr. Mars told him that once that had been completed, he could move back to his office any time he wanted."
- A Procter & Gamble executive recounted a late-night phone call he received several years ago. The executive had just been promoted to management at that time and the call was from his district sales

manager: "George, you've got a problem with a bar of soap down here." Down here, George explained, was three hundred miles away. "George, think you could get down here by six-thirty in the morning?" Our informant added, "It sounded like more than an invitation." And, finally, he concluded, "After you've finished your first three-hundred-mile ride through the back hills of Tennessee at seventy mile an hour to look at one damned thirty-four-cent bar of soap, you understand that the Procter & Gamble Company is very, very serious about product quality. You don't subsequently need a two-hundred-page manual to prove it to you."

Source: Adapted from Tom Peters and Nancy Austin, *A Passion for Excellence* (New York: Random House, 1985), pp. 278–279. Reprinted by permission.

people. For example, a highly decentralized organization suggests that leaders have confidence in the abilities of subordinate managers.

2. *Organizational systems and procedures:* Some very visible parts of organizational life are the daily, weekly, monthly, quarterly, and annual cycles of routines, procedures, reports to file, forms to fill out, and other recurring tasks that have to be performed repeatedly. For example, if the CEO asks for quarterly reports on all assistant managers, this requirement communicates the message that the organization values and is concerned with this group.
3. *Design of physical space, façades, and buildings:* Leaders who embrace a clear philosophy and management style often make that style manifest in their choice of architectural style, interior design, and décor. For example, if a leader believes in open communication, office space may be laid out such that very few private areas or barriers to the flow of traffic exist.
4. *Stories, legends, myths, and parables about important events and people:* As a group develops and accumulates a history, some of this history becomes embodied in stories about events and leadership behavior. The scenarios in Highlight 5.2 provide extended examples of this mechanism.
5. *Formal statements of organizational philosophy, creeds, and charters:* Explicit statements by leaders of organizations about their values are a final means of shaping organizational culture. For example, at General Motors, executives carry around "culture cards" that spell out their mission:

> The fundamental purpose of General Motors is to provide products and services of such quality that our customers will receive superior value, our employees and business partners will share in our success, and our stockholders will receive a sustained superior return on their investment.[9]

[9] Whiteside, "Roger Smith's Campaign to Change the GM Culture," p. 85.

There are, then, a variety of methods for developing, maintaining, or changing organizational cultures. However, changing an organizational culture is a difficult task that, if it can be done at all, may require many years to complete. Continuation, routine, or limited strategy changes must usually be implemented with the organizational culture that is already in place. In these situations, the strategies formulated must be implemented without a major change in the corporate culture. For radical strategy changes and organizational redirection, a long-term change in organizational culture may be necessary. However, it may frequently be more efficient to keep acquired firms with radically different cultures separated to avoid major cultural clashes and the potentially serious problems that can result.

Such cultural clashes in part account for the fact that between one-half and two-thirds of all mergers simply do not work. Steven Prokesch and William Powell, who have investigated corporate mergers, offer some insight into this sorry state of affairs.[10] They maintain that mergers and acquisitions that work seem to have several things in common. First, they usually involve companies in closely related businesses. Second, they are often financed by stock swaps or cash on hand, rather than by borrowing money. Finally, the price does not include a lofty premium, and the management of the acquired company usually stays on to run the business. Those that don't work often involve one or more of the following "seven deadly sins in mergers and acquisitions":

- Paying too much
- Assuming a boom market won't crash
- Leaping before looking
- Straying too far afield
- Swallowing something too big
- Marrying disparate corporate cultures
- Counting on key managers staying

SELECTING AN IMPLEMENTATION APPROACH

The manager's task at this stage is to determine an appropriate approach to implementing the strategy. On the basis of their research on management practices at a number of companies, David Brodwin and L. J. Bourgeois suggest five fundamental approaches to implementing strategies.[11] These approaches range from simply telling employees to implement the strategy that has been formulated to developing employees who can formulate and implement sound

[10] Steven E. Prokesch and William J. Powell, Jr., "Do Mergers Really Work?" *Business Week,* June 3, 1985, pp. 88–91. Also see Michael L. McManus and Michael L. Hergert, *Surviving Merger and Acquisitions* (Glenview, Ill.: Scott, Foresman and Company, 1988).

[11] The discussion that follows is based on David R. Brodwin and L. J. Bourgeois III, "Five Steps to Strategic Action," *California Management Review,* Spring 1984, pp. 176–190. Also see Paul C. Nutt, "Selecting Tactics to Implement Strategic Plans," *Strategic Management Journal* 10 (1989): 145–161.

strategies on their own. In each approach, the manager plays a somewhat different role and uses different methods of strategic management. Brodwin and Bourgeois call these five approaches the Commander Approach, the Organizational Change Approach, the Collaborative Approach, the Cultural Approach, and the Crescive Approach. Table 5.4 presents an overview of these approaches, and each is discussed below.

The Commander Approach

Under this approach, the manager concentrates on *formulating* strategy by applying rigorous logic and analysis. The manager may either develop the strategy alone or supervise a team of strategists charged with determining the optimal course of action for the organization. Tools such as growth–share matrices and industry and competitive analysis (see Chapter 4) are commonly used by managers who employ this approach. Once the "best" strategy is determined, the manager passes it along to subordinates who are instructed to execute the strategy. The manager does not take an active role in implementing the strategy.

In some organizations, the Commander Approach helps focus operations from a strategic perspective. However, three conditions must exist for this approach to result in successful implementation:

1. The manager must wield enough power to *command* implementation, or the strategy must pose little threat to the status quo. Implementation under this approach is resisted if the new strategy threatens the positions of employees.
2. Accurate and timely information must be available, and the environment must be reasonably stable. If the environment is changing so rapidly that information becomes dated before it can be assimilated, effective implementation under this approach is unlikely.
3. The manager formulating the strategy should be insulated from personal biases and political influences that might affect the content of the strategy.

A serious drawback to this approach is that it can reduce employee motivation, and employees who feel that they have no say in strategy formulation are unlikely to be a very innovative group. However, the approach can still be effective in smaller companies within stable industries. It works best when the strategy to be implemented requires relatively little change, such as strategy continuation or routine strategy changes.

Although the Commander Approach raises a number of problems, it is commonly advocated by certain business consultants and is used by some managers. Several factors account for its popularity. First, despite its drawbacks, it offers managers a valuable perspective and allows them to focus their energies on strategy formulation. By dividing the strategic management task into two stages—"thinking" and "doing"—the manager reduces the number of factors that have to be considered simultaneously. Second, young managers in

TABLE 5.4 Comparison of Five Approaches to Implementing a Strategy

	APPROACH				
Factor	Commander	Change	Collaborative	Cultural	Crescive
How are goals set? Where in the organization (top or bottom) are the strategic goals established?	Dictated from top	Dictated from top	Negotiated among top team	Embodied in culture	Stated loosely from top, refined from bottom
What signifies success? What signifies a successful outcome to the strategic planning/implementation process?	A good plan as judged on economic criteria	Organization and structure which fit the strategy	An acceptable plan with broad top management support	An army of busy implementers	Sound strategies with champions behind them
What factors are considered? What are the kinds of factors, or types of rationality, used in developing a strategy for resolving conflicts between alternative proposed strategies?	Economic	Economic, Political	Economic, Social, Political	Economic, Social	Economic, Social, Political, Behavioral
What is the typical level of organization-wide effort required? During the planning phase	Low	Low	High	High	High
During the implementation phase	N/A	High	Low	Low	Low
How stringent are the requirements placed on the CEO in order for the approach to succeed? Required CEO knowledge: To what extent must the CEO be able to maintain personal awareness of all significant strategic opportunities or threats?	High	High	Moderate	Low	Low
Required CEO power: To what extent must the CEO have the power to impose a detailed implementation plan on the organization?	High	High	Moderate	Moderate	Moderate

Source: David R. Brodwin and L. J. Bourgeois III, "Five Steps to Strategic Action," *California Management Review* 26, no. 3 (Spring 1984): 178.

particular seem to prefer this approach because it allows them to focus on the quantitative, objective aspects of a situation rather than on the qualitative, subjective elements of behavioral interactions. (Many young managers are better trained to deal with the former than with the latter.) Finally, such an approach may make some ambitious managers feel powerful in that their thinking and decision making affect the activities of thousands of people.

The Organizational Change Approach

Whereas the manager who adopts the Commander Approach avoids dealing directly with implementation, the Organizational Change Approach (or simply the Change Approach) focuses on how to get an organization to implement a strategy. Managers who apply the Change Approach assume that a good strategy has been formulated and view their task as getting the company moving toward new goals. The tools used to accomplish this task are largely behavioral and include such things as changing the organizational structure and staffing to focus attention on the organization's new priorities, revising planning and control systems, and invoking other organizational change techniques. The manager's role is that of an architect designing administrative systems for effective strategy implementation.

Because powerful behavioral tools are used in the Change Approach to implementation, it is often more effective than the Commander Approach and can be used to implement more difficult strategies. However, the Change Approach has several limitations that may restrict its use to smaller companies in stable industries. It doesn't help managers stay abreast of rapid changes in the environment. It doesn't deal with situations wherein politics and personal agendas discourage objectivity among strategists. And because it calls for imposing strategy in "top down" fashion, it is subject to the same motivational problems as the Commander Approach.

Finally, this approach can backfire in uncertain or rapidly changing conditions. The manager sacrifices important strategic flexibility by manipulating the systems and structures of the organization in support of a particular strategy. Some of these systems (particularly incentive compensation) take a long time to design and install. Should a change in the environment require a new strategy, it may be very difficult to change the organization's course, which has been firmly established to support the now obsolete strategy.

The Collaborative Approach

In the Collaborative Approach, the manager in charge of the strategy calls in the rest of the management team to brainstorm strategy formulation *and* strategy implementation. Managers with different perspectives are encouraged to contribute their points of view in order to extract whatever group wisdom emerges from these multiple perspectives. The role of the manager is that of a coordinator who uses his or her understanding of group dynamics to ensure that all good ideas are discussed and investigated. For example, several years ago General Motors formed "business teams" that consisted of managers from different functional areas. The role of the team was simply to bring out different points of view on whatever strategic problems cropped up. Exxon's major strategic decisions are made by its management committee, which comprises all of Exxon's inside directors and is led by the chairman of the board. Every committee member serves as a contact executive for the line managers of one or more of Exxon's 13 affiliates and subsidiaries.

The Collaborative Approach overcomes two key limitations of the other two approaches we have treated. By capturing information contributed by managers closer to operations, and by offering a forum for the expression of many viewpoints, it can increase the quality and timeliness of the information incorporated in the strategy. And to the degree that participation enhances commitment to the strategy, it improves the chances of efficient implementation.

Though the Collaborative Approach may gain more commitment than the foregoing approaches, it may also result in a poorer strategy. The fact that strategy is negotiated among managers with different points of view and possibly different goals may reduce management's chances of formulating and implementing superior strategies. For one thing, a negotiated strategy is likely to be less visionary and more conservative than one created by an individual or staff team. For another, gaming and empire building by various individual managers may result in a strategy that favors a particular functional area but is less sound from an overall strategic perspective. And the negotiation process can take so much time that an organization misses opportunities and fails to react quickly enough to changing environments.

Finally, a fundamental criticism of the Collaborative Approach is that it is not really collective decision making from an organizational viewpoint because upper-level managers often retain centralized control. In effect, this approach preserves the artificial distinction between thinkers and doers and fails to draw on the full human potential throughout the organization. When properly used, the Collaborative Approach can increase commitment to a strategy and encourage effective implementation. Yet it can also create political problems within the organization that can impede rapid and efficient strategy formulation and implementation.

The Cultural Approach

The Cultural Approach enlarges the Collaborative Approach to include lower levels in the organization. In this approach, the manager guides the organization by communicating and instilling his or her vision of the overall mission for the organization and then allowing employees to design their own work activities in accordance with this mission. Once the strategy is formulated, the manager plays the role of coach, giving general directions but encouraging individual decision making on the operating details of executing the strategy.

The implementation tools used in building a strong organizational culture range from such simple notions as publishing a company creed and singing a company song to much more complex techniques. These techniques involve what can be called "third-order control." First-order control is direct supervision; second-order control involves using rules, procedures, and organizational structure to guide behavior. Third-order control is more subtle—and potentially more powerful. It consists of influencing behavior by shaping the norms, values, symbols, and beliefs that managers and employees draw on as they make day-to-day decisions.

The Cultural Approach partially breaks down the barriers between thinkers and doers, because each member of the organization can be involved to some degree in both the formulation and the implementation of strategy. Hewlett-Packard is a well-known example of a company whose employees share a strong awareness of the corporate mission. They all know that the "HP way" encourages product innovation at every level. Matsushita, for its part, starts each work day with 87,000 employees singing the company song and reciting its code of values. The company creed at J. C. Penney is reprinted in Highlight 5.3.

The Cultural Approach appears to work best in organizations that have sufficient resources to absorb the cost of building and maintaining a supportive value system. Often these are high-growth firms in high-technology industries.

While this approach has a number of advantages, not the least of which is dedicated, enthusiastic implementation of strategies, it also has limitations. First, it tends to work only in organizations composed primarily of informed,

HIGHLIGHT 5.3

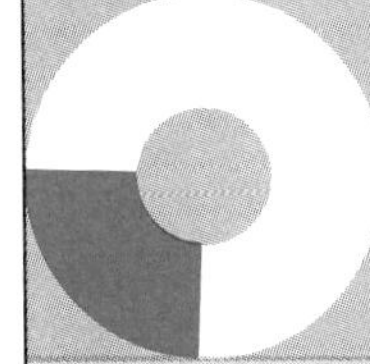

ILLUSTRATIVE EXAMPLE ■ J. C. Penney's Company Creed

J. C. Penney's company creed was adopted in 1913 and is called "The Penney Idea." It consists of the following seven points:

1. To serve the public, as nearly as we can, to its complete satisfaction.
2. To expect for the service we render a fair remuneration and not all the profit the traffic will bear.
3. To do all in our power to pack the customer's dollar full of value, quality, and satisfaction.
4. To continue to train ourselves and our associates so that the service we give will be more and more intelligently performed.
5. To improve constantly the human factor in our business.
6. To reward men and women in our organization through participation in what the business produces.
7. To test our every policy, method and act in this wise: "Does it square with what is right and just?"

Source: "Corporate Culture." Reprinted from October 27, 1980 issue of *Business Week* by special permission.

intelligent people. Second, it consumes enormous amounts of time to install. Third, it can foster such a strong sense of organizational identity that it becomes a handicap; for example, bringing outsiders in at top management levels can be difficult because they aren't accepted by other executives. Fourth, companies with excessively strong cultures often suppress deviance, discourage attempts to change, and foster homogeneity and inbreeding. To handle this conformist tendency, some companies (such as IBM, Xerox, and GM) have segregated their ongoing research units and their new product development efforts, sometimes placing them in physical locations far enough from other units to shield them from the corporation's culture.

The Crescive Approach

The manager who adopts the Crescive Approach addresses strategy formulation and strategy implementation simultaneously. (*Crescive* means "increasing" or "growing.") However, she or he does not focus on doing these tasks but on encouraging subordinates to develop, champion, and implement sound strategies on their own. This approach differs from the others in several ways. First, instead of strategy being delivered downward from top management or a strategy group, it moves upward from the doers (salespeople, engineers, production workers) and lower middle-level managers and supervisors. Second, "strategy" becomes the sum of all the individual proposals that surface throughout the year. Third, the top-management team shapes the employees' premises—that is, the employees' notions of what would constitute supportable strategic projects. Fourth, the chief executive, or manager in charge of strategy, functions more as a judge evaluating the proposals than as a master strategist.

Brodwin and Bourgeois advocate use of the Crescive Approach primarily for CEOs of large, complex, diversified organizations. In these organizations, the CEO cannot know and understand all the strategic and operating situations facing each division. Therefore, if strategies are to be formulated and implemented effectively, the CEO *must* give up some control to spur opportunism and achievement.

This approach has several advantages. First, it encourages middle-level managers to formulate effective strategies and gives them the opportunity to carry out the implementation of their own plans. This autonomy increases their motivation to make the strategy succeed. Second, strategies developed, as these are, by employees and managers closer to the strategic opportunity are likely to be operationally sound and readily implemented. However, this approach requires (1) that funds be available for individuals to develop good ideas unencumbered by bureaucratic approval cycles and (2) that tolerance be extended in the inevitable cases where failure occurs despite a worthy effort having been made. Furthermore, converting an organization that is accustomed to centralized, top-down systems to the Crescive Approach can be very difficult, expensive, and time consuming. Finally, the Crescive Approach does not specify how the managers who are in charge of implementing the strategy should do so. In sum, the Crescive Approach is a viable approach for complex organizations that exist in dynamic industries.

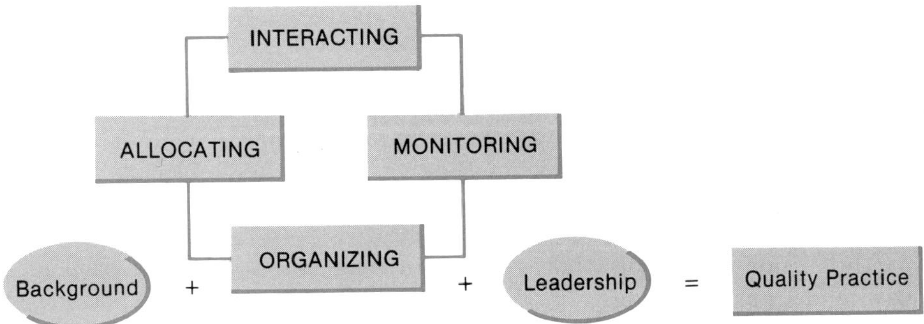

FIGURE 5.4 *Four Key Implementation Skills (Source: The Marketing Edge: Making Strategies Work by Thomas V. Bonoma. Copyright 1985 by The Free Press. Reprinted with permission.)*

IMPLEMENTING THE STRATEGY AND EVALUATING THE RESULTS

By this stage the manager has a clear idea of the level of strategic change that is to be implemented. In addition, having the benefit of an analysis of organizational structure and organizational culture, she or he has developed an understanding of the factors within the organization that will facilitate or impede implementation. An implementation approach has been selected that does the best job of capitalizing on the firm's strengths and overcomes, circumvents, or minimizes problems within the organization. The task at this stage is to execute the strategy and evaluate the results.

Professor Thomas V. Bonoma of the Harvard Business School suggests that successful implementation of strategies requires four basic types of execution skills.[12] These are shown in Figure 5.4 and are discussed below.

Interacting skills are expressed in managing one's own and others' behavior to achieve objectives. Depending on the level of strategic change required to implement a strategy, managers may need to influence others both within and outside of the organization. Bonoma suggests that managers who show empathy—the ability to understand how others feel—and have good bargaining skills are the best implementers.

Allocating skills are brought to bear in managers' abilities to schedule tasks and budget time, money, and other resources efficiently. Able managers avoid putting too many resources into mature programs and recognize that new, riskier programs often demand greater investment of resources.

Monitoring skills involve the efficient use of information to correct any problems that arise in the process of implementation. Good implementers have an efficient feedback system to analyze progress toward strategy execution and any problems that occur. For example, one general manager of a company

[12] Bonoma, *The Marketing Edge,* pp. 112–121. Also see Thomas V. Bonoma, "Making Your Marketing Strategy Work," *Harvard Business Review,* March–April 1984, pp. 69–76; and Thomas V. Bonoma and Victoria L. Crittenden, "Managing Marketing Implementation," *Sloan Management Review,* Winter 1988, pp. 7–14.

with 38 plants and 300,000 customers ran everything he considered crucial according to notations on two 3-by-5 index cards!

Organizing skills are exhibited in the ability to create a new informal organization or network to match each problem that occurs. Good implementers know people in every part of the organization (and outside of it) who, by virtue of mutual respect, attraction, or some other tie, can and will help however they can. In other words, good implementers "customize" the informal organization to facilitate good execution.

Thus, implementation often requires managers who possess particular skills tailored to overcoming obstacles and ensuring that tasks are performed efficiently. Throughout implementation, managers must also evaluate how well the strategy is being executed and whether it is accomplishing organizational objectives. Issues in strategy evaluation are the topic of the next chapter of this text.

SUMMARY

In this chapter we suggested that implementation is an important part of strategic management that is too frequently overlooked. After investigating how the quality of both strategy formulation and strategy implementation affects the chances that a strategy will succeed, we developed a five-stage model of the strategy implementation process.

First, it is important to analyze a proposed strategy in terms of how much the firm itself will have to change in order to implement it successfully. Strategies, we found, can range from the no-change continuation strategy through routine strategy change, limited strategy change, and radical strategy change all the way to organizational redirection. The latter consists of sweeping transformations that a firm usually undergoes only when it enters a new industry or takes part in a merger or acquisition.

The next step in the strategy implementation process is to analyze both the formal and the informal structure of the organization. Its formal structure may be simple (owner-manager and employees); the firm may be divided into functions (such as marketing, operations, and finance), divisions (reflecting different product lines, areas, distribution channels, or the like), or groups of divisions known as strategic business units; or, in the matrix organizational structure, functional responsibility and project responsibility may overlap. Each structure has strengths and weaknesses. Recognizing the probable impact of structure on successful strategy implementation is always important. The informal organization, too, can be used to facilitate successful implementation.

Analyzing organizational culture is important for both formulating and implementing strategies. The organizational culture consists of the values, beliefs, and attitudes toward the firm that employees share. Leader behaviors, criteria for recruiting and rewarding employees, rules and procedures, formal statements of a "company creed," oft-told tales about important events and people in the history of the organization, and even the physical layout of the buildings—all can contribute to effective organizational cultures and can be used to shape employee attitudes and behavior. Once ingrained, organizational culture is persistent, and strategic changes that run counter to it are often doomed to failure.

We then discussed several different approaches suggested by Brodwin and Bourgeois to implementing a given strategy. First there is the Commander Approach, in which the manager formulates a strategy and simply instructs subordinates to implement it. Also usable is the Organizational Change Approach, which works by assuming the strategy is good and behavioral approaches to changing organizational structure must be marshaled to implement it. The Collaborative Approach, in which a management team is invited to participate in both the formulation and the implementation of strategy, and the Cultural Approach, which democratizes the Collaborative Approach to

HIGHLIGHT 5.4

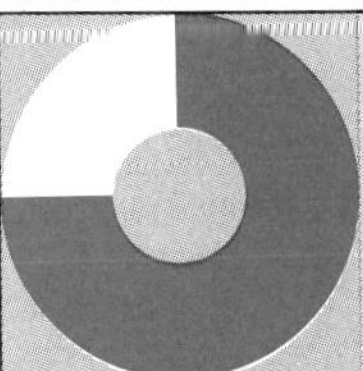

CHECKLIST ■ Analyzing Strategy Implementation in Problems and Cases

- ☐ 1. Is strategy implementation the major focus of the problem or case?
- ☐ 2. Is enough information available for managers to offer a detailed plan for implementation?
- ☐ 3. What level of strategic change does the problem or case involve?
- ☐ 4. Will the existing formal and informal organizational structures promote or impede successful implementation?
- ☐ 5. What could be done to redesign the formal organization or redirect the informal organization to facilitate efficient strategy implementation?
- ☐ 6. Will the organizational culture support or limit effective strategy implementation?
- ☐ 7. What type of implementation approach would probably be most successful?
- ☐ 8. Overall, does the management of the organization appear to have good implementation skills, such as skill in interacting, allocating, monitoring, and organizing?
- ☐ 9. Who has the responsibility for implementing the strategy and the authority to do so?
- ☐ 10. How, when, and where should the strategy be implemented?

include lower levels of the organization, can also be employed. Finally, in the Crescive Approach, subordinates are encouraged to develop, propose, and implement strategies of their own devising. We probed the merits and drawbacks of each approach and outlined the conditions under which each is most likely to be appropriate.

Finally, we noted the importance to the implementation process of managers' skills in interacting and empathizing with others, in allocating resources, in monitoring progress toward goals, and in organizing new informal networks as necessary to facilitate strategy implementation. Managers who have such skills are able to oversee the implementation of strategy effectively and to evaluate the implementation process as it unfolds, taking remedial action if necessary.

Highlight 5.4 is a checklist covering many of the points made in this chapter. Use it when you analyze cases and problems that involve the implementation of strategy.

ADDITIONAL READINGS

Barney, Jay B. "Organizational Culture: Can It Be a Source of Sustained Competitive Advantage?" *Academy of Management Review,* Vol. II no. 3 (1986):656–665.

Bennigson, Lawrence A. "Managing Corporate Cultures." *Management Review,* February 1985, pp. 31–32.

Drazin, Robert, and Peter Howard. "Strategy Implementation: A Technique for Organizational Design." *Columbia Journal of World Business,* Summer 1984, pp. 40–46.

Gresov, Christopher. "Designing Organizations to Innovate and Implement: Using Two Dilemmas to Create a Solution." *Columbia Journal of World Business,* Winter 1984, pp. 63–67.

Marcus, Alfred A. "Implementing Externally Induced Innovations: A Comparison of Rule-Bound and Autonomous Approaches." *Academy of Management Journal,* Vol. 31 no. 2 (1988): 235–256.

Nahavandi, Afsaneh, and Ali R. Malekzadeh. "Acculturation in Mergers and Acquisitions." *Academy of Management Review,* Vol. 13 no. 1 (1988):79–90.

Nutt, Paul C. "Implementation Approaches for Project Planning." *Academy of Management Review,* Vol. 8 no. 4 (1983):600–611.

————. "Tactics of Implementation." *Academy of Management Journal,* Vol. 29 no. 2 (1986):230–261.

Schwartz, Howard, and Stanley M. Davis. "Matching Corporate Culture and Business Strategy." *Organizational Dynamics,* Summer 1981, pp. 30–48.

Slevin, Dennis P., and Jeffrey K. Pinto, "Balancing Strategy and Tactics in Project Implementation," *Sloan Management Review*, Fall 1987, pp. 33–41.

Ranson, Stewart, Bob Hinings, and Royston Greenwood. "The Structuring of Organizational Structures." *Administrative Science Quarterly*, March 1980, pp. 1–17.

Trice, Harrison M., and Janice M. Beyer. "Studying Organizational Cultures Through Rites and Ceremonials." *Academy of Management Review*, October 1984, pp. 653–667.

HIGHLIGHT 5.5 ■ APPLICATION OF CHAPTER MATERIAL

Strategy Implementation at Cross Pens

Some of corporate America's most successful citizens have them clipped to their shirt pockets. They're Cross pens—status symbols and tools for the power elite. But now, after 15 years as the best seller in its price class, Cross is under attack from two rejuvenated competitors.

A. T. Cross Co., which has posted a return on equity of 20 percent or more for ten straight years, is a 140-year-old company that has maintained its enviable record by cultivating an image of timelessness. The company seldom introduces new models, and it offers a lifetime guarantee. "We prefer measured growth. We don't want to sit on our laurels, but we're not operating under a panic situation either," says Chairman Bradford R. Boss.

Because he faces stiffer competition ahead, Boss plans to expand the business by offering more gift items. Current items include clocks and leather goods such as briefcases. More new products are planned. They will inherit from the established line a reputation that has helped capture more than 50 percent of the U.S. market share in expensive pens.

To break into the premium gift business, Boss bought the Mark Cross leather goods stores in 1983. He also acquired Chelsea Clock Company in order to market nautical timepieces. And the company plans to intensify its efforts in the foreign pen market, which presently accounts for only 18 percent of its sales. Parker Pen Ltd., with 80 percent of its $155 million in sales in offshore markets, is the leader overseas.

The recent sale of Parker Pen to Manpower Inc. and the expansion of Scheaffer Eaton, Cross's other major competitor, are likely to increase competition. Scheaffer Eaton, for example, is adding to its 2,000-item product line—that's 20 times the size of the Cross line. Scheaffer's new products include an array of brightly colored pens with decorative pouches or ribbons for women. Murray R. Eisner, president of the penmaker, says he has long regarded Cross as vulnerable. As he notes, "I couldn't understand how people could continue to want a tired old design."

(*Continued*)

Boss says he is not worried about the increased competition and plans to continue to market mainly with the traditional Cross line of silver, gold, and black enamel pens in the pen market. Some retailers think Scheaffer's new products will cut into Cross's sales. Yet, as one analyst puts it, "I'd be very surprised if Scheaffer caused more than a ripple in the pond. A Cross Pen is a Cross Pen."

DISCUSSION QUESTIONS

1. What level of strategic change is being implemented by Cross Pens?
2. What problems do you think Cross Pens will have in implementing this strategy?
3. What recommendations would you make to Chairman Boss about implementation of this strategy?

Source: Based on Debra Michals, "How Cross Pens Keep the Black Ink Flowing," *Business Week*, August 18, 1986, p. 58.

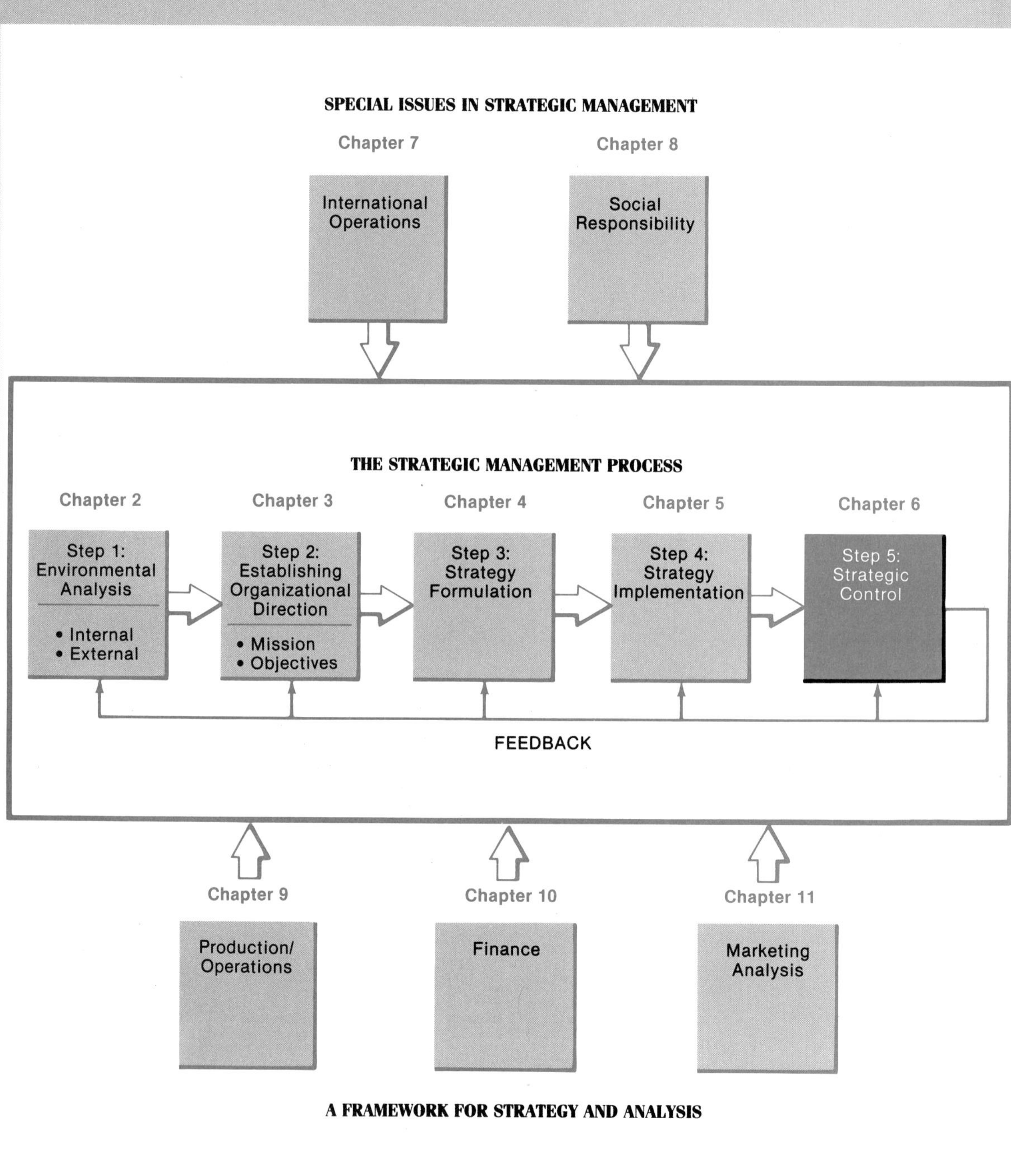
SPECIAL ISSUES IN STRATEGIC MANAGEMENT
Chapter 7
International Operations
Chapter 8
Social Responsibility
THE STRATEGIC MANAGEMENT PROCESS
Chapter 2
Step 1: Environmental Analysis
• Internal
• External
Chapter 3
Step 2: Establishing Organizational Direction
• Mission
• Objectives
Chapter 4
Step 3: Strategy Formulation
Chapter 5
Step 4: Strategy Implementation
Chapter 6
Step 5: Strategic Control
FEEDBACK
Chapter 9
Production/ Operations
Chapter 10
Finance
Chapter 11
Marketing Analysis
A FRAMEWORK FOR STRATEGY AND ANALYSIS
Chapter 12
An Approach to Solving Strategic Problems and Cases

CHAPTER 6

Strategic Control

Previous chapters in this section have discussed the strategic management process by focusing on the sequential and related steps of conducting an environmental analysis, establishing organizational direction, formulating organizational strategy, and implementing organizational strategy. This chapter emphasizes the last major step in the strategic management process, exerting strategic control, which consists of making certain that strategies unfold as they were intended to.

First we briefly examine the broader topic of organizational control in order to understand the context in which the more specific issues related to strategic control develop. Then we proceed to defining strategic control and outlining the purposes for which the strategic control process is undertaken.

The main part of the chapter is reserved for our treatment of the process of strategic control itself. We examine at length the use of the "strategic audit" in measuring organizational performance and differentiate between qualitative and quantitative measures. We discuss ways to compare actual organizational performance to goals and standards. And we explain how to determine whether corrective action is called for.

Our next major topic is the importance to strategic control of obtaining reliable information, and we explore the use of management information systems toward that end. Finally, we stress the need for top management to be firmly committed to making the strategic control process successful.

ORGANIZATIONAL CONTROL AND STRATEGIC CONTROL

Without an understanding of the broader issues involved in organizational control, it is impossible to appreciate the special issues that arise in strategic control. For this reason, we should briefly discuss the broader topic of control at the organizational level before narrowing our focus to the specific issues involved in strategic control.

A Broad View of Organizational Control

In organizations, controlling entails monitoring, evaluating, and improving various activities that take place within an organization. We will first define the term *control*—and then outline the general characteristics of the control process.

A Definition of Control

Exerting control is a major part of every manager's job. *Control* consists of making something happen the way it was planned to happen.[1] For example, if an organization plans to increase net profit by 10 percent in order to meet accelerating product demand, control entails monitoring organizational progress and making modifications, if necessary, to ensure that net profit does indeed increase by 10 percent.

In order to control, managers must have a clear understanding of the results a particular action is intended to have. Only then can they ascertain whether the anticipated results are occurring and make whatever changes are necessary to ensure that the desired results do occur. Managers control to ensure that plans become reality, so they need a clear understanding of what reality is planned.[2]

General Characteristics of the Control Process

In practice, managers actually control by following three general steps: measuring performance, comparing measured performance to standards, and taking corrective action necessary to ensure that planned events actually materialize.

Keep in mind that these steps are broad recommendations embracing the area of organizational control as a whole. More specific types of organizational

[1] For a comprehensive discussion of the control function see K. A. Merchant, "The Control Function of Management," *Sloan Management Review* 23 (Summer 1982): 43–55.

[2] Robert L. Dewelt, "Control: Key to Making Financial Strategy Work," *Management Review,* March 1977, p. 18. This link between planning and control is supported and illustrated in S. S. Cowen and J. K. Middaugh, "Designing an Effective Financial Planning and Control System," *Long Range Planning* 21 (December 1988): 83–92.

control (such as production control, inventory control, strategic control, and quality control) are based on these same three steps but must be tailored to the demands of the specific type of control being exercised.

A general model depicting how these broad steps of the control process are related appears in Figure 6.1. This model implies that when performance measurements are significantly different from standard or planned outcomes, management takes corrective action to ensure that expected outcomes actually occur. On the other hand, when performance does measure up to standard or planned outcomes, no corrective action is necessary and work continues without interference.

The Application of Strategic Control

Armed with a general understanding of control as management must apply it in organizations, we are now ready to discuss the specific application of strategic control. We will first define strategic control, then explain why strategic control is important, and finally trace the steps involved in the process of strategic control.

A Definition of Strategic Control

Strategic control is a special type of organizational control that focuses on monitoring and evaluating the strategic management process in order to make sure it is functioning properly. In essence, strategic control is undertaken to ensure that all outcomes planned during the strategic management process do indeed materialize. Although this definition oversimplifies strategic control and makes it sound somewhat mechanical, we will soon discover how challenging and intricate strategic control really is.

The Purposes of Strategic Control

Perhaps the most fundamental purpose of strategic control is to help top management achieve organizational goals through monitoring and evaluating

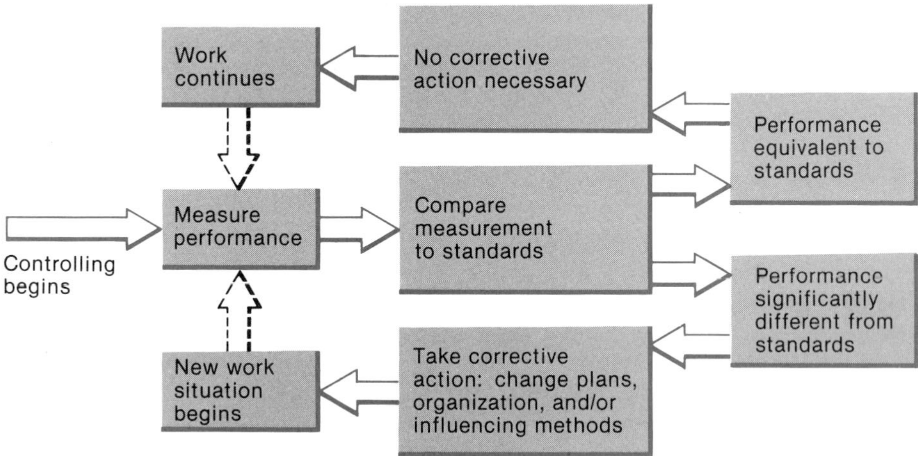

FIGURE 6.1 A General Model of the Control Process

the strategic management process. As we have seen, the strategic management process results in an assessment of organizational environment (environmental analysis), the establishment of organizational mission and goals (establishing organizational direction), the development of ways to deal with competition in order to reach these goals and fulfill the organization's mission (strategy formulation), and a plan for translating organizational strategy into action (strategy implementation). Strategic control provides feedback that is critical for determining whether all steps of the strategic management process are appropriate, are compatible, and are functioning properly.

This overview approaches strategic control primarily from the standpoint of ensuring organizational goal attainment by monitoring and evaluating the effectiveness of the strategic management process. There are, however, several other reasons for exerting strategic control.[3] A few of these additional purposes are presented in Table 6.1.

THE PROCESS OF STRATEGIC CONTROL

Three distinct but related steps must be taken to carry out the strategic control process within an organization. Because they constitute a special type of organizational control, these steps are closely related to the more general control model presented earlier. They are measuring organizational performance, comparing performance to goals and standards, and taking necessary corrective action.[4]

Step 1: Measure Organizational Performance

Before managers can determine what must be done to make the strategic management process more effective, they must take measures that reflect current organizational performance. In order to understand what strategic control performance measurements are and how a manager can take such measurements, we need to introduce two important topics: (1) strategic audits and (2) strategic audit measurement methods.

The Strategic Audit

A *strategic audit* is an examination and evaluation of areas affected by the operation of a strategic management process within an organization. Such an audit may be very comprehensive, emphasizing all facets of a strategic management process, or very focused, emphasizing only a single part of the process. In addition, the strategic audit can be quite formal, strictly adhering to established organizational rules and procedures, or quite informal, allowing

[3] Charles H. Roush, "Strategic Resource Allocation and Control," in William D. Guth (ed.), *Handbook of Business Strategy* (Boston: Warren, Gorham & Lamont, 1985), pp. 20-1–20-25.

[4] For an excellent discussion of the strategic control process see Charles H. Roush, Jr., and Ben C. Ball, Jr., "Controlling the Implementation of Strategy," *Managerial Planning,* November–December 1980, pp. 3–12.

TABLE 6.1 Additional Purposes of Strategic Control

1. To evaluate a business strategy for its validity and reality, testing it against the corporate goals, resource availability, and general strategic framework (assuming, of course, that top management has already developed its directions in these terms).
2. To ensure that the divisional general manager knows that the CEO knows that the general manager knows the business.
3. To evaluate the trade-offs general managers make in a changing environment—their risk-taking attitudes, their emphasis on long-term versus short-term goals, and the realism of their perception of the changes in cost and competitive patterns, particularly in an inflationary environment.
4. To forge a contract between top management and divisional management, whereby corporate management becomes committed to a certain resource allocation and the divisional general manager to delivering certain results; subsequent reviews, whether annual or quarterly, provide for monitoring and follow-up of this agreement.
5. To negotiate and integrate strategic issues among interdependent divisions—especially critical in organizations which operate in some form of matrix structure.
6. To broaden the scope of knowledge of all participants, including the chief executive; as one CEO put it: "The review forum could be the best device for education in realistic strategic thinking, business school seminars on the topic notwithstanding."
7. To provide a forum, sometimes hidden, but nonetheless real, where not only reviewers, but reviewees as well, can (and usually do) evaluate fellow executives' intellectual mettle, motivation, and attitudes.

Source: Ram Charan, "How to Strengthen Your Strategy Review Process," *The Journal of Business Strategy* 2, no. 3 (Winter 1982): 51–52. Reprinted by permission.

managers wide discretion in deciding what organizational measurements should be taken and when.

In short, no one method can be prescribed for performing a strategic audit, and each organization must design and implement its own audits to meet its own unique needs. Several thoughts of Vaughn L. Beals concerning recent events within his company appear in Highlight 6.1. Beals is the chief executive officer of Harley-Davidson, a motorcycle manufacturer. Beals's thoughts can be considered a description of and a reaction to a relatively simple and informal strategic audit that his company conducts. Naturally, the audit was designed to reflect Harley-Davidson's unique organizational situation. Other chief executive officers might conclude that more comprehensive and formal strategic audits are more appropriate for their companies than more simple and informal ones. Table 6.2 presents a set of worthwhile guidelines that such managers might follow in designing and implementing more comprehensive strategic audits.

Strategic Audit Measurement Methods

There are several generally accepted methods for measuring organizational performance. One way of categorizing these methods divides them into two

HIGHLIGHT 6.1

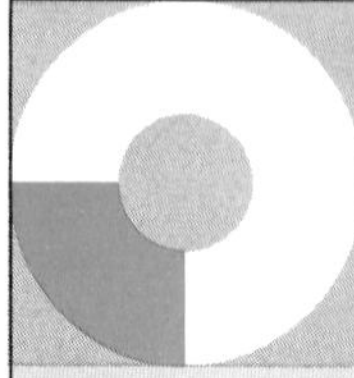

ILLUSTRATIVE EXAMPLE ■ Harley-Davidson's Strategic Audit Focuses on Customers

Harley-Davidson had two bad years back-to-back in 1981 and 1982. . . . Our difficulties in 1982 weren't all on the bottom line. While product improvements were underway, some Harleys, fresh off the assembly line, had a variety of problems. Meanwhile, the Japanese were making reliable machines and started riding all over us. Our share of the domestic market among motorcycles bigger than 850cc sank from 39 percent in 1979 to 23 percent in 1983.

We learned a painful, but vital, lesson: Your product is the most vital relationship you have with a customer. If you let anything disturb that relationship, trouble will follow. To turn Harley around, we had to turn to our customers for help. Taking cues from them, everyone—from our management team to people on the shop floor—rolled up his sleeves and contributed.

When we surveyed our customers, we found that bikers aren't particularly shy about letting us know what they like and don't like about Harleys. In the early days, we would come home with notebooks full of complaints. But it certainly shortened the correction time of problems.

Willie G. Davidson, a grandson of the company's founder and vice president of styling, started going to rallies to find out how bikers were using their Harleys. Many were customizing them. If the innovation looked promising, he'd figure out a way to come out with a factory version.

Customer complaints inspired us to rethink our manufacturing process. Just a few days before a brand-new model, the Cafe Racer, was to come off the production line, a service-department supervisor came to see me. Would I take a look at some of the earlier models that were coming back defective?

I was pretty ticked off at the magnitude of the problem and decided to make the Cafe Racer a symbol of the quality Harley should stand for. I sent a group of engineering, service, and manufacturing managers down to the Racer chassis plant with instructions to do whatever it took to make sure the Racers came out right. The first 100 cost us $100,000 to fix. But it made us concentrate on problems upstream. We later institutionalized that concept in the quality-audit program that's still an integral part of manufacturing, along with such procedures as the just-in-time program and statistical operator controls.

Harley has come roaring back. We're headed toward our sixth consecutive year of profits, which will set new records again. And we have 45 percent of the domestic market.

But we don't take our comeback for granted. If we ever fail to deliver what the customer wants, we'll be right back where we started. That's why my fellow officers and I spend most of our time on the road at rallies and stores, listening to the people who put us on the road to recovery.

TABLE 6.2 How to Conduct a Strategic Audit

A strateg[ic] audit is conducted in three phases: diagnosis to identify how, where, and in what priority in-depth analyses need to be made; focused analysis; and generation and testing of recommendations. Objectivity and the ability to ask critical, probing questions are key requirements for conducting a strateg[ic] audit.

Phase one: Diagnosis

The diagnostic phase includes the following tasks:

1. Review key documents such as:
   a. Strategic plan.
   b. Business or operational plans.
   c. Organizational arrangements.
   d. Major policies governing matters such as resource allocation and performance measurement.
2. Review financial, market, and operational performance against benchmarks and industry norms to identify key variances and emerging trends.
3. Gain an understanding of:
   a. Principal roles, responsibilities, and reporting relationships.
   b. Decision-making processes and major decisions made.
   c. Resources, including physical facilities, capital, management, technology.
   d. Interrelationships between functional staffs and business or operating units.
4. Identify strategic implications of strategy [for] organization structure, behavior patterns, systems, and processes.
   a. Define interrelationships and linkages to strategy.
5. Determine internal and external perspectives.
   a. Survey the attitudes and perceptions of senior and middle managers and other key employees to assess the extent to which these are consistent with the strategic direction of the firm. One way to accomplish this task is through carefully focused interviews and/or questionnaires, wherein employees are asked to identify and make trade-offs among the objectives and variables *they* consider most important.
   b. Interview a carefully selected sample of customers and prospective customers and other key external sources to gain an understanding of how the company is viewed.
6. Identify aspects of the strategy that are working well. Formulate hypotheses regarding problems and opportunities for improvement based on the findings above. Define how and in what order each should be pursued.

Phase two: Focused analysis

1. Test the hypotheses concerning problems and opportunities for improvement through analysis of specific issues.
   a. Identify interrelationships and dependencies among components of the strategic system.
2. Formulate conclusions as to weaknesses in strategy formulation, implementation deficiencies, or interactions between the two.

Phase three: Recommendations

1. Develop alternative solutions to problems and ways of capitalizing on opportunities.
   a. Test [these alternatives] in light of their resource requirements, risks, rewards, priorities, and other applicable measures.
2. Develop specific recommendations.
   a. Develop an integrated, measurable, and time-phased action plan to improve strategic results.

Source: Adapted from A. J. Prager and M. B. Shea, "The Strategic Audit," in *The Strategic Management Handbook*, ed. K. J. Albert (New York: McGraw-Hill, 1983), pp. 8–14. Copyright © 1983. Reproduced with permission.

distinct types: qualitative and quantitative. Although this scheme is useful for developing an understanding of strategic audit measurement methods, a few methods do not fall neatly into one or the other of these categories but rather are a combination of both types.

QUALITATIVE ORGANIZATIONAL MEASUREMENTS. These measurements are organizational assessments resulting in data that are subjectively summarized and organized before any conclusions are drawn on which to base strategic control action. Many managers believe that qualitative organizational measurements are best arrived at simply by answering a series of critical questions designed to reflect important facets of organizational operations. There is no universally endorsed list of such questions, but several that might be useful to the practicing manager are presented in Table 6.3.

Seymour Tilles has written a classic article on the qualitative assessment of organizational performance.[5] This article discusses several important issues involving one small facet of organizational performance: organizational routines that result in organizational strategy. The Tilles article can serve as the basis for generating several important questions to be asked during a qualitative organizational measurement that focuses on organizational procedures used to develop strategy. These questions are:

1. *Is organizational strategy internally consistent?* Internal consistency refers to the cumulative impact of various strategies on the organization. Are strategies conflicting in purpose? According to Tilles, a strategy must be judged not only in terms of itself, but also in terms of its relationship to other organizational strategies.
2. *Is organizational strategy consistent with its environment?* Organizational strategy must make sense in light of what is happening outside the organization. Is organizational strategy consistent with pending or new government regulations, changing consumer tastes, or trends in the labor supply? Most organizational problems that arise from inconsistency between strategy and environment are not due to extreme difficulty in matching these two variables. Rather, such problems crop up simply because organizations do not make a conscious effort to make strategy and environment consistent.
3. *Is organizational strategy appropriate given organizational resources?* Without appropriate resources, organizations simply cannot make strategies work. Are the resources the organization possesses sufficient to carry out a proposed strategy? Without enough money, people, materials, or machines, it is senseless to pursue any strategy, however well planned.
4. *Is organizational strategy too risky?* Strategy and resources, taken together, determine the degree of risk the organization is undertaking. Naturally,

[5] Seymour Tilles, "How to Evaluate Corporate Strategy," *Harvard Business Review,* July–August 1963, pp. 111–121.

TABLE 6.3 Sample Questions to Be Asked for a Qualitative Organizational Measurement

- Are the financial policies with respect to investment . . . dividends, and financing consistent with the opportunities likely to be available?
- Has the company defined the market segments in which it intends to operate sufficiently specifically with respect to both product lines and market segments? Has it clearly defined the key capabilities needed for success?
- Does the company have a viable plan for developing a significant and defensible superiority over competition with respect to these capabilities?
- Will the business segments in which the company operates provide adequate opportunities for achieving corporate objectives? Do they appear so attractive as to make it likely that an excessive amount of investment will be drawn to the market from other companies? Is adequate provision being made to develop attractive new investment opportunities?
- Are the management, financial, technical, and other resources of the company really adequate to justify an expectation of maintaining superiority over competition in the key areas of capability?
- Does the company have operations in which it is not reasonable to expect to be more capable than competition? If so, can the board expect them to generate adequate returns on invested capital? Is there any justification for investing further in such operations, even just to maintain them?
- Has the company selected business segments that can reinforce each other by contributing jointly to the development of key capabilities? Or are there competitors that have combinations of operations which provide them with an opportunity to gain superiority in the key resource areas? Can the company's scope of operations be revised so as to improve its position vis-à-vis competition?
- To the extent that operations are diversified, has the company recognized and provided for the special management and control systems required?

Source: Milton Lauenstein, "Keeping Your Corporate Strategy on Track," *The Journal of Business Strategy* 2, no. 1 (Summer 1981): 64. Reprinted by permission.

each organization must determine the amount of risk (or potentially lost resources) it wishes to incur. In this area, management must assess such issues as the total amount of resources a strategy requires, the proportion of the organization's resources that a strategy will consume, and the amount of time that must be committed.

5. *Is the time horizon of the strategy appropriate?* Every strategy is designed to bring about the accomplishment of some organizational goal within a certain time period. Is the time allotted for implementing the strategy and for reaching the related organizational goals realistic and acceptable, given organizational circumstances? Management must ensure that the time available to reach the goals and the time necessary to implement the strategy are consistent. Inconsistency between these two variables

can make it impossible to reach organizational goals in a satisfactory way.

Qualitative measurement methods can be very useful, but their application involves significant amounts of human judgment. Conclusions based on such methods must be drawn very carefully, because this subjective judgment, if exercised incorrectly, could easily render audit results invalid. Strategic control actions based on invalid audit results will certainly limit the effectiveness and efficiency of the strategic management process and could even become the primary reason for organizational failure.

QUANTITATIVE ORGANIZATIONAL MEASUREMENTS. These measurements are organizational assessments resulting in data that are numerically summarized and organized before conclusions are drawn on which to base strategic control action. Although data gathered via such measures are generally easier to summarize and organize than data gathered through more qualitative measurements, interpreting what quantitative measurements actually mean and what corrective action they signal can be very difficult and is highly subjective. Examples of the types of quantitative measurement that can be taken include the number of units produced per time period, the cost of production, the level of production efficiency, the levels of employee turnover and absenteeism, the levels of sales and sales growth, the amount of net profit earned, the level of dividends being paid, the return on equity being achieved, the proportion of market share possessed, and the level of earnings per share generated.[6]

In practice, each organization uses its own specially designed methods to measure organizational performance quantitatively. For an extended discussion of the quantitative measurement of organizational performance, see Chapter 10, "Financial Foundations for Strategic Management." Here, we will briefly discuss three measurements. They are:

1. *Return on investment* (*ROI*): This most commonly used measure of organizational performance divides net income by total assets. The result indicates the relationship between the amount of income generated and the amount of assets needed to operate the organization.[7] Naturally, an ROI value for one year alone may not provide the manager with much useful information. Comparing ROI values for consecutive years or consecutive quarters, or comparing ROI values to those of similar companies or competitors, usually generates a more complete picture of organizational performance in this area.

   Managers must keep in mind the several advantages and the

[6] Robert T. Justus, Richard J. Judd, and David B. Stephens, *Strategic Management and Policy: Concepts and Cases* (Englewood Cliffs, N.J.: Prentice-Hall, 1985), p. 144.

[7] See Joseph G. Louderback and George E. Manners, Jr., "Integrating ROI and CVP," *Management Accounting*, April 1981, pp. 33–39.

TABLE 6.4 Advantages and Limitations in Using ROI as a Measure of Organizational Performance

Advantages
1. ROI is a single comprehensive figure influenced by everything that happens.
2. It measures how well the division manager uses the property of the company to generate profits. It is also a good way to check on the accuracy of capital investment proposals.
3. It is a common denominator that can be compared with many entities.
4. It provides an incentive to use existing assets efficiently.
5. It provides an incentive to acquire new assets only when doing so would increase the return.

Limitations
1. ROI is very sensitive to depreciation policy. Depreciation write-off variances between divisions affect ROI performance. Accelerated depreciation techniques reduce ROI, conflicting with capital budgeting discounted cash-flow analysis.
2. ROI is sensitive to book value. Older plants with more depreciated assets have relatively lower investment bases than newer plants (note also the effect of inflation), thus increasing ROI. Note that asset investment may be held down or assets disposed of in order to increase ROI performance.
3. In many firms that use ROI, one division sells to another. As a result, transfer pricing must occur. Expenses incurred affect profit. Since, in theory, the transfer price should be based on the total impact on firm profit, some investment center managers are bound to suffer. Equitable transfer prices are difficult to determine.
4. If one division operates in an industry that has favorable conditions and another division operates in an industry that has unfavorable conditions, the former division will automatically "look" better than the other.
5. The time span of concern here is short range. The performance of division managers should be measured in the long run. This is top management's time-span capacity.
6. The business cycle strongly affects ROI performance, often despite managerial performance.

Source: James M. Higgins, *Organizational Policy and Strategic Management: Text and Cases*, 2nd ed.

limitations of ROI as a measure of organizational performance.[8] Several of these advantages and limitations are presented in Table 6.4. The limitations listed here should *not* discourage managers from using ROI; it is an extremely useful measure. Rather, management must thoroughly understand these limitations and supplement the ROI with such other performance measures as are needed.

[8] James M. Higgins and Julian W. Vincze, *Strategic Management and Organizational Policy: Text and Cases* (New York: Dryden Press, 1986), p. 228.

2. z *score:* This common quantitative measure results from an analysis that numerically weights and sums five measures to arrive at an overall score.[9] The score becomes a basis for classifying firms as "healthy" ones that are not likely to go bankrupt or as "sick" ones that are likely to go bankrupt. The formula itself is

$$z = 1.2\ X_1 + 1.4\ X_2 + 3.3\ X_3 + 0.6\ X_4 + 1.0\ X_5$$

Here z is defined as an index of overall corporate health. All other variables in the formula (X_1, X_2, etc.) are explained in Table 6.5.

[9] Edward I. Altman and James K. LaFleur, "Managing a Return to Financial Health," *The Journal of Business Strategy* 2, no. 1 (Summer 1981): 31–38.

TABLE 6.5 An Explanation of Variables Contained in Calculating a z Score

VARIABLES	DISCUSSION
$X_1 = \frac{\text{Working capital}}{\text{Total assets}}$	Frequently found in studies of corporate problems, this is a measure of the net liquid assets of the firm relative to the total capitalization. Working capital is defined as the difference between current assets and current liabilities. Liquidity and size characteristics are explicitly considered. Ordinarily, a firm experiencing consistent operating losses will have shrinking current assets in relation to total assets.
$X_2 = \frac{\text{Retained earnings}}{\text{Total assets}}$	This is a measure of cumulative profitability over time, and the balance sheet figure is used. The age of a firm is implicitly considered in this ratio. For example, a relatively young firm will probably show a low RE/TA ratio because it has not had time to build up its cumulative profits. Therefore, it may be argued that the young firm is somewhat discriminated against in this analysis, and its chance of being classified as bankrupt is relatively higher than [that of] another, older firm. But this is precisely the situation in the real world. The incidence of failure is much higher in a firm's earlier years; over 50 percent of firms that fail do so in the first five years of existence. It should be noted that the retained-earnings account is subject to manipulation via corporate quasi-reorganizations and stock dividend declarations. It is conceivable that a bias would be created by a substantial reorganization or stock dividend.
$X_3 = \frac{\text{Earnings before interest \& taxes}}{\text{Total assets}}$	This ratio is calculated by dividing the total assets of a firm into its earnings before interest and tax reductions. In essence, it is a measure of the true productivity of the firm's assets, abstracting from any tax or leverage factors. Since a firm's ultimate existence is based on the earning power of its assets, this ratio appears to be particularly appropriate for studies dealing with corporate

TABLE 6.5 (Continued)

VARIABLES	DISCUSSION
	failure. Furthermore, insolvency in a bankruptcy sense occurs when the total liabilities exceed a fair valuation of the firm's assets with value determined by the earning power of the assets.
$X_4 = \frac{\text{Market value of equity}}{\text{Book value of total liabilities}}$	Equity is measured by the combined market value of all shares of stock, preferred and common, while liabilities include both current and long-term. Book values of preferred and common stockholders' equity may be substituted for market values when the latter is not available. The substitution of book values, especially for the common stock component, should be recognized as a proxy without statistical verification, since the model was built using market values (price × shares outstanding). The measure shows how much the firm's assets can decline in value (measured by market value of equity plus debt) before the liabilities exceed the assets and the firm becomes insolvent. For example, a company with a market value of its equity of $1,000 and debt of $500 could experience a two-thirds drop in asset value before insolvency. However, the same firm with $250 in equity will be insolvent if its drop is only one-third in value.
$X_5 = \frac{\text{Sales}}{\text{Total assets}}$	The capital-turnover ratio is a standard financial ratio illustrating the sales-generating ability of the firm's assets. It is one measure of management's capability in dealing with competitive conditions.

It should be noted that variables X_1, X_2, X_3, and X_4 should be inserted into the model as *decimal fractions;* for example, a working capital/total assets of 20 percent should be written as 0.20. The variable X_5, however, is usually a ratio *greater than unity;* for example, where sales are twice as large as assets, the ratio is written as 2.0.

Source: Adapted from Edward I. Altman and James K. LaFleur, "Managing a Return to Financial Health," *The Journal of Business Strategy* 2, no. 1 (Summer 1981): 31–38. Reprinted by permission.

Using the *z* score typically results in a single number that ranges from −5 to 10. According to research investigating the *z* score, a score below 1.8 signals a relatively high probability of going bankrupt. Firms that score above 3.0 have a relatively low probability of going bankrupt. Firms that score between 1.8 and 3.0 are in a gray area. Knowing and understanding the *z* score for a particular firm can give top management an idea of the financial health of the firm and insights into how to improve it.

3. *Stakeholders' audit: Stakeholders* are people interested in a corporation's activities because they are significantly affected by accomplishment of the organization's objectives.[10] Organizational stakeholders include (a) stockholders interested in the appreciation of stock and dividends; (b) unions interested in favorable wage rates and benefit packages;

[10] R. E. Freeman, *Strategic Management: A Stakeholder Approach* (Boston: Pitman, 1984), p. 25.

(c) creditors interested in the organization's ability to pay its debts; (d) suppliers interested in retaining the organization as a customer; (e) governments, who see organizations as taxpayers contributing to the costs of running a society; and (f) social interest groups, such as consumer advocates and environmentalists.

Many managers believe that one very useful measure of organizational performance is a *stakeholders' audit,* a summary of the feedback generated by various stakeholder groups. The tone and content of such feedback can be an extremely valuable indicator of organizational progress toward various goals. Table 6.6 lists several stakeholder groups and related measures that can be used to assess both short-run and long-run organizational performance.

Highlight 6.2 will give you an opportunity to speculate about how various stakeholders are likely to react to a new plant that General Motors has announced plans to build.

As this section indicates, there are many different ways to measure organizational performance. Managers must establish and use whatever methods best suit their organization. There is, however, one important guideline that management should follow: Organizations should measure performance in all critical areas targeted by organizational goals.

Step 2: Compare Organizational Performance to Goals and Standards

After measurements of organizational performance are taken, they must be compared with two established benchmarks: organizational goals and standards. Organizational goals are simply the output of an earlier step of the strategic management process. They are fully discussed in Chapter 3, "Establishing Organizational Direction: Mission and Objectives."

Standards are developed to reflect organizational goals; they are "yardsticks" that indicate acceptable levels of organizational performance.[11] The specific standards that companies actually establish vary from firm to firm. As a rule, management must develop standards in all performance areas touched on by established organizational goals. Commonly used as an example, the following eight types of standards have been set by General Electric[12]:

1. *Profitability standards:* These standards indicate how much profit General Electric would like to make in a given time period.

[11] Norton M. Bedford, "Managerial Control," in Joseph W. McGuire (ed.), *Contemporary Management: Issues and Viewpoints* (Englewood Cliffs, N.J.: Prentice-Hall, 1974), pp. 507–514. For insights regarding how to construct worthwhile performance indicators see R. Kaufman, "Preparing Useful Performance Indicators," *Training and Development Journal* 42 (September 1989): 80–83.

[12] Robert W. Lewis, "Measuring, Reporting, and Appraising Results of Operations with Reference to Goals, Plans, and Budgets," in *Planning, Managing, and Measuring the Business: A Case Study of Management Planning and Control at General Electric Company* (New York: Controllership Foundation, 1955).

TABLE 6.6 Sample Stakeholder Groups and Suggestions for Measuring Their Activities for Both Near-Term and Long-Term Organizational Performance

STAKEHOLDER CATEGORY	POSSIBLE NEAR-TERM MEASURES	POSSIBLE LONG-TERM MEASURES
Customers	Sales ($ and volume) New customers Number of new customer needs met ("tries")	Growth in sales Turnover of customer base Ability to control price
Suppliers	Cost of raw material Delivery time Inventory Availability of raw material	Growth rates of: Raw materials costs Delivery time Inventory New ideas from suppliers
Financial community	EPS[1] Stock price Number of "buy" lists[2] ROE[3]	Ability to convince Wall Street of strategy Growth in ROE
Employees	Number of suggestions Productivity Number of grievances	Number of internal promotions Turnover
Congress	Number of new pieces of legislation that affect the firm Access to key members and staff	Number of new regulations that affect industry Ratio of "cooperative" [to] "competitive" encounters
Consumer advocate [CA]	Number of meetings Number of "hostile" encounters Number of times coalitions formed Number of legal actions	Number of changes in policy due to CA Number of CA-initiated "calls for help"[4]
Environmentalists	Number of meetings Number of hostile encounters Number of times coalitions formed Number of EPA [Environmental Protection Agency] complaints Number of legal actions	Number of changes in policy due to environmentalists Number of environmentalist "calls for help"

[1] Earnings per share.
[2] Lists from which financial brokers recommend stock purchases for their clients.
[3] Return on earnings.
[4] Calls in which CA attempts to enlist others in action against a company.

Source: Adapted from R. E. Freeman, *Strategic Management* (Boston: Ballinger Publishing, 1984), p. 179.

HIGHLIGHT 6.2

SKILLS MODULE ■ Assessing Stakeholder Attitudes Toward the New Saturn Plant

INTRODUCTION

Stakeholders are groups of individuals who are interested in a corporation's activities because they are significantly affected by the organization's accomplishment of its objectives. Review the following situation at General Motors, and then complete the skill development exercise that follows. Doing so will help you learn to analyze the reactions of various stakeholder groups to organizational strategy.

THE SITUATION

The General Motors Company recently announced its decision to construct a new, revolutionary automobile plant in Spring Hill, Tennessee. Important issues addressed by the designers of this new plant include quality of life, the use of work teams, modular assembly of products, and the use of computers to enhance organizational efficiency and effectiveness. The accompanying illustration shows how plant design addressed each of these areas.

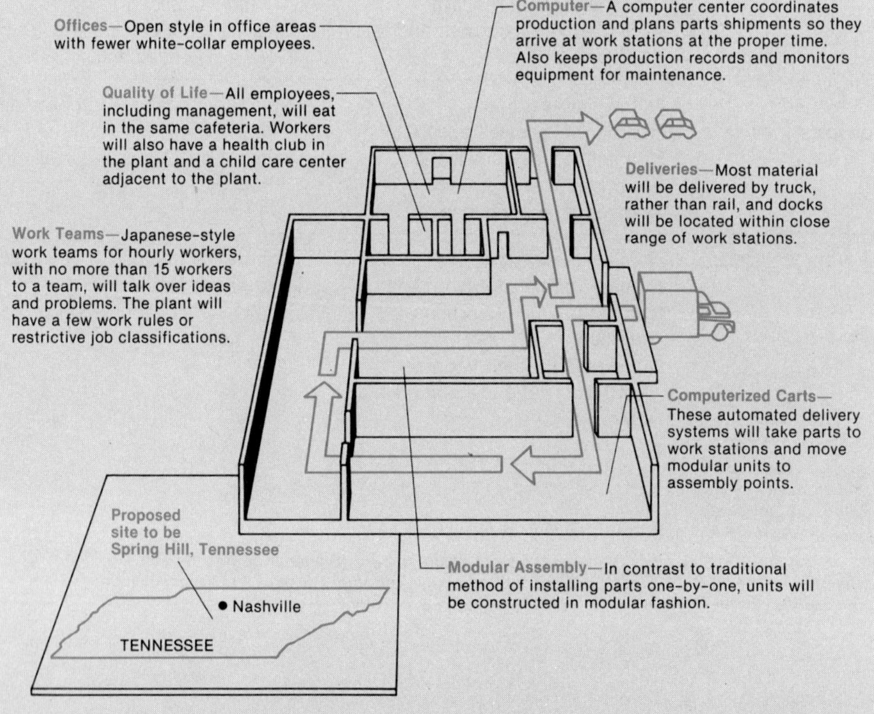

Source: Adapted from *Terre Haute Tribune–Star,* July 30, 1985, p. B4. Reprinted by permission.

SKILL DEVELOPMENT EXERCISE

The chief executive officer at General Motors is very supportive of the new Saturn plant design. He is also aware, however, that many different stakeholder groups are intently interested in the Saturn project and that some will probably respond positively to the project whereas others will probably respond negatively. List various GM stakeholder groups and predict which groups might react positively and which negatively to the development of the Saturn plant. Given your analysis, was the decision to develop the Saturn plant good for the company? Explain.

Source: Based on "GM Confirms Site of Saturn Plant" (Associated Press, Detroit), *Terre Haute Tribune Star,* July 30, 1985, p. B4.

2. *Market position standards:* These standards indicate the percentage of total product market that the company would like to win from its competitors.
3. *Productivity standards:* These production oriented standards indicate various acceptable rates at which final products should be generated within the organization.
4. *Product leadership standards:* Innovation is critical for long-run organizational success. Product leadership standards indicate what levels of product innovation would make people view General Electric products as leaders in the market.
5. *Personnel development standards:* The development of organization members in all areas is critical to continued organizational success. Personnel development standards list acceptable levels of progress in this area.
6. *Employee attitude standards:* These standards indicate attitudes that General Electric employees should adopt. Not only are workers evaluated for the degree to which they project these attitudes, but managers are evaluated for the extent to which they develop them in their subordinates.
7. *Public responsibility standards:* All organizations have certain obligations to society. General Electric's standards in this area indicate acceptable levels of activity within the organization directed toward living up to social responsibilities.
8. *Standards reflecting balance between short-range and long-range goals:* General Electric, like most organizations, feels that both long-run and short-run goals are necessary to maintain a healthy and successful organization. Standards in this area indicate what the acceptable long- and short-range goals are and the relationships among them.

Step 3: Take Necessary Corrective Action

Once managers have collected organizational measurements and compared these measurements to established goals and standards, they should take any corrective action that is warranted. *Corrective action* is defined as a change management makes in the way an organization functions in order to ensure that the organization can more effectively and efficiently reach organizational goals and perform up to standards that have been established. Corrective action may be as simple as changing the price of a product or as complicated as the recent boardroom struggle led by Laurence Tisch and William Paley to fire Thomas Wyman as the chief executive officer at CBS.[13]

As Highlight 6.3 illustrates, strategic control can also result in changes as dramatic as modifying the type of product a company offers the marketplace. The Honda Motor Company recently repositioned its compact car of the 1980s, the Accord, as a midsized car for the 1990s that will compete directly with other cars like Ford's Taurus and Sable. Perhaps because Honda recently had to offer discounts on its Accord in order to maintain a desirable sales volume, Honda top management concluded that product modification was necessary if they were to remain competitive within the industry.

Thoroughly understanding the steps of the strategic control process and how they are related to the major steps of the strategic management process is the basis for determining how corrective action should be taken. Figure 6.2 summarizes the main steps of the strategic control process and illustrates the relationship between it and the major steps of the strategic management process.

Assume that in a particular organization, appropriate organizational goals and standards are not being met and that corrective action is necessary. As Figure 6.2 implies, such action might include attempting to improve organizational performance by focusing on one or more of the major steps of the strategic management process. This analysis, of course, includes improving the strategic control process itself by enhancing the validity and reliability of measures of organizational performance.

In most situations, corrective action is not necessary if the organization is reaching the goals and standards that have been established for it. However, management must not automatically assume that this is the case. Goals and standards may have been set too *low,* in which case corrective action should promptly be taken to make them more challenging.

Highlight 6.4 will give you an opportunity to try your hand at incorporating the results of a survey of customer attitudes into the strategic control process at a well-known firm.

INFORMATION

The Importance of Information in Strategic Control

In order to be successful at strategic control, management must have valid and reliable information that reflects various measurements of organizational performance. Without such information, action taken to exert strategic control

[13] Bill Powell and Jonathan Alter, "The Showdown at CBS," *Newsweek,* September 22, 1986, pp. 54–58.

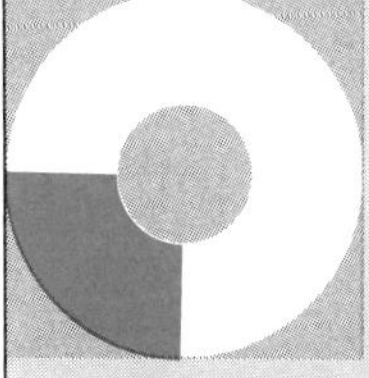

ILLUSTRATIVE EXAMPLE ■ **Strategic Control at Honda Results in Changes to the Accord**

Scott Whitlock, the ex-lawyer who manages Honda Motor Co.'s big assembly plant in Marysville, Ohio, looked out across the throng of workers at the end of the assembly line last Thursday to celebrate the launch of the 1990 Accord.

"This is the car that's going to support us and satisfy our customers for the next four years," Mr. Whitlock declared. "This is our future."

Mr. Whitlock wasn't exaggerating. The Accord accounts for nearly half of the company's annual U.S. sales. Its success is a must if Honda is to make its U.S. subsidiary a fully self-reliant operation, in everything from design to engineering to manufacturing. *And this year's Accord, the trend-setting compact car of the 1980s, enters the midsized market.*

For the first time, Ford Motor Co.'s competitive-analysis studies pit the Accord against Ford's twin flagships, the Taurus and Sable. The Japanese assault on the U.S. luxury-car market has grabbed the spotlight, but just beneath all that glitter, Honda is aiming its bread-and-butter Accord at the heart of Detroit's home market: midsized, midpriced, family cars.

Honda not only plans a new Accord sedan, but next fall will introduce an *Accord station wagon,* designed in part to answer the prayers of dealers who have pleaded for a vehicle that can keep Honda families from defecting to minivans or Taurus wagons. Other Japanese auto makers are taking aim at the same family market.

Until this year, the Accord's success and its image as a trend-setting automobile allowed Honda to boost its sales and market share without resorting to sales incentives. But that abruptly changed last April. To counter slumping sales, Honda was forced to offer its first-ever discounts on Accord, thinly disguised as $100 to $300 a car advertising subsidies paid to dealers. Then, in July, Honda offered as much as $350 a car in incentives to dealers who met certain sales quotas.

The money has allowed the Accord to maintain its record of seven straight years of sales growth since 1982. Honda will probably sell more than 370,000 Accords this year, compared with 195,000 in 1982. But incentives also have contributed to a rare earnings slide at Honda.

Thus the acid test for the new Accord will be whether Honda can avoid offering any more discounts. Honda officials insist that they won't have to do that. But they aren't taking many chances. "We're increasing the advertising budget 25% for 1990, even though our sales projection is only up 5% to 6%," says Thomas Elliot, Honda's top U.S. marketing official.

Source: Adapted from Joseph B. White, "Honda Takes Aim at Detroit's Heart," *The Wall Street Journal*, September 18, 1989, p. B1.

HIGHLIGHT 6.4

SKILLS MODULE ■ Skill in Operating the Strategic Control Process at Kellogg

INTRODUCTION

We have seen that the strategic control process consists of three major steps: measuring organizational performance, comparing measured organizational performance to goals and standards, and taking corrective action. Review the following situation at Kellogg, and then complete the skill development exercise that follows. Doing so will help you appreciate the skills involved in operating a strategic control process.

THE SITUATION

Assume that you are in charge of strategic planning for the Kellogg Company, a manufacturer of several different kinds of breakfast cereals. Your assistant has just come into your office and handed you the results of a survey on attitude toward nutritional content of foods, recently conducted by the Food Marketing Institute of Shoppers. The results of this survey are shown in the accompanying chart.

(Percentage answering very concerned)

	1986	1983
Total	58	64
Age 18-24	55	61
25-39	51	64
40-49	49	61
50-64		68
65 and over		65
Men	55	62
Women	58	65

	1986	1983
Chemical additives	16	27
Preservatives	15	22
Freshness, purity	8	14
Harmful ingredients	5	10
Overly processed	3	12
Excess food coloring dyes	2	6
Fat content	17	9
Cholesterol	13	5

SKILL DEVELOPMENT EXERCISE

After ample deliberation, you conclude that the results of this survey are valid and significant to the operation of your company. What special features should be built into the strategic control process at Kellogg to ensure that the survey results are properly considered? Discuss these features in detail.

Source: Data from *Food Marketing Institute Survey of Shoppers,* in Erik Larson, "What's for Dinner? Food Specialists Serve Up Some Unexpected Dishes," *The Wall Street Journal,* November 3, 1986, p. 37. Reprinted by permission of *The Wall Street Journal.*

will be highly subjective and will have little chance of consistently improving organizational performance. Information is the lifeblood of successful strategic control.

Information Systems

Because valid and reliable information about organizational performance is critical to strategic control, virtually all organizations develop and implement some type of system to generate this information. The following section discusses two such systems: management information systems (MIS) and management decision support systems (MDSS).

The Management Information System (MIS)

A *management information system* is a formal organizational network that is normally computer-assisted and is established within an organization to provide managers with information to help their decision making. Although there are many different uses for such information, a significant portion of it supports strategic control.

As Figure 6.3 illustrates, operating an MIS is largely a matter of performing six related steps. Let us interpret these steps in the context of using the MIS for strategic control purposes.

Once management establishes what information is needed for strategic control, appropriate data must be collected and analyzed, and the information this analysis yields must be disseminated to appropriate organization members, usually upper management. Next, upper management must formulate and implement strategic control activities in light of this information. Finally, and on a continuing basis, feedback on the effect of implementing these activities and on the functioning of the MIS system itself must be used as a basis for meeting the information needs of strategic control better in the future.

THE MIS AND MANAGEMENT LEVELS. Because managers at various levels of the organization are responsible for performing different kinds of activities, the MIS should be flexible enough to provide various management levels with the information that carrying out these activities requires. Table 6.7 summarizes typical activities performed by top-, middle-, and lower-level managers. This table illustrates that although strategic control and other strategic management tasks are the primary focus of top management, all management levels have some role in the strategic management process, and the MIS should provide them the supportive information they need.

SYMPTOMS OF AN INADEQUATE MIS. Because the effectiveness of the strategic control process is largely dependent on valid and reliable organizational performance measurements, managers should continually assess MIS functioning to ensure that it is meeting strategic control needs.[14] Most managers

[14] George S. Day, "Tough Questions for Developing Strategies," *Journal of Business Strategy,* Winter 1986, pp. 60–68.

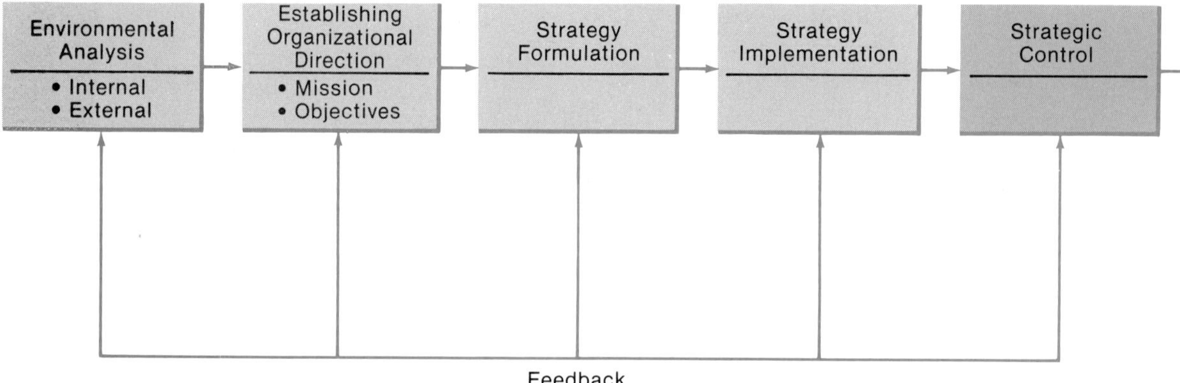

FIGURE 6.2 Relationships Between the Strategic Management Process and the Strategic Control Process

agree that they must constantly be alert for signals that an MIS is not operating effectively and efficiently. Naturally, once such symptoms are discovered, management must take steps to solve whatever problems plague the MIS. Once these problems are eliminated, the symptoms of trouble should disappear.

Sensing MIS-related problems can be quite difficult, or it may be as simple as listening to the comments of strategic control decision makers. Such individuals may complain that there is too much information of the wrong kind and not enough of the right kind, that information is so dispersed throughout the company that great effort must be expended to obtain simple facts, that others sometimes suppress vital information for personal reasons, that vital information frequently arrives too late to be useful, or that information often arrives in a form that gives no hint of how accurate it is and there is no one to turn to for confirmation.[15] Managers may bluntly worry that the

[15] J. Paul Peter and James H. Donnelly, Jr., *A Preface to Marketing Management* (Dallas, Tex.: Business Publications, 1985), p. 38.

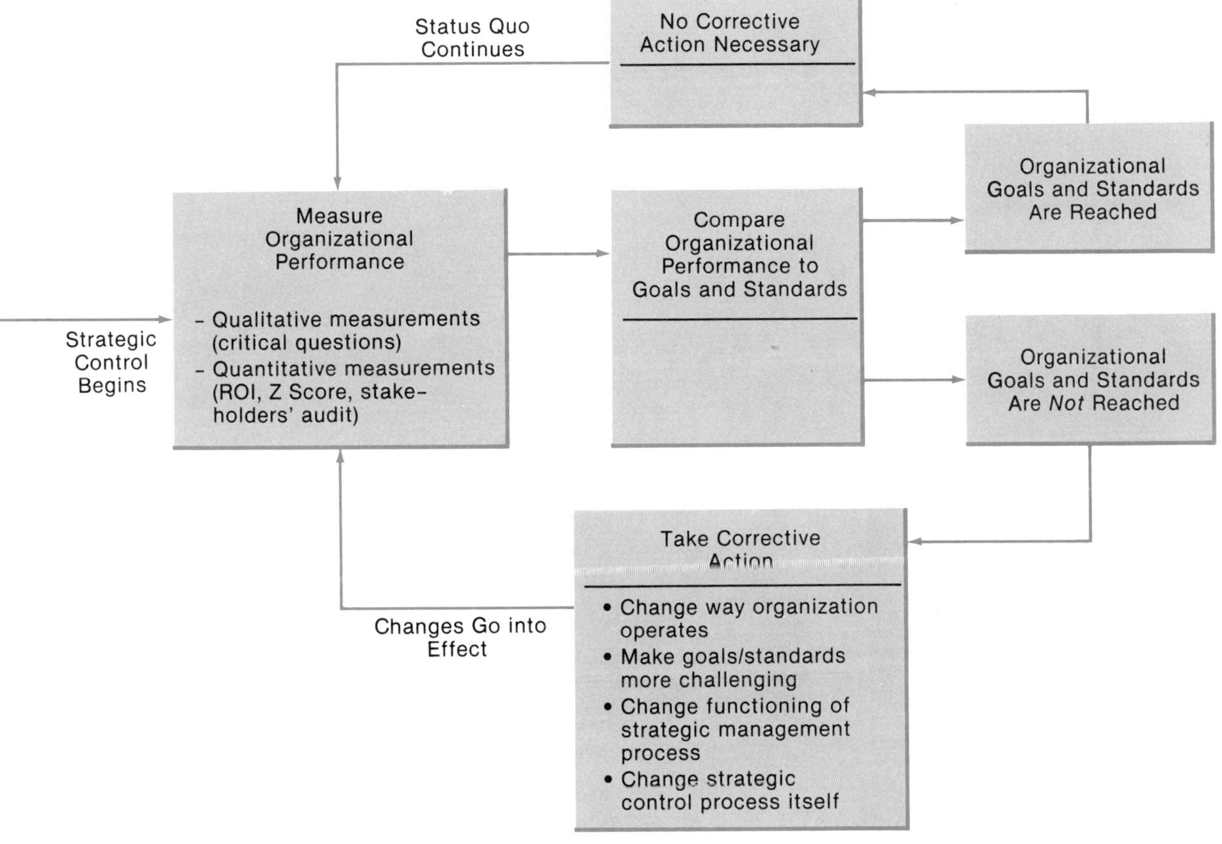

information they get may be moving them in the *wrong* strategic direction with all possible speed.[16]

Bertram A. Colbert, a principal of Price Waterhouse & Company, has indicated that other kinds of symptoms can also betray an MIS that is operating improperly. They are: (1) *operational symptoms,* which are related to the way an organization functions; (2) *psychological symptoms,* which reflect the feelings of organization members; and (3) *report content symptoms,* which are exhibited in the structure of reports generated by the MIS. Table 6.8 lists several organizational symptoms that fall in each of these three categories.

As soon as they become aware of symptoms of this sort, managers should take action to solve the MIS problems responsible. In practice, however, it may be quite difficult to determine exactly what problems within an organization are hampering the effectiveness of the MIS. Answering the five following

[16] Daniel H. Gray, "Uses and Misuses of Strategic Planning," *Harvard Business Review,* January–February 1986, pp. 89–97.

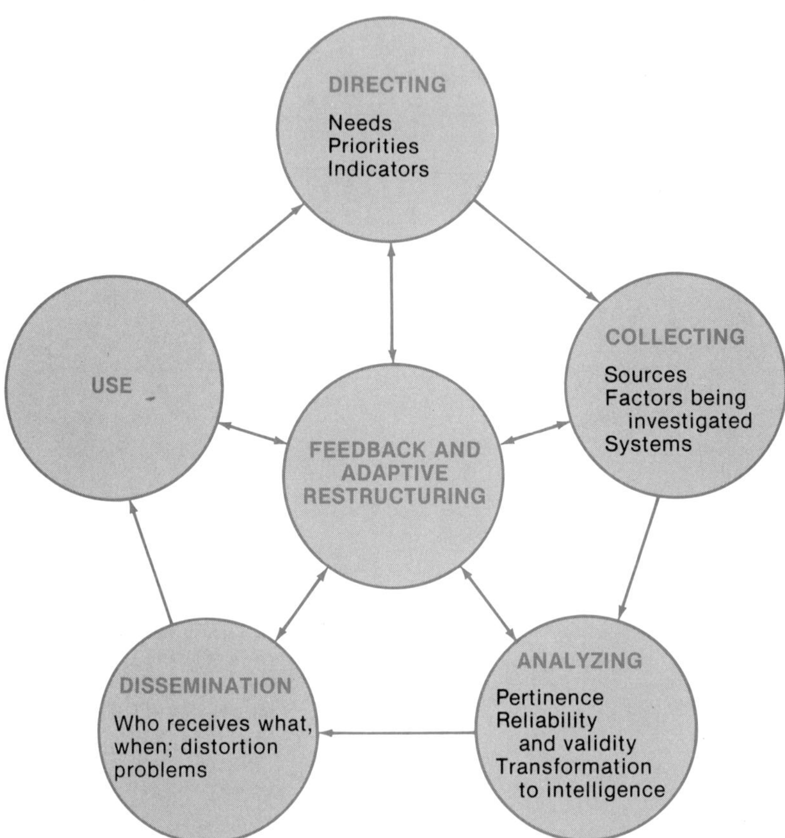

FIGURE 6.3 *Major Steps in Operating an MIS (Source: Toward Strategic Intelligence Systems, vol. 43, Fall 1979. Reprinted with permission.)*

questions may help the manager to pinpoint MIS-related strategic control problems.

1. Where and how do managers involved in the strategic control process get information?
2. Can managers involved in strategic control make better use of their contacts to get information?
3. In what strategic control areas is the knowledge of these managers weakest, and how can they be given information to minimize such weaknesses?
4. Do managers involved in strategic control tend to act before receiving enough information?
5. Do managers involved in strategic control wait so long for information that opportunities pass them by and they become "bottlenecks"?[17]

[17] Henry Mintzberg, "The Manager's Job: Folklore and Fact," *Harvard Business Review,* July–August 1975, p. 58. Some implications of this article from a strategic viewpoint are discussed in James Brian Quinn, Henry Mintzberg, and Robert M. James, *The Strategy Process: Concepts, Contexts, and Cases* (Englewood Cliffs, N.J.: Prentice-Hall, 1988), p. 21.

TABLE 6.7 Typical Activities Performed by Managers at Various Organizational Levels

ORGANIZATIONAL LEVEL	CHARACTERISTICS OF ACTIVITIES PERFORMED	SAMPLE ACTIVITIES
Top management	Activities are future oriented Activities involve significant amounts of uncertainty Activities involve significant subjective assessment Activities involve strategic management emphasis	Establishing organizational direction Performing an environmental analysis Developing organizational strategies
Middle management	Activities are somewhat future oriented but not so much as top-management activities Activities emphasize implementation of organizational strategies	Making short-term forecasts Budgeting Human resource planning
Source management	Activities emphasize daily production Activities emphasize daily performance that reflects organizational strategy and contributes to attainment of long-term organizational goals	Assigning jobs to specific workers Managing inventory Supervising workers Handling worker complaints Maintaining organizational procedures and rules

The Management Decision Support System (MDSS)[18]

Traditionally, an MIS that gathers data and provides information to managers electronically has been invaluable. This MIS assistance has been especially useful in areas where managers must make recurring decisions; the computer repeatedly generates the information they need. An example of such a structured decision might be using the computer to track cumulative population shifts in the market the organization serves. In such a case, the computer may be used to update environmental analysis reports automatically and even to remind management that additional salespeople should be deployed when the numbers of target customers in a specified market area increase substantially.

Closely related to the MIS is the management decision support system (MDSS). A *management decision support system* is an interdependent set of decision aids that helps managers make relatively unstructured, perhaps nonrecurring decisions. The computer (in conjunction with such software as the Lotus electronic spreadsheet) is the main element of the MDSS and is used as an analytic tool for making more subjective decisions. The MDSS, however, does not pretend to dictate the manager's decision or impose solutions to

[18] This section is based on Steven L. Mandell, *Computers and Data Processing: Concepts and Applications with BASIC* (St. Paul, Minn.: West Publishing Company, 1982), pp. 370–391.

TABLE 6.8 Operational, Psychological, and Report Content Symptoms of an Improperly Operating MIS

OPERATIONAL	PSYCHOLOGICAL	REPORT CONTENT
Large physical inventory adjustments	Surprise at financial results	Excessive use of tabulations of figures
Capital expenditure overruns	Poor attitude of executives about usefulness of information	Multiple preparation and distribution of identical data
Inability of executives to explain changes from year to year in operating results	Lack of understanding of financial information on part of nonfinancial executives	Disagreeing information from different sources
Uncertain direction of company growth	Lack of concern for environmental changes	Lack of periodic comparative information and trends
Cost variances unexplainable	Executive homework reviewing reports considered excessive	Lateness of information
No order backlog awareness		Too little or excess detail
No internal discussion of reported data		Inaccurate information
Insufficient knowledge about competition		Lack of standards for comparison
Purchasing parts from outside vendors when internal capability and capacity to make are available		Failure to identify variances by cause and responsibility
Record of some "sour" investments in facilities, or in programs such as R&D and advertising		Inadequate externally generated information

Source: Institute for Practitioners in Work-Study, Organization, and Methods, Middlesex, England, *Management Sciences* 4, no. 5 (September–October 1967): 15–24. Reprinted by permission.

problems. Many managers use an MDSS to help them make strategic control decisions and other types of strategic management decisions. For example, a manager may consider how best to implement strategy within an organization by determining all the different costs that various implementation alternatives will entail. The MDSS provides and organizes the information; the manager "factors it in" as she or he makes the decision.

Stunning technological advances in microcomputers have made the use of MDSS feasible and available to virtually all managers. And the continued development of extensive software to support information analysis related to more subjective decision making is contributing to the popularity of the MDSS. A set of components that might make up a typical MDSS system is shown in Figure 6.4.

TOP MANAGEMENT AND STRATEGIC CONTROL

Because strategic management is primarily the responsibility of top management, and because strategic control is a critical ingredient of successful

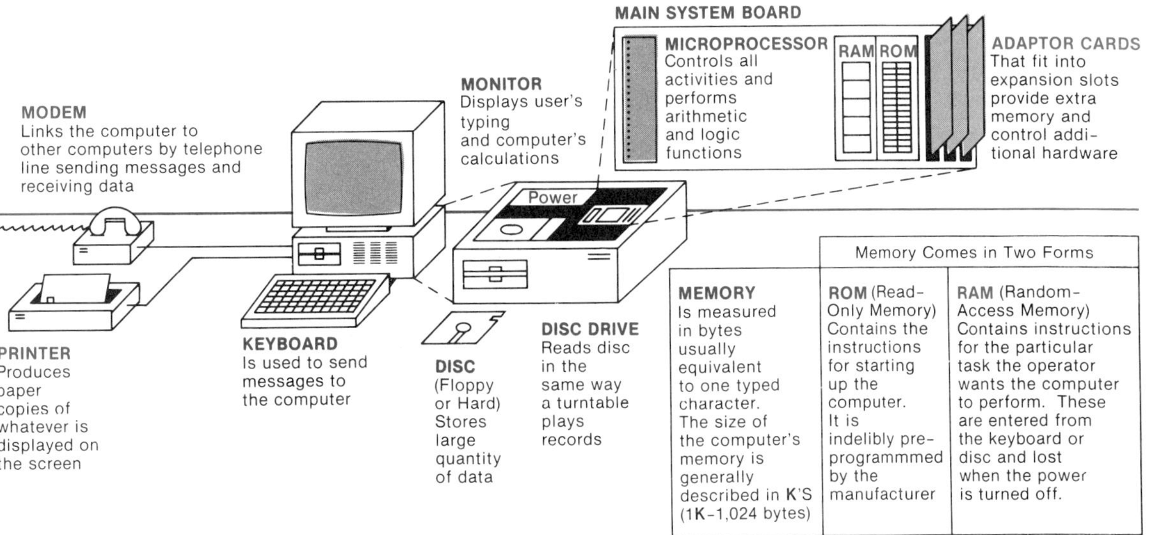

FIGURE 6.4 *Typical Components of a Management Decision Support System (Source: Time, January 3, 1983. Copyright 1982. Reprinted with permission.)*

strategic management, top management must be able to understand strategic control and know how to take the action implied by the strategic control process. Top management must make a firm and enduring commitment to the establishment and use of a strategic control system within the organization. And, of course, organizational resources must be committed to support such activity.

A model illustrating the variables that are important to maintaining successful strategic control is presented in Figure 6.5. According to this model, strategic control entails reaching either of two primary objectives: maintaining strategic momentum already achieved or "leaping" to a new strategy direction if and when such a new direction is appropriate.

According to this model, in order to reach either of these objectives, top management must ensure that four interrelated organizational variables are consistent and complementary: (1) organizational structure, (2) incentives, (3) information systems, and (4) organizational value systems and norms. To

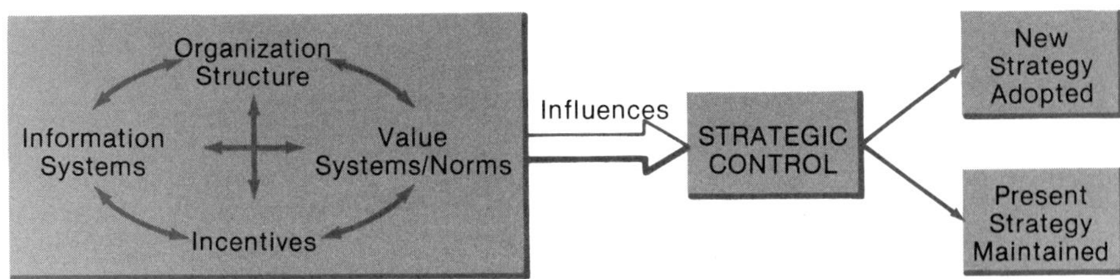

FIGURE 6.5 Variables Important to Maintaining Strategic Control

maintain strategic momentum or leap to a new strategy, top management must ensure the following:

1. Appropriate behavior within the organization is encouraged through the use of organizational incentives.
2. Organizational structure contributes to attainment of the objective.
3. Values and norms existing within the organizational culture are consistent with the objective being pursued.[19]
4. The information support needed to reach the objective is available.

SUMMARY

Exerting control in organizations entails monitoring, evaluating, and improving various types of activities occurring within organizations in order to make events unfold as planned. Strategic control, a special type of organizational control, focuses on monitoring and evaluating the strategic management process to ensure that what is supposed to happen as a result of the process actually does happen. Although strategic control has many different purposes within an organization, the most fundamental one is to help managers achieve organizational goals via control of strategic management.

There are three basic steps to the strategic control process. Step 1 is measuring organizational performance. Here management generally uses strategic audits to determine what is actually happening within the organization. Step 2 is comparing organizational performance to goals and standards. Here management builds a case for concluding whether what has happened as a result of the strategic management process is acceptable. Step 3 in the strategic control process is actually taking corrective action, if any is necessary. If events are occurring in line with organizational goals that were established within the strategic management process, no corrective action is probably necessary. If they are out of line, however, some type of corrective action is usually called for.

Information that reflects valid and reliable measurements of organizational activities is a prerequisite for successful strategic control. Recognizing the importance of acquiring and applying such information, most organizations establish both management information systems (MIS) and management decision support systems (MDSS). These systems typically use the computer in conjunction with specially tailored software to provide management with needed measurements of organizational performance. Once established, infor-

[19] Peter Linkow, "HRD at the Roots of Corporate Strategy," *Training and Development Journal*, May 1985, pp. 85–87.

mation systems must be constantly monitored to ensure that they continue to work properly.

Top management has an important role in making sure that strategic control is successful. Upper-level managers must design and implement the strategic control process so that appropriate strategic control behavior within the organization is encouraged through organizational incentives, so that organizational structure is consistent with strategic control objectives, so that organizational culture is consistent with strategic control, and so that the information needed to support strategic control is available.

Highlight 6.5 is a checklist of questions based on this chapter. Use it in analyzing strategic management problems and cases that focus on strategic control issues.

HIGHLIGHT 6.5

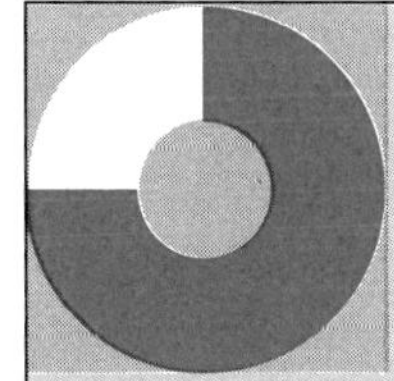

CHECKLIST ■ **Analyzing Strategic Control in Problems and Cases**

- ☐ 1. Does the case involve strategic control issues?
- ☐ 2. Is the strategic control described in the case fulfilling all of its purposes?
- ☐ 3. Do issues arise in the case about the appropriate role and conduct of strategic audits?
- ☐ 4. Have both qualitative and quantitative measures of organizational performance been appropriately employed?
- ☐ 5. Are the interests of various stakeholder groups being considered?
- ☐ 6. Are performance standards appropriate to the organization being set and compared to organizational performance?
- ☐ 7. Is any necessary corrective action being applied?
- ☐ 8. Is the management information system (MIS) established and operating appropriately?
- ☐ 9. Is a management decision support system (MDSS) being employed as it should be?
- ☐ 10. Are various levels of management appropriately involved in the strategic control process?

ADDITIONAL READINGS

Bennis, Warren, and Burt Nanus. *Leaders: Strategies for Taking Charge.* New York: Harper & Row, 1985.

Brown, Stephen W., and Martin D. Goslar. "New Information Systems for Marketing Decision Making." *Business*, July–September 1988, pp. 18–24.

Byars, Lloyd L. *Strategic Management: Planning and Implementation, Concepts and Cases.* New York: Harper & Row, 1987.

Donovan, John J. "Beyond Chief Information Officer to Network Manager," *Harvard Business Review*, September–October 1988, pp. 134–140.

Foster, Lawrence W. "From Darwin to Now: The Evolution of Organizational Strategies." *Journal of Business Strategy* 5, no. 4 (Spring 1985): 94–98.

Mainelli, Michael R., and David R. Miller. "Strategic Planning for Information Systems at British Rail." *Long Range Planning* 21 (August 1988): 65–75.

Nutt, P. C. "Identifying and Appraising How Managers Install Strategy." *Strategic Management Journal* 8, no. 1 (January–February 1987): 1–14.

Renier, James J. "Turnaround of Information Systems at Honeywell." *The Academy of Management Executive* 1, no. 1 (February 1987): 47–50.

Schreyogg, Georg, and Horst Steinmann. "Strategic Control: A New Perspective." *The Academy of Management Review* 12, no. 1 (January 1987): 91–103.

HIGHLIGHT 6.6 ■ APPLICATION OF CHAPTER MATERIAL

Strategic Control at Winnebago Industries

It hasn't been dull at Winnebago Industries, Inc. In 1971, the Forest City, Iowa, maker of recreational vehicles was the year's hottest stock, up 462 percent. Then came the first gas crunch and, as Winnebago was getting going again, the second gas crunch. Revenues dropped from 1978's $229 million to $92 million—and a $13.5 million deficit—in 1980. That was when founder and 45 percent owner John K. Hanson came out of retirement, laid off a mob of M.B.A.s, and got the company profitable again. In the process, his son John B. ended up leaving the company.

"We weren't making no money," exclaims Hanson, now seventy. "I saw mistakes, I returned to correct them. Simple as falling off a log." Hanson will not say much more than that about the past.

But Ron Haugen will. He's the local boy who joined Winnebago right out of high school. He is now its forty-two-year-old chief executive and is almost a surrogate son to Hanson. "The industry had gone from

140,000 units per year to not much over 26,000 in 1980," he recalls. "Survival was at stake. We brought employment down from four thousand to eight hundred and consolidated 29 percent of our manufacturing plants and office buildings. We went from $18 million in debt to $18 million cash in eighteen months." The major reason? Thanks to all the tightening, break-even fell from $240 million to just over $100 million.

But survival was only the beginning. "We knew the product was inadequate," Haugen concedes. Winnebago's basic design hadn't changed much since its 1965 introduction, and Coachmen and Fleetwood had driven it into third place. But Winnebago saw an opening. Nobody had a fuel-efficient vehicle in the new mileage-conscious market.

Haugen and Hanson went to work. "We wanted to get the thing lighter, improve aerodynamics, and thereby dramatically improve gas mileage," says Haugen. "We said we were going to find a vehicle that does all the things a conventional motor home does, but would be more affordable, more maneuverable, maybe multi-purpose." Haugen hoped to attract potential young buyers who got their licenses in time to wait on gas lines.

Renault of France proved to be the key. "We went to General Motors, Chrysler, and Ford," says Haugen. "They had nothing in that weight-carrying capacity, nor did they have anything on the drawing board. The Japanese had nothing for us either."

But Renault had recently finished a seven-year, $2 billion program to develop a heavy-duty, front-wheel-drive diesel engine. Hanson and Haugen went to Paris and negotiated a three-year exclusive contract.

In mid-1982, Winnebago introduced a new line of small motor homes with Renault diesels. These vehicles sell for close to $20,000 instead of over $40,000, the price of larger models, and get twenty-two plus miles per gallon instead of eight to twelve, the company's previous standard. They are selling like the Winnebagos of old. Despite production delays, parts shortages, and painful retooling—and dealers who had to be trained to repair Renault engines—Winnebago moved fifteen hundred units in fiscal 1983 ending in August.

Building on the breakthrough, Winnebago's research and development engineers took their aerodynamic gains and applied them toward a sorely needed, new, full-size motor home. Now analyst Steven Eisenberg of Bear, Stearns thinks Winnebago can sell six to seven thousand of its new-style vehicles, large and small, in fiscal 1984. What about Coachmen and Fleetwood? "We think Winnebago has at least a two-year lead time," says Eisenberg.

Meanwhile, Haugen has been attending to some money-making details, like licensing the Winnebago name to manufacturers of everything from sailboats to backpacks and coolers. In fiscal 1984, through existing

(Continues)

dealers, Haugen also hopes to provide two thousand motor homes as rental vehicles. Analysts think that could add fifteen cents per share to earnings. All in all, with the $3.3 billion recreational vehicle industry in a dramatic recovery, Winnebago's revenues could top $400 million. Earnings per share could hit $1.65.

That's good news for Forest City, Iowa, a community that was watching Winnebago's travail with more than ordinary concern. As John Hanson puts it, "We are the community." The sign that welcomes you to "The Recreational Vehicle Capital of America" is chipped and fading, but employment at Winnebago is over two thousand again, and the company is back on top, with over a third of the RV market.

What happens if another fuel shock comes along? It would be rough, but Winnebago feels it would survive. And surviving is the first step toward prevailing.

DISCUSSION QUESTIONS

1. Does this case focus on strategic control issues? Explain.
2. Which step of the strategic control process is most important to the future success of Winnebago? Give examples of how this step might affect the company.
3. Which step of the strategic control process is discussed most here? Give examples to support your answer.

Source: Jay Gissen, "Good Times in Forest City." Reprinted by permission of *Forbes* magazine, February 13, 1984.

SECTION THREE

Special Issues in Strategic Management

In Sections One and Two of this text, we introduced and analyzed the strategic management process. The knowledge and skills you developed in your study of Chapters 1–6 can be successfully applied to a variety of strategic management problems and cases. However, dealing with certain situations that arise in strategic management may require additional, specialized knowledge of particular areas. In the following section we discuss two such areas that strategic managers often need to be familiar with: international operations (Chapter 7) and social responsibility (Chapter 8). After carefully studying this section, you should understand the special problems that strategic managers confront when they deal with issues in these two important areas.

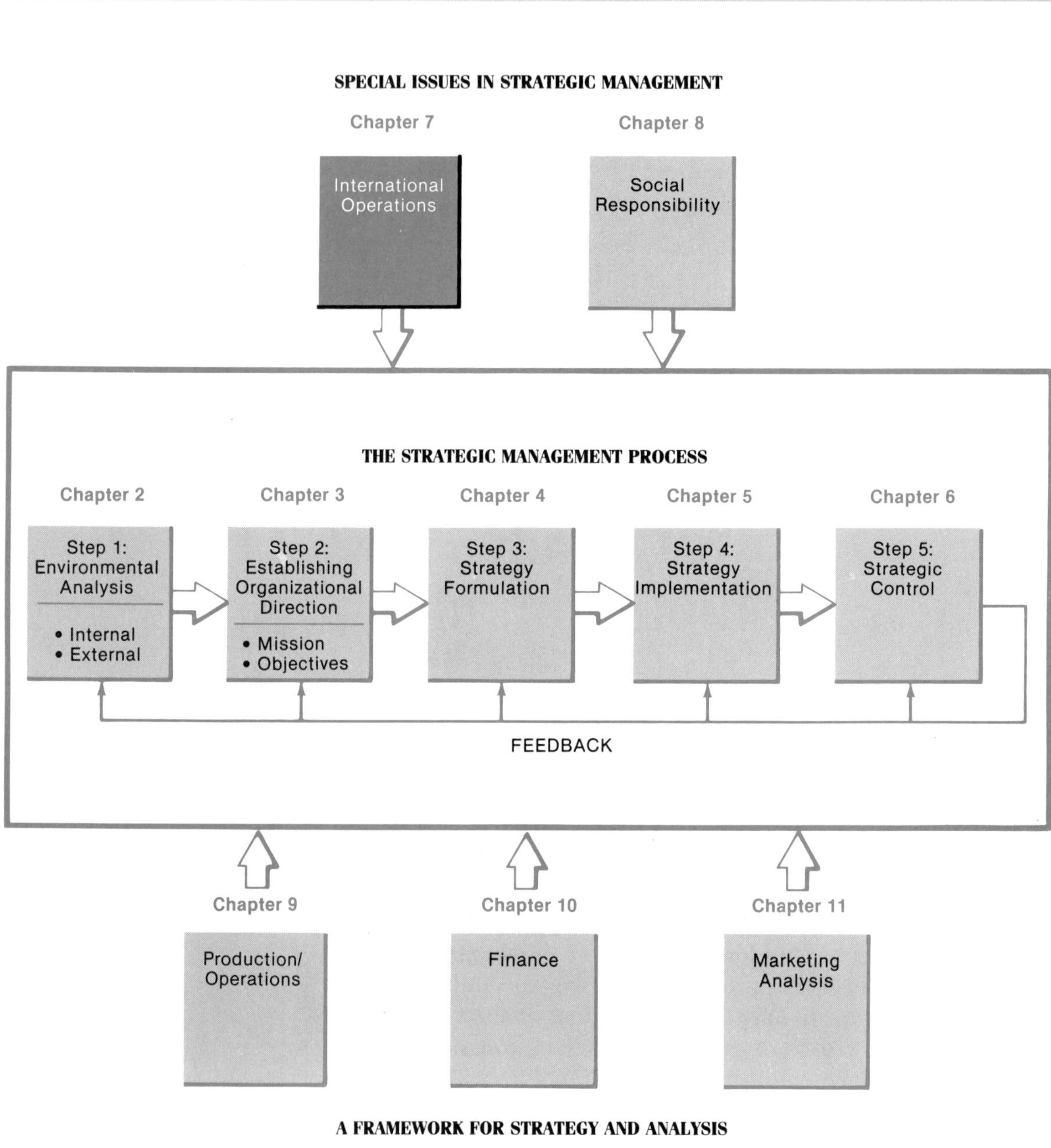

Chapter 12

An Approach to Solving Strategic Problems and Cases

CHAPTER 7

Strategic Management and International Operations

The subject of this chapter is strategic management for businesses that engage in international operations. Over the last several years, more and more businesses have become increasingly involved in the international arena. Because this trend is expected to continue, international issues will become increasingly important considerations in successfully designing and implementing organizational strategy.

This chapter is divided into two main parts. First we discuss the international business situation in general, including the complex nature of international management, the unique opportunities and risks involved in doing business internationally, and the several forms that multinational corporations can take. Then we trace the strategic management process through the five steps that have become familiar to us, noting the special considerations that managers must take into account when they perform strategic management activities in the international context.

FUNDAMENTALS OF THE INTERNATIONAL BUSINESS SITUATION

Before managers can learn how to practice strategic management successfully in the international context, they must have a thorough understanding of the basic principles of international management. We will cover these principles first by outlining the fundamentals of international management and then by discussing multinational corporations.

Fundamentals of International Management

Before we can discuss the potential impact of international operations on strategic management, we must be clear about what the term "international management" actually means. Then we will consider the potential advantages and disadvantages of conducting business internationally.

A Definition of International Management

To engage in *international management* is to perform management activities across national borders. That is, the firm accomplishes its organizational mission at least partially by conducting business activities in a foreign country. Such activities can be as simple as selling a product in a foreign country or as complicated as entering into an agreement with a foreign partner to manufacture and sell products throughout the world.

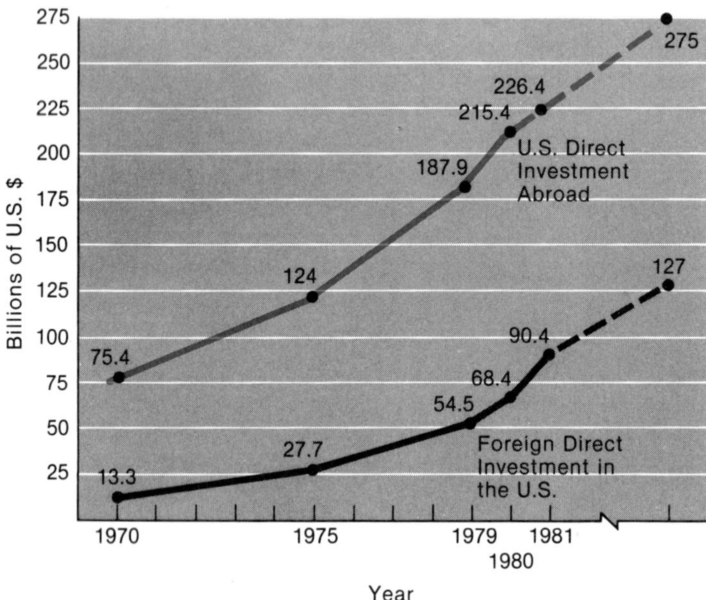

FIGURE 7.1 Growth in Foreign Investment Inside and Outside the United States *(Source: U.S. Census Bureau,* Statistical Abstracts of the United States, 1984 *[Washington, D.C.: Government Printing Office, 1985], pp. 822, 824.)*

* Author forecast given past trends.

Advances in transportation, technology, and communication have made international management more feasible, and continuing progress in these areas is expected to encourage companies to become even more involved with international business in the future. Figure 7.1 reflects this growth in international business. It shows a growing trend both in investments by the United States in foreign countries and in investments in the United States by foreign countries. Examples of foreign ownership of U.S. firms include French ownership of 46 percent of American Motors, Japanese ownership of 77 percent of the California First Bank, West German ownership of 23 percent of Clorox, Swiss ownership of 34 percent of the First Boston Bank, and United Kingdom ownership of 29 percent of Libbey-Owens-Ford.[1] The following excerpt from an Eastman Kodak quarterly performance bulletin illustrates the extent of the commitment U.S. firms can make to foreign investment:

> The company (Eastman Kodak) announced that it plans to spend $1.591 billion to expand and improve its worldwide facilities in 1986, up more than 6% from its 1985 spending level of $1.495 billion. "The objective of the capital commitment is to enhance Kodak's competitive position in the world marketplace," said Colby H. Chandler, chairman and chief executive officer.[2]

International Business: Pros and Cons

There are several potential advantages that management stands to gain by initiating, continuing, or increasing its involvement in the international sphere. For example, a firm might decide to pursue international business activities in order to achieve one or more of the following objectives:

- To *lower its operating costs relative to those of its competitors:* Management may be able to achieve lower operating costs by purchasing raw materials from foreign concerns that can offer them at lower than domestic prices or by manufacturing products in foreign factories that pay lower wages.[3] According to David C. Garfield, president of Ingersoll-Rand, a worldwide company that produces construction and mining equipment, wage rates are extremely significant in any attempt to price products competitively. Average U.S. wages for manufacturing workers approach $12 per hour, including the cost of fringe benefits, and such costs in the automobile industry are higher than $20 per hour. Comparable wages in the more industrialized European countries are about one-third less; in developing countries they may be less than $2 per hour.[4]
- *To increase its sales and profits by becoming involved in less competitive situations:* Management may find that the domestic market for its

[1] *Forbes,* July 29, 1985, pp. 180–186.
[2] *Kodak Highlights,* Fourth Quarter, 1985, p. 8.
[3] Ira C. Magaziner and Robert B. Reich, *Minding America's Business* (New York: Harcourt Brace Jovanovich, 1982), p. 82.
[4] David C. Garfield, "The International Challenge to U.S. Business," *The Journal of Business Strategy* 5, no. 4 (Spring 1985):26–29.

product is highly competitive. On the other hand, the market for its product in a foreign country might be much less competitive. In this situation, entry into a foreign market seems to hold great promise.

- *To ensure continued growth in relation to its competitors:* Management may be able to ensure company growth relative to its competition by becoming more involved in the international business arena. The advertising industry has recently seen several company mergers and acquisitions aimed at enhancing growth through the exploration of foreign markets. Since 1975, for example, the advertising firm of Foote, Cone & Belding has acquired agency interests in Europe, South America, and Asia. These acquisitions are calculated to ensure that the agency's growth will outstrip that of its competitors by offering clients a full-service, global marketing operation.[5]

There are also several potential disadvantages of becoming involved in international operations.[6] These potential disadvantages include the following:

- *Being confronted with many different political, economic, and cultural environments and with the different rates at which they are changing:* The managers of an internationally oriented company must handle many diverse environmental issues simultaneously. For example, assume that the chief executive officer of a major U.S. company has recently learned that the inflation rate within the economic environment of her Yugoslavian plant is soon expected to hit triple digits, that Swedes being hired to work in her Japanese banks are having difficulty adjusting to the Japanese culture, and that the political instability of Poland will probably prevent recently consummated deals from materializing.[7] Issues of this sort almost inevitably make the international situation much more complicated to manage than the purely domestic scene.
- *Becoming involved in a situation in which it is more difficult to keep track of competitors:* Keeping informed about competitors in two or more countries is simply harder than staying abreast of developments in a single nation. The distance between countries, the different languages spoken, and varying national attitudes exacerbate this difficulty.

  In addition, the varying presence of different communication media throughout different countries can make gathering and transmitting information more difficult in the international arena than on the purely domestic front. Table 7.1 illustrates what dramatic differences we find

[5] Janice Castro, "Heavy Duty Mergers," *Time,* May 12, 1986, pp. 72–73.

[6] Much of this section is based on W. A. Dymsza, *Multinational Business Strategy* (New York: McGraw-Hill, 1972), pp. 50–51.

[7] These examples are based on real, recently reported multinational corporation issues. See Scot J. Paltrow, "Occidental Petroleum Hasn't Always Thrived from East Bloc Deals," *The Wall Street Journal,* August 30, 1984, p. 1; Bernard Wysocki, Jr., "How Foreigners Hired by Japanese Adjust to a New Way of Life," *The Wall Street Journal,* March 24, 1986, p. 1; and Roger Thurow, "Political Drifting, An Economy in Chaos Prevails in Yugoslavia," *The Wall Street Journal,* May 8, 1986, p. 1.

TABLE 7.1 Distribution of Communication Media Throughout Several Parts of the World

	TELEPHONES PER 100 POPULATION	PIECES OF MAIL SENT (IN MILLIONS)	NEWSPAPER COPIES PER 1,000 POPULATION	RADIOS PER 1,000 POPULATION
United States	74.4	88,970	287	1,882
Western Europe				
France	32.9	11,382	214	330
Germany	37.4	12,368	312	329
Italy	28.5	3,031	113	232
Spain	26.1	3,578	98	259
Sweden	71.7	2,551	572	390
United Kingdom	41.5	8,840	388	706
Latin America				
Argentina	9.0	620	NA	838
Brazil	4.1	2,178	39	158
Colombia	5.6	119	NA	117
Ecuador	2.9	7	49	279
Mexico	5.9	1,068	NA	301
Peru	2.6	NA	NA	129
Asia				
India	0.3	7,421	16	24
Japan	42.4	12,186	526	530
Pakistan	0.3	502	NA	17
Philippines	1.3	630	NA	43
Sri Lanka	0.5	580	NA	58
Thailand	0.8	184	NA	131
Africa				
Egypt	1.4	205	21	138
Ghana	0.7	58	51	105
Madagascar	0.4	22	9	74
Nigeria	0.2	959	NA	79
South Africa	8.3	1,383	70	96
Zimbabwe	2.9	18	18	39

Source: U.S. Census Bureau, *Statistical Abstracts of the United States, 1980* (Washington, D.C.: Government Printing Office, 1981), pp. 922, 923.

in the distribution of communication media when we compare Western Europe, Latin America, Asia, and Africa with the United States.

- *Dealing with two or more monetary systems:* Dealing with two or more monetary systems, rather than just one, complicates the accounting process considerably. Such tasks as comparing the track records of operational units in different countries and transferring goods between these operational units can become very complex. Not only are different monetary units used to place a value on organizational assets and expenses, but the values of the units also change at different rates.

The Parker Hannifin Corporation is the world's leading supplier of hydraulic components and systems for the industrial, automotive, aviation, space, and marine markets. The following information from the 1984 *Parker Hannifin Corporation Annual Report* illustrates how complicated financial issues can become in multinational situations:

> The company's major foreign operations are located in West Germany, the United Kingdom, and France, and their business activities are conducted principally in their local currency. The assets and liabilities of these subsidiaries are translated at the current exchange rate at the balance sheet date. Income statement items are translated at the weighted average monthly rate. The strengthening of the U.S. dollar against these foreign currencies is reflected in the negative translation adjustments in shareholders' equity.[8]

- *Significantly increasing the political risk of doing business:* In this context, *political risk* is defined as the potential loss of control over ownership or benefits of enterprise due to action taken by a foreign government.[9] Table 7.2 lists conditions that spell political risk, groups that can generate political risk, and several possible effects of political risk on organizational operations.

  Let us look at an example of how this political risk can influence organizational operations. A small local competitor in a foreign country recently accused a Xerox subsidiary of underpricing. The Ministry of Commerce in this country responded by clamping new restrictions on Xerox and imposing tariffs on vital materials that Xerox was importing. Xerox's top officers revised the company's pricing policy, but ever since, unlike other foreign investors in that country, Xerox has had to obey special instructions on pricing. The incident convinced management that it should not have ignored the warnings of local managers who had tried to point out that the firm's pricing structure might cause political problems.[10]

Highlight 7.1 gives you an opportunity to weigh the advantages against the risks and decide whether you would have endorsed the decision of the Walt Disney Company to build its first international theme park.

Multinational Corporations

Now that we have defined international management and discussed some of the advantages and disadvantages of conducting international business, we are

[8] *Parker Hannifin Corporation Annual Report,* 1984, p. 37.

[9] Mark Fitzpatrick, "The Definition and Assessment of Political Risk in International Business: A Review of the Literature," *Academy of Management Review* 8, no. 2 (1983): 249–254.

[10] Thomas W. Shreeve, "Be Prepared for Political Changes Abroad," *Harvard Business Review,* July–August 1984, pp. 111–118.

TABLE 7.2 Political Risk and the International Business Arena

SOURCES OF POLITICAL RISK	GROUPS THROUGH WHICH POLITICAL RISK CAN BE GENERATED	POLITICAL RISK EFFECTS: TYPES OF INFLUENCE ON INTERNATIONAL BUSINESS OPERATIONS
Competing political philosophies (nationalism, socialism, communism) Social unrest and disorder Vested interests of local business groups Recent and impending political independence Armed conflicts, internal rebellions for political power, and terrorism New international alliances	Government in power and its operating agencies Parliamentary opposition groups Nonparliamentary opposition groups (e.g., anarchist or terrorist movements working from within or outside of country) Nonorganized common-interest groups: students, workers, peasants, minorities, and so forth Foreign governments or international governmental agencies such as the EEC Foreign governments willing to enter into armed conflict or to support internal rebellion	Confiscation: loss of assets without compensation Expropriation with compensation: loss of freedom to operate Operational restrictions: market shares, product characteristics, employment policies, locally shared ownership, and so forth Loss of transfer freedom: financial (e.g., dividends, interest payments), goods, personnel, or ownership rights Breaches or unilateral revisions [in] contracts and agreements Discrimination such as taxes, compulsory subcontracting Damage to property or personnel (kidnapping) from riots, insurrections, revolutions, wars, and terrorism

Source: Stefan H. Robock and Kenneth Simmons, *International Business and Multinational Enterprise,* 3rd ed. (Homewood, Ill.: Richard D. Irwin, 1983), p. 347. Reprinted by permission.

ready to focus on multinational corporations themselves: what they are and the different forms they can take.

What Are Multinational Corporations?

Having first appeared in the dictionary about 1975, the term "multinational corporation" is a relatively new word in our vocabulary. A *multinational corporation* is a company that has significant operations in more than one country. The company investing in international operations is called the *parent company;* the country in which the investment is made is called the *host country.*

Overall, the multinational corporation views itself as a whole and develops and implements a unified strategy to include all areas of international involvement. Table 7.3 lists the ten largest multinational corporations ranked by sales,

HIGHLIGHT 7.1

SKILLS MODULE ■ International Analysis at Tokyo Disneyland

INTRODUCTION

We have discussed some of the pros and cons of conducting international business. Review the following situation at Tokyo Disneyland, and then complete the skill development exercise that follows. Doing so will help you develop some skill in determining whether or not a company should become involved in international business.

THE SITUATION

Tokyo Disneyland, Disney's first international theme park, continues to prove that Disney entertainment is popular throughout the world. Mirroring the fantasy and fun of its American counterparts, the theme park, located on the fringes of Tokyo Bay, welcomed more than 10 million guests during its first year of operation. This attendance is nearly triple the number of guests who visited Disneyland during its first year of operation.

An all-time record for one-day attendance at any theme park was set at Tokyo Disneyland in 1984 when, on August 13, 111,467 guests visited the park. In addition to traditional Disneyland attractions, Tokyo Disneyland also highlights Japanese culture and tradition. Planned to be developed soon for Tokyo Disneyland are the Electric Parade, Tomorrowland Theatre, a Castle Tour, and Big Thunder Mountain Railroad.

SKILL DEVELOPMENT EXERCISE

Assume that Tokyo Disneyland has not been built and that you must decide whether or not it should be built. Your job is to outline the pros and cons of expanding into international business with a theme park in Tokyo. Be as specific as you can about the situation facing the Walt Disney Company, the organization for which you work. Given your analysis, would you have decided to build in Tokyo? If so, how would you counter the argument that genuine risks were involved?

Source: Based on *Walt Disney Productions Annual Report, 1984.*

and Table 7.4 shows how significant an impact international operations can have on company revenue, profits, and asset investments.

What Forms Do Multinational Corporations Take?

According to Neil H. Jacoby, a company would normally go through six stages on the way to its appearance on this top-ten list. These stages range from

TABLE 7.3 The Ten Largest Multinational Corporations

COMPANY	HEADQUARTERS	INDUSTRY	SALES ($000)
General Motors	Detroit	Motor vehicles and parts	96,371,700
Exxon	New York	Petroleum refining	86,673,000
Royal Dutch/Shell Group	The Hague/London	Petroleum refining	81,743,514
Mobil	New York	Petroleum refining	55,960,000
British Petroleum	London	Petroleum refining	53,100,765
Ford Motor	Dearborn, Mich.	Motor vehicles and parts	52,774,400
International Business Machines	Armonk, N.Y.	Computers, office equip.	50,056,000
Texaco	Harrison, N.Y.	Petroleum refining	46,297,000
Chevron	San Francisco	Petroleum refining	41,741,905
American Tel. & Tel.	New York	Electronics	34,909,500

Source: "The 50 Largest Industrials in the World," *Fortune,* August 4, 1986.

TABLE 7.4 Impact of Multinational Operations of Several Companies on Revenue, Profits, and Assets Owned

COMPANY	FOREIGN REVENUE AS PERCENT OF TOTAL	FOREIGN PROFIT AS PERCENT OF TOTAL PROFITS	FOREIGN ASSETS AS PERCENT OF TOTAL PROFITS
Coca Cola	38.0%	55.6%	25.3%
Exxon	69.4	55.4	43.0
Texaco	50.1	46.1	30.1
Gillette	51.8	54.0	45.5
IBM	40.4	39.4	36.1
Dow Chemical	53.6	55.3	45.9
Citicorp	49.8	51.2	53.7
Colgate Palmolive	52.3	48.1	38.4

Source: Excerpted by permission of *Forbes* magazine, July 19, 1985.

Stage I (a slightly multinationalized company that simply exports products to foreign countries) to Stage VI (a company that multinationalizes ownership of its corporate stock). Table 7.5 defines all six stages. In general, as an organization progresses from Stage I to Stage VI, the international issues its management must face become more complex and difficult to manage.

STRATEGIC MANAGEMENT AND THE INTERNATIONAL ARENA

This section explains how the strategic management process might be influenced by international issues. More specifically, it focuses on international

TABLE 7.5 Jacoby's Six Stages of Multinationalization

STAGE I	STAGE II	STAGE III	STAGE IV	STAGE V	STAGE VI
Exports its products to foreign countries	Establishes sales organizations abroad	Licenses use of its patents and know-how to foreign firms that make and sell its products	Establishes foreign manufacturing facilities	Multinationalizes management from top to bottom	Multinationalizes ownership of corporate stock

Source: Based on Neil H. Jacoby, "The Multinational Corporation," *The Center Magazine*, May 1970, pp. 37–55.

operations in terms of the main steps of the strategic management process: environmental analysis, establishing organizational direction, formulating strategy, implementing strategy, and evaluating strategy. Our remarks here are not meant to replace earlier chapters that discussed these steps of the strategic management process, but rather to supplement them.

Environmental Analysis and International Operations

In Chapter 2, "Environmental Analysis," we briefly discussed what we called the international component of the organizational environment. Here we will treat this international component in more detail by examining the complexity of international environmental analysis and various trends in the international environment.

Complexity of International Environmental Analysis

Environmental analysis, you will recall, is the process of monitoring an organizational environment to determine present and future threats and opportunities that are likely to affect organizational goal attainment. This process is generally quite complicated. It involves analyzing (1) the social, economic, technological, legal, and political components of the general environment; (2) the international, supplier, competition, customer, and labor components of the operating environment; and (3) all important components within the internal environment.

As one might expect, performing an environmental analysis for a multinational corporation is generally far more complicated than performing one for a purely domestic concern. It simply takes more time and effort to monitor the environments within which multinational corporations exist. According to Richard D. Robinson, the greater complexity of a multinational corporation's operating environment stems primarily from six factors[11]:

[11] Richard D. Robinson, *International Management* (New York: Holt, Rinehart & Winston, 1967), pp. 3–5.

1. Multinational corporations operate within different national sovereignties—that is, under different national governments.
2. Multinational corporations function under widely differing economic conditions.
3. Multinational corporations involve people with significantly different value systems within a single organization.
4. Multinational corporations operate in places that experienced the industrial revolution at different times—or may still be experiencing it.
5. Multinational corporations generally necessitate managing over great distances.
6. Multinational corporations normally conduct business in national markets that vary widely in population and area.

Figure 7.2 illustrates some of the relationships among these six factors that can lead to environmental complexity. For example, "different national sovereignties" normally generate "different legal, monetary, and political systems." In turn, each "legal system" implies a unique set of "rights and obligations" related to property, taxation, antitrust law, corporate law, and contract law. Hence the multinational corporation must acquire the skills necessary to assess such legal considerations. The purely domestic corporation does not encounter environmental complexities of this nature. But the internationally oriented organization must consider them thoroughly as part of its environmental analysis.

Trends in the International Environment

Several significant trends that are emerging in the international environment also have implications for international competition and consequently should be explored during the multinational corporation's environmental analysis. According to Michael Porter, the international environment is characterized by the following trends[12]:

- *A reduction in the differences among countries:* Differences in such areas as income, energy costs, marketing practices, and channels of distribution seem to be narrowing. The management of a multinational corporation should know whether the countries in which it does business are becoming more alike. An increasing similarity among such countries could significantly alter the potential advantages of doing business within any one of them, and organizational strategy should be adjusted accordingly.
- *More aggressive industrial policies:* Such countries as Japan, West Germany, and Taiwan have governments with very competitive orientations toward international business. The policies that such governments adopt

[12] Michael E. Porter, *Competitive Strategy* (New York: The Free Press, 1980), pp. 295–296.

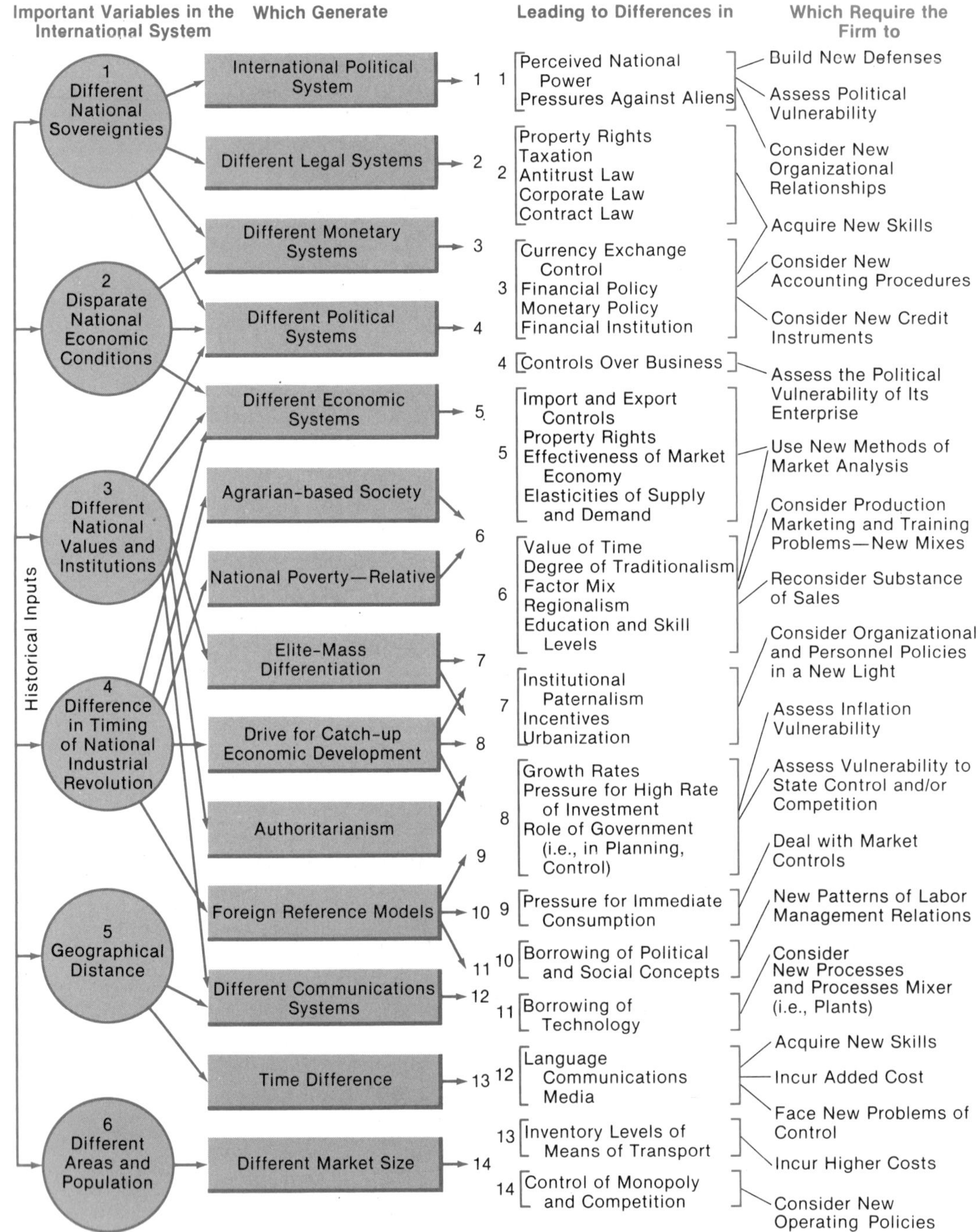

FIGURE 7.2 Six Variables and the Relationships Among Them That Contribute to Environmental Complexity for Multinational Corporations *(Source: Richard D. Robinson,* International Management *[New York: Holt, Rinehart, & Winston, 1967], pp. 4–5. Reprinted by permission.)*

in the future will probably be aimed at making the international business situation more and more competitive. Multinational corporations should monitor this trend carefully in choosing what countries to compete with.

- *Protecting distinctive assets:* More and more countries seem to be determining what unique assets they possess and using this uniqueness to best advantage. Perhaps the most obvious example is the formation of the cartel known as OPEC. Although the effectiveness of this cartel seems to vary over time, its primary purpose is clear: to protect the return generated on a scarce national resource, oil. Generally speaking, multinational corporations should carefully monitor this protectionist trend; it could influence the long-run availability and prices of distinctive assets owned by one country and used by others.
- *Freer flow of technology:* Technological improvements seem to be flowing more freely from country to country. Naturally, this increased flow of technology makes it easier for firms from other countries to upgrade their products or production processes in order to carve out a more advantageous competitive position. Environmental analysts for a multinational corporation should monitor this trend carefully to determine whether (and if so, when) its competitors may become stronger through the use of such technological advances.
- *Emerging, new, large-scale markets:* The opening up of countries such as India and Russia as possible markets establishes new, high-volume potential for successful products. One of the countries that has most recently opened for business dealings with the United States is the People's Republic of China. Eager to exploit the opportunities that such a new market might offer, several multinational corporations have entered into agreements to produce and sell goods in China. A list of these companies and the products they hope to market in China appears in Table 7.6. In line with this trend, environmental analysts for a multinational corporation should always be alert to new, emerging international markets.
- *Competition from newly developing countries:* Now more than ever before, smaller, developing countries are becoming competitors in the international arena. Consistent with this trend, environmental analysts for a multinational corporation should evaluate not only the larger, more established foreign competitors, but also the smaller, evolving countries.

Organizational Direction and International Operations

We have noted that the international environment is complex and that several significant trends need to be considered in the international firm's analysis of its environment. This section focuses on the strategic management step that follows environmental analysis: establishing direction for the organization that participates in the international arena.

Like the purely domestic organization, after carefully evaluating the results of environmental analysis, the multinational organization must chart a course

TABLE 7.6 Companies and the Products They Will Market in China

COMPANY	PRODUCT
American International Group	Insurance
American Motors Corporation	Four-wheel drive vehicles
Baker Marine Corporation	Oil rig construction and leasing
Beatrice Foods	Processed foods
Brown & Root Inc.	Offshore engineering services
Dresser Industries	Oil exploration services
Florasynth Inc.	Flavors and fragrances
Foxboro Company	Electronic process-control instruments
Gillette Company	Razor blades
Korwin Xian Hotel Company	Hotel
Parker-Hannifin Corporation	O-ring seals
R. J. Reynolds Tobacco International Inc.	Cigarettes
Seahorse Inc.	Supply vessels for South China Sea oil exploration
E. R. Squibb & Sons Inc.	Pharmaceuticals
United Technologies-Otis Elevator Div.	Elevators

Source: John D. Daniels, Jeffrey Krug, and Douglas Nigh, "U.S. Joint Ventures in China: Motivation and Management of Political Risk," *California Management Review* 27, no. 4 (Summer 1985): 47. Copyright © 1985 by the Regents of the University of California. By permission of The Regents.

consistent with its organizational mission. The type and extent of international involvement desired must be designated, because appropriate organizational goals must be established on that basis.

The SmithKline Beckman Corporation provides an example of how international emphasis can be indicated in a company's mission statement:

> SmithKline Beckman is a technology-intensive health care company. We market worldwide a broad line of prescription and proprietary products for human and animal care as well as diagnostic and analytical products and services that facilitate the detection and treatment of disease and the advancement of biomedical research.[13]

In addition, the products on the front cover of the company's 1985 Annual Report—Contac and Tagament with Japanese labels and Ecotrin with a Korean label—depict the growing importance of East Asia to the SmithKline Beckman Corporation. These materials give all organization members and stockholders an understanding that the future of this company will involve a substantial commitment to international business.

The managers of the multinational organization provide further direction for their company by developing long-term and short-term goals. Naturally, these goals reflect the type and extent of international involvement outlined in the company mission statement. Host countries often impose certain con-

[13] *SmithKline Beckman Annual Report,* 1985, p. 1.

TABLE 7.7 Sample Organizational Goals for Multinationals and Constraints That Host Countries Might Place on Their Development

TYPE OF ORGANIZATIONAL GOAL	CONSTRAINT
Ownership goal	The host country may require a major or controlling interest in multinational operations.
Employment goal	Host countries commonly demand certain management and technology positions for host country citizens.
Profit goal	Host countries normally set profits at some maximum level.
Training goal	Host countries normally set some acceptable level of training for all host country citizens who are employed.
Technology goal	Most host countries seek technology based businesses and strive to raise the technology levels of multinational organizations which exist within their borders.

Source: R. Hal Mason, "Conflicts Between Host Countries and the Multinational Enterprise," *California Management Review*, Fall 1974, pp. 5–14.

straints, however, that can affect the goals that management of a multinational corporation sets. Table 7.7 lists several categories of goals and some of the constraints that host countries commonly impose on multinational organizations in these areas.

Strategy Formulation and International Operations

Following the general model of strategic management outlined in this text, strategy developed for an organization should reflect organizational goals, which in turn reflect organizational mission, which reflects the results of environmental analysis. Appropriate strategies are actions the organization can take in order to deal successfully with competitors.

Regardless of whether the organization focuses purely on domestic operations or enters into international operations as well, the purpose of strategy is the same: dealing with competition. Over the years, numerous internationally oriented strategies have been formulated and successfully followed by many different companies. Four of the most widely used of these strategies are direct investment, license agreements, joint ventures, and importing/exporting.

Direct Investment

Direct investment is simply use of the assets of a company to acquire additional operating assets. The purchase of presently operating assets (such as existing factories and equipment) is direct investment, as is the construction of new plants and the purchase of new equipment. In the international arena, this strategy entails the purchase of operating or new assets in one country by a firm in another country.

An interesting example of this direct investment strategy involves the Kawasaki motorcycle. Two decades ago, Kawasaki motorcycles were made principally in Japan for the Japanese market. When domestic sales started to level off, management looked for other growth opportunities. In 1965 Kawasaki established a U.S.-based sales arm to encourage growth in foreign sales, and in 1974 it established the first Japanese motorcycle assembly plant in the United States. This new plant in Lincoln, Nebraska, was a sister plant to Kawasaki's Akashi, Japan, plant. In recent years, Kawasaki's U.S. production has accounted for about one-third of its global output.[14]

License Agreements

A *license agreement* is a right granted by one company to another to use its brand name, product specifications, and the like in the sale of goods or services. The purchaser of the license hopes to profit from sale of the products being sold, whereas the seller of the license profits from the fee charged for the license itself. At the international level, the purchaser and the seller of a license are from different countries, or the purchaser of the products will sell them in a different country from the one where it bought them.

One good example of an organization aggressively pursuing license agreements is Hoffmann-LaRoche, a multinational pharmaceutical company. Historically, this company depended mainly on internal research and development to generate new products. In 1971, however, a small, three-member license team was organized. Its purpose? To scan international markets for new pharmaceutical compounds that would be available to market through the purchase of license agreements. Since its creation, this license team has acquired a number of products that it is conservatively estimated will account for sales of more than $50 million over the next few years.[15]

Joint Ventures

A *joint venture* is a partnership formed between two companies for the purpose of pursuing some mutually desirable business venture. International joint ventures involve companies from different countries.

Since 1979 when the People's Republic of China approved the Law on Joint Ventures Using Chinese and Foreign Investment, many U.S. firms have established joint ventures with Chinese organizations. The Gillette Company and the R. J. Reynolds Tobacco Company are prominent names among them. U.S. companies that become party to such joint ventures enjoy the advantage of reduced transportation costs in getting U.S. products to the Chinese market.

[14] David C. Shanks, "Strategic Planning for Global Competition," *The Journal of Business Strategy* 5, no. 3 (Winter 1985): 80–89.

[15] Robert Ronstadt and Robert J. Kramer, "Internationalizing Industrial Innovation," *The Journal of Business Strategy* 3, no. 3 (Winter 1983): 3–15.

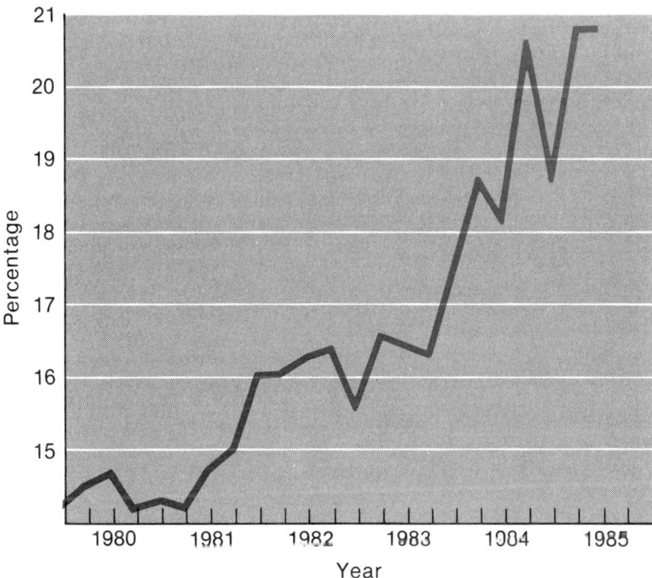

FIGURE 7.3 Imports' Share of the U.S. Market for Industrial Goods *(Source:* Fortune, *August 19, 1985, p. 29. Copyright © 1985 Time Inc. All rights reserved.)*

The Chinese companies gain access to U.S. technology and an opportunity to "position themselves" for eventually entering the potentially profitable U.S. market.[16]

Importing/Exporting

Importing is buying goods or services produced in a foreign country; *exporting* is selling goods or services to customers in a foreign country. Companies of virtually all sizes are involved in both importing and exporting today. People's Car Company, which consists mainly of two individuals, imports the hard-to-find Volkswagen "beetle" from Mexico to be resold to American automobile dealers.[17] At the other end of the scale, very large organizations like General Motors export certain carefully chosen products for sale in other countries.

Many U.S. firms are concerned with the rising impact that foreign goods are having in the domestic market. As Figure 7.3 implies, from 1980 to 1985 the impact of imports on the U.S. market for industrial goods was significant.

One strategy has been suggested, however, that can help U.S. firms compete with imports.[18] Firms can counter foreign competitors by penetrating *their*

[16] John D. Daniels, Jeffrey Krun, and Douglas Nigh, "U.S. Joint Ventures in China: Motivation and Management of Political Risk," *California Management Review* 27, no. 4 (Summer 1985): 46–58.

[17] "The Bug Comes Back," *Newsweek,* April 4, 1983, p. 60.

[18] Ellen C. Fingerhut and Daryl G. Hatano, "Principles of Strategic Planning Applied to International Corporations," *Managerial Planning,* September–October 1985, pp. 4–14.

domestic markets before they have an opportunity to attempt penetration of the U.S. market. This action should sap the foreign firm's cash flow and other resources necessary for its entry into the U.S. market. For example, IBM's 25 percent share of the Japanese mainframe computer market has drained Fujitsu's and Hitachi's resources in this way, making it impossible for them to invade the U.S. marketplace.[19]

Highlight 7.2 gives you a chance to apply what you have learned about international strategy to counter a threat felt by a major U.S. firm from a foreign competitor.

Strategy Implementation and International Operations

After conducting an environmental analysis, establishing the organization's direction, and devoting careful attention to formulating strategy, managers involved in the international arena must implement the strategy they have devised.

Implementing an internationally based strategy is generally considered a much greater challenge than implementing a purely domestic strategy. The domestic operations of a typical U.S. multinational corporation are normally organized differently from its foreign operations. As a result, in order to be successful in implementing an internationally oriented organizational strategy, management must understand the way *both* domestic and foreign organizational segments operate and respond to them appropriately. Table 7.8 summarizes several general elements of company operations and suggests how they might differ between U.S. and foreign operations. Naturally, each of these differences has implications for the manner in which strategy might best be implemented.

As another example, compare our ways of carrying out management functions in the Western world with those prevalent in the Middle East. Dramatic differences exist in how organizations are designed, how decisions are made, how performance is evaluated and controlled, how policies are developed and used, how organizations are led, how communication takes place, and what management methods are applied. (Table 7.9 characterizes these differences in more detail.) Successfully implementing an internationally oriented strategy that sought to combine a Western organization with a Middle Eastern organization would be a difficult task.

Strategy Evaluation and the International Arena

The evaluation of internationally based strategy follows its implementation. The strategy must be evaluated to determine whether it has been effective, given organizational conditions. Comparing this effectiveness to some predetermined standard and making changes if necessary are part of managerial control.

The financial standards used to establish the appropriateness of perfor-

[19] Craig M. Watson, "Counter Competition Abroad to Protect Home Markets," *Harvard Business Review* 60, no. 1 (January–February 1982): 41.

HIGHLIGHT 7.2

SKILLS MODULE ■ International Strategy at Briggs & Stratton

INTRODUCTION

We have discussed various kinds of organizational strategies that can be developed for the international arena. Review the following situation at Briggs & Stratton, and then complete the skill development exercise that follows. Doing so will help you develop some ability in formulating strategy that focuses on international issues.

THE SITUATION

For over a quarter of a century now, the Wisconsin-based Briggs & Stratton Corporation has enjoyed a General Motors-like domination of the 12-million-unit U.S. small-engine market. These are the engines that power lawn mowers, garden tractors, and snow blowers. Briggs & Stratton is a dominant force not only in the United States but in the rest of the world as well.

Today, however, Briggs & Stratton is a company "on the run." And it is running not from traditional competitors but from the Japanese. As the market for motorcycles peaked in the early 1980s, Honda in particular concluded that small engines offered a logical extension to its business. As a result, Honda has gone after Briggs & Stratton markets in a big way. It has been reported that in 1984, Honda spent $12.5 million to advertise its lawn and garden equipment. Industry analysts contend that this is 20 percent of the industry's total advertising budget, though Honda now has only 2 percent of the sales in that market.

According to Fred Stratton, grandson of one of the company's cofounders, there is no Japanese home market for lawn mowers. Stratton feels sure that Honda is aiming right at his company.

SKILL DEVELOPMENT EXERCISE

You are Fred Stratton. What strategy or strategies would you use to fight Honda? Be sure to explain why you chose this plan of attack.

Source: Based on James Cook, "We Are the Target," *Forbes,* April 7, 1986, pp. 54–56.

mance at the international level are commonly used at the domestic level as well. The financial standard often mentioned by businesspeople as the most important financial measurement used to evaluate the performance of foreign operations is return on investment (ROI).[20]

[20] J. D. Daniels, E. W. Ogram, Jr., and L. H. Radenbaugh, *International Business: Environments and Operations,* 3rd ed. (Reading, Mass.: Addison-Wesley, 1982), p. 552.

TABLE 7.8 Major Operational Factors and How They Differ in U.S. Versus International Operations

FACTOR	U.S. OPERATIONS	INTERNATIONAL OPERATIONS
Language	English used almost universally.	Local language must be used in many situations.
Culture	Relatively homogeneous.	Quite diverse, both between countries and within a country.
Politics	Stable and relatively unimportant.	Often volatile and of decisive importance.
Economy	Relatively uniform.	Wide variations among countries and between regions within countries.
Government interference	Minimal and reasonably predictable.	Extensive and subject to rapid change.
Labor	Skilled labor available.	Skilled labor often scarce, requiring training or redesign of production methods.
Financing	Well-developed financial markets.	Poorly developed financial markets. Capital flows subject to government control.
Market research	Data easy to collect.	Data difficult and expensive to collect.
Advertising	Many media available; few restrictions.	Media limited; many restrictions; low literacy rates rule out print media in some countries.
Money	U.S. dollar used universally.	Must change from one currency to another; changing exchange rates and government restrictions are problems.
Transportation/communication	Among the best in the world.	Often inadequate.
Control	Always a problem. Centralized control will work.	A worse problem. Centralized control won't work. Must walk a tightrope between overcentralizing and losing control through too much decentralizing.
Contracts	Once signed, are binding on both parties, even if one party makes a bad deal.	Can be voided and renegotiated if one party becomes dissatisfied.
Labor relations	Collective bargaining; can lay off workers easily.	Often cannot lay off workers; may have mandatory worker participation in management; workers may seek change through political process rather than collective bargaining.
Trade barriers	Nonexistent.	Extensive and very important.

Source: R. C. Murdick, R. H. Eckhouse, and T. W. Zimmerer, *Business Policy: A Framework for Analysis.*

TABLE 7.9 Differences in Carrying Out Management Functions in the Mideast Versus the West

MANAGERIAL FUNCTION	MIDEASTERN	WESTERN
Organizational design	Highly bureaucratic, over-centralized with power and authority at the top. Vague relationships. Ambigious and unpredictable organization environments.	Less bureaucratic, more delegation of authority. Relatively decentralized structure.
Patterns of decision making	Ad hoc planning, decisions made at the highest level of management. Unwillingness to take high risk inherent in decision making.	Sophisticated planning techniques, modern tools of decision making, elaborate management information systems.
Performance evaluation and control	Informal control mechanisms, routine checks on performance. Lack of vigorous performance evaluation systems.	Fairly advanced control systems focusing on cost reduction and organizational effectiveness.
Manpower policies	Heavy reliance on personal contacts and getting individuals from the "right social origin" to fill major positions.	Sound personnel management policies. Candidates' qualifications are usually the basis for selection decisions.
Leadership	Highly authoritarian tone, rigid instructions. Too many management directives.	Less emphasis on leader's personality, considerable weight on leader's style and performance.
Communication	The tone depends on the communication. Social position, power, and family influence are ever-present factors. Chain of command must be followed rigidly. People relate to each other rightly and specifically. Friendships are intense and binding.	Stress usually on equality and a minimization of differences. People relate to each other loosely and generally. Friendships are not intense and binding.
Management methods	Generally old and outdated.	Generally modern and more scientific.

Source: M. K. Badawy, "Styles of Mideastern Management," *California Management Review* 22, no. 2 (1980): 57.

Applying such financial measurements, however, is complicated when one is evaluating performance for operations in different countries. Having to take into account different currencies, different rates of inflation, and different tax laws contributes to this complexity. In the final analysis, comparing operations in different countries in terms of their financial performance is very difficult and commonly becomes somewhat subjective.

SUMMARY

This chapter focuses on strategic management for organizations that are involved in international business. International management is defined as performing management functions across national borders. The trend toward businesses becoming more involved in the international arena is on the upswing because of such potential advantages as lower operating costs, increased sales and profits, and continued growth. The drawbacks of international involvement include operating in many different environments, having difficulty keeping track of competitors, coping with different monetary systems, and exposing oneself to the risk of political interference or upheaval.

Multinational corporations (companies with significant operations in more than one country) face special problems during the strategic management process. Such factors as different national sovereignties (governments) and different national values make environmental analysis for such organizations very complex. In addition, environmental trends on an international scale (such as a reduction in the differences between countries) must be monitored very closely during the environmental analysis process. The multinational corporation must establish international as well as domestic direction through organizational mission statements and organizational goals. The special organizational strategies that have been formulated for multinational corporations include direct investment, license agreements, joint ventures, and importing/exporting. But because domestic and foreign units commonly operate differently, implementing such strategies for multinational corporations presents formidable challenges. In evaluating strategy, the management of multinational corporations must set standards and ensure that the strategy implemented meets them. Here too, however, different (and often unstable) monetary systems and tax laws can make this evaluation process very complex and somewhat subjective.

Highlight 7.3 contains a summary checklist of questions based on this chapter. Use it in analyzing strategic management problems and cases that revolve around international operations issues.

ADDITIONAL READINGS

Cheape, Charles W. *Family Firm to Modern Multinational Company: A New England Enterprise.* Boston: Harvard University Press, 1985.

HIGHLIGHT 7.3

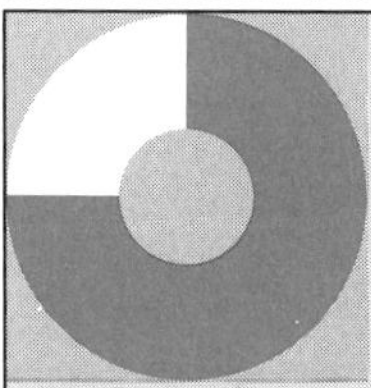

CHECKLIST ■ Analyzing International Operations in Problems and Cases

- ☐ 1. Does the problem or case involve international management issues?
- ☐ 2. Does the problem or case involve a multinational corporation?
- ☐ 3. After considering both the advantages and the disadvantages of pursuing international activities, do you think the company should be involved in the international arena?
- ☐ 4. Does the form of the multinational corporation being considered seem appropriate for the situation?
- ☐ 5. Have managers responsible for the international operations of the organization adequately considered environmental trends on the international scene and acknowledged the complexity of operating in the international environment?
- ☐ 6. Is there evidence that the organizational mission provides clear direction regarding international involvement?
- ☐ 7. Do organizational goals adequately focus on international operations and reflect organizational mission?
- ☐ 8. Does the strategy formulation process within the organization adequately reflect international issues?
- ☐ 9. Are international issues within the problem or case appropriately considered in the course of strategy implementation?
- ☐ 10. Does the strategy evaluation process take international issues into account?

Daniels, John D., Robert Pitts, and Marietta J. Tretter. "Strategy and Structure of U.S. Multinationals: An Exploratory Study." *The Academy of Management Journal* 27, no. 2 (1984): 292–307.

Doz, Yves L. "Strategic Management in Multinational Companies." *Sloan Management Review,* Winter 1980, pp. 27–44.

Lewis, James. *Excellent Organizations: How to Develop and Manage Them Using Theory Z.* Westbury, N.Y.: Wilkerson Publishing Company, 1985.

Mills, Daniel Quinn. *New Competitors: A Report on American Managers.* New York: John Wiley & Sons, 1985.

Popoff, Frank P. "Planning the Multinational's Future." *Business Horizons,* March–April 1984, pp. 64–68.

Rowe, Alan J. *Strategic Management: A Methodological Approach.* Reading, Mass.: Addison-Wesley, 1985.

Thurow, Lester (ed.). *Management Challenge: Japanese Views.* Boston: MIT Press, 1985.

Wheelwright, Steven C. "Restoring the Competitive Edge in U.S. Manufacturing." *California Management Review,* Spring 1985, pp. 26–41.

HIGHLIGHT 7.4 ■ APPLICATION OF CHAPTER MATERIAL

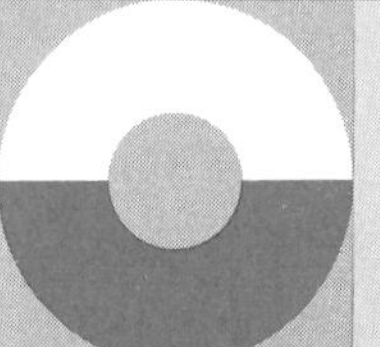

Small World Greetings Fights the Taiwanese

Fast-talking Alan Levenson, founder of Los Angeles' $23 million (1985 sales) Small World Greetings, couldn't care less where the dollar is headed. "My strategy," says Levenson, "is to get in, do my game, perfect it, then walk away after I've had my 18 months."

Levenson's Small World, privately owned by him and his brother Edward and childhood friend Jack Shaw, grinds out vinyl gift and stationery items ranging from checkbook covers, briefcases and scratch pads to wall clocks and personal organizers, all of which retail below $40.

This is the sort of stuff that flows from Asian factories by the boatload. Yet Levenson makes almost all of his products in his factory in central Los Angeles. He can't cut vinyl cheaper than the Taiwanese, but he can do it faster and with more variety. That, in the faddish gift business, is his edge.

"You take checkbook covers," Levenson says. "You go to Taiwan, you're committing to 5,000 red [covers], 'cause that's all they'll do as a minimum run of red. I have 48 different colors in the line. We're trying to make to order. So if we can just keep 100 [of each item] on the shelves, we keep our inventories down and we can price better."

To help keep prices low, Levenson's factory taps the pool of cheap labor in East Los Angeles' barrios, where he can hire a set of nimble hands for $35 a day. But Levenson's real point is that the gift game is jungle war. He looks for one big product line a year. He mass-produces and moves it, then gets out before the fad fades. In 1981 and 1982 it was personalized night-lights for kids, then children's sticker books. At the moment it's organizers, vinyl wall clocks and a line of fashionably colored mock-suede briefcases and accessories aimed at working women. These three items will account for 70% of revenues this year, which Levenson estimates will top $33 million. Profits? He hopes at least $2 million.

Levenson says he can bring an item to market in three months, compared with 18 or 24 months for his major U.S. competitors, Hallmark and American Greetings. "They're knocking off last year's hits," he scoffs. "By the time they're big in vinyl clocks, we'll be into 20 new things."

We are not talking high concept here. Levenson's notepads and gift cards are adorned with cutesie cartoon Scottie dogs, penguins, bears and elephants. Hearts are big. No royalty payments for these. Levenson doesn't try to start trends: He waits for a trend to start, then jumps aboard with a better, or cheaper, product.

Take those organizers, the purse-size binders that young career women [and, to a lesser extent, men] are convinced will add hours to their productive time. Levenson's competitors retail their organizers at anywhere from $40 to $100 and more. Small World's vinyl-bound organizers go for $25 and are easy to figure out. His competitors' organizers, he says, "were either too basic, or you needed a Ph.D. to figure them out."

Organizers have something else going for them: the refills. Levenson has designed a store display offering 104 refill inserts in seven categories, including health and fitness, gourmet, household and financial. Concept: Customers can design organizers around their own lifestyles. "The Taiwanese wouldn't understand 90% of the inserts," Levenson says, "but you would because they're geared to you."

Moving swiftly and surely through the gift fads has bought Levenson, still only 38, a Southern California life only *Lifestyles of the Rich and Famous* could fully appreciate. He started Small World in 1969 with a $3,600 loan from his father, Sol, a Santa Monica jeweler. His entire line consisted of 12 greeting cards based on black and white photos of smiling children. He moved up to posters, which students loved, and followed the students out of school with boxed stationery. In the mid-1970s he started cutting vinyl checkbook covers and address books decorated with pen-and-ink drawings of animals.

Today Levenson lives in a 35-room Tudor mansion in South Pasadena, built in the 1920s. There is a lot of 18th- and 19th-century French furniture and a couple of 18th-century English paintings. He owns six cars, including a 1964 Rolls-Royce Flying Spur he says was once owned by Joseph Kennedy, Sr. But he's not a total sybarite. Levenson is a generous supporter of the Make-A-Wish Foundation, which grants the final wishes of terminally ill children.

After organizers, what? Levenson doesn't know. Mirrors, maybe, or beveled glass items. The product doesn't matter. The mindset does. Levenson's parting advice: "We try to take the obvious and make it better. Briefcases? I brought briefcases out of the dungeon and boutiqued them. Clocks? They told me wall clocks were dead. I'm going to sell a million this year."

DISCUSSION QUESTIONS

1. How has Alan Levenson beaten his foreign competition, the Taiwanese?
2. What strategy should the Taiwanese use to better compete with

(Continues)

Small World Greetings? Are the Taiwanese positioned to better compete with Hallmark and American Greetings? Explain.

3. From what you can tell, in which of the six stages of multinationalization does Small World Greetings presently exist (see Table 7.5)? Explain. In which stage is the Taiwanese company? Explain.

Source: Marc Beauchamp, "Cut Vinyl," *Forbes,* March 24, 1986, p. 88. Reprinted by permission of *Forbes* magazine.

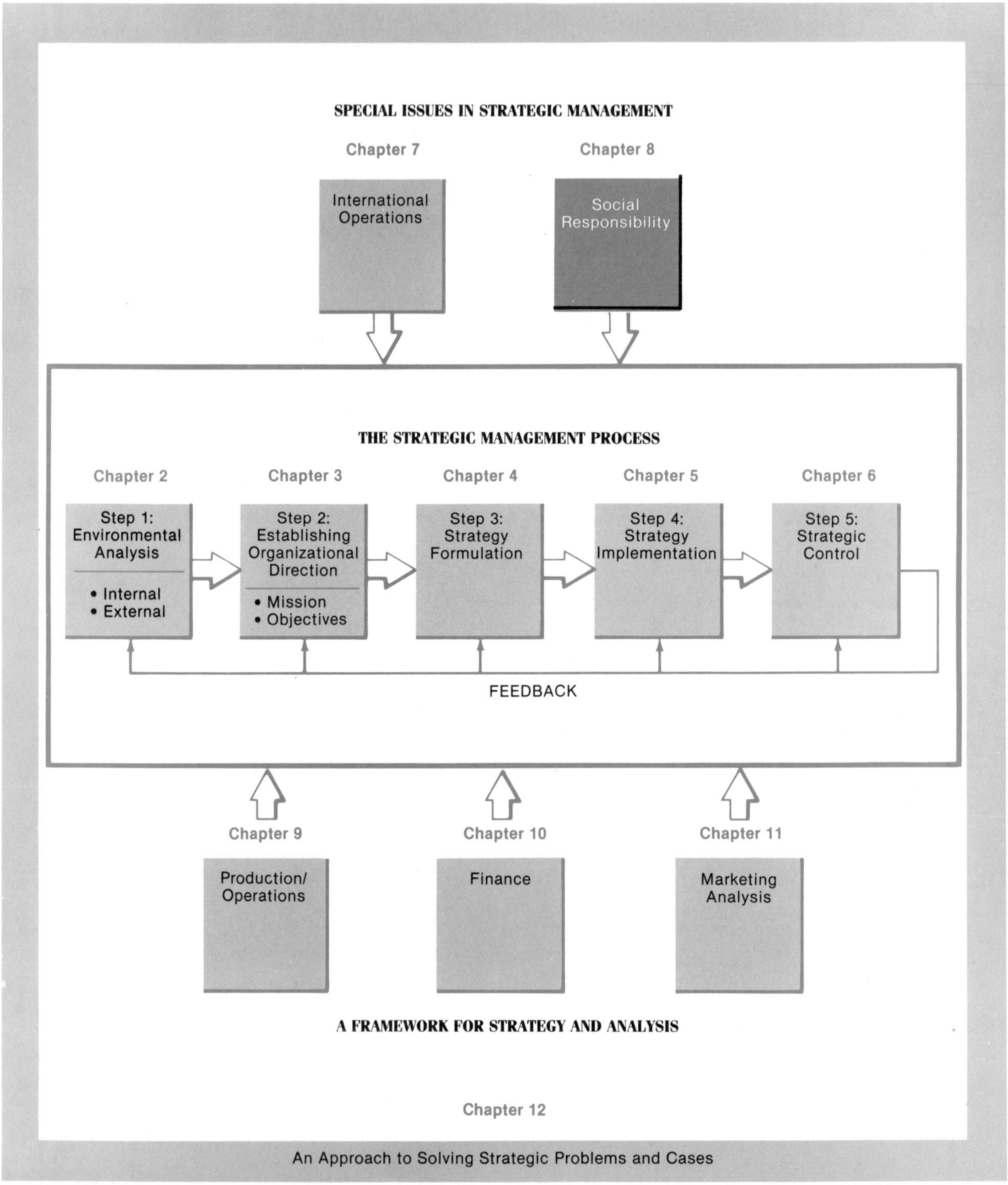

SPECIAL ISSUES IN STRATEGIC MANAGEMENT

Chapter 7

International Operations

Chapter 8

Social Responsibility

THE STRATEGIC MANAGEMENT PROCESS

Chapter 2

Step 1: Environmental Analysis

- Internal
- External

Chapter 3

Step 2: Establishing Organizational Direction

- Mission
- Objectives

Chapter 4

Step 3: Strategy Formulation

Chapter 5

Step 4: Strategy Implementation

Chapter 6

Step 5: Strategic Control

FEEDBACK

Chapter 9

Production/ Operations

Chapter 10

Finance

Chapter 11

Marketing Analysis

A FRAMEWORK FOR STRATEGY AND ANALYSIS

Chapter 12

An Approach to Solving Strategic Problems and Cases

CHAPTER 8

Strategic Management: Social and Ethical Dimensions

The stakeholders of an organization are individuals or groups who have a stake in the consequences of management decisions and can influence those decisions. The managers of successful corporations have obligations to many different stakeholders.[1] For example, they are responsible to:

- The *stockholders* or *owners* of the corporation to attempt to increase the value of the firm
- The *suppliers* of materials and *resellers* of products to deal fairly with them
- *Lenders* of capital to repay them
- *Government agencies* and society to abide by laws
- *Political groups* to consider their arguments
- *Employees* and *unions* to provide safe work environments and recognize their rights
- *Consumers* to provide safe products and market them efficiently
- *Competitors* to avoid practices that restrain trade
- The *local community* and *society at large* to avoid practices that harm the environment

[1] Portions of this chapter are based on Samuel C. Certo, *Principles of Modern Management*, 4th ed. (Boston: Allyn & Bacon, 1989), chap. 19; and J. Paul Peter and Jerry C. Olson, *Consumer Behavior and Marketing Strategy*, 2nd ed. (Homewood, Ill.: Richard D. Irwin, 1990), chapter 20.

Some analysts argue that one or the other of these obligations is most important, but we believe all of them must be considered. The reason is that successful business firms are powerful forces in society, and because of their power they incur certain responsibilities. For example, consider the rights of businesses (sellers) relative to consumers[2]:

1. Sellers have the right to introduce any product in any size, style, color, or shape so long as it meets minimum requirements of health and safety.
2. Sellers have the right to price the product as they please so long as they avoid certain discriminatory forms of pricing that undermine competition.
3. Sellers have the right to promote the product using any amount of resources, any media, and any message so long as no deception or fraud is involved.
4. Sellers have the right to introduce any buying schemes they wish so long as these are not discriminatory.
5. Sellers have the right to alter product offerings at any time.
6. Sellers have the right to distribute products in any reasonable manner.
7. Sellers have the right to limit product guarantees or post-sale services that they offer.

Although this list is not exhaustive, it does serve to illustrate that businesses have a good deal of power. Consumers, on the other hand, are generally accorded four basic rights: the right to safety, the right to be informed, the right to choose, and the right to be heard. However, these rights depend on the ability and willingness of consumers to be highly involved in purchases, and many consumers are neither able nor willing to become so involved. For example, young children, a number of the elderly, and many uneducated consumers lack the experience or cognitive capacity to process information well enough to protect themselves.

In this chapter we investigate the responsibility of business to society. In the first part of the chapter, we review arguments against and arguments in favor of business performing activities undertaken to discharge social responsibility. Then we discuss a number of specific areas in which questions about social responsibility are raised and investigate four influences on the social responsibility of business: legal, political, competitive, and ethical influences. Finally, we suggest a model for analyzing social responsibility issues from a strategic management viewpoint.

THE SOCIAL RESPONSIBILITY DEBATE

Consensus has not been reached on the precise meaning of social responsibility or on the degree to which businesses have obligations to society. However, for

[2] Philip Kotler, "What Consumerism Means for Marketers," *Harvard Business Review*, May–June 1972, pp. 48–57.

the purposes of this text, we define *social responsibility* as the degree to which managers of an organization perform activities that protect and improve society beyond the extent required to serve the direct economic and technical interests of the organization. In other words, exhibiting corporate social responsibility involves performing activities that may help society even if they do not directly contribute to the firm's profits.

A major debate rages in the strategic management literature over whether firms should be involved in activities undertaken primarily to live up to social responsibilities. In short, the classical view is that businesses should not be involved, whereas the contemporary view is that they often should. We shall discuss and compare these two views.

The Classical View

The classical view holds that businesses should not assume any social responsibility beyond making as much money as possible for the owners of the firm. The managers of organizations are the employees of the stockholders, the argument runs, and have obligations only to them. The noted economist Milton Friedman, a proponent of this view, argues that

> there is one and only one social responsibility of business—to use its resources and engage in activities designed to increase its profits so long as it stays within the rules of the game, which is to say, engages in open and free competition, without deception or fraud. . . . Few trends could so thoroughly undermine the very foundations of our free society as the acceptance by corporate officials of a social responsibility other than to make as much money for their stockholders as possible. This is a fundamentally subversive doctrine.[3]

Thus, in the classical view, the role of managers is to produce and market goods efficiently—that is, in such a way that owners of the firm receive the greatest economic profits. Performing other social responsibility activities is seen as disturbing fundamental economic relationships.

The Contemporary View

The contemporary view is that businesses, as important and influential members of society, are responsible to help maintain and improve the society's overall welfare. A strong advocate of corporate social responsibility, Keith Davis, has elaborated on this view.[4] It can be summarized in terms of the following five propositions:

[3] Milton Friedman, *Capitalism and Freedom* (Chicago, Ill.: University of Chicago Press, 1962), p. 133, as reported in George A. Steiner and John F. Steiner, *Business, Government, and Society* (New York: Random House, Inc., 1985), p. 236.

[4] Keith Davis, "Five Propositions for Social Responsibility," *Business Horizons,* June 1975, pp. 19–24. Also see Peter F. Drucker, "The New Meaning of Corporate Social Responsibility," *California Management Review,* Winter 1984, pp. 53–63; Jerry W. Anderson, "Social Responsibility and the Corporation," *Business Horizons,* July–August 1986, pp. 22–27; and Jean B. McGuire, Alison Sundgren, and Thomas Schneeweis, "Corporate Social Responsibility and Firm Financial Performance," *Academy of Management Journal* 31 (December 1988): 854–872.

- *Proposition 1: Social responsibility arises from social power.* This proposition is built on the premise that business has a significant amount of influence or power over such critical social issues as minority employment and environmental pollution. In essence, the collective action of all businesses determines the proportion of minorities employed and the prevailing condition of the environment. Thus, because business has power over society, society can and must hold business responsible for social conditions affected by the use of this power.
- *Proposition 2: Business shall operate as a two-way open system with open receipt of inputs from society and open disclosure of its operations to the public.* Business must be willing to listen to societal representatives concerning what must be done to improve societal welfare. Davis suggests that continuing, honest, and open communications between business and societal representatives must exist if the overall welfare of society is to be maintained or improved.
- *Proposition 3: Both the social costs and the social benefits of an activity, product, or service shall be thoroughly calculated and considered in order to decide whether or not to proceed with it.* Technical feasibility and economic profitability are not the only factors that should influence business decision making. Business should also consider both the long- and short-term societal consequences of all business activities before such activities are undertaken.
- *Proposition 4: Social costs related to each activity, product, or service shall be passed on to the consumer.* Business cannot be expected to finance all activities that are economically disadvantageous but socially advantageous. The cost of maintaining socially desirable activities within business should be passed on to consumers through higher prices for the goods or services that are directly related to those socially desirable activities.
- *Proposition 5: As citizens, business institutions have the responsibility to become involved in certain social problems that are outside their normal areas of operation.* If a business possesses the expertise to solve a social problem with which it may not be directly associated, it should be held responsible for helping society solve the problem. Business will eventually receive increased profits from a generally improved society, so business should share in the responsibility of all citizens to improve that society.

Table 8.1 summarizes the major arguments for, and those against, businesses exhibiting social responsibility.

Comparison of the Two Views

The classical view conceives of businesses as economic entities, whereas the contemporary view conceives of businesses as members of society. Although business organizations clearly are both, recognizing this does not always answer the question of how involved companies should be in social responsi-

TABLE 8.1 Summary of Major Arguments For and Against Business Social Responsibility

FOR SOCIAL RESPONSIBILITY

1. It is in the best interest of the business to promote and improve the communities where it does business.
2. Social actions can be profitable.
3. It is the ethical thing to do.
4. It improves the public image of the firm.
5. It increases the viability of the business system. Business exists because it gives society benefits. Society can amend or take away its charter. This is the "iron law of responsibility."
6. It is necessary to avoid government regulation.
7. Sociocultural norms require it.
8. Laws cannot be passed for all circumstances. Thus, business must assume responsibility to maintain an orderly legal society.
9. It is in the stockholders' best interest. It will improve the price of stock in the long run because the stock market will view the company as less risky and open to public attack and therefore award it a higher price–earnings ratio.
10. Society should give business a chance to solve social problems that government has failed to solve.
11. Business, by some groups, is considered to be the institution with the financial and human resources to solve social problems.
12. Prevention of problems is better than cures—so let business solve problems before they become too great.

AGAINST SOCIAL RESPONSIBILITY

1. It might be illegal.
2. Business plus government equals monolith.
3. Social actions cannot be measured.
4. It violates profit maximization.
5. Cost of social responsibility is too great and would increase prices too much.
6. Business lacks social skills to solve societal problems.
7. It would dilute business's primary purposes.
8. It would weaken U.S. balance of payments because price of goods will have to go up to pay for social programs.
9. Business already has too much power. Such involvement would make business too powerful.
10. Business lacks accountability to the public. Thus, the public would have no control over its social involvement.
11. Such business involvement lacks broad public support.

Source: R. Joseph Mansen, Jr., "The Social Attitudes of Management," in Joseph W. McQuire, ed., *Contemporary Management* (Englewood Cliffs, N.J.: Prentice-Hall, 1974), p. 616. Reprinted by permission of the author.

TABLE 8.2 Areas of Social Responsibility Concern

CONCERN FOR CONSUMERS

1. Are products safe and well designed?
2. Are products priced fairly?
3. Are advertisements clear and not deceptive?
4. Are customers treated fairly by salespeople?
5. Are credit terms clear?
6. Is adequate product information available?

CONCERN FOR EMPLOYEES

1. Are employees paid a fair wage?
2. Are employees provided a safe work environment?
3. Are workers hired, promoted, and treated fairly without regard to sex, race, color, or creed?
4. Are employees given special training and educational opportunities?
5. Are handicapped people given employment opportunities?
6. Does the business help rehabilitate employees with physical, mental, or emotional problems?

CONCERN FOR THE ENVIRONMENT

1. Is the environment adequately protected from unclean air and water, excessive noise, and other types of pollution?
2. Are products and packages biodegradable or recyclable?
3. Are any by-products that pose a safety hazard to society (such as nuclear waste or commercial solvents) carefully handled and properly treated or disposed of?

CONCERN FOR SOCIETY IN GENERAL

1. Does the firm support minority and community enterprises by purchasing from them or subcontracting to them?
2. Are donations made to help develop and support education, art, health, and community development programs?
3. Is the social impact of plant locations or relocations considered by the managers who make those decisions?
4. Is appropriate information concerning business operations made public?

bility activities. In many cases, however, both views lead to the same conclusion about whether a firm should engage in a particular activity of this nature. For example, when the activity is required by law, both approaches support engaging in it. And in situations in which it is profitable, both approaches support engaging in the activity.

It is only in situations in which the social responsibility activity (1) is not required by law *and* (2) is not profitable that the two views diverge. Here the classical view would argue against performing the activity, but the contemporary view would argue in favor of performing the activity if the costs were not too great.

Overall, the degree to which a firm should seek to advance societal versus economic objectives depends on many factors, including the size of the firm, its ability to invest in social responsibility programs, the competitiveness of the industry, and the consequences of forgoing or engaging in the activity. Furthermore, these decisions depend on the specific problem and kind of social responsibility involved.

SPECIFIC AREAS OF SOCIAL RESPONSIBILITY

Questions have been raised about the social responsibility of business in many areas. Table 8.2 presents four of the more commonly discussed areas of concern and several specific questions related to each. As you review these questions, keep two points in mind.

First, business firms are considered socially responsible entities to the degree that they *voluntarily* act to maintain or increase societal welfare rather than being forced to do so by government regulations. For example, voluntarily removing products from the market when tampering is suspected, rather than being forced to do so, is considered socially responsible behavior.

Second, precise standards for determining whether a business is acting in a socially responsible manner seldom exist. In some cases, a firm's social responsibility activities can be compared with those of other firms in the same industry. However, this measure is not always a good one. For example, consider the issue of product safety. Though it might be argued that all products should either be completely safe or not be allowed on the market, imposing such a standard would be impractical. Bicycles often head the list of the most hazardous products, and every year many consumers are injured while riding them. Yet few would argue that bicycles should be banned from the market. Much of the problem in resolving product safety issues involves the question of whether the harm done results from an inherent lack of product safety or from unsafe use by the consumer. Similarly, answers to many of the questions listed in Table 8.2 depend on subjective social judgments rather than on precise standards of business conduct.

INFLUENCES ON THE SOCIAL RESPONSIBILITY OF BUSINESS

As noted, business firms have considerable power and can markedly influence society. However, built into our social system are a number of checks and balances designed to ensure that business power is not misused. Figure 8.1 illustrates four major influences that can inhibit the inappropriate use of business power. These include legal, political, competitive, and ethical influences.

Legal Influences

Legal influences consist of federal, state, and local legislation and the agencies and processes by which these laws are upheld. For example, Table 8.3 presents

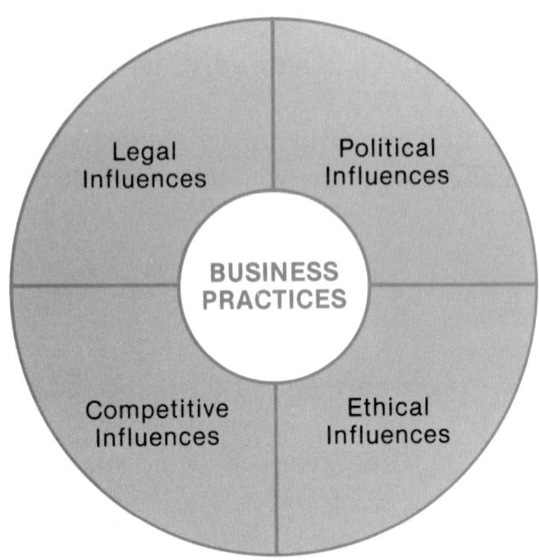

FIGURE 8.1 Major Influences on Business Practices

a list of several bills enacted by Congress that influence business practices. Some of this legislation is designed to control business practices in specific industries, such as toys or textiles; other laws are aimed at controlling functional areas, such as packaging or product safety.

A variety of government agencies are involved in enforcing these laws and investigating business practices. In addition to state and local agencies, a number of federal agencies are empowered to regulate particular areas of social responsibility. Table 8.4 presents a capsule summary of the activities of several of these federal agencies.

Table 8.4 makes it clear that federal agencies have broad and diverse powers to influence business practices and a variety of remedies to impose for improper business conduct. For example, the Federal Trade Commission has dealt with deceptive advertising—advertising that misleads consumers—by requiring firms to run corrective ads. These corrective ads are designed to clear up any misconceptions fostered by previous ads. The FTC has found advertising for several products to be misleading. For example,

- Profile Bread's advertising misled consumers to believe it was effective in weight reduction.
- Domino Sugar's advertising misled consumers to believe it was a special source of strength, energy, and stamina.
- Ocean Spray Cranberry Juice Cocktail misled consumers about food energy.
- Sugar Information, Inc., misled consumers about the benefits of eating sugar.

Highlight 8.1 presents the text of the corrective ads these firms were required by the FTC to run to correct these false impressions.

TABLE 8.3 Examples of Recent Federal Legislation Affecting Business Practices

YEAR	LEGISLATION	MAJOR PROVISION OF LAW
1988	Toxic Substances Control Act Amendment	Provides adequate time for planning and implementation of school asbestos management plans.
1988	Federal Food, Drug and Cosmetic Act Amendment	Bans reimportation of drugs produced in the U.S. Places restrictions on distribution of drug samples, bans certain resales of drugs by health care facilities.
1986	Truth in Mileage Act	Amends the Motor Vehicle Information and Cost Savings Act to strengthen, for the protection of consumers, the provisions respecting disclosure of mileage when motor vehicles are transferred.
1986	Petroleum Overcharge Distribution and Restitution Act	Provides for distribution to injured consumers of escrow funds remaining from oil company settlements of alleged price allocation violations under the Emergency Petroleum Allocation Act of 1973.
1986	Superfund Amendments and Reauthorization Act	Extends and amends the Comprehensive Environmental Response Compensation and Liability Act of 1980. Authorizes appropriations for and revises the EPA Hazardous Substance Response Trust Fund program for financing cleanup of uncontrolled hazardous waste sites.
1986	Anti-Drug Abuse Act	Amends the Food, Drug and Cosmetic Act to revise provisions on regulation of infant formula manufacture.
1986	Processed Products Inspection Improvement Act	Amends the Meat Inspection Act to eliminate USDA continuous inspection requirements for meats, poultry, and egg processing plants for a six-year trial period.
1986	Emergency Response Act	Amends the Toxic Substances Control Act to require the EPA to promulgate regulations pertaining to inspections, development of asbestos management plans and response actions.
1986	Safe Drinking Water Act Amendments	Amends the Safe Drinking Water Act. Authorizes appropriations for and revises EPA safe drinking water programs, including grants to states for drinking water standards enforcement and groundwater protection programs.
1986	Drug Export Amendments Act	Amends the Food, Drug and Cosmetic Act to remove restrictions on export of human and veterinary drugs not yet approved by FDA or USDA for use in the U.S. and establishes conditions governing export of such drugs.
1986	Comprehensive Smokeless Tobacco Health Education Act	Provides for public education concerning the health consequences of using smokeless tobacco products. Prohibits radio and television advertising of smokeless tobacco.
1986	Recreational Boating Safety Act Amendment	Enhances boating safety by requiring a report relating to informational displays on gasoline pumps.

Source: John R. Nevin, "Consumer Protection Legislation: Evolution, Structure and Prognosis," Working paper, University of Wisconsin–Madison, Madison, Wis., August 1989.

TABLE 8.4 Some Important Federal Regulatory Agencies

AGENCY	RESPONSIBILITIES
Federal Trade Commission (FTC)	Enforces laws and develops guidelines regarding unfair business practices
Food and Drug Administration (FDA)	Enforces laws and develops regulations to prevent the distribution and sale of adulterated or misbranded foods, drugs, cosmetics, and hazardous consumer products
Consumer Product Safety Commission (CPSC)	Enforces the Consumer Product Safety Act, which covers any consumer product not assigned to other regulatory agencies
Interstate Commerce Commission (ICC)	Regulates interstate rail, bus, truck, and water carriers
Federal Communications Commission (FCC)	Regulates interstate wire, radio, and television
Environmental Protection Agency (EPA)	Develops and enforces environmental protection standards in such areas as water, air, and noise pollution
Office of Consumer Affairs	Handles consumer complaints
Equal Employment Opportunity Commission (EEOC)	Investigates and conciliates employment discrimination complaints that are based on race, sex, or creed
Office of Federal Contract Compliance Programs	Insures that employers holding federal contracts grant equal employment opportunity to people regardless of race or sex
Occupational Safety and Health Administration (OSHA)	Regulates safety and health conditions in nongovernmental workplaces
National Highway Safety Administration (NHSA)	Attempts to reduce traffic accidents through the regulation of transportation-related manufacturers and products
Mining Enforcement and Safety Administration	Attempts to improve conditions for mine workers by enforcing all mine safety and equipment standards

HIGHLIGHT 8.1

ILLUSTRATIVE EXAMPLE ■ Examples of Corrective Ads

PROFILE BREAD

"Hi, (celebrity's name) for Profile Bread. Like all mothers, I'm concerned about nutrition and balanced meals. So, I'd like to clear up any misunderstanding you may have about Profile Bread from its advertising or even its name.

"Does Profile have fewer calories than any other breads? No. Profile has about the same per ounce as other breads. To be exact, Profile has seven fewer calories per slice. That's because Profile is sliced thinner.

But eating Profile will not cause you to lose weight. A reduction of seven calories is insignificant. It's total calories and balanced nutrition that count. And Profile can help you achieve a balanced meal because it provides protein and B vitamins as well as other nutrients.

"How does my family feel about Profile? Well, my husband likes Profile toast, the children love Profile sandwiches, and I prefer Profile to any other bread. So you see, at our house, delicious taste makes Profile a family affair."

(To be run in 25% of brand's advertising, for one year.)

AMSTAR

"Do you recall some of our past messages saying that Domino Sugar gives you strength, energy, and stamina? Actually, Domino is not a special or unique source of strength, energy, and stamina. No sugar is, because what you need is a balanced diet and plenty of rest and exercise."

(To be run in one of every four ads for one year.)

OCEAN SPRAY

"If you've wondered what some of our earlier advertising meant when we said Ocean Spray Cranberry Juice Cocktail has more food energy than orange juice or tomato juice, let us make it clear: we didn't mean vitamins and minerals. Food energy means calories. Nothing more.

"Food energy is important at breakfast since many of us may not get enough calories, or food energy, to get off to a good start. Ocean Spray Cranberry Juice Cocktail helps because it contains more food energy than most other breakfast drinks.

"And Ocean Spray Cranberry Juice Cocktail gives you and your family Vitamin C plus a great wake-up taste. It's . . . the other breakfast drink."

(To be run in one of every four ads for one year.)

SUGAR INFORMATION, INC.

"Do you recall the messages we brought you in the past about sugar? How something with sugar in it before meals could help you curb your appetite? We hope you didn't get the idea that our little diet tip was any magic formula for losing weight. Because there are no tricks or shortcuts; the whole diet subject is very complicated. Research hasn't established that consuming sugar before meals will contribute to weight reduction or even keep you from gaining weight."

(To be run for one insertion in each of seven magazines.)

Source: William L. Wilkie, Dennis L. McNeill, and Michael B. Mazis, "Marketing's 'Scarlet Letter': The Theory and Practice of Corrective Advertising," *Journal of Marketing,* Spring 1984, p. 13. Reprinted from *Journal of Marketing,* published by the American Marketing Association.

Legal influences and the power of government agencies to regulate business practices grew dramatically during the 1970s. However, the 1980s witnessed a decline in many regulatory activities. In fact, deregulation of business has been a major trend recently, and many government agencies have considerably reduced their involvement in controlling business practices.

Political Influences

By political influences we mean the pressure exerted by special-interest groups in society to control business practices. These groups use a variety of methods to influence business, such as lobbying to persuade various government agencies to enact or enforce legislation and working directly with employees or consumers. Table 8.5 lists some organizations that are designed to serve consumer interests. These are but a few examples; one tally found over 100 national organizations and over 600 state and local groups involved in consumer advocacy.[5]

Consumerism is concerned with augmenting the rights of consumers in dealing with business. Paul Bloom and Stephen Greyser argue that consumerism has reached the mature stage of its "product life cycle" and that its impact has been fragmented.[6] Yet they believe consumerism will continue to have some impact on business, and they suggest three strategies for coping with it. First, businesses can try to accelerate the decline of consumerism by *reducing demand* for it. This could be done by improving product quality, expanding services, lowering prices, and/or toning down advertising claims.

Second, businesses can *compete* with consumer advocacy groups by having active consumer affairs departments to offer consumer education and assistance in seeking redress of grievances. Alternatively, businesses can fund and coordinate activities designed to "sell" deregulation and other pro-business causes.

Third, businesses can *cooperate* with consumer advocacy groups by providing financial and other support. All of these strategies would be likely to further reduce the impact of political influences on business's approach to social responsibility. However, to the degree that following these strategies leads business firms to step up their social responsibility activities in the long run, consumers and other stakeholder groups could benefit.

Competitive Influences

Competitive influences are the actions that competing firms take to affect each other and society. These actions can be taken in many ways. For example, one firm might sue another firm or publicly allege that it engaged in fraudulent activities. Johnson & Johnson has frequently gone to court to prevent competitors from showing its Tylenol brand of pain relievers in comparative

[5] Ann P. Harvey, *Contacts in Consumerism 1980–1981* (Washington, D.C.: Fraser/Associates, 1980).
[6] Paul N. Bloom and Stephen A. Greyser, "The Maturing of Consumerism," *Harvard Business Review*, November–December 1981, pp. 130–139.

TABLE 8.5 Some Political Groups Concerned with Business Practices

BROAD-BASED NATIONAL GROUPS
Consumer Federation of America
National Wildlife Federation
Common Cause
SMALLER MULTI-ISSUE ORGANIZATIONS
National Consumer's League
Ralph Nader's Public Citizen
SPECIAL-INTEREST GROUPS
Action for Children's Television
American Association of Retired Persons
Group Against Smoking and Pollution
LOCAL GROUPS
Public-interest research groups
Local consumer protection offices
Local broadcast and newspaper consumer "action lines"

Source: Based on Paul N. Bloom and Stephen A. Greyser, "The Maturing of Consumerism," *Harvard Business Review*, November–December 1981, pp. 130–139.

ads. Burger King has publicly accused McDonald's of overstating the weight of its hamburgers.

Competitors also influence one another by diluting each other's political, economic, and market power. For example, in a business environment with many competitors, a single firm usually cannot dominate the flow of information to consumers. Conflicting competitive claims and price deals offered by various firms may help consumers resist the influence of a single firm.

Highlight 8.2 offers you an opportunity to analyze a situation wherein some people feel two giant firms are unfairly exploiting their competitive edge to further increase their dominance of a huge industry.

Society may also benefit from the better, safer, more efficient products and services that are often spawned by competitive pressure. Overall, then, competition may help balance business power within an industry and stimulate the development of better market offerings.

Ethical Influences

The last type of influence on business practices that we will discuss involves ethical decision making and the self-regulation of business conduct. Many professions have codes of ethics, and many business firms have their own offices to handle employee and consumer complaints.

HIGHLIGHT 8.2

SKILLS MODULE ■ Competitive Influence Analysis for Coke and Pepsi

INTRODUCTION

Our discussion of social responsibility has included competitive influences and their role in controlling the power of businesses. Review the following situation, and then complete the skill development exercise that follows. Doing so should help you develop some ability in analyzing this influence.

THE SITUATION

In your supermarket's soft drink aisle, you may have noticed that Coca-Cola and Pepsi-Cola bottlers are fighting a ferocious war. Stacks of eight-packs and two-liter bottles adorned with signs shouting out specials clutter the aisle. Coke and Pepsi's sales account for as much as 50 percent of a store's total soft-drink volume, and in the battle between them for space, Royal Crown, Dr Pepper, 7 Up, and others are getting lost.

Aggressive marketing and the success of their diet colas have pushed Coke and Pepsi's combined market share from 64.7 to 66.3 percent in a recent year. That is a gain of $420 million in the $26-billion-a-year soft drink industry. Some of the competitors lost up to 0.4 percent market share during this period.

Every time a bottler loses a fraction of a percentage point of market share, it may also lose some shelf space, because grocers generally assign space by sales per square foot. As one competitor complained, "Pretty soon Coke and Pepsi are going to squeeze everyone else out—it's just a matter of time."

Coke and Pepsi bottlers secure the supermarkets' high-volume selling display areas by giving grocers huge price breaks and promotional allowances. For example, one estimate is that the Kroger chain received about $2 million worth of discounts by Coke and Pepsi in 1984 for store advertising and promotion. The other soft drink companies compete for shelf space in the same way, but lesser sales mean smaller clout. Although some of these companies have sued Coke and Pepsi, alleging unfair competition, no action has been taken against the industry leaders.

SKILL DEVELOPMENT EXERCISE

Coke and Pepsi dominate the soft drink industry, and smaller competitors complain that these companies have too much market power. Prepare a detailed argument either supporting or disputing the idea that Coke and Pepsi are competing unfairly.

Source: Based on Ford S. Worthy, "Coke and Pepsi Stomp on the Little Guys," *Fortune*, January 7, 1985, pp. 67–68.

A difficult problem in discussing ethical influences is the lack of a single, universal standard for judging whether a particular action is ethical. Gene Laczniak summarizes five ethical standards that have been proposed[7]:

1. *The Golden Rule:* Act in the way you would expect others to act toward you.
2. *The utilitarian principle:* Act in a way that results in the greatest good for the greatest number.
3. *Kant's categorical imperative:* Act in such a way that the action you take could be a universal law or rule of behavior under the circumstances.
4. *The professional ethic:* Take actions that a disinterested panel of professional colleagues would view as proper.
5. *The TV test:* Ask, "Would I feel comfortable explaining to a national TV audience why I took this action?"

Applying these diverse standards could result in many different interpretations of what an ethical business practice is. For example, applying them to the scenarios presented in Highlight 8.3 illustrates the problem of interpreting appropriate ethical conduct.

Overall, then, what constitutes ethical business practices is a matter of social judgment. Even product safety decisions are not always clear-cut. For example, thousands of people are killed and injured every year by automobiles. Air bags installed in automobiles could reduce the deaths and serious injuries. However, because consumers are not willing to pay the additional cost of this safety feature, very few automobiles are equipped with them. In other words, the public's social judgment has not been that air bags are necessary for reasonable product safety in automobiles.

MANAGING SOCIAL RESPONSIBILITY

Many managers have accepted the idea that corporate social responsibility is an integral part of a company's overall strategy. The key elements of managing social responsibility are discussed below.

Environmental Analysis and Organizational Direction

Like every element of strategy development, social responsibility begins with environmental analysis. Managers analyze both problems and opportunities in the environment in terms of their impact on society and then decide what areas require further investigation. Organization mission statements and

[7] Gene R. Laczniak, "Framework for Analyzing Marketing Ethics," *Journal of Macromarketing*, Spring 1983, pp. 7–18. Also see Harvey C. Bunke, "Should We Teach Business Ethics?" *Business Horizons*, July–August 1988, pp. 2–8; LaRue Tone Hosmer, "Adding Ethics to the Business Curriculum," *Business Horizons*, July–August 1988, pp. 9–15; and Bruce H. Drake and Eileen Drake, "Ethical and Legal Aspects of Managing Corporate Cultures," *California Management Review*, Winter 1988, pp. 107–123.

HIGHLIGHT 8.3

ILLUSTRATIVE EXAMPLE ■ Business Scenarios That Raise Ethical Questions

SCENARIO 1

The Thrifty Supermarket Chain has 12 stores in the city of Gotham, U.S.A. The company's policy is to maintain the same prices for all items at all stores. However, the distribution manager knowingly sends the poorest cuts of meat and the lowest-quality produce to the store located in the low-income section of town. He justifies this action based on the fact that this store has the highest overhead due to factors such as employee turnover, pilferage, and vandalism. *Is the distribution manager's economic rationale sufficient justification for his allocation method?*

SCENARIO 2

The Independent Chevy Dealers of Metropolis, U.S.A. have undertaken an advertising campaign headlined by the slogan: "Is your family's life worth 45 MPG?" The ads admit that while Chevy subcompacts are *not* as fuel efficient as foreign imports and cost more to maintain, they are safer according to government-sponsored crash tests. The ads implicitly ask if responsible parents, when purchasing a car, should trade off fuel efficiency for safety. *Is it ethical for the dealers association to use a fear appeal to offset an economic disadvantage?*

SCENARIO 3

A few recent studies have linked the presence of the artificial sweetener subsugural to cancer in laboratory rats. While the validity of these findings has been hotly debated by medical experts, the Food and Drug Administration has ordered products containing the ingredient banned from sale in the United States. The Jones Company sends all of its sugar-free J. C. Cola (which contains subsugural) to European supermarkets because the sweetener has not been banned there. *Is it acceptable for the Jones Company to send an arguably unsafe product to another market without waiting for further evidence?*

SCENARIO 4

The Acme Company sells industrial supplies through its own sales force, which calls on company purchasing agents. Acme has found that providing the purchasing agent with small gifts helps cement a cordial relationship and creates goodwill. Acme follows the policy that the bigger the order, the bigger the gift to the purchasing agent. The gifts range from a pair of tickets to a sporting event to outboard motors and snowmobiles. Acme does not give gifts to personnel at companies which they know have an explicit policy prohibiting the acceptance of such gifts. *Assuming no laws are violated, is Acme's policy of providing gifts to purchasing agents morally proper?*

SCENARIO 5

The Buy American Electronics Company has been selling its highly rated System X Color TV sets (21, 19, and 12 inches) for $700, $500, and $300, respectively. These prices have been relatively uncompetitive in the market. After some study, Buy American substitutes several cheaper components (which engineering says may slightly reduce the quality of performance) and passes on the savings to the consumer in the form of a $100 price reduction on each model. Buy American institutes a price-oriented promotional campaign which neglects to mention that the second-generation System X sets are different from the first. *Is the company's competitive strategy ethical?*

SCENARIO 6

The Smith & Smith Advertising Agency has been struggling financially. Mr. Smith is approached by the representative of a small South American country which is on good terms with the U.S. Department of State. He wants S & S to create a multimillion dollar advertising and public relations campaign which will bolster the image of the country and increase the likelihood that it will receive U.S. foreign assistance and attract investment capital. Smith knows the country is a dictatorship which has been accused of numerous human rights violations. *Is it ethical for the Smith & Smith Agency to undertake the proposed campaign?*

Source: Gene R. Laczniak, "Framework for Analyzing Marketing Ethics," *Journal of Macromarketing,* Spring 1983, p. 8. Reprinted by permission of the publisher, Business Research Division, University of Colorado, Boulder.

objectives provide guidance in determining in what areas social responsibility is of special concern.

Strategy Formulation

Once areas of concern about social responsibility have been identified and studied, strategy formulation for social responsibility begins. The object is to develop appropriate actions for dealing with the issues. Many alternatives are available for dealing with most social responsibility issues. For example, improving guarantees, installing consumer complaint hotlines, offering more detailed label information, removing products from the market, and modifying products are all ways of dealing with problems associated with poor product performance.

Strategy Implementation

Implementation involves putting the formulated strategy into action, which entails assigning responsibility to individuals or groups, providing adequate information, and establishing controls to make sure the strategy is implemented efficiently. For example, Procter & Gamble developed its own consumer service department to handle consumer complaints and requests for information. In a recent year, it received over 670,000 mail and telephone contacts about its products. The consumer service department consists of 75 employees—30 to answer calls and the rest to answer letters and analyze the data. Clearly, implementing this strategy entailed considerable expense and effort. Management considers the system very effective in providing "a distant, early warning signal" of product problems.[8]

Strategic Control

Strategic control activities undertaken to fulfill social responsibility involve measuring the results of the implemented strategy and changing it if necessary. The specific areas in which individual companies actually take such measurements vary with their specific social responsibility objectives, but four general areas should probably be considered.[9]

1. *The economic functional area:* A measurement should be made to indicate whether or not the organization is performing such activities as producing goods and services that people need, creating jobs, paying fair wages, and ensuring worker safety. This measurement gives some indication of the economic contribution the organization is making to society.
2. *The quality-of-life area:* In this area, measurement should focus on determining whether the organization is improving or degrading the general quality of life in society. Producing high-quality goods, dealing fairly with employees and customers, and making an effort to preserve the natural environment could all be indicators that the organization is upholding or improving the general quality of life. As an example, some people believe that because cigarette companies produce goods that actually damage the health of society overall, these companies are socially irresponsible.
3. *The social investment area:* This area deals with the degree to which the organization is investing both money and human resources to solve community social problems. The socially responsible organization might be involved in assisting community organizations that promote education, charities, and the arts.
4. *The problem-solving area:* Measurement in this area should focus on the degree to which the organization deals with social problems themselves,

[8] "Customers: P&G's Pipeline to Product Problems," *Business Week,* June 11, 1984, p. 167. Also see Brian Dumaine, "P&G Rewrites the Marketing Rules," *Fortune,* November 6, 1989, pp. 34–48.
[9] Frank H. Cassell, "The Social Cost of Doing Business," *MSU Business Topics,* Autumn 1974, pp. 19–26.

HIGHLIGHT 8.4

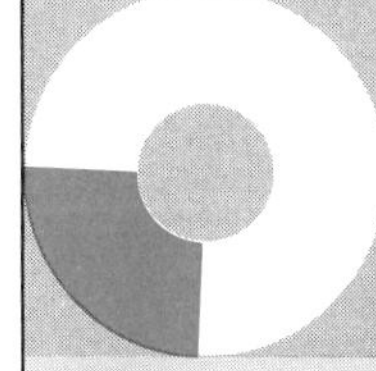

ILLUSTRATIVE EXAMPLE ■ A Social Audit Report for Bank of America

MNB Social Performance Report
Part 1—Mainstream Issues

PRIORITY—CONSUMER ISSUES

Issue—Discrimination in Credit—Women

Potential Growing public awareness of issue. Consumer Finance Commission Report should stimulate legislation within two years. Class actions a possibility.

Progress New guidelines instituted for credit cards and small loans (under $5,000). Women's full income and employment now considered. No restrictions on married women obtaining credit in own name.

Problems No change in real estate or larger personal loans because of Michigan's community property laws.

Position Well ahead of competition. Better advertising of this fact would generate considerable new business.

Issue—Complaints and Errors

Potential Errors prime reason for customers leaving bank. Five percent reduction in closed accounts would be equal to raising profits by $280,000. Quick handling of complaints could increase this to $400,000.

Progress Instituted double-check system. Check-processing errors down 27 percent. Cost: $110,000. Instituted 800 line to handle complaints and questions. Good results. Cost for line, officer, and advertising: $90,000.

Problems No progress in credit card billing errors.

Position Reputation for personalized service improved. Closed accounts down 4.3 percent.

PRIORITY—EMPLOYEE DEVELOPMENT

Issue—Affirmative Action

Potential Close monitoring by government and others assured. Recent class actions indicate severe penalties for nonaction. Potential liability $1 million to 10 million. Upgrading large pool of underutilized talent in bank (especially women) could significantly increase productivity. Growing number of qualified minorities in Detroit.

Progress Strong minority program instituted during year with goals, timetables, and enforcement mechanism. The record is good: *1968,* 18.3 percent of employees minority; *1970,* 20.5 percent; *1972,* 24.1 percent; *1975* goal is population parity (31.7 percent). Similar program for women (now 62 percent of labor force) will be ready in mid-1973.

Problems Minorities and women still concentrated in lower rank:

Percent Bank Officers Who Are:	1968	1970	1972	1975 Goal
Minority	5.6%	6.1%	7.3%	12.0%
Women	18.2%	20.8%	23.3%	30.0%

To reach 1975 goals, we must develop a better system of isolating promotables, training and placing them. Difficulty of attracting top minorities to banking. Some resentment from white males expected.

Position This effort largely required. Other Detroit banks at essentially the same position. No competitive advantage or disadvantage.

Source: Bernard Butcher, "Anatomy of a Social Performance Report," *Business and Society Review,* Autumn 1973, p. 29. Reprinted by permission. Copyright © 1973 *Business and Society Review.*

as opposed to the symptoms of those problems. Such activities as participating in long-range community planning and conducting studies to pinpoint social problems would generally be construed as dealing with social problems rather than merely addressing their symptoms.

Conducting a *social audit* is the process of taking social responsibility measurements such as those we have listed. The basic steps in a social audit are monitoring, measuring, and appraising all aspects of an organization's social responsibility performance. The audit itself can be performed either by organization personnel or by outside consultants. Highlight 8.4 is a portion of a social audit prepared by Bernard Butcher, the executive vice president for social policy at the Bank of America in San Francisco. The format of social audits varies with the company, of course, but this example provides a clear summary of the issues Bank of America faced at the time this social audit was completed.

SUMMARY

In this chapter, we investigated strategic management and social responsibility. First we outlined the classical view that companies should not assume any social responsibility beyond their obligation to make a profit and the contemporary view that businesses do have a responsibility to maintain and advance the welfare of society at large. We found that many businesses' activities are supported by both viewpoints and that the degree to which a firm should seek to achieve purely societal objectives depends on many considerations. Then we noted several areas in which firms can exhibit social responsibility, such as concern for consumers, for employees, for the environment, and for society in general.

Next we investigated four major influences on business that act to promote social responsibility and curb the inappropriate use of business's considerable power. These include legal influences, such as laws and government regulatory agencies; the political pressure brought to bear by various groups such as consumer advocates; the controls that competing firms exert on one another, acting, for example, as "watchdogs" to prevent misleading advertising; and the ethical influences that are exhibited in many firms' self-regulation of their

HIGHLIGHT 8.5

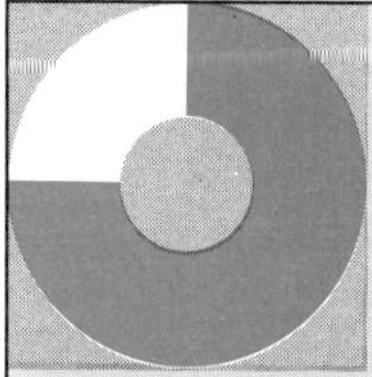

CHECKLIST ■ Analyzing Social Responsibility in Problems and Cases

- ☐ 1. Does this problem or case involve an area wherein social responsibility is an important concern?
- ☐ 2. Is there any legislation requiring the organization to perform in a socially responsible manner?
- ☐ 3. Would performing social responsibility activities be economically profitable to the firm in the long run?
- ☐ 4. Can the organization afford to engage in social responsibility activities, and would they result in goodwill or other noneconomic benefits from one or more stakeholder groups?
- ☐ 5. What specific stakeholders and area(s) of social responsibility are of concern in this problem or case?
- ☐ 6. Are there any political forces attempting to change the firm's activities? If so, do they have sound arguments?
- ☐ 7. Are there any competitive influences that the firm should take into consideration?
- ☐ 8. Does the problem or case involve an ethical dilemma in which a decision has to be made?
- ☐ 9. Does the organization have a well-developed program for dealing with social responsibility issues?
- ☐ 10. Would a social audit be useful for identifying problems and suggesting appropriate solutions?

business conduct. (In the final analysis, of course, what is "ethical" comes down to a social judgment.)

Finally, we analyzed the process of managing social responsibility issues in terms of our strategic management model, offering examples of ways in which social responsibility can be taken into account in the course of conducting an environmental analysis and in formulating, implementing, and controlling strategy. And we examined the social audit as an effective means of appraising an organization's performance in the area of social responsibility.

Highlight 8.5 contains a summary checklist of questions based on this chapter. Use it in analyzing strategic management problems and cases that revolve around social responsibility issues.

ADDITIONAL READINGS

Aaker, David A., and George S. Day. *Consumerism: Search for the Consumer Interest*, 4th ed. New York: The Free Press, 1982.

Donaldson, Thomas, and Patricia H. Werhane. *Ethical Issues in Business*, 2nd ed. Englewood Cliffs, N.J.: Prentice-Hall, 1983.

Foote, Susan Bartlett. "Corporate Responsibility in a Changing Legal Environment." *California Management Review*, Spring 1984, pp. 217–228.

Magnet, Myron. "The Decline and Fall of Business Ethics." *Fortune*, December 8, 1986, pp. 65–72.

Steiner, George A., and John F. Steiner. *Business, Government, and Society*, 4th ed. New York: Random House, 1985.

Sturdivant, Frederick D. *Business and Society*, 3rd ed. Homewood Ill.: Richard D. Irwin, 1985.

HIGHLIGHT 8.6 ■ APPLICATION OF CHAPTER MATERIAL

A Social Responsibility Concern for Suzuki Motor Company

Suzuki Motor Co. entered the U.S. automobile market in November 1985 with a single model, the Samurai. The Samurai is a cross between a jeep and an economy car and was initially promoted as a fun car for the youth market. In one ad, for example, four witty and attractive people in a Samurai are shown playfully negotiating a test track. The ad ends with a "brake" test, that is, the driver says, "Let's break for lunch."

Suzuki sold 47,732 Samurais in 1986 and sales jumped to 81,349 in 1987. Apparently, the car was successfully filling the niche left by American Motors's removal of the Jeep CJ5 a few years earlier. However, in December 1987 and January 1988, sales of the Samurai had declined a total of 16.6 percent from this period a year earlier. Auto market analysts blamed the decrease on increases in insurance rates. Apparently, insurance companies had concluded that the Samurai was prone to accidents and expensive to repair.

Questions about the Samurai's safety continued to mount. In February 1988, the Center for Auto Safety, a Washington, D.C.–based consumer group, filed a petition with the National Highway Traffic Safety Administration, charging that the Samurai's high center of gravity made it unstable on the road. The center said it had evidence of 11 accidents in which Samurais had rolled over, causing 3 deaths and leaving 8 other people injured.

Suzuki reacted to this by changing its advertising messages. The new ads, shot almost entirely in black and white, featured laudatory quotes from car enthusiast magazines. For example, the following quote was used from *Off-Road* magazine: "We gave the Samurai good points for maneuverability, engine performance, and chassis balance." The ads helped: sales of the Samurai in May 1988 were 6,074 units.

In June 1988, Consumers Union published an article in its *Consumer Reports* magazine stating that the Samurai had a "dangerous propensity" to roll over when its driver attempted to make a sharp turn. Consumers Union charged that the vehicle was too tall for its small wheelbase and called for the immediate recall of all 160,000 Samurais on U.S. roads and reimbursement to their owners. Sales of the Samurai dropped to 2,199 units in June 1988, compared with 7,479 in June 1987.

At this point, Suzuki took some extraordinary marketing measures to try to stop the sales plunge of its car. First, it offered dealers $2,000 incentives on each Samurai. The company didn't require dealers to cut the Samurai's price with the incentive, but many dealers immediately

(Continues)

lopped off 25 percent from the base price of $7,995. Second, the company boosted its advertising budget by $1.5 million per week to try to counter consumer fears raised by the tests. Third, some dealers began offering free $1 million life insurance policies for Samurai buyers. The policy lasted for one year after purchase and covered only the death of the driver in a rollover accident. As one dealer put it: "We can't run enough ads to convince the public that our cars are safe. But with the insurance we can draw attention by saying we're willing to pay $1 million to back up the Samurai's safety." Fourth, Suzuki hinted that it might sue the critics of its car.

By August 1988 sales of the Samurai had rebounded sharply. In fact, in August a two-month inventory was wiped out as Suzuki sold 12,208 Samurais, the best month it had since entering the U.S. market. Suzuki also announced that it was introducing two new models in the U.S. market.

DISCUSSION QUESTIONS

1. Describe and evaluate Suzuki's strategy in terms of its reactions to changes in consumers and other elements of the environment.
2. Do you think there are ethical problems with Suzuki's responses to criticism of its Samurai?

Sources: "Suzuki Takes Extraordinary Measures to Halt Sales Plunge of the Samurai Model," *The Wall Street Journal*, July 11, 1988; "Suzuki Reverses Ad Strategy to Combat Claims That Samurai Vehicle Isn't Safe," *The Wall Street Journal*, March 3, 1988; "Suzuki Samurai Sales Have Plunged Since Consumers Union Called It Unsafe," *The Wall Street Journal*, July 7, 1988; "Suzuki Vehemently Defends Its Samurai," *Capital Times*, June 10, 1988; and "Sudden Deceleration," *American Way*, January 1989, pp. 20–23.

SECTION FOUR

Foundations for Strategic Management

Section Three of this text discussed two special topics in strategic management: international operations and social responsibility. The following section also focuses on more specialized areas in strategic management by examining three of the major functional areas of organizations. These are operations (Chapter 9), finance (Chapter 10), and marketing (Chapter 11). Students who have had recent coursework in all three areas should approach these chapters as a review or "refresher course" on major topics, issues, and techniques. For students who have not taken a recent course in one or more of these areas, Chapters 9, 10, and 11 can serve as a basic overview of operations, finance, and marketing. Additional information on these and other functional areas, of course, appears throughout the text.

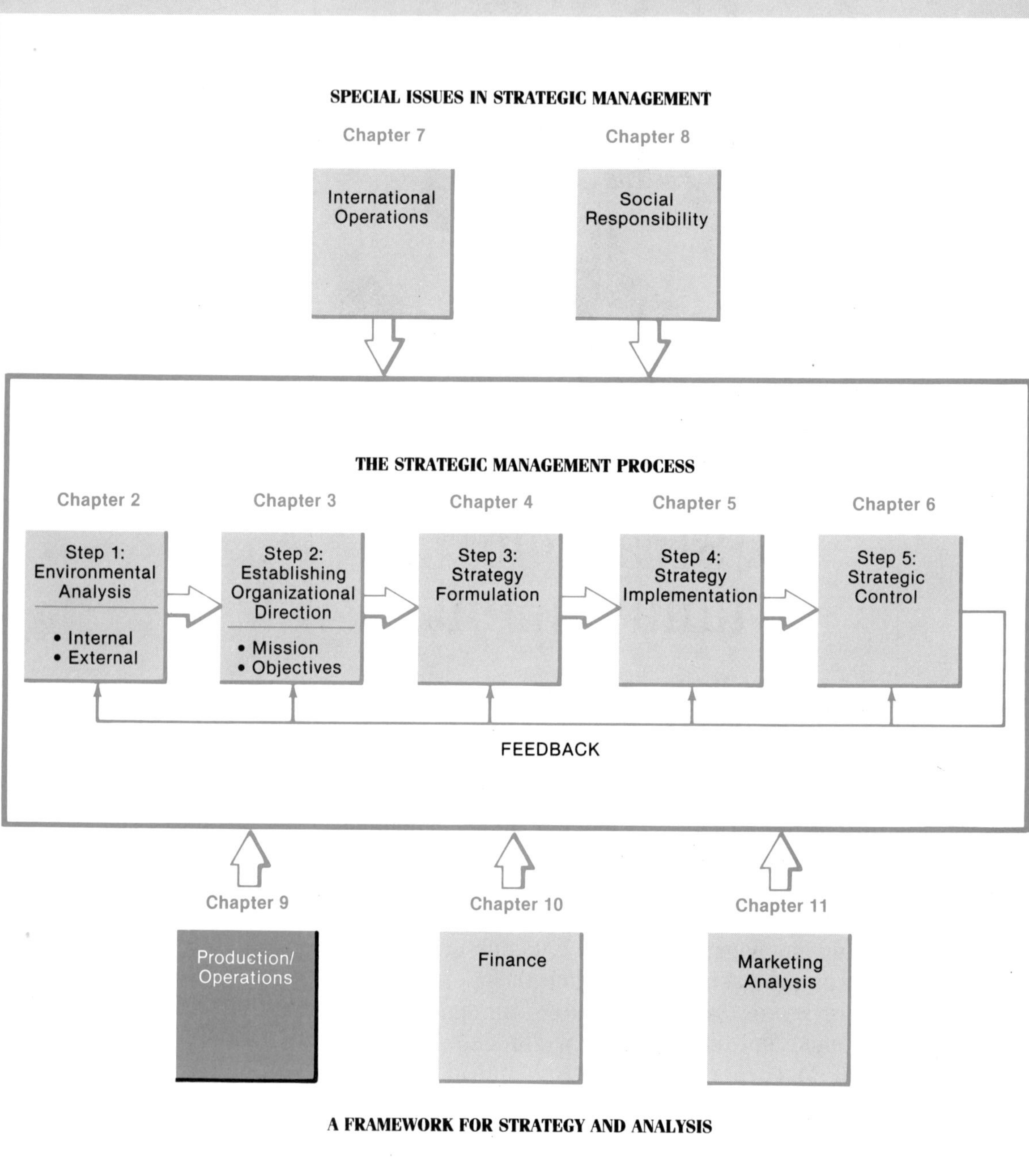

An Approach to Solving Strategic Problems and Cases

CHAPTER 9

Operations Foundations for Strategic Management[1]

The subject of this chapter is the operations function, one of the major functional areas of organizations. In the first part of the chapter, we explain what the operations function is, put it in context by briefly reviewing the other functions in the organization, and describe the various operations systems that have evolved in the production of goods or the provision of services in manufacturing and nonmanufacturing settings.

The second part of the chapter addresses the relationship of operations to strategic management. We note the vital association between marketing strategy and type of operations function, for example, and the importance of considering the firm's operations capabilities when formulating corporate strategy. Next we discuss strategy decisions for the operations function itself, focusing especially on deciding which production characteristics the operations function will emphasize. The final factor we analyze in terms of operations strategy is product design.

[1] This chapter is a combination of chapter 1 ("Zeroing in on Operations") and chapter 2 ("Operations Strategy") in James B. Dilworth, *Production and Operations Management: Manufacturing and Nonmanufacturing* (New York: Random House, 1986). This book is now available in a 1989 version from McGraw-Hill Book Company. The authors would like to express their sincere appreciation to Professor James B. Dilworth for his important contribution to this text.

ESSENTIALS OF ORGANIZATIONAL OPERATIONS

The Operations Function

The *operations function* is performed by those people in a business who are responsible for producing the goods or providing the services that the business offers to the public. The operations function, also called the *production function,* is one of three primary functions within a business, the other two being finance and marketing. But in a typical business, it is the operations function that employs the greatest number of people and is responsible for the greatest portion of the firm's controllable assets. You can quickly see, then, that operations is a very important function and certainly worthy of study. Our purpose in this chapter is to discuss the various activities that take place in the operations function and to explore how these activities can affect strategic management.

Other Functions

The operations function is only one part of a larger system—the entire organization. As such, it is interrelated with other functions in the organization. Plans and actions of all components of the business must be kept in concert if the total organization is to achieve its full potential. Before we discuss the operations function in greater detail, let us briefly review the other primary business functions—marketing and finance—as well as some secondary or supporting functions.

Marketing

The *marketing function* consists of the group of people who are responsible for discovering or developing a need or demand for the company's goods and services. They also seek to maintain a responsive working relationship with consumers or potential consumers. Profit-seeking companies cannot long survive without a market for their goods or services. Nonprofit organizations, such as governmental agencies, may survive without a genuine need or demand for their services, but such situations represent a misapplication of economic resources. Nonbusiness enterprises are performing a marketing activity when they determine the extent and location of the need for their services and when they make the availability of their services known to the public. The marketing function is discussed in detail in Chapter 11, "Marketing Foundations for Strategic Management."

Finance

The *finance function* consists primarily of those activities aimed at obtaining funds for an organization and guiding the wise use of those funds. The finance function exists in nonbusiness enterprises and may include lobbying for support or seeking public contributions through the efforts of volunteers. Included in the finance function are budgeting and allocation of funds to the various subdivisions of the firm and review of their expenditures. The finance function is discussed in detail in Chapter 10, "Financial Foundations for Strategic Management."

Supporting Functions

Naturally functions other than operations, marketing, and finance exist within organizations, and they receive varying emphasis, depending on the organization's purposes, its external environment, and the persons within the organization who shape its responses to the environment. If a company produces a tangible product, some research and development, design, and engineering functions must be performed. Similar functions must be performed in nonmanufacturing companies, but in these organizations such functions consist of deciding on the services to offer and the manner in which they will be provided. A restaurant, for example, must decide whether to provide food for patrons through service at tables or at self-service cafeteria counters.

Because organizations require human effort, they must recruit personnel, train employees, and distribute benefits to them so that they may share in the profits generated by the organization's work. Some management scholars claim that the personnel or human resource function is so important to the organization that it should be listed as a fourth major business function. A very strong case can be made for this argument. Our purpose here is not to debate this issue, but merely to indicate that the human resource function is of critical importance to the organization in general and to the operations function in particular. Additional information on the human resource function and its relationship to strategic management is integrated into various chapters of this text.

Interdependence of Functions

Public relations are important to all the primary and secondary functions. Public attitude affects the success of attempts to sell stock or to borrow money. The public's attitude also affects the company's ability to sell its product and to obtain competent employees to produce the goods and services that the company exists to provide.

Public relations activities illustrate some of the interrelationships among functions within businesses. We may divide a company into smaller units so that each unit is within the human capacity to understand and to supervise, but the parts still are only *parts*. They must work together if the total organization is to function properly.

The three major functions within a business are interdependent. Having the financial resources and the ability to produce a product are of little value if there is no market for the product. Having the finance resources and a market for a product are of little value if one cannot provide the product. The ability to produce a product and a market for the product are not sufficient if one does not have the necessary capital to employ personnel, buy raw material, and put the other capabilities into action. All of the functions in an organization

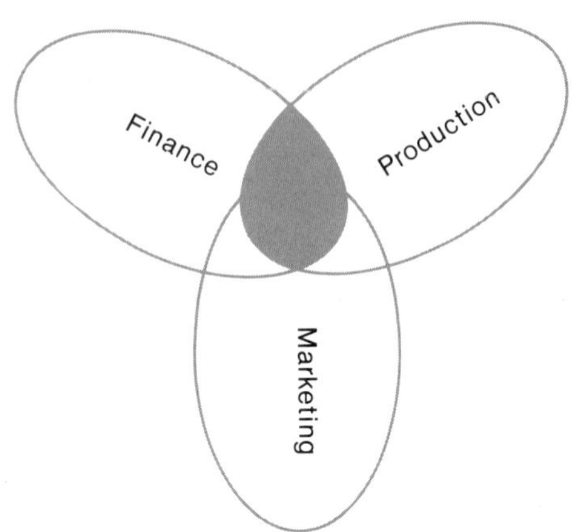

FIGURE 9.1 Major Functions within Organizations

both contribute to the whole and depend on the remainder of the organization. We consider each function separately so that we may study a manageable unit, but it is important to keep in mind that the other functions are at the same time necessary to, and dependent on, the function being studied. Figure 9.1 illustrates the interrelatedness of some functions within businesses.

Today's Broader View of the Operations Function

The operations function is sometimes called the production function, or the production and operations function. In the past, the term "production" was considered by some persons to connote only the manufacture of tangible items; later the term "operations" was added or substituted to include references to nonmanufacturing operations. Today the term "production" is often used with a broader meaning to refer to the production of goods or of services. It was stated earlier that the operations function is responsible for producing goods or providing services. In this chapter the terms "production," "operations," and "production and operations" are used to refer to the function in either manufacturing or nonmanufacturing settings.

Manufacturing operations perform some physical or chemical processes such as sawing, sewing, machining, welding, grinding, blending, or refining to convert some tangible raw materials into tangible products. All other operations that do not actually make goods can be called *nonmanufacturing* or *service operations*. Customers deal with some of these nonmanufacturing companies to obtain purely intangible services such as advice or instruction; they may seek help in completing tax forms, for example. Customers deal with other nonmanufacturing companies, such as wholesalers or retailers, to obtain goods—but these companies do not make the goods. These companies primarily serve their customers by transporting, packaging, storing, and the like, rather than by performing manufacturing processes. Thus, our major criterion for classifying operations lies in whether these operations manufacture goods or provide some type of service operation, even though they may provide tangible goods or some less tangible service to customers.

Operations: Providing a Product or Service

When viewed at a general or conceptual level, all types of production operations have some common characteristics. The most obvious common ground is the system's purpose or function; that is, the production system is responsible for providing the goods or services offered by the organization. The production system must transform some set of inputs into a set of outputs. This is the element that all production systems have in common; it is illustrated schematically in Figure 9.2. The types of inputs, transformations, and outputs will vary among operations.

Manufacturing operations transform or convert such inputs as raw materials, labor skills, management skills, capital, and sales revenue into some product, which is then sold. Other outputs are wages that flow into the economy, environmental effects, social influences, and other, even less obvious factors. The production system is a part of a larger system—the company. The company is a part of a larger system—the community. As the system boundaries expand, it becomes more difficult to determine all of the inputs, outputs, and transformations.

Service operations also transform a set of inputs into a set of outputs. A restaurant uses such inputs as meat, potatoes, lettuce, the chef's skills, servers' skills, and many others. Some of the transformation processes involve storing supplies, blending ingredients into desirable combinations, and altering the form of the inputs by cooking, freezing, heating, and transporting them to the proper tables at the proper time. Less tangible operations involve the provision of a pleasant atmosphere, perhaps even by offering entertainment. The outputs include, one hopes, a satisfied patron. Other outputs include wages and purchase payments sent into the economy and refuse sent into the refuse collection system (which is yet another service system).

Educational institutions use such inputs as books, students, and instructional skills to produce knowledgeable and skilled individuals as their output. Hospitals use scientific equipment, professional skills, and tender loving care to transform sick people into well ones. Repair shops use repair parts, equipment, and worker skills to transform malfunctioning inputs into properly functioning outputs. All types of operations, then, transform inputs into outputs.

When the output is a tangible product, the transformations performed by the operations function are intended to increase the utility of the inputs by changing either the physical form of the inputs or the time or place at which the outputs are available. Operations that change the physical form of the inputs include factories, landscapers, restaurants, upholstery shops, ice cream

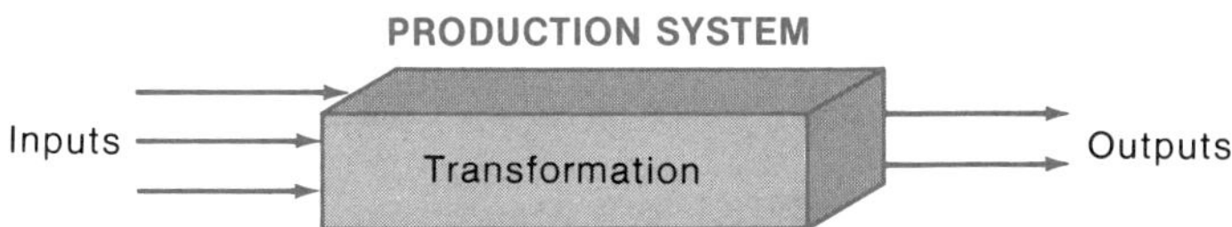

FIGURE 9.2 Conceptual Diagram of a Production System

shops, and laundries. Some operations provide special skills or convenience by providing services for customers. Operations such as wholesalers, retailers, transporters, and the postal system provide materials-handling operations to change the place at which the output is made available. Banks, public warehouses, and cold-storage plants for food or fur storage perform an inventory function to make the output available at a different time. Even though the inputs, transformations, and outputs may vary, the general characteristic of the transformation of inputs into more usable outputs holds true for all operations.

Manufacturing Operations

The type of production facility and production methods that a manufacturing company uses are sometimes referred to as its production system. The production system that a company finds most appropriate is frequently related to the way in which the company conducts its business. More specifically, it is related to the stage at which the company plans to hold inventory so it can serve its customers more quickly than the full lead time required to purchase all of the materials and convert them into the final product. At the time a customer's order is received, the items used to fill that order might intentionally be (1) held as finished goods, (2) held as standard modules waiting to be assembled, or (3) held or ordered as basic inputs without any processing performed on them. The terms presented in the following paragraph are used to characterize the degree of processing that is done after the customer's order is received.

Some companies are *make-to-stock producers;* that is, they make items that are completed and placed in stock prior to receipt of the customer's order. The end item is shipped "off the shelf" from finished-goods inventory after receipt of a customer order. In contrast, some companies make to order. In the case of a *make-to-order producer,* the end item is completed after receipt of the customer's order for the item. If the item is fully a unique, custom-designed item, the customer will probably have to wait for many of the materials to be purchased and for the production work to be performed, because the producer cannot anticipate what each customer might want and have the necessary raw materials and components on hand to shorten the production lead time. If some components or materials are frequently used by the business, however, the producer may keep some of them in stock—particularly if the lead time to purchase or produce these items is long. When the company produces standard-design, optional modules ahead of time and assembles a particular combination of these modules after the customer orders it, the business is said to be an *assemble-to-order producer.*[2] An example of an assemble-to-order producer is an automobile factory that, in response to a dealer's order, provides an automatic or manual transmission, air conditioner, sound system, interior options, and specific engine options as well as the specified body style

[2] These terms are defined in accordance with Thomas F. Wallace, *APICS Dictionary,* 5th ed. (Falls Church, Va.: American Production and Inventory Control Society, 1984).

and color. Many of the components would already have been ordered or started into production when the dealer placed the order. Otherwise the lead time to deliver the automobile would be much longer. With these terms in mind, we will now discuss the two major categories of production facilities and methods.

CONTINUOUS PRODUCTION. A *continuous production* system is one in which the equipment and work stations are arranged in a sequence according to the steps used to convert the input raw materials into the desired component or assembly. The routings of jobs are fixed, and the setup of the equipment is seldom changed from one product to another. The flow of materials is relatively continuous during the production process. This type of production is sometimes called *repetitive manufacturing*, which is high-volume production of discrete units, usually with a fixed sequence of material flow. Since the material flow path and processing steps are fixed, this type of production is frequently used with standard products that are make-to-stock items. Examples are production lines or assembly lines for the production of radios, televisions, refrigerators, or other products that may be produced and stocked in perhaps a few standard models. The customer selects the particular standard model he or she wants. Continuous production might be used for items that are made to order or assembled to order if the volume is sufficient to justify having a fixed, special-purpose production system for the items.

Some continuous production operations produce a product that blends together in bulk rather than being in discrete units. Some products of this type of operation include petroleum products, flour, cement, and liquid chemicals. The industries that produce these types of products are sometimes called *process industries*, particularly if some physical or chemical reaction is used. (Chemical processing can also occur with batches of material, and this is sometimes called batch-process production.)

INTERMITTENT PRODUCTION OR JOB SHOP. An *intermittent production* system or *job shop* differs greatly from the continuous system in that it is designed to provide much more flexibility. This type of production system is one in which the production equipment or work stations are grouped and organized according to the function or process they perform. Different types of products flow in batches corresponding to individual orders. Each batch or lot might have a different routing through the functional work centers, depending on the requirements of the type of product being made. Products could be made for stock or to order, but generally this type of production is associated with make-to-order businesses.

Continuous and intermittent production systems are points near opposite ends of a continuum representing the degree of specificity of the production system (see Figure 9.3). At one end of the continuum are production facilities designed specifically to produce one particular standard item and optimized for the materials movement and production steps required to make that item. Near the other end of the continuum are job shops; they are not ideal for any single product but are capable of producing a wide variety of items. Many

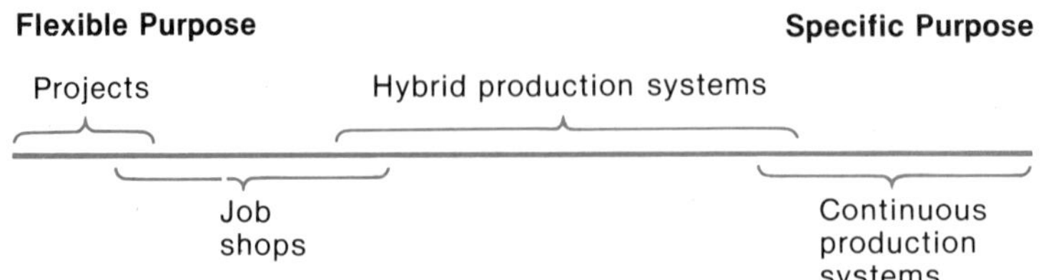

FIGURE 9.3 Degree of Specificity of Production Systems

production facilities embody features of both of these production approaches. That is, they lie somewhere on the continuum between a job shop and continuous production.

Lying at the flexibility end of the continuum is the low-volume type of operation often referred to as a *project.* Usually, projects are of relatively long duration, and the same personnel often are assigned to a project for a significant part of this time. In the manufacturing category, projects include such items as ships, bridges, buildings, and large, special machines.

Nonmanufacturing Operations

Nonmanufacturing operations—also known as *service operations*—are operations that do not produce tangible outputs. Like manufacturing operations, nonmanufacturing operations can be subdivided according to the degree of standardization of their outputs—that is, whether they are *standard services* or *custom services*—and/or the processes they perform. Some nonmanufacturing activities might be thought of as projects because they involve the activities of a team of people over a period of time. In the nonmanufacturing category, a project might be a software package or a training program. Table 9.1 displays a classification system for manufacturing and nonmanufacturing operations based on the degree of standardization of their output.

Nonmanufacturing operations can be divided into categories according to another classification scheme that provides useful insights into the management issues they face. Some nonmanufacturing operations deal primarily with tangible outputs, even though these operations do not manufacture the items. These types of operations include wholesale distributors and transportation companies and they can utilize many of the materials management principles and techniques that a manufacturing operation might use. The ideas vital to materials handling are also important in some operations that deal with tangible items.

Other nonmanufacturing operations deal in intangible products, or services, as their primary outputs. These are *service operations,* but one should recognize that an operation does not necessarily provide *only* services or *only* goods. Facilitating goods may be provided with services, and facilitating services may be provided with goods. For example, we can obtain the same goods (although in a different form) from a grocery store or from a restaurant. We think of a

TABLE 9.1 Classification of Types of Operations

TYPES OF OPERATIONS	MANUFACTURING, OR GOODS-PRODUCING, OPERATIONS	NONMANUFACTURING, OR NON-GOODS-PRODUCING, OPERATIONS
Project: activities of long duration and low volume	Building a bridge, dam, or house; preparing for a banquet	Research projects, development of software
Unit or batch: activities of short duration and low volume, producing custom goods or services	Job shop: making industrial hardware; printing personalized stationery; making drapes	Custom service: offering charter air or bus service; cleaning carpets; repairing autos; providing health care or counseling services; providing hair care; translating a foreign-language book for a publisher; designing costumes for a theatrical production; public warehousing; providing special-delivery mail service
Mass production: activities of short duration and high volume, producing standard goods or services	Continuous operation: making light bulbs, refrigerators, television sets, automobiles	Standard service: providing fast food, standard insurance policies, scheduled air or bus service, dry cleaning, personal checking accounts, regular mail service, distribution and wholesaling of standardized products; processing photographic film
Process industries: continuous processing of a homogeneous material	Continuous operation: processing chemicals, refining oil, milling flour, manufacturing paper	

grocery store as primarily providing goods. We trade with a restaurant primarily for the services it provides in selecting, preparing, and serving food, which is actually a tangible good. When we have a car "serviced," the process may include the installation of some parts. The service is provided by someone who knows which parts to replace and how to replace them and who spends the time to perform this service.

Operations that deal primarily in services can be further divided according to the degree to which the customer is a participant in the process. Many services are custom services, so the customer often has some contact with the service provider. The customer, however, does not have to be present during the process for some types of service, such as having clothes laundered or a watch repaired. Professor Richard Chase states that systems with a greater

TABLE 9.2 A Classification of Nonmanufacturing Operations

NONMANUFACTURING (NON-GOODS-PRODUCING) OPERATIONS		
PROVIDERS OF TANGIBLE PRODUCTS	PROVIDERS OF SERVICES	
Mail service Library service Wholesale and retail distributors Examples: Television sets Radios Watches Refrigerators Air conditioners	Services in which the customer is not a participant. Examples: Preparing tax forms Architectural design Landscaping Cleaning clothes Repairing watches, automobiles, appliances, etc. Rating and issuing insurance	Services in which the customer is a participant. Examples: Health care Hair care Travel Legal advice Financial advice Marriage counseling

percentage of customer contact are more difficult to understand and control.[3] Table 9.2 displays a classification of nonmanufacturing operations, with some examples of each type of operation.

OPERATIONS AND STRATEGIC MANAGEMENT

Different Operations, Different Strategies

A company's overall strategy addresses many broad issues and can even include plans for social responsibility, stockholder relations, and employee relations. One important aspect of the overall direction of a firm is its *competitive strategy* for marketing. At a very general level, one can identify some characteristics of marketing strategies often associated with the types of operations functions previously introduced in this chapter. Primarily, strategies of companies with a custom product will tend to differ from those of companies with a more standardized product. Table 9.3 shows some general features of marketing strategy for various types of operations.

Generally, companies can compete on three primary features of their goods or services:

1. *Quality*: Do all of the characteristics of a product make it suitable and reliable for the customer's intended use?
2. *Price*: Is the cost to the customer over the life of the product affordable

[3] Richard B. Chase, "Where Does the Customer Fit in a Service Operation?" *Harvard Business Review*, November–December 1978, p. 138.

TABLE 9.3 Marketing Strategies Associated with Various Types of Operations

TYPE OF OPERATION	TYPE OF PRODUCT	TYPICAL PROCESS CHARACTERISTICS	TYPICAL CHARACTERISTICS OF MARKETING STRATEGY
Service Project Job shop	Make to order as customer specifies	Use of broadly skilled workers and general-purpose equipment; emphasis on good initial planning of work, quality, flexibility	Selling diversity of capabilities and ability to provide features customers desire, ability to perform a quality job, ability to achieve reasonable delivery times
Continuous Process	Make for inventory a product designed to have features desired by many potential customers	Use of workers with narrower skills, specialized equipment, perhaps automation; emphasis on efficiency and cost control; good distribution system to make items readily available	Selling the desirability of features that are already designed into the product plus the desirability of the price, availability, service. Market research is important to ensure that product features are appropriate for the market

and considered reasonable when compared to the quality of the product and other quality-to-price ratios available in the marketplace?

3. *Availability*: Can the product be obtained within a reasonable and competitive time?

To succeed in the marketplace, the product must be judged as at least adequate on all three measures.

Operations: A Vital Element in Strategy

The operations function has great value as a competitive weapon in a company's strategy. Because it is the part of the firm that must produce the goods or provide the services that the consumer buys, the operations function plays an important role in implementing strategy. The operations function establishes the level of quality as a product is manufactured or as a service is provided. The operations function often is responsible for the largest part of a company's human and capital assets. Thus, much of a product's cost is incurred within operations, and this cost affects the price that must be charged and the profit margin that can be achieved. Finally, the ability of the operations function to perform determines to a great extent the ability of the company to have sufficient products available to meet delivery commitments.

It is clear, then, that the operations function has an important influence on the cost, quality, and availability of the company's goods or services.

Operations strengths and weaknesses can have a great impact on the success of the company's overall strategy. Therefore, the capabilities of operations must be carefully considered when corporate strategy is formulated, and operations decisions must be consistent with corporate strategy so that the full potential of operations' resources can be harnessed in pursuit of the company's goals.

This important relationship between strategy and operations is certainly recognized at General Motors. According to Roger B. Smith, chairman of GM, a serious attempt is made in his company to integrate strategic management into everyday "working lives." According to Smith, true integration involves tying together strategic management with the operating organization. Highlight 9.1 offers more information on the relationship between strategic management and operations at GM.

Strategy Decisions for Operations

Positioning Decisions

Strategy decisions at the top-management level and within the operations function affect how well the operations function will contribute to the competitive effectiveness of a company. One broad strategy decision that is important in guiding and coordinating the actions of operations is related to positioning. *Positioning* establishes the extent to which the production system will emphasize certain characteristics in order to achieve the greatest competitive advantage. Regardless of how desirable it may sound, a company cannot simultaneously have a product that is lowest in cost, highest in quality, and instantly available in abundance at numerous convenient locations. Professor Steven Wheelwright recommends that a manufacturing company explicitly establish the relative priorities it will give to the four performance characteristics: cost efficiency, quality, dependability, and flexibility.[4] These performance characteristics can be briefly described as follows:

- *Cost efficiency:* A company that emphasizes cost efficiency will see that its capital, labor, and other operating costs are kept low relative to those of other, similar companies.
- *Quality:* A company that emphasizes quality will consistently strive to provide a level of quality that is significantly superior to that of its competitors, even if it has to pay extra to do so.
- *Dependability:* A company that stresses dependability can be relied on to have its goods available for customers or to deliver its goods or services on schedule, if it is at all possible.
- *Flexibility:* A company that develops flexibility can quickly respond to changes in product design, product mix, or production volume.

[4] Steven C. Wheelwright, "Reflecting Corporate Strategy in Manufacturing Decisions," *Business Horizons,* February 1978, pp. 57–66.

HIGHLIGHT 9.1

ILLUSTRATIVE EXAMPLE ■ Smith Tries to Integrate Strategy and Operations at General Motors

Only eight years ago, General Motors Corp. had no strategic planners in its divisions, let alone in a lowly car plant. But as Raymond K. Fears, the strategic planner for GM's Buick City complex in Flint, Mich., amply demonstrates, times have changed. Fears, who turns 30 in mid-September, moved from GM's corporate strategic-planning group in 1983 to Buick City—the trio of 60-year-old plants that GM aspires to turn into the world's most efficient auto factory. His assignment: "To get [operating managers], who are used to thinking in terms of nuts and bolts, to think in strategic terms." That, he concedes, "is a major educational job."

Fears's transfer is part of GM Chairman Roger B. Smith's master plan to integrate strategic planning "into our daily lives." In Smith's book, that means "true integration with the operating organization."

MARCHING IN STEP

Fears served as a product planner for three years in GM's Chevrolet Motor Division before moving in 1982 to corporate, where he worked as a business-plan consultant to nine GM divisions. At Buick City, which will begin cranking out full-size 1986 cars a year from now, Fears's job is to aid in devising and implementing its piece of Buick Motor Division's strategy.

Chairman Smith insists that "the guy in charge of strategic planning is the general manager." Indeed, Fears's job will probably be phased out next year when the plant manager assumes all strategic-planning duties. One of Fears's tasks is to coordinate the strategic committee charged with ensuring that all corporate groups involved in pilot production are marching in step. He also has helped to scout the competition to make sure Buick City will not be made obsolete—even by newer GM plans that adopt the facility's manufacturing practices.

Does he have regrets about moving from headquarters to the down-in-the-trenches atmosphere of a car plant? Absolutely none, says Fears, who aspires to an operating job. "I see the move as getting closer to the action."

Source: "How GM Takes Planning to the Trenches," *Business Week,* September 17, 1984.

Positioning might be visualized as selecting a particular volume within a pyramid, such as the one shown in Figure 9.4, that the company consistently operates within. The pyramid defines the relative priorities that can be assigned to each of the four performance characteristics. However, the portion of the pyramid that the company will try to occupy is a strategic decision that must rest with the top management. If each part of a company tries to move in any direction in which that part of the company believes a competitor is outperforming it, then overall the company's money, talents, and efforts will not be effectively expended. By trying to move in several directions simultaneously, such a company would not be recognized as having a distinctive competence that would attract and retain customers, and customers could not rely on it for consistent treatment.

Although a company cannot be simultaneously at all corners of the pyramid shown in Figure 9.4, a company can expand the range of the pyramid that it covers. This is quite different from the company or parts of the company bouncing inconsistently from one location to another within the pyramid. Expanding the range within the pyramid that a company consistently covers can be thought of as shortening one or more legs of the pyramid or making the pyramid smaller (that is, shrinking the pyramid). The effect is that a company can then cover a larger relative percentage of its pyramid than its competitors and leave less space for a competitor to develop a distinctive competence.

An example of shrinking the pyramid can be found in the operation of numerous Japanese companies. Through very careful and diligent efforts, these companies have controlled processes to prevent defects and have achieved greatly improved quality. These actions have reduced the cost of screening and repairing defective work in the factory and the cost of warranty work in the field. In effect, the companies simultaneously improve quality and cost so that they cover a larger relative portion of the cost–quality leg of their pyramid. We can think of this as reducing the length of the cost–quality leg of the pyramid, as shown in Figure 9.5(a). Many Japanese manufacturers have also provided extensive training and cross training of their workers so that they

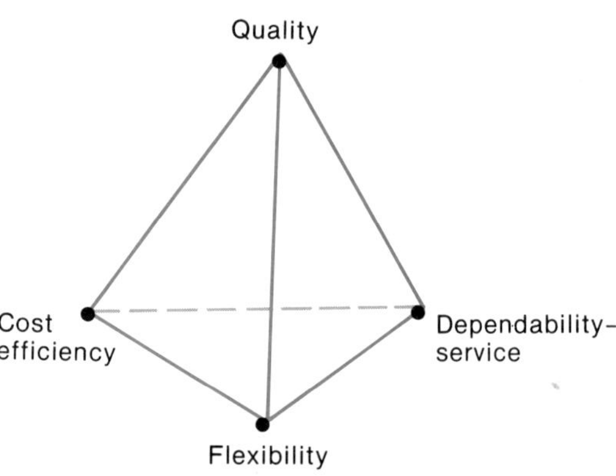

FIGURE 9.4 Possible Positions of an Operations Function

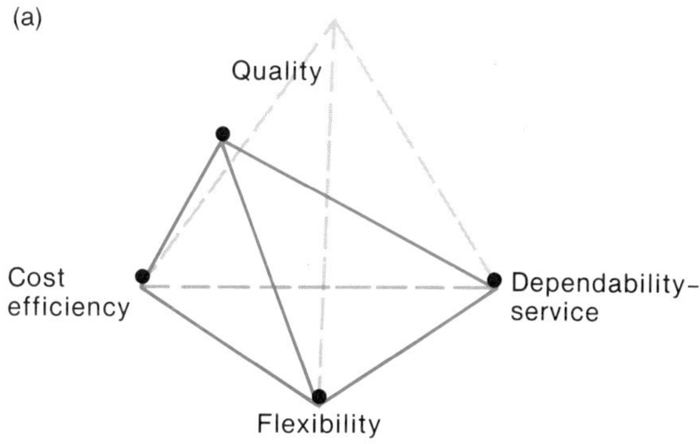

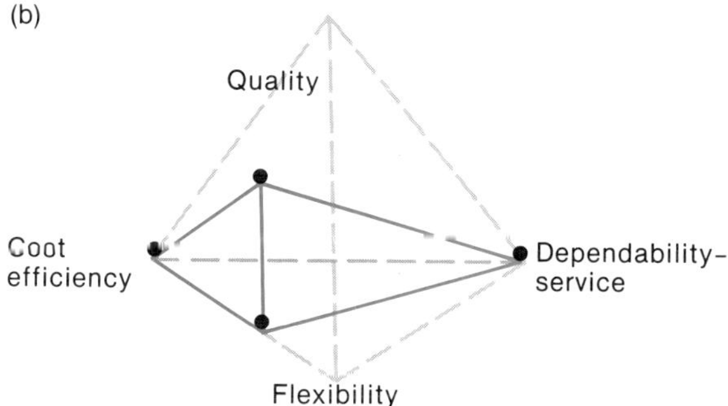

FIGURE 9.5 Shrinking the Pyramid

will have multiskilled workers. This versatile work force, coupled with plant arrangements and equipment that can easily be changed over from one product to another, provides greater flexibility without a significant increase in cost. The flexibility–cost leg of the pyramid is thereby shortened, as shown in Figure 9.5(b). Companies can employ these or other means to shrink various legs of their pyramids. Companies that are resourceful and succeed in shrinking their pyramids can serve their markets well. And their competitors will have difficulty finding a spot in which to try to establish their own distinctive competence.

Table 9.4 shows the four performance characteristics we have mentioned and some of the supporting features that are desirable in the operations function of a manufacturing company to help achieve a particular performance characteristic. Comments in the third column of the table indicate the degree to which this feature might also be appropriate to support that performance characteristic in a nonmanufacturing company.

Other Decisions

Once a company has selected its intended position and internally communicated this intention, all parts of the company can be more consistent in their decisions. That is, the decisions of any given part of the company will be more consistent with its own decisions over time and more consistent with the

TABLE 9.4 Operations Features That Support Particular Performance Characteristics

PERFORMANCE CHARACTERISTIC TO BE EMPHASIZED	FEATURES THAT MANUFACTURING OPERATIONS MIGHT PROVIDE	APPLICABILITY TO SERVICE OPERATIONS
Cost efficiency	Low overhead	Yes
	Special-purpose equipment and facilities	Yes
	High utilization of capacity	Yes
	Close control of materials	Maybe
	High productivity	Yes
	Low wage rates	Yes
Quality	Skilled workers	Yes
	Adequate precision of equipment	Maybe
	Motivation for pride of workmanship	Yes
	Effective communication of standards or job requirements	Yes
Dependability	Effective scheduling system	Yes
	Low equipment failure	Yes
	Low absenteeism, low turnover, no strikes	Yes
	High inventory investment	Maybe
	Commitment of personnel to perform as required	Yes
Flexibility	Dependable, rapid suppliers	Yes
	Reserve capacity	Yes
	Multiskilled workers who can be shifted	Yes
	Effective control of work flow	Yes
	Versatile processing equipment	Yes
	Low setup time and cost	Maybe
	Integration of design and production	Maybe

decisions made in other parts of the company. The company will be more likely to achieve its strategic objectives when all parts of the company are making concerted efforts to support these objectives in all of their decisions and activities.

Numerous decisions within the operations function are related to the positioning decision as well as to each other. Robert Hayes and Steven Wheelwright present eight major categories of strategy decisions for a manufacturing company, as shown in Table 9.5.[5] The first four categories are normally recognized as long-term decisions that are difficult to reverse and therefore more likely to be considered strategic. The last four categories appear to deal with "tactical" matters—that is, with decisions that are more concerned with day-to-day operating issues. It is important to recognize, however, that even these matters have long-run strategic impact.

Highlight 9.2 contains an interesting account of how plant location, the second item in Hayes and Wheelwright's list, is a long-run decision with

[5] Robert H. Hayes and Steven C. Wheelwright, *Restoring Our Competitive Edge* (New York: John Wiley & Sons, 1984), p. 31.

TABLE 9.5 Categories of Strategy Decisions in Manufacturing Operations

1. **Capacity**—amount, timing, type
2. **Facilities**—size, location, specialization
3. **Technology**—equipment, automation, linkages
4. **Vertical integration**—direction, extent, balance
5. **Work force**—skill level, wage policies, employment security
6. **Quality**—defect prevention, monitoring, intervention
7. **Production planning materials control**—sourcing policies, centralization, decision rules
8. **Organization**—structure, control/reward systems, role of staff groups

significant strategic impact for an automobile manufacturer such as the Honda Motor Company.

Product Design: An Important Strategy Factor

One of the basic decisions a company must face is what goods or services it will offer in the marketplace. Identification of the general type of product helps narrow the search for a niche in the market where the company might stimulate sufficient demand to achieve success. Beyond the broad question of what business it will be in, the company must address many details regarding what specific product or service it will offer and how. Decisions about the product's design specifications affect the selection of process technology (one of the decision categories in Table 9.5), which in turn affects the company's expenditures for equipment and facilities. Product design also affects the ease with which the product can be fabricated and assembled, so it has an effect on operating costs. Design also affects the ease with which a product can be produced with few defects, so that it has an effect on market acceptance and the customer's perception of the company. Product design, then, has serious implications for the company's long-range success and therefore is of strategic importance. Let us now consider the relationship between design and operating decisions in manufacturing and nonmanufacturing operations.

Product Design in Nonmanufacturing Operations

The product, or output, desired from the operations system of a nonmanufacturing firm will certainly affect the type of inputs needed and the capabilities that must be available to transform the inputs into the desired goods or services. The processing technology and kinds of skills that must be available in the operations function may be significantly affected even by what appear to be small differences in the characteristics of the product or of the way it is delivered.[6] The decision of a food establishment to provide buffet meals rather than cafeteria-style service, for example, will mean that fewer people will be

[6] Dan R. E. Thomas, "Strategy Is Different in Service Businesses," *Harvard Business Review*, July–August 1980, pp. 158–165.

HIGHLIGHT 9.2

ILLUSTRATIVE EXAMPLE ■ Plant Location and Strategy at Honda

When Americans grouse that Japanese auto companies loot American jobs, the Japanese have a ready answer: look how American we've become. In the last five years the Japanese opened four plants in the United States and another four were planned. But they are mainly factories that assemble engines and other parts manufactured in Japan. Last week the Honda Motor Co. said it will take a big step toward making the most American of Japanese cars. It plans to invest $450 million to expand its Anna, Ohio, plant to make engines, transmissions and other parts. By 1990, Honda promises, two-thirds or more of each American-made car will contain American-made parts. . . .

POLITICAL SAVVY

Moving production to the United States makes good political and economic sense. Honda and the other Japanese car companies know that Congress, now controlled by the Democrats, might pass a restrictive trade bill. And the yen's continued strength against the dollar means Japanese auto companies have lost their historic cost advantage over Americans. In fact, Accords are so inexpensive to make in Marysville that Honda may export them to Taiwan next year.

For Honda, being ahead of the curve has paid off handsomely. Producing 235,000 cars a year in Ohio helped shelter the company from the voluntary restraints that Tokyo placed on car exports to the United States. Honda was the top-selling Japanese car here in 1986—passing Toyota and Nissan—and is now the fourth largest automaker in America, behind Detroit's Big Three. With less than 10 percent of the Japanese market, Honda is more dependent on the U.S. market than its Japanese rivals. For that reason, many analysts expect the company will move most of its operations here within five years. And that may be the ultimate answer to protectionism.

Source: Adapted from Jeff B. Copeland and Ginny Carroll, "Honda: Made in the U.S.A.," *Newsweek*, January 19, 1987, p. 42.

needed behind the counter to serve patrons. It will, however, require the establishment to have extra food available or to be able to prepare additional food quickly, because management will no longer be able to control the size of each portion.

Levitz Furniture Corporation operated for years with cavernous 170,000-square-foot buildings that were combination warehouse–showrooms located near rail sidings in large cities. Customers could select furniture and haul it home. More recently, the company has added a chain of satellite stores that serve only as showrooms; the warehouses are located about twenty-five miles away. As a result of this change in merchandising strategy, the company must keep better inventory records so the people at the showrooms know what is available at various locations, and the company must have a more extensive fleet of vehicles and personnel to move the product between locations and make deliveries to the customers.

To take another example of the operating implications that result from a product characteristic, consider a decision by Wendy's Old-Fashioned Hamburgers chain. Wendy's had the choice of serving fresh or frozen french-fried potatoes. Serving fresh potatoes would have required each location to select, purchase, store, peel, store again, then cook and serve the potatoes. The use of preprocessed and frozen potatoes would have required each location only to store, then cook and serve the potatoes. Preprocessed potatoes also provide a more uniform product. Therefore, preprocessed frozen french fries were selected, reducing the number of employees and the amount of space required at each location and reducing quality control and waste-disposal problems at each location.

Product Design in Manufacturing Operations

A manufacturing firm must balance the need to make its product marketable with the need to produce it economically. Product design can affect appearance, so the designer must work for an appealing look. Because some aspects of the product design may necessitate particular processes and equipment in production, the best time to begin a cost-reduction program is while the product is on the drawing board. As the product is designed, a cost–benefit evaluation should be performed, taking into account the kind and amount of materials, labor, and processing equipment that each alternative design will require. The company must also recognize that the potential consumer will also perform some sort of cost–benefit evaluation before deciding whether to purchase the product. Some processes and materials are more expensive and should be used only if the functions of the product make them necessary or the aesthetic appeal of the results justifies the expense.

Myriad alternative designs for a product are usually possible, and alternative production methods may be possible even after the product is designed. Production engineers often serve as advisers to designers, helping them develop product designs that are reasonably economical to produce. A brief discussion of product design ideas will provide some appreciation of the complex nature of this topic. In selecting the raw material for a product, the designer must consider such properties as hardness, wear resistance, fatigue strength, tensile strength, weight, transparency, and ductility. Although a designer might consider the use of an inexpensive raw material, a more expensive material such as a free-machining alloy might result in a net saving when the processing costs are considered. After the material is selected, other design parameters must be evaluated. Economy can result from such ideas as:

HIGHLIGHT 9.3

SKILLS MODULE ■ Operations and Product Design at Apple

INTRODUCTION

We have noted that product design is an important operations and strategy issue. Review the following situation, and then complete the skill development exercise that follows. Doing so will help you develop some ability in appropriately managing product design as a component of strategy as well as considering its relationship to operations.

THE SITUATION

According to Clement Mok, a creative director at Apple Computer, Inc., Apple sees itself as a company that designs tools to help people communicate, learn, work, and create. Over the years, Apple seems to have prided itself on being "product design conscious." The company has long recognized and acted in terms of the concept that product design, as a part of strategy, must be integrally related and complementary to operations if a company is to be successful. In short, Apple appreciates the critical relationship between (1) how a product looks and how it works as indicators of its appropriateness for the marketplace and (2) the efficiency and effectiveness with which it can be manufactured.

The development of the Macintosh is a good example of how product design and operations are planned to be compatible at Apple. At the start, simplicity was the primary ingredient for the new computer. Do we really need that circuit board? Could we get along without that key? Do we really need that extra menu? Can we build this feature with present production facilities? Facing and reacting to hard questions of this type helped the company achieve a simply operated product that was suited to its customers and that could be feasibly produced given Apple production resources.

SKILL DEVELOPMENT EXERCISE

Assume that Apple Computer has just developed the strategy of selling a powerful new computer specially designed for the sophisticated computer user. Unlike the Macintosh, this new computer will emphasize intricacy and the ability to handle complex and unique problems. Also, unlike most Macintosh users, a significant proportion of the users of this new computer will be very familiar with computer technology and will appreciate the depth of the computer's capacity. According to this strategy, the new computer will not replace the Macintosh but will complement it in the Apple product line.

(Continues)

Apple management is concerned, however, about potential operational problems that will inevitably occur as a result of manufacturing this new computer. But management feels confident that careful planning of design for the computer will help minimize the effects of several such potential problems. List three potential operational problems that Apple could face as a result of manufacturing the new computer, and explain how careful product design might help the company overcome them.

Source: Based on Stephen MacDonald, "Looking Good: More Firms Place Higher Priority on Product Design," *The Wall Street Journal*, January 22, 1987, p. 33.

- Using a different process to achieve basic shape—for example; casting instead of machining
- Requiring machined surfaces only where necessary
- Requiring close tolerances only when necessary
- Ensuring that surfaces are easily accessible to the types of processes to be used
- Considering less costly ways of joining materials, such as spot welding rather than riveting
- Requiring thinner materials or less severe bends so that light-capacity machines can be used for forming operations

As indicated earlier, the most effective time to consider a product's manufacturability is while the product is being designed. Close coordination between the design and manufacturing departments is desirable if a company wants to develop economical and effective designs. One characteristic that was found to be common during a comparison of some of America's best-managed factories was a close linkage between design and manufacturing departments so that easily producible designs could be rapidly developed. (Other similarities noted were that the companies excelled in the ability to "build in quality, make wise choices about automation, get close to the customer and handle their work forces."[7])

Highlight 9.3 will give you an opportunity to consider how product design is a strategic management and an operations issue at Apple Computer.

SUMMARY

The operations function is performed by the people in an organization who produce the goods or services that the firm offers to the marketplace. The

[7] Gene Bylinsky, "America's Best-Managed Factories," *Fortune*, May 28, 1984, pp. 16–24.

operations function must be compatible and consistent with other important organizational functions, such as marketing and finance, in order for any organization to be successful. In our discussion of the operations function, we distinguished manufacturing functions from nonmanufacturing, or service, functions. We further characterized manufacturing firms as make-to-stock, make-to-order, or assemble-to-order producers and differentiated between continuous and intermittent production. Turning to nonmanufacturing operations, we drew a distinction between those that deal in (though they do not manufacture) tangible outputs and those that deal in intangible outputs, or services.

HIGHLIGHT 9.4

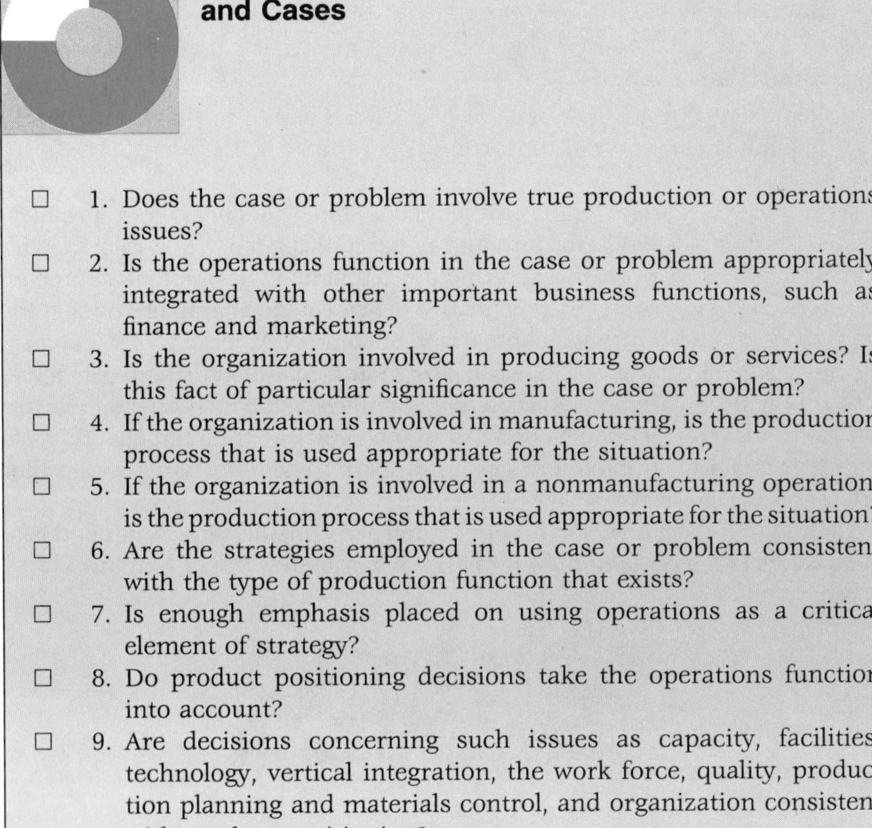

CHECKLIST ■ **Analyzing Operations in Problems and Cases**

- ☐ 1. Does the case or problem involve true production or operations issues?
- ☐ 2. Is the operations function in the case or problem appropriately integrated with other important business functions, such as finance and marketing?
- ☐ 3. Is the organization involved in producing goods or services? Is this fact of particular significance in the case or problem?
- ☐ 4. If the organization is involved in manufacturing, is the production process that is used appropriate for the situation?
- ☐ 5. If the organization is involved in a nonmanufacturing operation, is the production process that is used appropriate for the situation?
- ☐ 6. Are the strategies employed in the case or problem consistent with the type of production function that exists?
- ☐ 7. Is enough emphasis placed on using operations as a critical element of strategy?
- ☐ 8. Do product positioning decisions take the operations function into account?
- ☐ 9. Are decisions concerning such issues as capacity, facilities, technology, vertical integration, the work force, quality, production planning and materials control, and organization consistent with product positioning?
- ☐ 10. Is product design as a strategic factor appropriately linked to operations?

Because a firm's competitive strategy for marketing is such an important part of its overall direction, managers must understand the relationship between type of operation and marketing strategy. Strategy decisions about which production characteristic(s)—cost efficiency, quality, dependability, or flexibility—the operations function will emphasize can also be crucial to the firm's success. Product design is a third key strategy factor. It affects the selection of process technologies, the cost of equipment and facilities, the ease with which the product can be produced, the quality of the product, and hence the customer's perception of the firm.

Highlight 9.4 contains a summary checklist of questions based on this chapter. Use it in analyzing strategic management problems and cases that revolve around operations issues.

ADDITIONAL READINGS

Buffa, Elwood A. *Meeting the Competitive Challenge.* Homewood, Ill.: Richard D. Irwin, 1984.

Hall, Robert W. *Zero Inventories.* Homewood, Ill.: Dow Jones–Irwin, 1983.

Harmon, Roy L., and Leroy D. Peterson. *Reinventing the Factory: Productivity Breakthroughs in Manufacturing Today.* New York: The Free Press, 1989.

Hayes, Robert H., Steven C. Wheelwright, and Kim B. Clark. "The Power of Positive Manufacturing." *Across the Board,* October 1988, pp. 24–30.

Lubar, Robert. "Rediscovering the Factory." *Fortune,* July 13, 1981, pp. 52–64.

Plossl, George W. *Production and Inventory Control: Applications.* Atlanta, Ga.: George Plossl Educational Services, 1983.

Schonberger, Richard J. *Japanese Manufacturing Techniques: Nine Hidden Lessons in Simplicity.* New York: The Free Press, 1982.

———. *The World Class Company.* New York: The Free Press, 1990.

Wright, Oliver W. *MRP II: Unlocking America's Productivity Potential.* Boston: CBI Publishing, 1984.

HIGHLIGHT 9.5 ■ APPLICATION OF CHAPTER MATERIAL

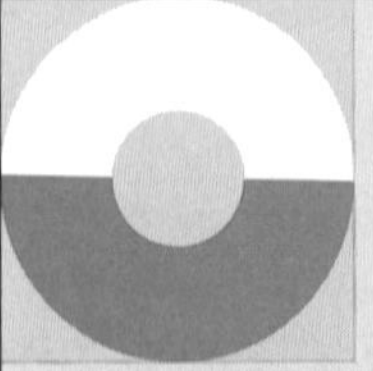

The Coming of the "Brewpub"

Allan Paul's friends loved the rich, amber lager he brewed in five-gallon batches at his apartment on San Francisco's Telegraph Hill. They urged him to start a brewery, but that was out of the question as long as California prohibited brewers from selling draft on their premises. Then the law changed—and, armed with a carefully researched business plan and a cooler of his product, Paul raised $400,000 to convert a turn-of-the-century saloon into the city's first "brewpub." Recently Mayor Dianne Feinstein cut a red ribbon on the hand-hammered copper brew kettle at Paul's San Francisco Brewing Co. Taking a long draft of his Emperor Norton lager, the visitor from city hall pronounced it "the best I've every tasted."

Weary of watery, mass-market brands, beer lovers across the country are thirsting for the kind of stout libation found in brewpubs and limited-production "microbreweries." Since the nation's first brewpub, the Hopland Brewery, opened in Mendocino, Calif., in 1983, more than a dozen others have sprouted across the country. Meantime the number of microbreweries, which sell their product both in bottles and at brewpublike taprooms, has grown from 40 in 1980 to 63 in 1985. While total beer sales have gone flat in recent years, the consumption of beer from microbreweries grew by 80 percent in 1985 and at least that much in 1986. So far only 10 states have passed the kind of direct-sales law that makes such establishments possible. But 10 other states are considering it. And Bill Owens, the feisty owner of Buffalo Bill's Brewery in Hayward, Calif., and publisher of a microbrewing trade magazine, is pressing for legislation that could open the spigots for a nationwide surge of brewpubs and microbreweries.

The atmosphere of brewpubs can differ as much as the flavor of the beer they serve. Paul's bar, with its polished mahogany and brass, has the appeal of a quiet English pub. Owens's establishment recalls a funky, frontier saloon. In New York City, The New Amsterdam Brewery's Tap Room boasts a tasteful Continental ambience. And in Portland, Oreg., Mike (Captain Neon) McMenamin invited local neon artists to decorate the fermentation room of his Hillsale Brewery and Public House. Most brewpubs feature traditional pub food—hearty, filling and inexpensive. Beer is the main attraction. Brewed in full view of customers and consumed in traditional pint glasses, it is generally a full-flavored beverage that bears little resemblance to mass-produced beers made from grain. "We make beer with water, malted barley, hops and yeast," says Paul, pausing for effect, "and nothing else."

For the moment, most large brewing companies are wagering that the American market will continue to favor lighter beers. But the success of brewpubs and microbreweries is causing a few to hedge their bets. Both Heileman and Coors have begun brewing "specialty beers." And Arnie Winograd, a beer-industry consultant, predicts this will be the growth sector of the industry for the next 10 years. "In the old days taverns were like clubs where people gathered to drink beer and talk," Winograd recalls. "We're coming back to that. People come to brewpubs for *Gemütlichkeit*—and good beer."

DISCUSSION QUESTIONS

1. What kind of manufacturing operation is used in brewpubs?
2. Do you think that manufacturing operations and organizational strategy are related in brewpubs? Explain.
3. If you were managing the Coors Brewing Company, would you be doing anything in response to the appearance of brewpubs? Explain.

Source: Gerald C. Lubenow, "A New Thirst for 'Brewpubs,'" *Newsweek*, February 9, 1987, p. 49.

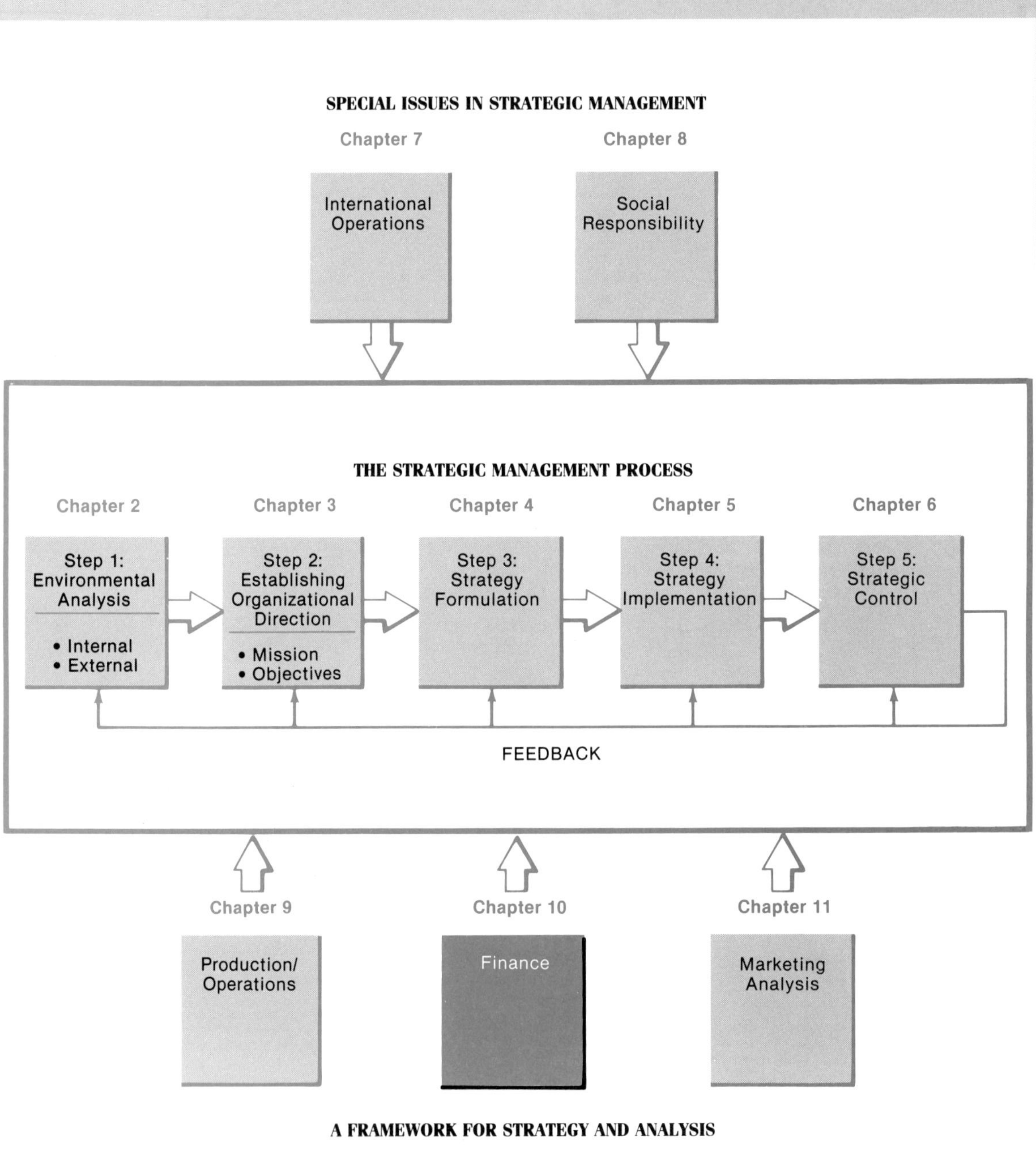
SPECIAL ISSUES IN STRATEGIC MANAGEMENT
Chapter 7
International Operations
Chapter 8
Social Responsibility
THE STRATEGIC MANAGEMENT PROCESS
Chapter 2
Step 1: Environmental Analysis
• Internal
• External
Chapter 3
Step 2: Establishing Organizational Direction
• Mission
• Objectives
Chapter 4
Step 3: Strategy Formulation
Chapter 5
Step 4: Strategy Implementation
Chapter 6
Step 5: Strategic Control
FEEDBACK
Chapter 9
Production/ Operations
Chapter 10
Finance
Chapter 11
Marketing Analysis
A FRAMEWORK FOR STRATEGY AND ANALYSIS
Chapter 12
An Approach to Solving Strategic Problems and Cases

CHAPTER 10

Financial Foundations for Strategic Management

Many types of financial analyses are useful for strategic management decision making. In this chapter, we investigate several financial tools that are commonly used in analyzing strategic management problems and cases.[1] First, we discuss financial ratio analysis, which is a useful tool for investigating the overall financial condition of an organization. Next, we examine break-even analysis, a simple financial tool for investigating the potential value of an investment. Finally, we describe net present value analysis, a more sophisticated method of examining investment alternatives.

[1] This chapter is based in part on J. Paul Peter and James H. Donnelly, Jr., *Marketing Management: Knowledge and Skills*, 2nd ed. (Homewood, Ill.: BPI/Irwin, 1989), section 3.

FINANCIAL RATIO ANALYSIS

A useful first step in analyzing an organization from a financial standpoint is to perform a financial ratio analysis. A *financial ratio analysis* is based on information provided in the organization's balance sheet and income statement. These two financial statements are frequently included in strategic management cases, and performing a financial ratio analysis is a convenient way to examine the condition of the firm. In this section, we first review the balance sheet and income statement and then propose a four-step process for performing a financial ratio analysis.

Table 10.1 presents the balance sheet for the MoPower Robotics Company, a manufacturer of specialized robots for industrial use. The *balance sheet* is a summary of the assets of an organization and the claims against its assets at a particular time. Actually, Table 10.1 represents a *comparative balance sheet;* the assets and liabilities of MoPower are given for more than one time. Note that two types of assets are shown. *Current assets* are those that are expected to be converted to cash within one year, whereas *fixed assets* are expected to be held for a longer time. Similarly, *current liabilities* are amounts of money that are owed and are expected to be paid out within one year; other obligations are more long term in nature.

TABLE 10.1 MoPower Robotics Company Illustrative Balance Sheet
(in thousands of dollars)

ASSETS	DEC. 31, 1988	DEC. 31, 1989
Cash	$ 30	$ 25
Marketable securities	40	25
Accounts receivable	200	100
Inventories	430	700
Total current assets	$ 700	$ 850
Plant and equipment	1,000	1,500
Long-term investments	500	900
Other assets	200	250
Total assets	$2,400	$3,500
LIABILITIES AND NET WORTH	**DEC. 31, 1988**	**DEC. 31, 1989**
Trade accounts payable	$ 150	$ 200
Notes payable	100	100
Accruals	25	100
Provision for federal taxes	40	50
Total current liabilities	$ 315	$ 450
Bonds	500	1,000
Debentures	85	50
Stockholders' equity	1,500	2,000
Total liabilities and stockholders' equity	$2,400	$3,500

TABLE 10.2 MoPower Robotics Company Illustrative Income Statement for the Year Ending December 31, 1989 (in thousands of dollars)

Sales		$3,600
Cost of goods sold		2,700
Gross profit		$ 900
Less operating expenses:		
Selling	$40	
General and administrative	60	100
Gross operating revenue		$ 800
Less depreciation		250
Net operating income (NOI)		$ 550
Less other expenses		50
Earnings before interest and taxes (EBIT)		$ 500
Less interest expense		200
Earnings before taxes (EBT)		$ 300
Less federal and state income taxes (40%)		120
Earnings after taxes (EAT)		$ 180

Table 10.2 presents MoPower's income statement. The *income statement* shows the financial results of an organization's operations during an interval of time, usually one year. The income statement lists net sales (sales minus returns and allowances) at the top and then proceeds to subtract various amounts to determine earnings after tax (net income). The amounts subtracted from net sales on this income statement include cost of goods sold, operating expenses, depreciation, other expenses, interest, and taxes. Various organizations may have different entries and labels, but these two financial statements are representative of commonly used reporting procedures.

These financial statements contain a tremendous amount of useful information for strategic managers. However, it is very difficult to simply look at the statements and determine how well the organization is doing. For example, is MoPower currently in a solid financial position, or do these financial statements suggest that the company has problems? In order to answer this question, we need a method of comparing MoPower's financial situation (across time), with that of other firms of similar size in the same industry, and with industry averages. These comparisons are the basis for financial ratio analysis.

Performing a financial ratio analysis can be divided into four steps: (1) choosing the appropriate ratios, (2) calculating the ratios, (3) comparing the ratios, and (4) checking for problems and opportunities. We will discuss each of these steps in turn.

Choosing the Appropriate Ratios

The many types of financial ratios include liquidity ratios, leverage ratios, activity ratios, profitability ratios, growth ratios, and valuation ratios. All have important uses in evaluating the financial well-being of an organization. Though strategic managers may use all of these types of ratios, some of them are very specialized, and applying them in a meaningful way requires an extensive financial management background.[2] However, there are several types of financial ratios that should be applied routinely in analyzing *any* strategic management case that includes financial statements. These types—the liquidity, activity, and profitability ratios—are especially useful for uncovering symptoms of problems in cases you are called on to analyze and for supporting the arguments you advance about the major issues in the case and the solutions you propose. There are many ratios of each of these types; we will discuss only a few of the most useful ones.

Liquidity Ratios

One of the first financial considerations we must take into account when analyzing a strategic case problem is the liquidity of the organization. *Liquidity* refers to the ability of the organization to pay its short-term obligations. If the organization cannot even meet its short-term obligations, it can do little else until this problem is corrected. In other words, a firm that cannot meet its current financial obligations must resolve this problem before long-term strategic planning can be effective.

The two most commonly used ratios for investigating liquidity are the current ratio and the quick ratio (or acid test ratio). The *current ratio* is found by dividing current assets by current liabilities and is a measure of the overall ability of an organization to meet its current obligations. A common rule of thumb is that the current ratio should be about 2:1, although what is acceptable depends greatly on the industry and the situation.

The *quick ratio* is determined by subtracting inventory from current assets and dividing the remainder by current liabilities. Because inventory is the least liquid current asset, the quick ratio gives an indication of the degree to which an organization has funds readily available to meet short-term obligations. A common rule of thumb is that the quick ratio should be at least 1:1, although, again, it depends on the industry and the situation.

Activity Ratios

Activity ratios, also called asset management ratios, investigate how well the organization handles its assets. For strategic management purposes, two of the most useful activity ratios measure inventory turnover and total asset utilization.

Inventory turnover is determined by dividing sales by inventories. If the firm is not turning over its inventory as rapidly as it did in the past, or as rapidly as other firms in the industry, it may have a problem. Perhaps too

[2] For cases that require a detailed ratio analysis of issues such as leverage, growth, and evaluation, consult J. Fred Weston and Eugene F. Brigham, *Essentials of Managerial Finance,* 7th ed. (Hinsdale, Ill.: The Dryden Press, 1985), pp. 59–101; and James C. Van Horne, *Financial Management and Policy,* 7th ed. (Englewood Cliffs, N.J.: Prentice-Hall, 1986), pp. 766–798.

much money is being tied up in unproductive or obsolete inventory, or the organization may be failing to market its products as well as it did in the past.

A second useful activity ratio is total asset utilization. *Total asset utilization* is calculated by dividing sales by total assets and is a measure of how productively the firm's assets have been used in generating sales. If this ratio is well below the industry average, management may not be using its assets effectively.

Profitability Ratios

The profitability of an organization is an important measure of its effectiveness. Although financial analysts suggest that a firm's goal is to maximize shareholder wealth, profitability is a common yardstick for assessing the firm's success. Two key profitability ratios are profit margin on sales and return on investment (ROI). *Profit margin on sales* is calculated by dividing earnings before interest and taxes (EBIT) by sales. Serious questions about an organization should be raised if this figure is declining across time or is well below that found for other firms in the industry.

Return on investment is calculated by dividing earnings after taxes (EAT) by total assets. This ratio is also called return on assets, and earnings after taxes are sometimes referred to as profit after taxes, net profit, or net income. This ratio gives an indication of how productively the organization has acquired, used, and managed assets. Return on investment is a commonly discussed measure of corporate performance.

Calculating the Ratios

The next step in ratio analysis is to calculate the ratios. Below we have calculated each of the six ratios we have discussed, using data derived from the financial statements for the MoPower Robotics Company, for the year 1989.

LIQUIDITY RATIOS

$$\text{Curent ratio} = \frac{\text{Current assets}}{\text{Current liabilities}} = \frac{850}{450} = 1.89$$

$$\text{Quick ratio} = \frac{\text{Current assets} - \text{inventory}}{\text{Current liabilities}} = \frac{150}{450} = 0.33$$

ACTIVITY RATIOS

$$\text{Inventory turnover} = \frac{\text{Sales}}{\text{Inventory}} = \frac{3{,}600}{700} = 5.14$$

$$\text{Total asset utilization} = \frac{\text{Sales}}{\text{Total assets}} = \frac{3{,}600}{3{,}500} = 1.03$$

PROFITABILITY RATIOS:

$$\text{Profit margin on sales} = \frac{\text{EBIT}}{\text{Sales}} = \frac{500}{3{,}600} = 0.14$$

$$\text{Return on investment} = \frac{\text{EAT}}{\text{Total assets}} = \frac{180}{3{,}500} = 0.05$$

Comparing the Ratios

We cannot overemphasize the fact that no single ratio has meaning by itself. In other words, it is the comparison of ratios that is critical for using this tool effectively. Ratios can be compared across time for the same firm, compared with those of similar firms in the industry, or compared with industry averages. The following examples illustrate each of these different types of comparisons.

First, suppose that in 1988 MoPower had sales of $3,300,000, earnings before interest and taxes of $600,000, and earnings after taxes of $200,000. With this information, and the balance sheet information for December 31, 1988 (supplied in Table 10.1), we can compute the ratios for 1988 and then compare them with those for 1989 to investigate trends. Table 10.3 presents this comparison.

To compare an organization's ratios with those of similar firms in the industry or with industry averages, the analyst must look up the industry information. (Highlight 10.1 lists some widely available sources of financial ratios.)

Table 10.4 presents a comparison of MoPower's 1989 ratios with those of firms of similar size in the industry and with the industry medians. (Financial sources often report the industry median rather than the mean to avoid the distorting effects of outliers, or values that lie far beyond the area where most tend to cluster.) Once the analyst has prepared comparative statements such as those shown in Table 10.3 and Table 10.4, it is time to interpret what all of the information means. This is the final step in ratio analysis.

TABLE 10.3 Comparison of Financial Ratios for MoPower Robotics Company, 1988 and 1989

FINANCIAL RATIOS	1988	1989
Liquidity		
Current ratio	2.22	1.89
Quick ratio	0.86	0.33
Activity		
Inventory turnover	7.67	5.14
Total asset utilization	1.38	1.03
Profitability		
Profit margin on sales	0.18	0.14
Return on investment	0.08	0.05

HIGHLIGHT 10.1

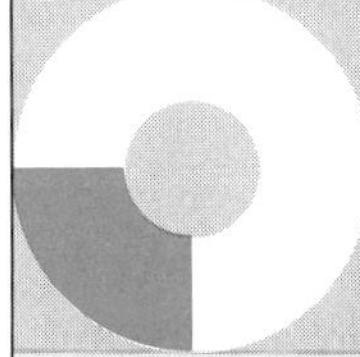

ILLUSTRATIVE EXAMPLE ■ Financial Ratios: Where to Find Them

1. *Annual Statement Studies.* Published by Robert Morris Associates, this work includes 11 financial ratios computed annually for over 150 lines of business. Each line of business is divided into 4 size categories.
2. Dun and Bradstreet provides 14 ratios calculated annually for over 100 lines of business.
3. *The Almanac of Business and Industrial Financial Ratios.* This work, published by Prentice-Hall, Inc., lists industry averages for 22 financial ratios. Approximately 170 businesses and industries are listed.
4. *The Quarterly Financial Report for Manufacturing Corporations.* This work, published jointly by the Federal Trade Commission and the Securities and Exchange Commission, contains balance-sheet and income-statement information by industry groupings and by asset-size categories.
5. Trade associations and individual companies often compute ratios for their industries and make them available to analysts.

Source: James C. Van Horne, *Financial Management and Policy,* 7th ed. Copyright © 1986, pp. 767–768. Reprinted by permission of Prentice-Hall, Inc., Englewood Cliffs, New Jersey.

TABLE 10.4 Comparison of Financial Ratios for MoPower with Industry Figures

FINANCIAL RATIOS	MOPOWER COMPANY	INDUSTRY FIRMS, ASSETS 1–10 MILLION	INDUSTRY MEDIAN
Liquidity			
Current ratio	1.88	1.8	1.8
Quick ratio	0.33	0.9	1.0
Activity			
Inventory turnover	5.14	7.8	7.9
Total asset utilization	1.03	1.7	1.8
Profitability			
Profit margin on sales	0.14	0.13	0.15
Return on investment	0.05	0.15	0.16

Checking for Problems and Opportunities

The comparisons between ratios shown in Tables 10.3 and 10.4 suggest that MoPower is not in a strong financial position and that its position has declined since the previous year. In terms of liquidity, although MoPower was in good shape in 1988, its position in 1989 was not favorable. Particularly, given the quick ratio of 0.33, MoPower could be in serious trouble if its creditors demanded quick payment. What appears to have happened is a large inventory buildup. This may mean that MoPower's products have been superseded in an area experiencing the effects of rapid technological change and are not selling well. Alternatively, MoPower may be building inventory for an expected increase in demand. In either case, its liquidity position needs to be improved.

The buildup in inventory is also reflected in the decrease in activity ratios. Inventory turnover and total asset utilization have slipped and are now well below industry averages. Perhaps MoPower has also accumulated some other unproductive or outdated assets that should be disposed of.

In terms of profitability, although profit margin on sales has decreased from 18 percent to 14 percent, it is still above that of firms of similar size in the industry. However, the company's return on investment is far below industry figures and has shrunk significantly. This could be a very important problem for MoPower, particularly if it is trying to attract new investors. However, much depends on other factors, such as whether MoPower is a new company that is expected to have a large increase in future earnings.

What should be clear from the foregoing analysis is that ratios offer a convenient way to investigate the financial well-being of an organization. Calculating various ratios and comparing them can alert analysts to what areas of strategic management should be investigated more fully. However, financial ratios only indicate symptoms of problems; the real problems are the *reasons* for poor financial performance. You can generally discover these underlying causes by carefully considering other information contained in a case or strategic management situation.

Finally, even in cases where a firm's financial ratios appear to conform to industry averages, this conformity does not mean that the firm has no financial or other strategic management problems. For example, perhaps the firm has a clear differential advantage that could be exploited to far *outstrip* average industry performance but is not taking advantage of it. Alternatively, perhaps the firm looks good from a financial point of view at the moment, but a serious competitive threat could wipe it out in the near future. In short, financial ratio analysis is a very useful tool for analyzing strategic management cases, but it cannot replace other types of analysis and careful consideration of the issues present in the case.

BREAK-EVEN ANALYSIS

Break-even analysis is a simple method for investigating the potential value of a proposed investment. It is useful in the analysis of three important types of strategic management decisions:

1. When one is making new product decisions, break-even analysis can help determine how large the sales of a new product must be for the firm to achieve profitability.
2. Break-even analysis can be used as a broad framework for studying the effects of a general expansion in the level of a firm's operations.
3. When the firm is considering modernization and automation projects where the investment in equipment is increased in order to lower variable costs, particularly the cost of labor, break-even analysis can help management analyze the consequences of the action.[3]

The *break-even point* is that level of sales in either units or sales dollars at which a firm covers all the costs of investing in a project. In other words, it is the level at which total sales revenue just equals the total costs necessary to achieve these sales.

In order to compute the break-even point, an analyst must obtain three values. First, the analyst needs to know the selling price per unit of the product (*SP*). For example, after extensive market analysis, MoPower Robotics Company plans to sell its new, multifunction industrial robot for $5,000.

Second, the analyst needs to know the level of fixed costs (*FC*). Fixed costs are all costs relevant to the project that do not change regardless of how many units are produced and sold. For example, whether MoPower produces and sells 1 robot or 10,000, MoPower executives will collect their salaries, machinery must be purchased, and a plant must be constructed. Other fixed costs include interest payments, lease payments, and sinking fund payments. MoPower has tallied all of its fixed costs to produce the new robot and estimates the total to be $10,000,000.

Third, the analyst needs to know the variable costs per unit produced (*VC*). Variable costs, as the name implies, are those that vary directly with the number of units produced. For example, for each robot produced, there are costs for electrical and mechanical components, labor to assemble the robot, and machine costs such as electricity. MoPower estimates that for each robot produced, the variable costs will be $3,000.

Armed with this information, the analyst can determine the break-even point by dividing total fixed costs by the contribution margin. The *contribution margin* is simply the difference between the selling price per unit and the variable costs per unit. Algebraically,

$$\text{Break-even point (in units)} = \frac{\text{Total fixed costs}}{\text{Contribution margin}}$$

$$= \frac{FC}{SP - VC}$$

[3] Weston and Brigham, *Essentials of Managerial Finance,* p. 143.

Substituting the MoPower estimates, we find that

$$\text{Break-even point (in units)} = \frac{10{,}000{,}000}{5{,}000 - 3{,}000}$$

$$= \frac{10{,}000{,}000}{2{,}000}$$

$$= 5{,}000 \text{ units}$$

In other words, MoPower must sell 5,000 robots in order to just break even—that is, for total sales to equal total costs. This is a very useful number. It informs the analyst that if sales projections at this price level are less than 5,000 units, the project may not be viable.

Alternatively, the analyst may want to know the break-even point in terms of total sales dollars rather than units. Of course, if the preceding analysis has been done, one can simply multiply the break-even point in units by the selling price: 5,000 units × \$5,000 = \$25,000,000. However, the break-even point in dollars can be computed directly with the following formula:

$$\text{Break-even point in dollars} = \frac{FC}{1 - \frac{VC}{SP}}$$

$$\frac{10{,}000{,}000}{1 - \frac{3{,}000}{5{,}000}}$$

$$= \frac{10{,}000{,}000}{1 - 0.6}$$

$$= \$25{,}000{,}000$$

Thus, MoPower must produce and sell 5,000 robots, which equals \$25,000,000 in sales, to just break even on this project. Of course, MoPower does not want to just break even but to make a profit. The logic of break-even analysis can easily be extended to include profits (P). For example, suppose MoPower decided that a 20 percent return on fixed costs was the minimum that the project would have to generate to make it worth investing in. MoPower would need 20% × \$10,000,000 = \$2,000,000 in additional income to make the project worth the investment. To calculate how many units MoPower must sell to achieve this level of profits, we add the profit figure to fixed costs in the foregoing formulas. In our example,

$$\text{Break-even plus profits} = \frac{FC + P}{SP - VC}$$

$$= \frac{10{,}000{,}000 + 2{,}000{,}000}{5{,}000 - 3{,}000}$$

$$= \frac{12{,}000{,}000}{2{,}000}$$

$$= 6{,}000 \text{ units}$$

And in terms of the formula for sales dollars,

$$\text{Break-even plus profits} = \frac{FC + P}{1 - \dfrac{VC}{SP}}$$

$$= \frac{10{,}000{,}000 + 2{,}000{,}000}{1 - \dfrac{3{,}000}{5{,}000}}$$

$$= \frac{12{,}000{,}000}{1 - 0.6}$$

$$= \$30{,}000{,}000$$

MoPower must produce and sell 6,000 robots, which equals $30,000,000 in sales, if it is to achieve its minimum acceptable profit level. This is a very useful figure to calculate, because it invites the analyst to consider the probability of obtaining this level of sales. For example, if the entire market were 10,000 units, is it likely that MoPower could obtain a 60 percent market share, given the competition? If so, the project would be worth investing in. If not, MoPower should seek other opportunities or change its strategic plan. If it lowered the price of the robots, for example, sales increases might result in economies of scale and a profitable project.

Graphs constructed for presenting break-even analysis can give a clear overall picture of the relationships we have been discussing. Figure 10.1 is a graph of our MoPower break-even example. Such graphs provide an easy-to-understand, visual representation of the various relationships among sales,

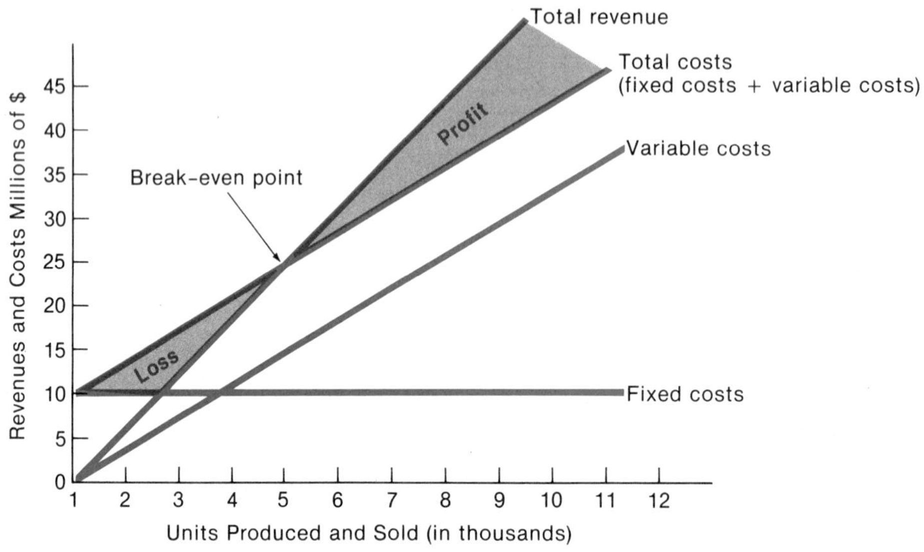

FIGURE 10.1 Graphical Presentation of Break-even Analysis

fixed costs, and variable costs, and they illustrate levels of losses and profits under various conditions. Highlight 10.2 offers you an opportunity to perform a break-even analysis.

Although break-even analysis is a useful tool, it does have limitations. For example, a whole series of break-even analyses are necessary if the analyst wishes to consider different price levels or different estimates of fixed or variable costs. Similarly, many costs are likely to change at different volume levels. For example, at higher volume levels, more employees may have to be hired and more machines may have to be purchased, which would change the various cost curves. Break-even analysis is useful (and in some cases, it is the only technique that can be applied), but more detailed analyses are often recommended for probing investment alternatives. One of these is net present value analysis.

NET PRESENT VALUE ANALYSIS

A detailed treatment of net present value analysis is beyond the scope of this text. Even so, we should review, in general terms, its use in strategic management case analysis. *Net present value analysis* can be used to investigate the value of a proposed investment to an organization or to compare alternative investments to determine which is better from a financial point of view.

This analysis is based on the idea that money has a time value. For example, \$10 today is worth more than \$10 one year from today because it could be invested for the year. If the \$10 were put in a money market account

HIGHLIGHT 10.2

SKILLS MODULE ■ **Break-even Analysis at Timex Corp.**

INTRODUCTION

We have discussed break-even analysis in some detail. Review the following situation, and then complete the skill development exercise that follows. Doing so will help you develop this important skill.

SITUATION

Timex Corp. sold 50 percent of the watches in America and had 20 percent of worldwide sales in the late 1960s. Yet by 1983, Timex's U.S. market share had plummeted to about 17 percent and operating losses approached $100 million. Part of the problem was the failure of Timex executives to recognize the importance of electronic watches marketed by competitors. When Timex finally introduced electronic watches, they were so big and clumsy that employees named them "quarter pounders" and their prices ended up 50 percent above those of the competition's much more attractive entries. At this point, Timex decided to try to rebuild its watch market and spent over $100 million to retool and redesign its watch and clock lines. One of the resulting watch lines was the Timex Elite collection, consisting of watches designed to sell in department and jewelry stores for $120.

SKILL DEVELOPMENT EXERCISE

Assume that Timex Elite watches have a variable cost of $30 apiece and that total fixed costs for the collection amount to $18 million. If Timex sells directly to retailers, and retailers mark watches up 50 percent, what is Timex's break-even point for Elite watches? How many Elite watches would Timex have to sell to make a profit of $3.6 million?

Source: Based on "Timex Takes the Torture Test," *Fortune,* June 27, 1983, pp. 112–120; "Can Timex Take a Licking and Keep on Ticking?" *Business Week,* February 20, 1984, p. 102; J. Paul Peter and James H. Donnelly, Jr., *Marketing Management: Knowledge and Skills,* 2nd ed. (Homewood, Ill.: BPI/Irwin, 1989), pp. 281–283.

and earned 6 percent interest, it would be worth $10.60 a year from today. Thus, a financial analyst who is considering cash inflows and outflows that will occur in the future can use net present value analysis to "discount them"—that is, to reflect their value in today's dollars.

In order to calculate the net present value of an investment, the analyst needs several figures. First, the total initial cost of the investment must be determined. This includes all payments made today to begin the project.

Second, the firm's cost of capital must be estimated. The cost of capital is often given in cases for which net present value analysis is appropriate. If not, one can estimate it by using the approaches suggested in financial management texts.[4] Third, the project's expected life must be determined. And fourth, the net cash flows from the project must be estimated. *Net cash flows* are the net amount (cash inflows minus cash outflows) that the firm receives from the project each year; they include earnings after taxes (net income) and depreciation.

The basic equation for calculating net present value is:

$$NPV = \frac{NCF_1}{(1 + k)^1} + \frac{NCF_2}{(1 + k)^2} + \cdots + \frac{NCF_n}{(1 + k)^n} - I$$

where

NPV = net present value
NCF = net cash flows each year of the project's life
I = total initial investment
k = cost of capital

This equation states that the net present value of an investment is equal to the net cash flows discounted by the cost of capital, minus the initial investment outlay. For example, suppose MoPower is deciding whether to get into the market for home robots and has available the following financial information:

Initial investment in equipment	\$1,500,000
Useful life of the equipment	10 years
Depreciation	10 percent per year
Salvage value	\$200,000
Net income per year	\$150,000
Cost of capital	10 percent

Because financial management texts include net present value tables, actually solving for the net present value is much easier than working through the formula above. Table 10.5 presents the net cash flows—net income (\$150,000 per year) plus depreciation (\$150,000 per year) equals \$300,000 and an additional \$200,000 in year ten for salvage value; the appropriate discount factors for a cost of capital of 10 percent; and the present value of these cash flows. The present value of the net cash flows is \$1,920,450, and subtracting the initial investment of \$1,500,000 results in a net present value of \$420,450. The net present value is positive, so MoPower should invest in entering the home robot market.

[4] Ibid., chapter 15.

TABLE 10.5 Present Value Calculations for the MoPower Robotics Company

YEAR	NET CASH FLOW	10% DISCOUNT FACTOR	PRESENT VALUE
1	$300,000	.9091	$ 272,730
2	300,000	.8264	247,920
3	300,000	.7513	225,390
4	300,000	.6830	204,900
5	300,000	.6209	186,270
6	300,000	.5645	169,350
7	300,000	.5132	153,960
8	300,000	.4665	139,950
9	300,000	.4241	127,230
10	500,000	.3855	192,750
			$1,920,450

Because the net cash flows for the first nine years are the same, it would be much easier to calculate the present value by treating these nine years as an annuity and multiplying by the total of the discount factors for nine years—that is, $300,000 × 5.7590 = $1,727,700. Adding the tenth year ($500,000 × 0.3855 = $192,750) to this amount makes it easier to obtain the present value of $1,920,450.

Net present value analysis is a useful method for examining investment alternatives. Employing it requires some background in financial management, but net present value analysis should be applied to strategic management cases when the required information is available or can be estimated. Table 10.6 presents some commonly used present value discount factors to assist you, and again, complete tables can be found in most financial management texts.

TABLE 10.6 Selected Present Value Discount Factors

YEAR	8%	10%	12%	14%	16%	18%
1	.9259	.9091	.8929	.8772	.8621	.8475
2	.8573	.8264	.7972	.7695	.7432	.7182
3	.7938	.7513	.7118	.6750	.6407	.6086
4	.7350	.6830	.6355	.5921	.5523	.5158
5	.6806	.6209	.5674	.5194	.4761	.4371
6	.6302	.5645	.5066	.4556	.4104	.3704
7	.5835	.5132	.4523	.3996	.3538	.3139
8	.5403	.4665	.4039	.3506	.3050	.2660
9	.5002	.4241	.3606	.3075	.2630	.2255
10	.4632	.3855	.3220	.2697	.2267	.1911

SUMMARY

This chapter investigated three financial tools that are useful for strategic management. We discussed financial ratio analysis and examined three types of financial ratios: liquidity, activity, and profitability ratios. We suggested that these types of ratios should be applied routinely to strategic management cases that include balance sheet and income statement information. Then we discussed break-even analysis as a method for investigating the potential value of an investment to an organization. It enables the firm to determine at what level of sales the total revenue generated by a project just equals the costs incurred to achieve those sales and can be extended to include desired profit levels. Finally, we presented net present value analysis as a sophisticated but useful method for analyzing investment alternatives. It enables the firm to determine the value in today's dollars of cash flows that will occur in the future.

Highlight 10.3 is a summary list of the main points made in this chapter. Use it when you analyze problems and cases that focus on financial issues.

ADDITIONAL READINGS

Brealey, Richard A., and Stewart C. Myers. *Principles of Corporate Finance*, 3rd ed. New York: McGraw-Hill, 1988.

Brigham, Eugene F., and Louis C. Gapenski. *Financial Management: Theory and Practice*, 5th ed. Chicago: The Dryden Press, 1988.

Campsey, B. J., and Eugene F. Brigham. *Introduction to Financial Management*, 2nd ed. Chicago: The Dryden Press, 1989.

HIGHLIGHT 10.3

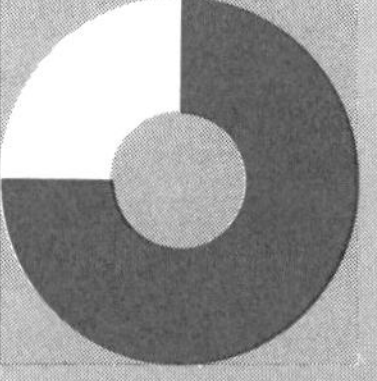

CHECKLIST ■ Analyzing Finances in Problems and Cases

- ☐ 1. Does this problem or case include financial statements so that we can perform a ratio analysis?
- ☐ 2. Would a ratio analysis help us develop a better understanding of the firm and its problems?
- ☐ 3. What is the financial condition of the company? That is, how does it compare with other firms in the industry in terms of such measures as liquidity, activity, and profitability ratios, and what are the implications for alternatives appropriate for solving the firm's problems?
- ☐ 4. Does the problem or case include the information we need to perform a break-even analysis?
- ☐ 5. Would a break-even analysis help us evaluate a proposed project for the company?
- ☐ 6. Given a break-even point, is the firm likely to be able to sell enough units to reach that point and be profitable?
- ☐ 7. Does the problem or case include the information we need to perform a net present value analysis?
- ☐ 8. Would a net present value analysis help us evaluate the firm's investment opportunities?
- ☐ 9. Given a positive net present value, is there any reason why the firm should not invest in the project?
- ☐ 10. If we do not have enough information to perform a break-even or net present value analysis, could such analyses be performed if a few reasonable assumptions were made? For example, could we assume the cost of capital in order to perform the analysis?

HIGHLIGHT 10.4 ■ APPLICATION OF CHAPTER MATERIAL

Financial Analysis for Polaroid Corporation

The Polaroid Corporation designs, manufactures, and markets a variety of products primarily in instant image-recording fields. These include instant cameras and films, magnetic media, light-polarizing filters and lenses, and diversified chem-

(*Continues*)

ical, optical, and commercial products. The principal products of the company are used in amateur and professional photography, industry, science, medicine, and education. Selected financial data for 1985 include the following (in millions):

Current assets	$1,035.7	Sales	$1,295.2
Inventory	335.0	EBIT	62.5
Total assets	1,384.7	EAT	36.9
Current liabilities	337.9		

Some of Polaroid's major products are cameras that focus and control exposure automatically. These cameras use advanced computerlike circuitry to make more than 30 complex focusing and exposure decisions within fifty-thousandths of a second. The cameras, film, accessories, and services involved are collectively called the Spectra System. This system was Polaroid's major product innovation for 1986.

DISCUSSION QUESTIONS

1. Calculate the current ratio, quick ratio, inventory turnover, total asset utilization, profit margin on sales, and return on investment for Polaroid for 1985.
2. Compare Polaroid's ratios with the following industry averages. What conclusions about Polaroid's financial condition do these comparisons suggest?

Current ratio	2.2	Total asset utilization	1.1
Quick ratio	1.0	Profit margin on sales	0.067
Inventory turnover	4.3	Return on investment	0.039

3. Suppose Polaroid were considering the development of an even more technologically advanced camera system. Say the total investment required was to be $2.5 million, and net cash flows were expected to be $750,000 for the first year, $1,500,000 for the second year, and $2,000,000 for the third year. Because the technology would be superseded after the third year, the project would end then and there would be no salvage value. If Polaroid's cost of capital were 12 percent, what would be the net present value of this investment?

Source: Based on *1985 Polaroid Corporation Annual Report.*

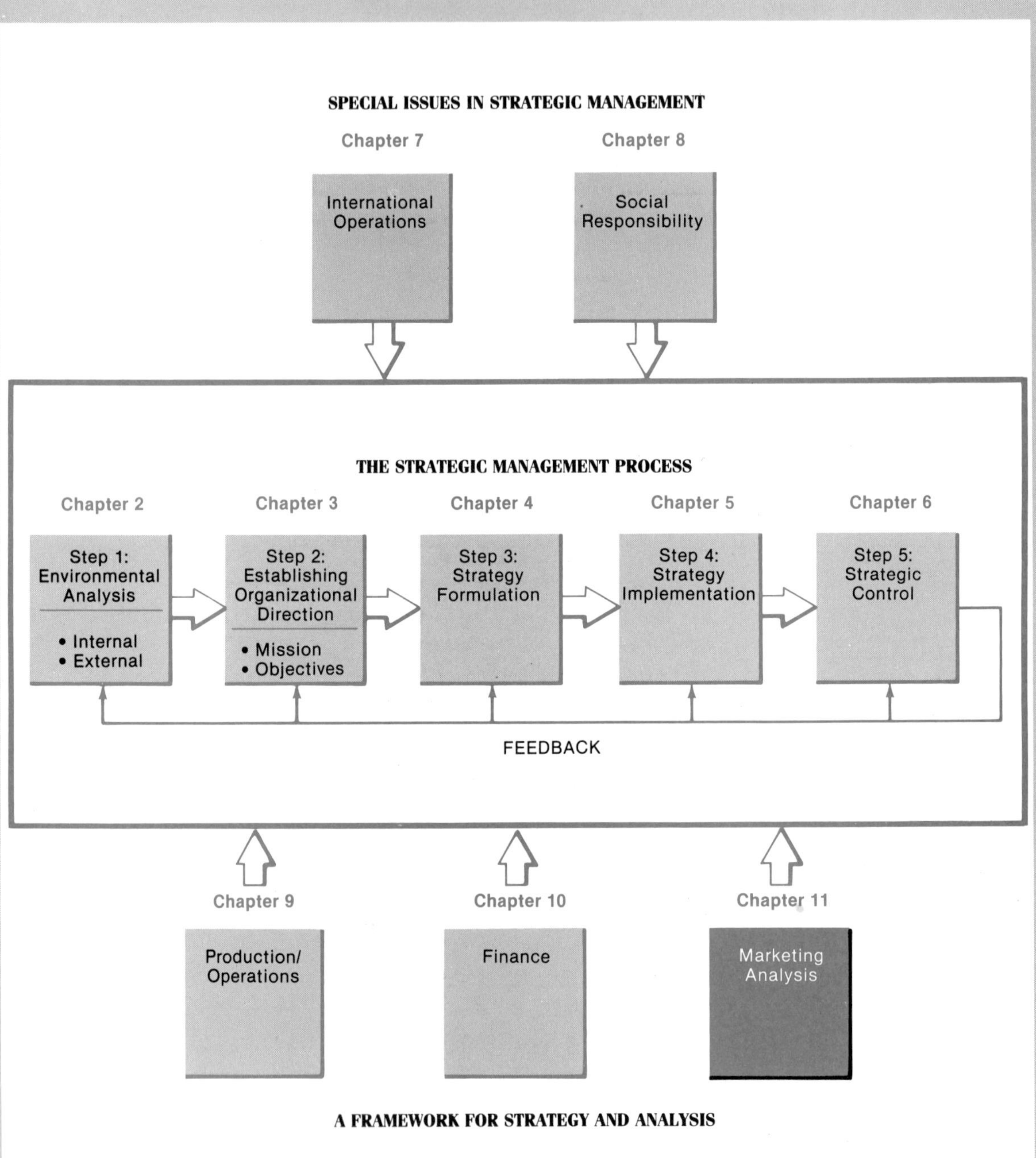
SPECIAL ISSUES IN STRATEGIC MANAGEMENT
Chapter 7
International Operations
Chapter 8
Social Responsibility
THE STRATEGIC MANAGEMENT PROCESS
Chapter 2
Step 1: Environmental Analysis
• Internal
• External
Chapter 3
Step 2: Establishing Organizational Direction
• Mission
• Objectives
Chapter 4
Step 3: Strategy Formulation
Chapter 5
Step 4: Strategy Implementation
Chapter 6
Step 5: Strategic Control
FEEDBACK
Chapter 9
Production/ Operations
Chapter 10
Finance
Chapter 11
Marketing Analysis
A FRAMEWORK FOR STRATEGY AND ANALYSIS
Chapter 12
An Approach to Solving Strategic Problems and Cases

CHAPTER 11

Marketing Foundations for Strategic Management

The marketing function involves facilitating exchanges between an organization and either industrial buyers or end users.[1] It is obviously an important function; profit-seeking organizations must create and keep customers in order to generate sales and profits.[2] Nonprofit organizations also develop marketing strategies to attract donations of time, money, and other resources in order to maintain their operations and achieve their objectives.

Many of the strategic management issues that we have discussed in this text contribute to the creation of successful marketing strategies. Environmental analysis is a critical aspect of marketing strategy development, because changes in an organization's environment can lead to both marketing opportunities and constraints on successful marketing. In particular, changes in the marketing strategies of competitors have a very direct impact on the marketing opportunities available to an organization.

[1] This chapter is based on J. Paul Peter and James H. Donnelly, Jr., *Marketing Management: Knowledge and Skills*, 2nd ed. (Homewood, Ill.: BPI/Irwin, 1989), section 1; and J. Paul Peter and Jerry C. Olson, *Consumer Behavior and Marketing Strategy*, 2nd ed. (Homewood, Ill.: Richard D. Irwin, 1990), section V.

[2] Theodore Levitt, *The Marketing Imagination* (New York: The Free Press, 1983), p. 5.

Organizational mission and objective statements provide the framework and direction for designing marketing objectives and strategies. For example, if a firm adopts an organizational objective of increasing net profits by 15 percent per year, this goal has important implications for the development of new products and the marketing of existing products.

Finally, the development of marketing strategies involves strategic management functions such as planning, analysis, implementation, and control. Although there is no clear distinction between some aspects of strategic management and marketing strategy, the major focus of marketing strategy is on knowing, adapting to, and influencing consumers in an effort to achieve organizational objectives. Marketing strategies are usually designed to increase sales and market share in order to increase long-run profits.

In this chapter, we investigate the process of developing successful marketing strategies. We focus on those issues that are most commonly considered marketing tasks and avoid many of the more general strategic management issues discussed previously in the text. Figure 11.1 provides an overview of this process (and also outlines the contents of the chapter). We begin by discussing the analysis of consumer/product relationships, a critical aspect of the development of marketing strategy. We next consider the different ways in which it is possible to "segment a market" or divide it into groups of similar consumers. Then we investigate the process of designing a marketing mix strategy. Finally, we examine the implementation and control of the firm's marketing strategy.

ANALYZING CONSUMER/PRODUCT RELATIONSHIPS

The first step in preparing a marketing strategy is to analyze consumer/product relationships. This analysis entails investigating why consumers buy a particular product, what the product means to them, what consequences they expect from using the product, how involved are they in purchasing the product, and in what situations the product is purchased and used. Test marketing and primary market research may help answer these questions, and one can often gain considerable insight by investigating secondary sources of information and studying general buying habits.

In performing this analysis, it is useful first to classify products as either consumer or industrial products. *Consumer products* are those that are purchased by the final user, whereas *industrial products* are purchased to aid in the production of other products or services. Each of these types of products can be divided into the categories shown in Table 11.1. Consumer goods are commonly classified as convenience, shopping, or specialty goods on the basis of the degree of involvement consumers have with the product and how much time and effort they will invest in purchasing it. Industrial goods are divided into five basic categories in terms of their role in the production process. Table 11.1 also suggests some of the basic characteristics of these products and some considerations to take into account when marketing them. Thus simply

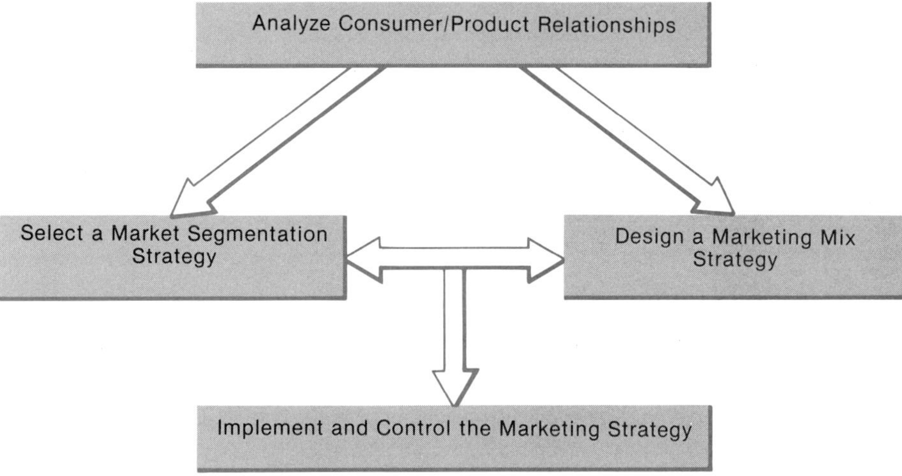

FIGURE 11.1 The Strategic Marketing Process

classifying a product offers some useful direction for developing marketing strategy.

Whereas classifying products is a useful starting point in analyzing consumer/product relationships, research and study of consumers of the product are critical. Consider a simple product such as toothpaste. What are some of the reasons why consumers buy this product? It seems clear that different consumers are seeking different benefits from the product. Decay prevention, fresh breath, sex appeal, whiter teeth, and plaque removal may differ in their importance to various consumers. Similarly, performance, economy, status, and styling vary in importance across groups of consumers who intend to purchase an automobile. Thus, performing the analysis of consumer/product relationships may yield some initial idea of the appropriate market segments an organization should seek to satisfy with its products.

Highlight 11.1 gives you a chance to try your hand at performing an analysis of consumer/product relationships.

SELECTING A MARKET SEGMENTATION STRATEGY

The logic of market segmentation is quite simple: it is based on the idea that a single product item does not usually appeal to all consumers. Consumers' purchasing goals, product knowledge, involvement, and purchase behavior vary. For this reason, marketing strategists typically focus their marketing effort on specific groups of consumers rather than on the whole population. *Market segmentation* is the process of dividing a market into groups of similar consumers and selecting the most appropriate group(s) for the organization to serve. Markets are selected on the basis of their size, their profit potential, and how well they can be defined and served by the organization.

TABLE 11.1 Categories of Products and Marketing Strategy Considerations

A. CONSUMER PRODUCTS

CHARACTERISTICS AND MARKETING CONSIDERATIONS	TYPE OF PRODUCT		
	Convenience	Shopping	Specialty
Characteristics:			
1. Time and effort devoted by consumer to shopping	Very little	Considerable	Cannot generalize; consumer may go to nearby store and buy with minimum effort or may have to go to distant store and spend much time and effort
2. Time spent planning the purchase	Very little	Considerable	Considerable
3. How soon want is satisfied after it arises	Immediately	Relatively long time	Relatively long time
4. Are price and quality compared?	No	Yes	No
5. Price	Low	High	High
6. Frequency of purchase	Usually frequent	Infrequent	Infrequent
7. Importance	Unimportant	Often very important	Cannot generalize
Marketing considerations:			
1. Length of channel	Long	Short	Short to very short
2. Importance of retailer	Any single store is relatively unimportant	Important	Very important
3. Number of outlets	As many as possible	Few	Few; often only one in a market
4. Stock turnover	High	Lower	Lower
5. Gross margin	Low	High	High
6. Responsibility for advertising	Manufacturer's	Retailer's	Joint responsibility
7. Importance of point-of-purchase display	Very important	Less important	Less important
8. Advertising used	Manufacturer's	Retailer's	Both
9. Brand or store name important	Brand name	Store name	Both
10. Importance of packaging	Very important	Less important	Less important

TABLE 11.1 (Continued)

B. INDUSTRIAL PRODUCTS					
	TYPE OF PRODUCT				
CHARACTERISTICS AND MARKETING CONSIDERATIONS	Raw Materials	Fabricating Parts and Materials	Installations	Accessory Equipment	Operating Supplies
Example:	Iron Ore	Engine Blocks	Blast Furnaces	Storage racks	Paper Clips
Characteristics:					
1. Unit price	Very low	Low	Very high	Medium	Low
2. Length of life	Very short	Depends on final product	Very long	Long	Short
3. Quantities purchased	Large	Large	Very small	Small	Small
4. Frequency of purchase	Frequent delivery; long-term purchase contract	Infrequent purchase, but frequent delivery	Very infrequent	Medium frequency	Frequent
5. Standardization of competitive products	Very much; grading is important	Very much	Very little; custom-made	Little	Much
6. Limits on supply	Limited; supply can be increased slowly or not at all	Usually no problem	No problem	Usually no problem	Usually no problem
Marketing considerations:					
1. Nature of channel	Short; no middlemen	Short; middlemen only for small buyers	Short; no middlemen	Middlemen used	Middlemen used
2. Negotiation period	Hard to generalize	Medium	Long	Medium	Short
3. Price competition	Important	Important	Not important	Not main factor	Important
4. Presale/postsale service	Not important	Important	Very important	Important	Very little
5. Demand stimulation	Very little	Moderate	Sales people very important	Important	Not too important
6. Brand preference	None	Generally low	High	High	Low
7. Advance buying contract	Important; long-term contracts used	Important; long-term contracts used	Not usually used	Not usually used	Not usually used

Source: William J. Stanton and Charles Futrell, *Fundamentals of Marketing,* 8th ed. (New York: McGraw-Hill 1987), pp. 195, 198. Reprinted by permission.

HIGHLIGHT 11.1

SKILLS MODULE ■ Consumer Analysis for Admiral Home Appliances

INTRODUCTION

We have noted the importance of analyzing consumer/product relationships as the starting point for developing sound marketing strategies. Review the following situation, and then complete the skill development exercise that follows. Doing so will help you develop this important skill.

THE SITUATION

Product innovation was not a very important part of the refrigerator business for many years. Other than frost-free units introduced in 1954 and automatic ice makers in 1956, the only thing that changed much was the colors. John Green, president of Admiral Home Appliances, a division of Magic Chef, Inc., stated that "the industry pretty much has operated on the theory that all consumers want is a reliable and economic box to keep food fresh." Green changed that view by introducing two upscale refrigerator models. The first, called the Entertainer, features a built-in wine rack and microwave storage trays. This model quickly became Admiral's best-selling unit (it had sales of $10 million in the first year), increasing Admiral's fourth-place share of the market by 50 percent. The second, called the A la Mode, was priced at $1,299 and could make ice cream, soup, and chilled drinks. These products have a blast freezer that, among other functions, can make ice cubes in 45 minutes. Admiral's new products have given it an estimated 15 percent of the more than $4.5-billion-a-year refrigerator and freezer market.

SKILL DEVELOPMENT EXERCISE

Admiral Home Appliances was clearly successful in introducing expensive, upscale refrigerators that included several modifications in product design. These models were the direct result of consumer surveys that revealed a trend toward increased entertaining at home. Explain how you would analyze the consumer/product relationships for these new models of refrigerators. Be sure to consider whether consumers are willing to pay high prices simply for the additional features, or whether product image and social factors influence these purchases.

Source: Based on John Koten, "Innovative, Upscale Iceboxes Mark a Sales Coup for Admiral," *The Wall Street Journal,* April 19, 1984, p. 29.

Markets can be segmented on a variety of dimensions, or bases. Table 11.2 lists some of the more commonly used dimensions for segmenting consumer and industrial markets. Often a number of these dimensions are used together to segment markets and to develop "profiles" of the consumers in them. Typically, considerable market research is done to define particular markets very carefully. We will briefly describe four types of market segmentation: geographic, demographic, psychographic, and benefit segmentation.

Geographic Segmentation

For many products, geographic segmentation offers a useful basis for initially defining markets. For example, the markets for such products as snowmobiles, ice fishing equipment, engine block heaters, and snow skiing equipment are concentrated in northern areas. Fast-food restaurants such as McDonald's and Burger King use information on population size and population density to help them select restaurant locations. Because data on geographic segmentation bases are available from public sources, collecting such information is an inexpensive way to explore market potential.

Demographic Segmentation

Demographic variables are commonly used to segment markets. Many products are designed for groups defined on the basis of sex (clothes, cosmetics), age (toys), or income (automobiles). Demographic variables are also used in conjunction with other segmentation bases to describe particular markets more thoroughly. For example, a major market for light beer consists of men in their thirties who are eager to stay healthy and trim. In this market profile, both sex and age are demographic variables, and concerns about health and weight are psychographic variables.

Psychographic Segmentation

Psychographic, or *lifestyle, segmentation* involves the study of consumers' activities (such as work, hobbies, and vacations), interests (such as family, job, and community), and opinions (about such things as politics, social issues, and business). Consumers are grouped together empirically, on the basis of the similarity of their responses, into various lifestyle groups. A well-known psychographic segmentation was developed at SRI International in California. The original segmentation divided consumers in the United States into nine groups and was called VALS,™ which stands for "values and lifestyles." However, while this segmentation was commercially successful, it tended to place the majority of consumers into only one or two groups and SRI felt it needed to be updated to reflect changes in society. Thus, SRI developed a new typology called VALS 2™.[3]

VALS 2 is based on two national surveys of 2,500 consumers who responded to 43 lifestyle questions. The first survey developed the segmentation, and the

[3] This discussion is based on Martha Farnsworth Riche, "Psychographics for the 1990s," *American Demographics,* July 1989, pp. 24–26 ff.

TABLE 11.2 Useful Segmentation Bases for Consumer and Industrial Markets

CONSUMER MARKETS	
Segmentation Base	Base Categories
Geographic:	
Region	Pacific, Mountain, West North Central, West South Central, East North Central, East South Central, South Atlantic, Middle Atlantic, New England
City, county, or SMSA size	Under 5,000, 5,000–19,999, 20,000–49,999, 50,000–99,999, 100,000–249,999, 250,000–499,999, 500,000–999,999, 1,000,000–3,999,999, 4,000,000 or over
Population density	Urban, suburban, rural
Climate	Warm, cold
Demographic:	
Age	Under 6, 6–12, 13–19, 20–29, 30–39, 40–49, 50–59, 60+
Sex	Male, female
Family size	1–2, 3–4, 5+
Family life cycle	Young, single; young, married, no children; young, married, youngest child under 6; young, married, youngest child 6 or over; older, married, with children; older, married, no children under 18; older, single; other
Income	Under \$5,000, \$5,000–\$7,999, \$8,000–\$9,999, \$10,000–\$14,999, \$15,000–\$24,999, \$25,000–\$34,999, \$35,000 or over
Occupation	Professional and technical; managers, officials, and proprietors; clerical, sales; craftsmen, foremen, operatives; farmers; retired; students; housewives; unemployed
Education	Grade school or less, some high school, graduated high school, some college, graduated college, some graduate work, graduate degree
Religion	Catholic, Protestant, Jewish, other
Race	White, black, oriental, other
Nationality	American, British, French, German, Italian, Japanese, and so on

second validated it and linked it to buying and media behavior. The questionnaire asked consumers to respond to whether they agreed or disagreed with statements such as "My idea of fun at a national park would be to stay at an expensive lodge and dress up for dinner" and "I could stand to skin a dead animal." Consumers were then clustered into the eight groups shown and described in Figure 11.2.

The VALS 2 groups are arranged in a rectangle and are based on two dimensions. The vertical dimension represents resources, which include income, education, self-confidence, health, eagerness to buy, intelligence, and energy level. The horizontal dimension represents self-orientations and includes three different types. *Principle-oriented consumers* are guided by their views of how the world is or should be; *status-oriented consumers* by the actions and

TABLE 11.2 (Continued)

CONSUMER MARKETS	
Segmentation Base	**Base Categories**
Psychographic:	
Social class	Lower-lower, upper-lower, lower-middle, upper-middle, lower-upper, upper-upper
Lifestyle	Traditionalist, sophisticate, swinger
Personality	Compliant, aggressive, detached
Cognitive and behavioral:	
Attitudes	Positive, neutral, negative
Benefits sought	Convenience, economy, prestige
Readiness stage	Unaware, aware, informed, interested, desirous . . . intention to purchase
Perceived risk	High, moderate, low
Innovativeness	Innovator, early adopter, early majority, late majority, laggard
Involvement	Low, high
Loyalty status	None, some, total
Usage rate	None, light, medium, heavy
User status	Nonuser, ex-user, potential user, current user

INDUSTRIAL BUYER MARKETS	
Segmentation Base	**Base Categories**
Source loyalty	Purchase from one, two, three, four, or more suppliers
Size of company	Small, medium, large relative to industry
Average size of purchase	Small, medium, large
Usage rate	Light, medium, heavy
Product application	Maintenance, production, final product component, administration
Type of business	Manufacturer, wholesaler, retailer; SIC categories
Location	North, East, South, West; sales territories
Purchase status	New customer, occasional purchaser, frequent purchaser, nonpurchaser
Attribute importance	Reliability of supply, price, service, durability, convenience, reputation of supplier

opinions of others; and *action-oriented consumers* by a desire for social or physical activity, variety, and risk taking.

Each of the VALS 2 groups represents from 9 to 17 percent of the United States adult population. Marketers can buy VALS 2 information for a variety of products and can have it tied to a number of other consumer databases.

Benefit Segmentation

Underlying this segmentation approach is the concept that the *benefits* people seek in consuming a given product are the real reasons for the existence of true market segments. This approach attempts to measure consumer value systems and perceptions of various brands in a product class. The classic

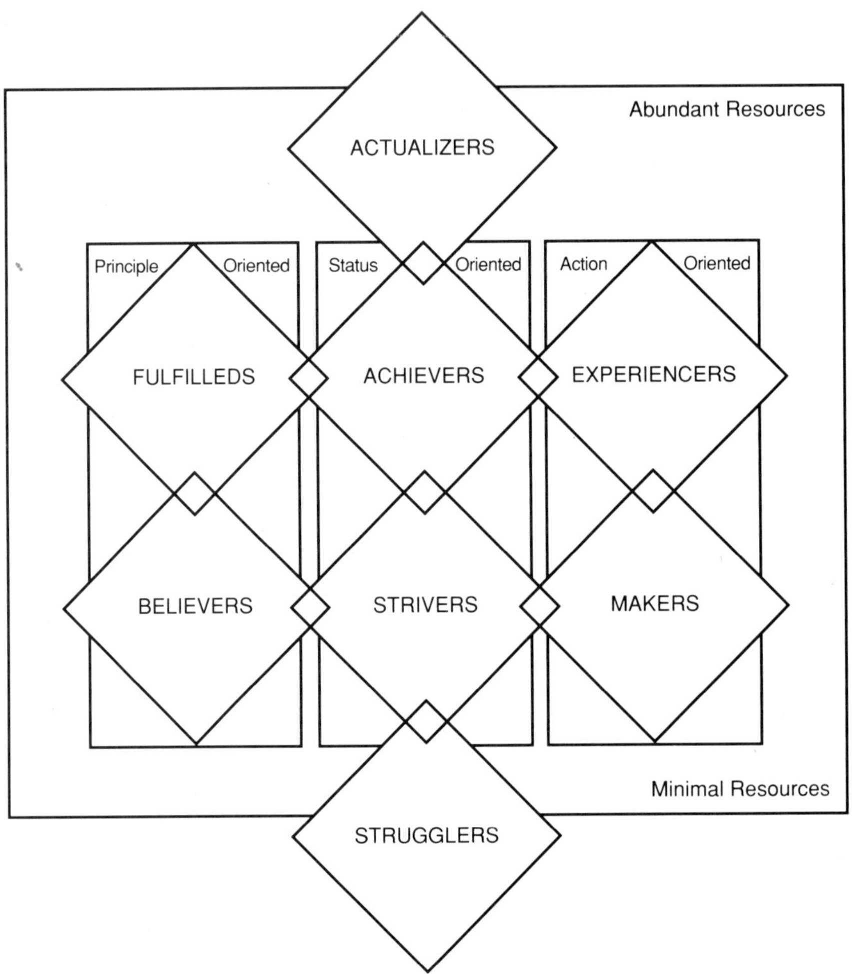

FIGURE 11.2 VALS 2™ Eight American Lifestyles

example of a benefit segmentation is drawn from the toothpaste market.[4] As shown in Table 11.3, four basic segments were identified: the Sensory, Sociable, Worrier, and Independent segments.

The segments shown in Table 11.3 have important implications for many aspects of marketing strategy, including the selection of advertising copy and

[4] See Russell I. Haley, "Benefit Segmentation: A Decision-Oriented Research Tool," *Journal of Marketing*, July 1968, pp. 30–35. Also see Russell I. Haley, "Benefit Segmentation—20 Years Later," *Journal of Consumer Marketing*, no. 1 (1983):5–13.

FIGURE 11.2 *(Continued)*

Actualizers. These consumers have the highest incomes and such high self-esteem and abundant resources that they can indulge in any or all self-orientations. They are located above the rectangle. Image is important to them as an expression of their taste, independence, and character. Their consumer choices are directed toward the finer things in life.

Fulfilleds. These consumers are the high resource group of those who are principle-oriented. They are mature, responsible, well-educated professionals. Their leisure activities center on their homes, but they are well-informed about what goes on in the world and they are open to new ideas and social change. They have high incomes but are practical consumers.

Believers. These consumers are the low resource group of those who are principle-oriented. They are conservative and predictable consumers who favor American products and established brands. Their lives are centered on family, church, community, and the nation. They have modest incomes.

Achievers. These consumers are the high-resource group of those who are status-oriented. They are successful, work-oriented people who get their satisfaction from their jobs and families. They are politically conservative and respect authority and the status quo. They favor established product and services that show off their success to their peers.

Strivers. These consumers are the low-resource group of those who are status-oriented. They have values very similar to Achievers but have fewer economic, social, and psychological resources. Style is extremely important to them as they strive to emulate people they admire and wish to be like.

Experiencers. These consumers are the high-resource group of those who are action-oriented. They are the youngest of all the segments with a median age of 25. They have a lot of energy, which they pour into physical exercise and social activities. They are avid consumers, spending heavily on clothing, fast foods, music, and other youthful favorites—with particular emphasis on new products and services.

Makers. These consumers are the low-resource group of those who are action-oriented. They are practical people who value self-sufficiency. They are focused on the familiar—family, work, and physical recreation—and have little interest in the broader world. As consumers, they appreciate practical and functional products.

Strugglers. These consumers have the lowest incomes. They have too few resources to be included in any consumer self-orientation and are thus located below the rectangle. They are the oldest of all the segments with a median age of 61. Within their limited means, they tend to be brand-loyal consumers.

Source: Martha Farnsworth Riche, "Psychographics for the 1990s," *American Demographics*, July 1989, pp. 24–26.

media, length of a commercial, packaging, and new product design. For example, colorful packages might be appropriate for the Sensory segment, aqua packages (to indicate fluoride) for the Worrier group, and gleaming white packages for the Sociable segment because of their interest in white teeth. Benefit segmentation is a useful approach for investigating the meaning and value of products and brands to consumers.

Table 11.4 lists several questions that it is helpful to ask when analyzing consumer/product relationships and segmenting markets.

TABLE 11.3 Benefit Segmentation in the Toothpaste Market

	SENSORY SEGMENT	SOCIABLE SEGMENT	WORRIER SEGMENT	INDEPENDENT SEGMENT
Principal benefit sought	Flavor and product appearances	Brightness of teeth	Decay prevention	Price
Demographic strengths	Children	Teens, young people	Large families	Men
Special behavioral characteristics	Users of spearmint-flavored toothpaste	Smokers	Heavy users	Heavy users
Brands disproportionately favored	Colgate	Macleans, Ultra Brite	Crest	Cheapest brand
Lifestyle characteristics	Hedonistic	Active	Conservative	Value-oriented

Source: Based on Russell I. Haley, "Benefit Segmentation: A Decision-Oriented Research Tool," *Journal of Marketing*, July 1968, pp. 30–33. From J. Paul Peter and James H. Donnelly, Jr., *Marketing Management: Knowledge and Skills*, 2nd ed. (Homewood, Ill.: BPI/Irwin, 1989), p. 96. Reprinted by permission.

TABLE 11.4 Some Questions to Ask When Analyzing Consumer/Product Relationships and Segmenting Markets

1. Why do consumers purchase this product?
2. What does this product mean to consumers, and how important to them is the purchase of it?
3. What does the product do for consumers in a functional, organizational, or social sense?
4. In what situations is the product purchased and used?
5. What are the appropriate dimensions for segmenting the market for this product?
6. Is market segmentation research necessary, and if so, what are its costs and benefits?
7. Is this market segment large enough for the firm to serve profitably?
8. Can this market segment be reached efficiently, given the organization's resources?
9. Is competition too strong for the organization to attract consumers in this target market?
10. What are the implications of this analysis for marketing strategy?

DESIGNING A MARKETING MIX STRATEGY

The marketing mix consists of product, price, promotion, and channels of distribution (or place). These four elements are the controllable variables that organizations use to adapt to target markets or to influence them. Organizations must develop strategies in which all four of these elements are synchronized to achieve the same objectives. We will discuss each of these elements in some detail, inasmuch as they are the primary techniques that organizations use to obtain sales, profits, and market share.

Product Strategy

The survival of many organizations depends on their developing and marketing successful new products and managing them throughout the product life cycle. In this section we explain the process of developing and marketing new products in terms of a seven-stage product life cycle. This life cycle includes both stages that precede and stages that follow introduction of the product to the market. Then we discuss several product characteristics that influence the success of new or existing products.

Stages in a Product's Life

The life of a successful product can be divided into seven stages, as shown in Figure 11.3. The stages from concept generation and screening to commercialization/introduction represent the process of new product development; the stages from commercialization/introduction to market decline/product deletion represent the phases of the traditional product life cycle. We will briefly describe each of these seven stages.

CONCEPT GENERATION AND SCREENING. New products start as ideas or concepts. Thus the first step in new product development involves generating concepts and screening out those that have little potential. New product concepts can come from a variety of sources, including consumers, competitors, salespeople, and the firm's own research and development department. Typically, the industry a firm is in determines the types of products it seeks to develop for consumers.

Some evidence suggests that firms are becoming more efficient in concept generation and screening. Research on 13,000 new product introductions has revealed that in 1968 it took an average of 58 ideas to generate one product. In 1981, however, it took only 7 ideas to generate a product. This is partly because firms are spending more money in the earlier phases of product development—up from 10 to 21 percent of their total new product dollars.[5]

PRODUCT PLANNING AND DEVELOPMENT. This stage involves further evaluation, planning, and development of product concepts that have passed the initial screening. These concepts are formalized into a product plan that includes analysis in terms of production, marketing, financial, and competitive factors, as well as the results of prototype testing. If the product plan supports the feasibility of producing the product and results in favorable sales and profit estimates, then it is time to investigate consumer reactions to the product. This is commonly done through test marketing or a market simulation.

[5] Jeremy Main, "Help and Hype in the New-Products Game," *Fortune*, February 7, 1983, pp. 60–64.

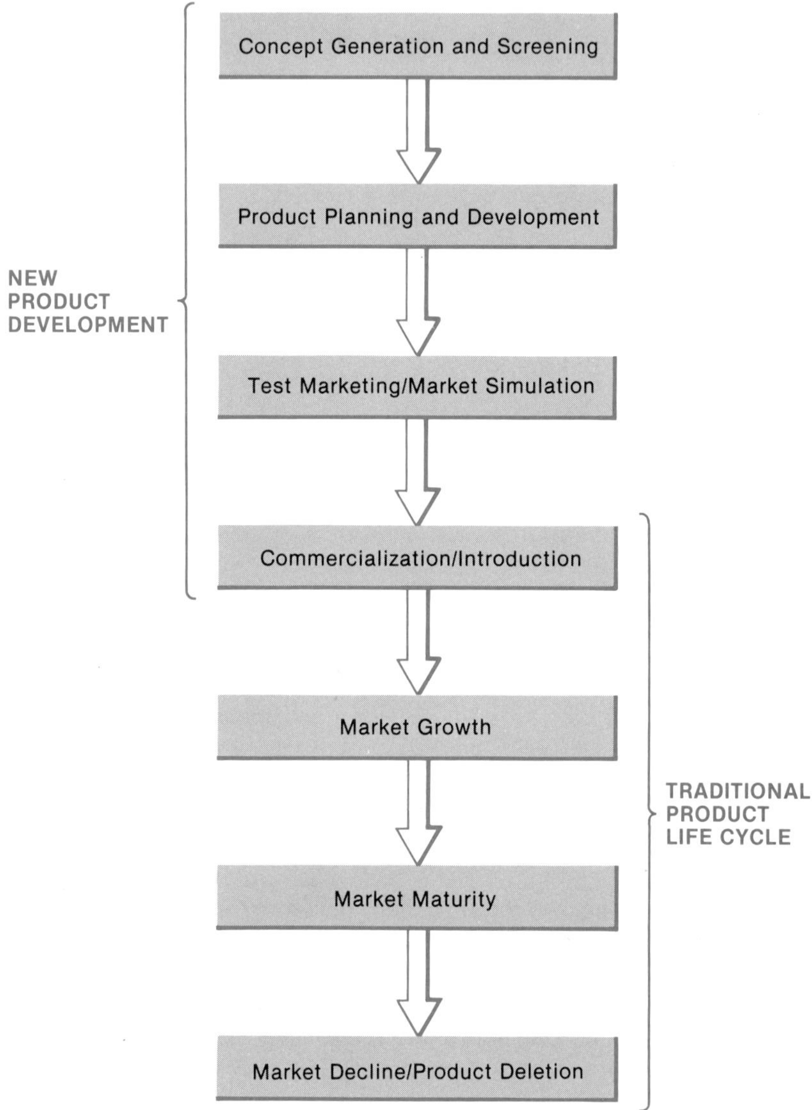

FIGURE 11.3 Stages in a Product's Life

TEST MARKETING/MARKET SIMULATION. In this stage, consumer reactions to the product are investigated. Traditionally, products have been test marketed in particular cities to determine their sales potential. However, as one analyst explains, there are a number of problems with test marketing:

> While a test market . . . sounds realistic, in fact almost everything can go wrong to mess up the findings. Competitors can distort the results of a test by slashing

prices in the test city, promoting their brand heavily, or even buying up all the items put out for the test sale, which is what happened some years ago when General Foods tried to test frozen baby food. Gerber, Libby, and Heinz bought it all. And though tests may not always be realistic, they're always expensive. They can cost up to $1.5 million.[6]

For these reasons, some firms have purchased or developed simulated market tests. These tests are based on a small sample of the public. Members of this sample are shown ads and promotions for a variety of products, including the one being tested. The shoppers are then taken to a mock-up store or a real store where their purchases are recorded. The behavior of shoppers and their willingness to rebuy the item are then analyzed via computerized models. These models consist of sets of equations designed to simulate the market. This service ranges in cost from about $35,000 to $75,000 and can be run in eight weeks without giving competitors a look at the product. Some of these models have been credited with making very accurate predictions of product successes and failures, but their overall accuracy is sometimes disputed.

COMMERCIALIZATION/INTRODUCTION If test market results and other elements of business planning are favorable, the product is introduced to the market. This is the last stage of the new product development process and the first stage of the traditional product life cycle. The main objectives at this stage are to make consumers aware of the product and to get them to try it. Figure 11.4 shows a typical sales curve generated as a product passes through the traditional product life cycle. The tabular portion of this figure shows the way several other characteristics and strategies change as the product "ages."

Many estimates of the percentage of new products that fail after introduction have been offered; they range from 33 to 90 percent. However, an extensive review of this question found that about 30 to 35 percent of new consumer products fail to meet the expectations of their developers.[7]

MARKET GROWTH. In this stage, sales of the product begin to increase rapidly and the product may become profitable. The market may expand because of increased repurchases by original buyers and a large set of new buyers who were influenced by them. As shown in Figure 11.4, a major objective at this point is to establish a strong position with distributors and users of the product.

MARKET MATURITY. At this stage, sales begin to grow less rapidly, eventually level off, and perhaps decline. Most of the consumers who are ever going to purchase the product have tried it and are either continuing to purchase it or have abandoned it. Competition becomes most intense and some competitors

[6] Ibid., p. 64.

[7] See C. Merle Crawford, *New Products Management,* 2nd ed. (Homewood, Ill.: Richard D. Irwin, 1987).

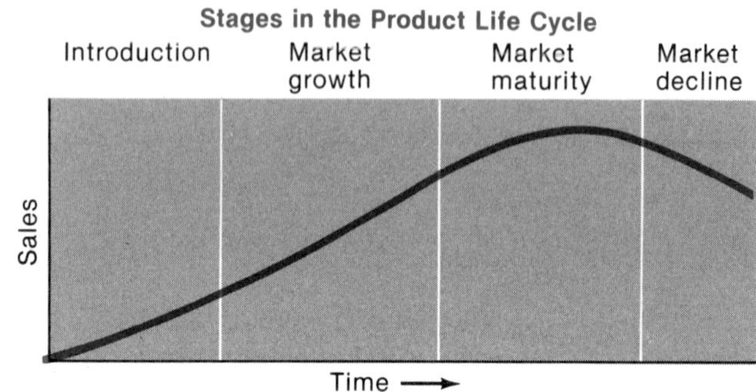

FIGURE 11.4 Elements of Marketing Strategy in the Product Life Cycle

	INTRODUCTION	MARKET GROWTH	MARKET MATURITY	MARKET DECLINE
Competition	None of importance	Some emulators	Many rivals competing for a small piece of the pie	Few in number with a rapid shakeout of weak members
Overall strategy	Market establishment; persuade early adopters to try the product	Market penetration; persuade mass market to prefer the brand	Defense of brand position; check the inroads of competition	Preparations for removal; milk the brand dry of all possible benefits
Profits	Negligible because of high production and marketing costs	Reach peak levels as a result of high prices and growing demand	Increasing competition cuts into profit margins and ultimately into total profits	Declining volume pushes costs up to levels that eliminate profits entirely
Retail prices	High, to recover some of the excessive costs of launching	High, to take advantage of heavy consumer demand	What the traffic will bear; need to avoid price wars	Low enough to permit quick liquidation of inventory

are forced out of the market or merge with other firms. Most products today are in the mature stage of the product life cycle. As Figure 11.4 suggests, a major objective at this point is to maintain and strengthen customer loyalty to the firm's products.

MARKET DECLINE/PRODUCT DELETION. At this stage, the product has run its normal course and sales begin to decline rapidly. Eventually, the product is deleted because it is no longer profitable to maintain it. Of course, attempts can be made to revitalize the product. These attempts may include seeking new markets for the product, finding new uses for the product, or adding new features to the product. However, if opportunities to revitalize a product do

FIGURE 11.4 ***(Continued)***

	INTRODUCTION	MARKET GROWTH	MARKET MATURITY	MARKET DECLINE
Distribution	Selective, as distribution is slowly built up	Intensive; employ small trade discounts since dealers are eager to store	Intensive; heavy trade allowances to retain shelf space	Selective; unprofitable outlets slowly phased out
Advertising strategy	Aim at the needs of early adopters	Make the mass market aware of brand benefits	Use advertising as a vehicle for differentiation among otherwise similar brands	Emphasize low price to reduce stock
Advertising emphasis	High, to generate awareness and interest among early adopters and persuade dealers to stock the brand	Moderate, to let sales rise on the sheer momentum of word-of-mouth recommendations	Moderate, since most buyers are aware of brand characteristics	Minimum expenditures required to phase out the product
Consumer sales and promotion expenditures	Heavy, to entice target groups, with samples, coupons, and other inducements to try the brand	Moderate, to create brand preference (advertising is better suited to do this job)	Heavy, to encourage brand switching, hoping to convert some buyers into loyal users	Minimal, to let the brand coast by itself

Source: Adapted from William Zikmund and Michael D'Amico, *Marketing,* 3rd ed. (New York: John Wiley & Sons), Copyright © John Wiley & Sons, Inc. Reprinted by permission of the publisher.

exist, they should be considered long before a product is under consideration for deletion.

Reasons for Product Success

Why do some products have long, profitable lives while others are expensive failures? There is no simple answer to this question, but several factors partially account for product acceptance by consumers. Two of the most important are competitive differential advantage and product symbolism.

COMPETITIVE DIFFERENTIAL ADVANTAGE. From a marketing strategy perspective, competitive differential advantage derives from the characteristics of a product that make it superior to competitive products. We believe that competitive differential advantage is a most important reason for product success and should be considered whenever product strategy is analyzed.

In some situations, a competitive differential advantage can be obtained through technological developments. For example, at the product class level, RCA introduced the videodisc player that showed programs on any TV set. The disc player cost half as much as cassette machines, and the discs were cheaper than videocassettes. However, videocassettes had a competitive differential advantage over the disc player: Cassette machines can record programs and disc players cannot. RCA assumed that recording ability was not an important factor to consumers—and lost more than $500 million learning otherwise.

At the brand level, however, it is often difficult to maintain a competitive differential advantage based on superior technology because competitors promptly copy new or improved technology. For example, Sony pioneered the Betamax system of videotape recorders and, in 1975, had the entire VCR market. Yet by 1982 Sony held only 14 percent of the market and was fighting for survival as competitors simply copied the technology and, having spent little on R&D, could sell at a lower price. Thus, although competitive differential advantage is a most important element of profitable marketing strategies, for such an advantage to be sustained, it often must derive from something other than technology or product modifications. One important source of sustainable competitive differential advantage is product symbolism.

PRODUCT SYMBOLISM. Product symbolism is what the product means to consumers and what consumers experience in purchasing and using it. At the brand level, it refers to the image that a particular item evokes in the minds of consumers. Marketing researchers recognize that products possess symbolic features and that consumption of some goods may depend more on their social meaning than on their functional utility.

For many product classes, the products and brands offered are relatively homogeneous in their "use value" to the consumer. Yet these products and brands differ widely in market share. For example, it is well known that few consumers can differentiate among the tastes of various brands of beer. Yet market shares vary dramatically, partly because of the brand images that have been created. Similarly, brands of jeans such as Levi's, Lee, and Wrangler are very similar in appearance, price, and quality. Yet it seems clear that these brand names have important meanings for consumers and symbolize different values, resulting in differences in market share. Guess? jeans obtained sales of $200 million in the first three years. A large portion of the market for these jeans consisted of teenagers who may have sought to present an identity different from that of wearers of traditional brands, such as their parents. Thus, the differential advantage of this brand of jeans may have been that Guess? products were a symbol of a new generation of jeans wearers.

Product symbolism and appropriate brand images can actually be more important than technological superiority. For example, the IBM personal computer was not the fastest, most advanced PC on the market and its keyboard layout was criticized. IBM was not the first in the PC market and had little experience in marketing consumer goods. IBM dominated the PC market, however, perhaps because it had a superior company image as a computer manufacturer. That is, IBM *meant* computers to many consumers and probably still does.

Table 11.5 lists several questions that it is helpful to ask when analyzing product strategies.

Product symbolism and brand images are often created by other elements of the marketing mix, including pricing, promotion, and channels of distribution. We will now discuss strategy in terms of each of these elements.

Pricing Strategy

Pricing strategy comes into play in three situations: (1) when an organization is introducing a new product and is establishing its initial price; (2) when an organization is considering a long-term price change for an existing product; and (3) when an organization is considering a short-term price change, usually a decrease to stimulate demand. Three important influences on pricing strategy are consumer characteristics, organization characteristics, and competitive characteristics.

Consumer Characteristics

The nature of the target market and its expected reactions to a given price or price change are major considerations in pricing strategy. For some products, consumers may use price as an indicator of quality, so a low price does *not* stimulate demand. For many products, price is used to segment consumers into prestige, mass, and economy markets. Price is also used for creating product and brand images. For example, Old Milwaukee beer is promoted as

TABLE 11.5 Some Questions to Ask When Analyzing Product Strategies

1. What process does the organization use to develop new products?
2. How are new products evaluated?
3. What previous success has the organization had in developing new products?
4. In what stage of the product life cycle is the product?
5. What consumers make up the target market, and what are their reactions to the product?
6. What is the competitive differential advantage of this product?
7. Can this competitive differential advantage be sustained, or can it be easily copied by competitors?
8. Is product symbolism or brand image an important factor in the market, and what is the image of the organization's product among consumers?
9. What product strategies are competitors using, and how successful are they?
10. What changes in product characteristics could be made to improve the sales, profits, and market share of this product?

tasting just as good as Budweiser but as being available at a lower price. Thus, it is positioned as a bargain for the consumer. Other products, such as Chivas Regal scotch, Cadillac automobiles, and Gucci handbags, are positioned as prestige products partly on the basis of their high prices.

Organization Characteristics

There are several organization characteristics that influence pricing strategies. First, the variable cost for a product usually sets the lower limit on the price of a product. The price of a product must at least cover the variable costs of production, promotion, and distribution and should provide some profit in order for the product to be offered to the market. Second, the objectives of the organization influence pricing strategy. A common pricing objective is to achieve a target return on investment consistent with the organization's objectives. Third, the nature of the product influences pricing strategy. Distinctive products often have higher prices, for example, and perishable products must often be priced lower to promote faster sales.

Finally, the stage of the product life cycle that a product has reached may influence pricing strategy. A *skimming pricing strategy* involves setting a relatively high price early in the product life cycle and then gradually decreasing the price when competitors enter the market. Generally, skimming is used when the organization has a temporary monopoly and when demand for the product is not very sensitive to price. A *penetration pricing strategy* involves setting a relatively low price early in the product life cycle, in anticipation of raising it at a later stage. Penetration is used when the firm expects competition to move in rapidly and when demand is strongly influenced by price. Penetration is also used to obtain large economies of scale and to create a large market rapidly.

Competitive Characteristics

The nature of competitors—their number, size, cost structures, and historical reactions to price changes—influences pricing strategy. An organization can price at, below, or above competition, depending on such factors as its own cost structure, competitive differential advantage, and financial and marketing abilities.

Table 11.6 lists several questions that it is helpful to ask when analyzing pricing strategies.

Promotion Strategy

Designing promotion strategies involves selecting the appropriate mix of promotion tools to accomplish specific objectives. Four types of promotion tools can be used to inform, persuade, and remind consumers or industrial buyers:

1. *Advertising* is any paid form of nonpersonal presentation and promotion of ideas, goods, or services by an identified sponsor. (Examples include TV and radio commercials and magazine and newspaper ads.)

TABLE 11.6 Some Questions to Ask When Analyzing Pricing Strategies

1. How important is price to the target consumers of this product?
2. Do consumers of this product use price as an indicator of quality?
3. How will various prices affect the product or brand image?
4. What are the variable costs of the product, and will consumers pay a price that will cover them plus the desired level of profit?
5. What are the organization's objectives, and what price must be charged to obtain these objectives?
6. Is the product distinctive or perishable to the degree that pricing strategies are affected?
7. What is the product's life cycle stage, and what influence does this have on pricing strategy?
8. Do conditions warrant a penetration or skimming pricing strategy?
9. What are the prices of competitive products?
10. How will competition react to the initial price or to the price change contemplated?

2. *Sales promotion* is a short-term incentive to encourage the purchase or sale of a product or service. (Examples include contests, games, premiums, and coupons.)
3. *Publicity* is any unpaid form of nonpersonal presentation of ideas, goods, or services. (An example is the discussion of a new product on a TV talk show.)
4. *Personal selling* is direct, face-to-face communication between sellers and potential buyers for the purpose of making an exchange.

As shown in Table 11.7, each of these promotion tools has a variety of advantages and disadvantages. No single method is always superior, and promotion mix decisions depend on several factors. For example, although sales of complex products such as insurance and computers are influenced by advertising, some personal selling is usually required to close sales.

Simpler products such as cereal and shampoo can be marketed to consumers via advertising and sales promotion, but salespeople are often required for selling the product to retailers. In general, designing promotion strategies involves three steps: determining promotion objectives, formulating the promotion plan, and developing promotion budgets.

Determining Promotion Objectives

Table 11.8 lists some general objectives of promotion. Which of these and other promotion objectives is appropriate depends in part on the results of the company's earlier analysis of consumer/product relationships. There are, of course, many possible relationships between consumers and products, and they lead to different promotion objectives. For example, consider the following situations:

- *Situation 1: Consumers are unaware of our brand but have a need for the product.* In this situation, an appropriate promotion objective is to inform

TABLE 11.7 Advantages and Disadvantages of Major Promotion Tools

ADVERTISING	
Advantages	**Disadvantages**
Can reach many consumers simultaneously Offers relatively low cost per exposure Is excellent for creating brand images Offers high degree of flexibility and variety of media to choose from; can accomplish many different types of promotion objectives	May waste promotion dollars if consumers reached are not potential buyers Is a major target of marketing critics because of high visibility Offers very brief exposure time of advertising message Can be quickly and easily screened out by consumers
SALES PROMOTION	
Advantages	**Disadvantages**
Can stimulate demand by short-term price reductions Offers a large variety of tools to choose from Can be effective for changing a variety of consumer behaviors Can be easily tied in with other promotion tools	May influence primarily brand-loyal customers to stock up at the lower price and result in few new customers May have only short-term impact May hurt brand image and profits by overuse of price-related sales promotion tools If effective, may be easily copied by competitors
PUBLICITY	
Advantages	**Disadvantages**
Can be positive and stimulate demand at no cost as "free advertising" May be perceived by consumers as more credible because it is not paid for by the seller May be paid more attention because messages are not quickly "screened out," as many advertisements are	Content of messages cannot be completely controlled Not always available Seldom a long-term promotion tool for brands, since messages are repeated only a limited number of times Can be negative and hurt sales as well as company, product, and brand images
PERSONAL SELLING	
Advantages	**Disadvantages**
Can be the most persuasive promotion tool, since salespeople can directly influence purchase behaviors Allows two-way communication Is often necessary for technically complex products Allows direct one-on-one targeting of promotional effort	Is high in cost per contact Can be expensive and difficult since it involves training and motivation Has a poor image as a career, making recruitment difficult Can hurt sales as well as company, product, and brand images if done poorly

TABLE 11.8 Some General Objectives of Promotion Strategies

1. Increase brand awareness
2. Increase consumer knowledge of product and brand
3. Change consumer attitudes about company
4. Change consumer attitudes about brand
5. Increase short-term sales
6. Increase long-term sales
7. Build corporate image
8. Build brand image and positioning
9. Announce a price reduction
10. Inform consumers of place of sale
11. Develop brand loyalty
12. Reassure consumers of brand quality
13. Close a sale
14. Prospect for customers
15. Obtain product trial
16. Inhibit purchase of competitive brands
17. Inform consumers of favorable credit terms
18. Increase store patronage and store loyalty
19. Reduce dissonance
20. Inform, persuade, and remind consumers

consumers of the existence of the brand and demonstrate its benefits and uses. Companies promoting new products frequently employ advertising and free samples to accomplish this objective. Promotion objectives in this situation are stated in terms of a particular percentage increase in awareness of a product.

- *Situation 2: Consumers are aware of our brand but purchase a competing brand.* In this situation, an appropriate promotion objective is to demonstrate the superiority of the firm's brand. For example, Burger King employed a series of comparative ads emphasizing flame broiling to induce McDonald's customers to come to Burger King. Promotion objectives in this situation may be stated in terms of increases in market share or changes in consumer behaviors.
- *Situation 3: Consumers are aware of our brand and purchase it, but they sometimes purchase competing brands also.* In this situation, a primary promotion objective may be to develop a higher degree of brand loyalty. For example, cereal manufacturers frequently enclose cents-off coupons in packages in order to encourage repeat purchase of the same brand.
- *Situation 4: Consumers are aware of our brand and purchase it consistently.* In this situation, a primary promotion objective may be to reinforce purchase via reminder advertising or phone calls. For example, automobile salespeople frequently call past customers to encourage them to rebuy the same brand. Similarly, promotion can be used to inform

consumers of new uses of the product. For example, Arm & Hammer dramatically increased sales of its baking soda by demonstrating its use in freshening refrigerators and carpets.

These brief sketches of a few of the possible situations and promotion objectives illustrate three important points. First, what objectives are appropriate depends on the relationships between consumers and various products and brands. Second, promotion tools vary in their effectiveness for achieving specific objectives. Advertising is more effective for achieving awareness in a mass market, yet sales promotion and personal selling may be more effective for closing sales and developing brand loyalty. Third, promotion objectives change over time to reflect changes in consumers, competitors, and other elements of the environment. Highlight 11.2 illustrates how Kellogg Company adapted its promotion and marketing strategy to changes in the environment.

Formulating the Promotion Plan

At this stage, decisions are made concerning the desired structure of the promotion mix, and a promotion plan is developed. These decisions and plans are based on the objectives determined in the previous stage, which in turn depend on the analysis of consumer/product relationships.

As we have noted, the promotion mix consists of advertising, sales promotion, publicity, and personal selling. The task at this stage is determining to what degree, and in what situations, each of these tools will be used. In addition, appropriate promotion messages, media, and scheduling are determined on the basis of the firm's promotion objectives for the product, the nature of the product, and the purchasing habits and use of the media that target consumers exhibit.

Many of these decisions depend on whether the product is new or has reached a later stage of the life cycle. If the product is new, consideration must be given to whether a sales force is needed, what its size should be, and what territories it will cover, as well as to compensation and management issues. Similarly, for new products, appropriate brand images and appeals must be developed.

This does not mean that management of the sales force or advertising decisions can be ignored for existing products. The structure and sales organization that are already in place should be reviewed. Similarly, for an existing product, many decisions about the appropriate messages, media, and scheduling for other forms of promotion have usually been carefully considered. Decision making in this situation involves investigating alternative promotion methods that could boost the efficiency of the promotion mix.

Developing Promotion Budgets

There are many methods of establishing promotion budgets. For example, some firms use the *affordable method,* which amounts to allocating to promotion as much as the firm can afford. Other firms use a *percentage of sales method,* selecting a particular percentage (such as 5 percent) of current or anticipated

HIGHLIGHT 11.2

ILLUSTRATIVE EXAMPLE ■ **Developing a Successful Marketing Strategy at Kellogg Company**

In the early 1980s, Kellogg Company was in a slump. The cereal maker had gotten out of touch with consumers too old to send in a Fruit Loops box top and 50¢ for a Toucan Sam doll. It was underspending its competition in marketing and product development and by 1983 its U.S. market share hit a low of 36.7 percent. A prominent Wall Street analyst summed up Kellogg's as "A fine company that's past its prime."

Kellogg's, however, did not concede the battle for cereal supremacy and by 1987 had staged a remarkable comeback. It picked up almost 5 percentage points of market share to reach 41.2 percent in a market where every point is worth about $42 million in revenues to the manufacturer. Its next largest competitor was General Mills with 21 percent of the market, followed by General Foods with 13.2 percent, Quaker Oats with 7.7 percent, and Nabisco and Ralston Purina with 5.5 percent each.

How did Kellogg's engineer this comeback? Several changes were critical. First, there was a renewed commitment to product quality and innovation. For example, in a recent year, Kellogg's introduced 47 new cereals worldwide and had a research and development budget of $40 million.

Second, marketing became a much more important item in the company's budget. For example, annual spending tripled between 1983 and 1987 to an estimated $865 million, or 20 percent of sales. Most of this marketing money went into brand-building advertising because Kellogg's, the largest cereal company, does not have to pay retailers for shelf space to stock new items as their competitors do.

Third, Kellogg's zeroed in on the expanding adult population, particularly the 80 million baby boomers. Kellogg's has helped persuade consumers aged 25 to 49 to eat, on the average, 26 percent more cereal than people that age consumed five years ago. Frosted Flakes, for example, have been sold to grown-ups since 1984 with a campaign that claims "Frosted Flakes have the taste adults have grown to love." Ad spending on the 36-year-old brand has doubled and sales have roared ahead more than 40 percent.

Overall, the supposedly "no growth" U.S. ready-to-eat cereal market, worth $3.7 billion at retail in 1983, totalled $5.4 billion by 1988, and has expanded three times as fast as the average grocery category. William E. LaMothe, chairman of Kellogg's, says proudly, "We're driving the cereal industry's growth."

Source: Based on Patricia Sellers, "How King Kellogg Beat the Blahs," *Fortune*, August 29, 1989, pp. 54–64.

sales and allocating that amount to promotion. Still others use a *competitive parity method*, setting promotion budgets to match competitors' outlays. Each of these methods has its advantages and disadvantages, but most promotion experts argue for what is called the *task method*, or *objective and task method*.

The task method is a three-stage approach that corresponds to the three stages outlined in this section. A firm that uses the task method first determines its promotion objectives. Then it formulates a promotion plan detailing the specific promotion tasks that must be performed to achieve the promotion objectives. The third step is to estimate the costs of performing all of the promotion tasks that have been selected. The sum of these costs represents the appropriate promotion budget. Of course, if the resulting figure is more than the organization can afford, or more than management is willing to invest, some reduction must be made in the planned promotion strategy.

Table 11.9 lists several questions that it is helpful to ask when analyzing promotion strategies.

Channel Strategy

A channel of distribution is the combination of institutions through which a seller markets products to industrial buyers or ultimate consumers. In *direct channels*, manufacturers sell directly to end users. In *indirect channels*, manufacturers use one or more middlemen to sell to end users. Table 11.10 lists some of the types of marketing intermediaries commonly used in channels of distribution.

TABLE 11.9 Some Questions to Ask When Analyzing Promotion Strategies

1. What is the target market for this product, and what sources of product information do these consumers use?
2. What are the overall promotion objectives, and what are the specific objectives of each promotion tool?
3. What is the appropriate promotion mix of advertising, sales promotion, publicity, and personal selling?
4. Who is responsible for planning, organizing, implementing, and controlling the promotion strategy?
5. What should the various forms of promotion communicate about the product?
6. What are the appropriate types and combinations of personal and nonpersonal media to use? Consider salespeople, television, radio, billboards, magazines, newspapers, and direct mail.
7. How long should the firm use this promotion strategy before changing its focus or methods?
8. What is the appropriate schedule for sales calls, advertisements, sales promotions, and publicity releases?
9. How much should be spent on each of the various forms of promotion, and how much should be spent in total?
10. How will the effectiveness of promotion be measured?

TABLE 11.10 Major Types of Marketing Intermediaries

Middleman—an independent business concern that operates as a link between producers and ultimate consumers or industrial buyers.

Merchant middleman—middleman who buys the goods outright and necessarily takes title to them.

Agent—a business unit which negotiates purchases, sales, or both but does not take title to the goods in which it deals.

Wholesaler—merchant establishment operated by a concern that is primarily engaged in buying, taking title to, usually storing and physically handling goods in large quantities, and reselling the goods (usually in smaller quantities) to retailers or to industrial or business users.

Retailer—merchant middleman who is engaged primarily in selling to ultimate consumers.

Broker—a middleman that serves as a "go-between" for the buyer or seller; assumes no title risks, does not usually have physical custody of products, and is not looked upon as a permanent representative of either the buyer or the seller.

Sales agent—an independent channel member, either an individual or a company, that is responsible for the sale of a firm's products or services but does not take title to the goods sold.

Distributor—a wholesale middleman, especially in lines where selective or exclusive distribution is common at the wholesale level in which the manufacturer expects strong promotional support; often a synonym for wholesaler.

Jobber—a middleman who buys from manufacturers and sells to retailers; a wholesaler.

Facilitating agent—a business firm that assists in the performance of distribution tasks other than buying, selling, and transferring title (i.e., transportation companies, warehouses, etc.).

Source: Based on Peter D. Bennett (ed.), *Dictionary of Marketing Terms* (Chicago: American Marketing Association, 1988).

Manufacturers use intermediaries because they can perform marketing functions more efficiently than the manufacturer or because the manufacturer does not have the financial resources or expertise to market directly to consumers. Table 11.11 lists the major functions performed in channels of distribution. It is important to note that, whether the manufacturer or one or more middlemen performs them, all of these functions must usually be assumed by someone. Thus it is necessary to decide who will do these tasks and to what extent.

From the consumer's viewpoint, channels provide form, time, place, and possession utility. To create *form utility* is to convert raw materials into finished goods and services that consumers seek to purchase. Creating *time utility* means making products available when consumers want to buy them. In creating *place utility* channels make products available where consumers can purchase them. And in creating *possession utility*, channels facilitate the transfer of ownership of products from manufacturers to consumers.

TABLE 11.11 Marketing Functions Performed in Channels of Distribution

Buying—purchasing products from sellers for use or for resale.
Selling—promoting the sale of products to ultimate consumers or industrial buyers.
Sorting—a function performed by intermediaries in order to bridge the discrepancy between the assortment of goods and services generated by the producer and the assortment demanded by the consumer. This function includes four distinct processes: sorting out, accumulation, allocation and assorting.
Sorting out—a sorting process that breaks down a heterogeneous supply into separate stocks which are relatively homogeneous.
Accumulation—a sorting process that brings similar stocks from a number of sources together into a larger homogeneous supply.
Allocation—a sorting process which consists of breaking a homogeneous supply down into smaller and smaller lots.
Assorting—a sorting process which consists of building an assortment of products for use in association with each other.
Concentration—the process of bringing goods from various places together in one place.
Financing—providing credit or funds to facilitate a transaction.
Storage—maintaining inventories and protecting products to provide better customer service.
Grading—classifying products into different categories on the basis of quality.
Transportation—physically moving products from where they are made to where they are purchased and used.
Risk-taking—taking on business risks involved in transporting and owning products.
Marketing research—collecting information concerning such things as market conditions, expected sales, consumer trends, and competitive forces.

Source: Based on Peter D. Bennett (ed.), *Dictionary of Marketing Terms* (Chicago: American Marketing Association, 1988).

Given the variety of types of middlemen, functions performed, and types of utilities provided to consumers by channels, the task of selecting and designing a channel of distribution may at first appear overwhelming. However, in many industries all competitors use essentially the same channel structure and the same types of intermediaries. In these industries, a manufacturer may *have* to use the traditional channels in order to compete in the industry. For example, nationally branded consumer food products are typically sold in a variety of grocery stores, and automobiles are typically sold through franchised dealers. These channels are likely to be highly efficient and thus appropriate for a manufacturer. In addition, no other types of middlemen may be available to market the product. This is not to say that channel design allows no room for innovation. For example, health and beauty aids are commonly sold in a variety of retail stores. Yet Mary Kay Cosmetics sells such products door-to-door, often very profitably.

The four major concerns in designing channels of distribution are distribution coverage, channel control, total distribution cost, and channel flexibility.

Distribution Coverage

Because of the characteristics of the product, the environment needed to sell the product, and the needs and expectations of potential buyers, products vary in the intensity of distribution coverage called for. Distribution coverage varies on a continuum from intensive through selective to exclusive distribution. *Intensive distribution* involves selling the product through as many wholesalers and retailers as possible. Intensive distribution is appropriate for most convenience goods because of their low unit value and high frequency of purchase. *Selective distribution* involves the use of a limited number of middlemen in a particular geographic area. Appliances and home furnishings are usually distributed selectively, on the basis of the reputation and service quality of particular retailers. *Exclusive distribution* involves the use of only one middleman in a particular territory and is commonly employed to increase the selling effort for a manufacturer's product. Automobile dealerships and beer distributors are examples of exclusive distribution arrangements.

Channel Control

One important influence in the design of channel strategies is the amount of control an organization wants over the marketing of its products. Typically, the more direct and exclusive a channel is, the more control a manufacturer has. Often, however, a channel is controlled by an intermediary rather than by the manufacturer. For example, a large retailer such as Sears, Roebuck may control small manufacturers who produce Sears-labeled products.

Total Distribution Cost

The concept of total distribution cost suggests that channels should be designed to minimize costs, other things being equal. Thus, if using a system of wholesalers and retailers is cheaper than marketing directly to consumers, such a system should be selected, other things equal. However, it is also important to consider the effects of a particular channel on sales, on profits, on the total marketing mix, and on the level of consumer service that is needed for the product to be successful.

Channel Flexibility

One reason why channel strategies must be chosen so carefully is that they usually involve long-term commitments to a particular course of action. Channels are typically not changed as frequently as other elements of the marketing mix. For example, long-term leases for retail store space and long-term agreements with wholesalers limit the flexibility of an organization. In general, the more uncertain the environment, the less favorable are channel alternatives that involve long-term commitments.

Table 11.12 lists several questions that it is helpful to ask when analyzing channel strategies.

TABLE 11.12 Some Questions to Ask When Analyzing Channel Strategies

1. What is the target market for this product, and where do these consumers usually purchase?
2. What is the nature of the product, and what problems and opportunities does this information suggest for distribution?
3. How do competitors distribute products like this, and how successful have they been?
4. What is the total distribution cost of various channel alternatives?
5. What degree of market coverage is needed to reach the target market?
6. How competent is the organization to manage various types of channels?
7. How much control over the channel does the organization want?
8. Are appropriate middlemen available and willing to distribute and market the product?
9. What is the relative market power of the manufacturer versus different types of middlemen?
10. Can the manufacturer afford to perform all of the marketing functions, and can it do so efficiently?

IMPLEMENTING AND CONTROLLING THE MARKETING STRATEGY

Implementing a marketing strategy involves putting it into action according to a predefined schedule. Even the most carefully developed strategies often cannot be executed with perfect timing. Thus, the organization must closely monitor and coordinate implementation. In some situations, adjustments may have to be made in the basic strategy because of changes in the environment. For example, a competitor's introduction of a new product may make it desirable to speed up or delay implementation. The reaction of the market to the withdrawal of the original-formula Coke certainly required a change in planned marketing strategies for the Coca-Cola Company. In almost all situations, some "fine tuning" is necessary.

Controlling the marketing strategy involves three steps. First, the results of the implemented strategy are measured. Second, the results are compared with the objectives of the strategy. Third, managers determine whether the strategy is achieving its stated objectives. If so, they must decide whether some change in strategy would improve it. If not, they must decide whether the objectives were unrealistic or the strategy is simply not effective. If the strategy is judged ineffective, a new one must be developed.

Measuring the effects of a particular strategy can involve considerable market research. For example, measuring the effects of a strategy designed to "increase awareness of the product by 25 percent" usually involves primary market research on members of the target market to estimate changes in awareness. However, marketing strategies designed to achieve other objectives, such as increases in sales, profits, or market share, can often be evaluated by examining secondary information, such as the organization's sales records.

SUMMARY

This chapter investigated the process of marketing analysis and its role in strategic management. The first step in preparing a marketing strategy is to analyze consumer/product relationships. Classifying goods as either consumer or industrial products is often helpful. Consumer products can be further divided into convenience, shopping, and specialty goods on the basis of how much trouble and expense the consumer will go to in order to purchase them. Similar classification schemes exist to help firms market industrial goods. Any research that sheds light on the reasons why consumers buy certain products can help businesses understand their target markets better.

Market segmentation is the process of dividing a market into groups of similar consumers and selecting the most appropriate group or groups to serve. For some products, geographic segmentation is best. For others, segmentation is most effectively based on a demographic variable such as sex, age, or income. Segmentation based on lifestyle, or the psychographic characteristics of a market, is sometimes appropriate, as is segmentation in terms of the benefits people seek in consuming a given product.

The marketing mix consists of product, price, promotion, and channels of distribution. Which of the seven stages of a product's life cycle (concept generation through deletion) the product is in profoundly affects the way it is marketed. Other significant factors include any competitive differential advantage that can be established either functionally or through product symbolism. Pricing strategy, for its part, is influenced by consumer characteristics, organization characteristics, and competitive characteristics. There are cases where a low price is called for and cases where a high price is best. The major approaches to promoting products are advertising, sales promotion, publicity, and personal selling. All are beneficial in seeking different objectives and under different conditions. Choosing one or more promotion techniques is a key part of the marketing mix decision. Selecting a channel of distribution—that is, the combination of intermediaries through which the firm markets products to the consumer—is another crucial decision. Channels convert products into the form in which consumers want them, they make products available where and when consumers want to buy them, and they facilitate the transfer of ownership of products from manufacturers to consumers. The "middleman" can sometimes be eliminated, but the functions it performs cannot.

In the course of implementing a marketing strategy, it is important to try to keep a plan on schedule and to be flexible enough to adjust it if changes in the environment make it advisable to do so. Controlling the marketing strategy involves measuring the results of the strategy, determining whether it is achieving its objectives, and then deciding what changes are called for to correct an ineffective strategy or (perhaps) to improve a successful one.

Highlight 11.3 is a summary list of the main points made in this chapter. Use it when you analyze problems and cases that focus on marketing.

ADDITIONAL READINGS

Kotler, Philip. *Marketing Management: Analysis, Planning, and Control,* 6th ed. Englewood Cliffs, N.J.: Prentice-Hall, 1988.

McCarthy, E. Jerome, and William D. Perrault. *Basic Marketing,* 9th ed. Homewood, Ill.: Richard D. Irwin, 1987.

Peter, J. Paul, and James H. Donnelly, Jr. *A Preface to Marketing Management,* 4th ed. Plano, Tex.: Business Publications, Inc., 1988.

———. *Consumer Behavior: Marketing Strategy Perspectives.* 2nd ed. Homewood, Ill.: BPI/Irwin, 1989.

Peter, J. Paul, and Jerry C. Olson. *Marketing Management: Knowledge and Skills,* 2nd ed. Homewood, Ill.: Richard D. Irwin, 1990.

Shapiro, Benson P., Robert J. Dolan, and John A. Quelch. *Marketing Management: Strategy, Planning, and Implementation.* Homewood, Ill.: Richard D. Irwin, 1985.

HIGHLIGHT 11.3

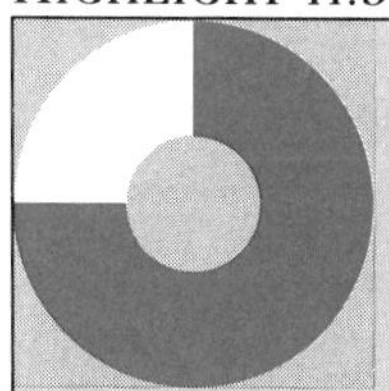

CHECKLIST ■ Analyzing Marketing in Problems and Cases

- ☐ 1. Does the problem or case involve relationships between an organization and consumers of the organization's product(s)?
- ☐ 2. Why should consumers purchase the organization's product(s) rather than competitive offerings? That is, what is the organization's competitive differential advantage from the consumer's point of view?
- ☐ 3. What are the appropriate market segments for the organization's products, and has the firm identified them?
- ☐ 4. Are these market segments large enough to serve profitably, and can the organization serve them efficiently?
- ☐ 5. What are the strengths and weaknesses of the organization's current marketing strategy?
- ☐ 6. Are all elements of the marketing strategy consistent and designed to achieve the organization's objectives?
- ☐ 7. Which elements of marketing strategy are of greatest concern in this problem or case? That is, is this a very general problem concerning the development and implementation of a marketing strategy, or is it focused on a particular type of decision?
- ☐ 8. Does the organization have good marketing skills, and is it capable of formulating and implementing a sound marketing strategy?
- ☐ 9. How would the marketing strategy have to be changed to achieve the organization's objectives?
- ☐ 10. What is the probable long-term impact on the organization of following the current or suggested marketing strategy?

HIGHLIGHT 11.4 ■ APPLICATION OF CHAPTER MATERIAL

Marketing Analysis of the 7 Up Company

7 Up was first introduced in 1929 under the name "Bib-Label Lithiated Lemon-Lime Soda." It was soon renamed "7 Up" and handily outsold the more than 600 other lemon-lime drinks on the market. It is still the traditional lemon-lime soft drink and the number-one seller in that category. It has been promoted

(*Continues*)

over the years in various campaigns under the banner of such slogans as "Nothing does it like 7 Up," "Wet and Wild," "The Uncola," "America is turning 7 Up," and "Never had it, never will." (This last campaign focused on the fact that 7 Up does not have caffeine in it, as most colas do.) The most successful by far of these campaigns was the "Uncola" campaign, which positioned 7 Up as an alternative to colas, clearing up any misconception that it was just a mixer or a medicinal product.

The 7 Up Company was purchased in 1978 by Philip Morris, a company well known for the marketing skill it has demonstrated with such successful products as Marlboro cigarettes and Miller Lite beer. However, 7 Up lost money in four of the first five years that it was a Philip Morris company. For example, in 1983, 7 Up had an operating loss of $10.8 million on revenues of $650 million.

The soft drink industry is growing at a rate of about 4 percent per year and is dominated by colas, which account for 62 percent of the $17-billion-a-year U.S. soft drink market. About 17 percent of adults in the United States drink lemon-lime soft drinks, but this category accounts for only about 12 percent of total soft drink sales. 7 Up's market share varies; in 1983 it captured 5.6 percent of the soft drink market. Though it is traditionally the number-three soft drink behind Coke and Pepsi, it slid to fourth place behind Diet Coke in 1984.

Just as 7 Up faces fierce competition from colas, it also has a variety of competitors in the lemon-lime market. In addition to Bubble-Up and Teem, the Coca-Cola Company aggressively promotes Sprite, a 7 Up equivalent, with the stated goal of converting 7 Up users. In 1981 Sprite was mentioned in twice as many ads as 7 Up. In 1984 PepsiCo introduced its own lemon-lime drink, Slice, which contains 10 percent real fruit juice, and aggressively promoted it against both 7 Up and Sprite.

As we noted, 7 Up promotion in 1984 focused on the fact that 7 Up is caffeine-free. Research conducted by the company indicated that 66 percent of American adults and 47 percent of teenagers would be interested in buying a soda without caffeine. 7 Up also introduced its own cola, Like, in 1982, using the same caffeine-free positioning. Although the introduction was supported with a $50 million advertising campaign, Like did not capture a large market share. The anticaffeine position was easily neutralized when both Coke and Pepsi introduced caffeine-free versions of most of their colas.

7 Up is distributed by 464 bottlers. Of these, 337 also distribute a competing cola such as Coke, Pepsi, or Royal Crown. It has been reported that there may be more conflict between 7 Up and its bottlers than between Coke and Pepsi and their bottlers. For one thing, many of the bottlers viewed 7 Up's anticaffeine promotion as a threat to them and to the soft drink industry. Also, it is alleged that Coke and Pepsi offer more and better discounts to bottlers than does 7 Up. Finally, at the retail level,

many restaurants prefer to deal with only one bottler that has a full line of soft drinks. For example, McDonald's has elected to standardize the beverages in its 6,250 U.S. restaurants and approves only three drinks: Coke, Sprite, and an orange flavor. However, McDonald's managers can still stock Diet 7 Up, because it appears on the company-authorized list of optional beverages.

DISCUSSION QUESTIONS

1. What are the major environmental factors affecting 7 Up?
2. What is 7 Up's competitive differential advantage?
3. What is the target market for 7 Up?
4. What should 7 Up do to regain market share and profitability?

Source: Based on "A Slow Rebound for Seven-Up," *Business Week,* October 12, 1981, pp. 107–108; "Seven-Up's Sudden Taste for Cola," *Fortune,* May 17, 1982, pp. 101–103; "Knocked from Third Place, 7 Up Is Going Flat," *Fortune,* May 14, 1984, p. 96; and J. Paul Peter and James H. Donnelly, Jr., *Marketing Management: Knowledge and Skills,* 2nd ed. (Homewood, Ill.: BPI/Irwin, 1989), pp. 339–341.

SECTION FIVE

A Framework for Strategic Analysis

This section explains a detailed approach to analyzing strategic management problems and cases. It is designed primarily for the analysis of comprehensive problems and cases, although the general logic of the approach can also be used to identify and analyze more specialized issues. Skilled case analysts are flexible in their thinking and able to adapt this approach in order to apply it to the analysis of specific problems or cases. You will find the approach helpful when you analyze the cases in this text and when you set out to solve the actual strategic management problems you will face as a practicing manager.

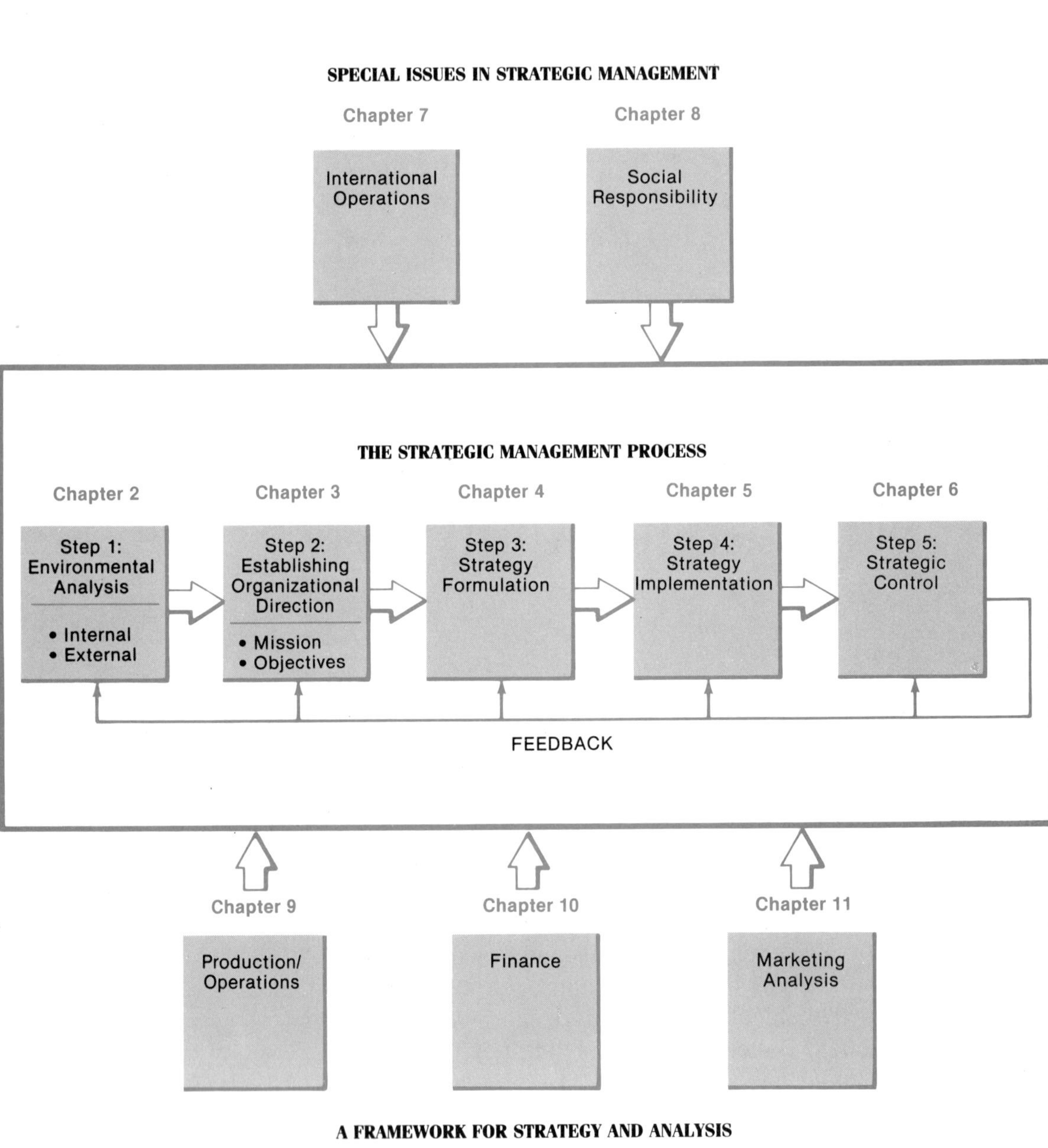
SPECIAL ISSUES IN STRATEGIC MANAGEMENT
Chapter 7
International Operations
Chapter 8
Social Responsibility
THE STRATEGIC MANAGEMENT PROCESS
Chapter 2
Step 1: Environmental Analysis
• Internal
• External
Chapter 3
Step 2: Establishing Organizational Direction
• Mission
• Objectives
Chapter 4
Step 3: Strategy Formulation
Chapter 5
Step 4: Strategy Implementation
Chapter 6
Step 5: Strategic Control
FEEDBACK
Chapter 9
Production/ Operations
Chapter 10
Finance
Chapter 11
Marketing Analysis
A FRAMEWORK FOR STRATEGY AND ANALYSIS
Chapter 12
An Approach to Solving Strategic Problems and Cases

CHAPTER 12

A Comprehensive Approach to Analyzing Strategic Problems and Cases

Since its development at the Harvard Business School in the 1920s, case analysis has become a major tool of management education.[1] *Cases* are detailed descriptions or reports of strategic management problems. They are often written by trained observers who were actually involved with the organization and the problems or issues described in the case. Cases usually include both qualitative and quantitative data that students must analyze in order to determine appropriate alternatives and solutions.

Since there are many different types of strategic management problems, there are many different types of cases. Some cases involve large, diversified companies; others involve small, single-product companies. Some cases involve very successful companies seeking to maintain industry leadership; others focus on failing companies about to go bankrupt. Some cases involve a complicated mixture of strategic management problems; others focus on only a single issue.

[1] This chapter is based on J. Paul Peter and James H. Donnelly, Jr., *A Preface to Marketing Management*, 4th ed. (Plano, Tex.: Business Publications, Inc., 1988), pp. 245–262.

A primary advantage of the case method is that it introduces a measure of realism into strategic management education. Rather than emphasizing the learning of concepts, the case method stresses the *application* of concepts and sound logic to real-world problems. In this way students learn to bridge the chasm between abstraction and application and to appreciate the value of both.

The purpose of this chapter is to outline a general approach to the analysis of strategic problems and cases. In addition, we suggest some common pitfalls to avoid in case analysis and some approaches to presenting cases. Remember, however, that although following the approach offered here is a logical and useful way to develop sound analyses, no single approach can be applied routinely or mechanically to all cases. Cases differ widely in scope, context, and amount of information available. Analysts must always be ready to "customize" this approach to the particular situation they face.

For example, in our approach, we offer a number of worksheets to assist analysts in various stages of case analysis. These worksheets are designed for broad, general cases and may have to be adapted to more specialized cases and problems. In short, there is no "magic formula" to guarantee an effective case analysis, and there is no substitute for logical, informed thinking on the part of the case analyst.

A major reason why instructors use the case method is that analyzing cases helps students develop and improve their skill at identifying problems and creating sound solutions to them. If this process required nothing more than routinely plugging information into a formula, there would be no need for strategic managers! Managers are paid to recognize problems and to formulate and implement sound solutions to them. Having a successful career in management depends on developing these skills. Highlight 12.1 lists some of the skills that case analysis helps student analysts develop.

A CASE ANALYSIS FRAMEWORK

The basic approach to case analysis that we propose is shown in Figure 12.1. This four-stage process suggests that analysts first clearly define the problem or issue to be resolved. Second, they should formulate reasonable alternatives that could potentially solve the problem. Third, analysts should evaluate each of the alternatives and compare them to find an effective solution. Finally, the alternative judged to be most effective and efficient should be selected and implemented to solve the problem.

When this process is carried out in a real situation, an additional step is included. Analysts would evaluate the effects of implementing the alternative to determine whether the problem had been solved. If so, they would continue to monitor the situation to ensure the sustained effectiveness of the alternative. If not, they would go "back to the drawing board" (to problem definition) and begin the whole process again in search of an effective solution.

This problem-solving approach to case analysis is the approach we advocate. However, for students who are not experienced in the analysis of strategic

HIGHLIGHT 12.1

ILLUSTRATIVE EXAMPLE ■ A Case for Case Analysis

Cases assist in bridging the gap between classroom learning and the so-called real world of strategic management. They provide us with an opportunity to develop, sharpen, and test our analytical skills at:

- Assessing situations
- Sorting out and organizing key information
- Asking the right questions
- Defining opportunities and problems
- Identifying and evaluating alternative courses of action
- Interpreting data
- Evaluating the results of past strategies
- Developing and defending new strategies
- Interacting with other managers
- Making decisions under conditions of uncertainty
- Critically evaluating the work of others
- Responding to criticism

Source: Adapted from David W. Cravens and Charles W. Lamb, Jr., *Strategic Marketing: Cases and Applications,* 3rd ed. (Homewood, Ill.: Richard D. Irwin, 1990), p. 55. Reprinted by permission.

problems and cases, this basic framework may be inadequate and oversimplified because it does not explain how to approach each of these tasks.

For example, consider the first stage, problem definition. What is desired here is a clear, unambiguous statement of the major problems or issues that the case hinges on. Yet just as in real situations that confront practicing managers, few cases offer a direct statement of what these pivotal problems are. In fact, after their initial reading of a case, students often conclude that the case is no more than a description of events in which there are no problems or important issues for analysis. Even in those cases that do include a direct statement about the problems or issues, there is almost always more of a problem than what first meets the eye, and much more analysis must be done.

For these reasons we have developed the more detailed framework for case analysis shown in Figure 12.2. This framework is designed to help students recognize case problems and issues and sequentially approach devising appropriate solutions to them.

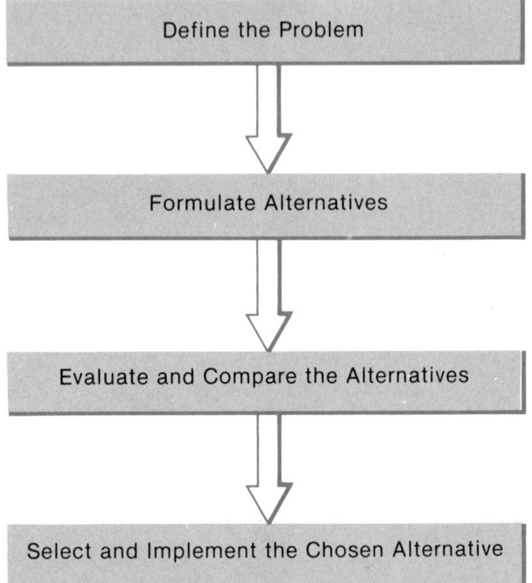

FIGURE 12.1 Stages in Case Analysis

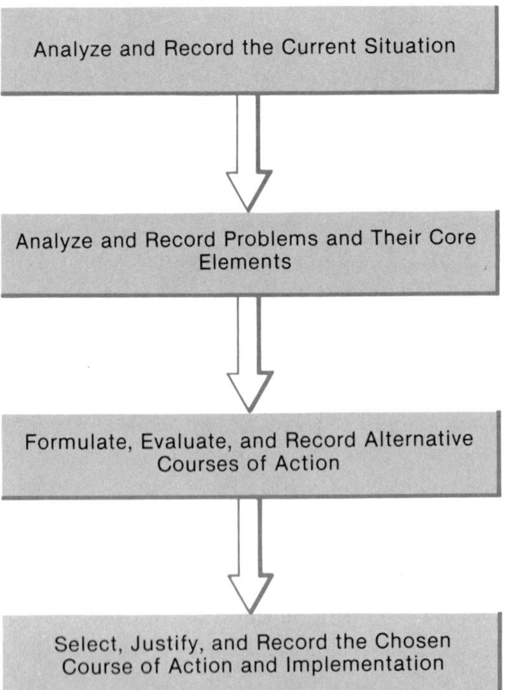

FIGURE 11.2 An Expanded Framework for Case Analysis

Analyze and Record the Current Situation

Whether the analysis of a strategic problem is conducted by a manager, a student, or an outside consultant, the first step is to analyze and record the current situation. This does not mean writing up a history of the organization or rewriting the case material. It involves the type of environmental analysis described below.

Analyzing and recording the current situation is critical for three reasons. First, until we have developed a clear understanding of the current situation, it is impossible to determine what courses of action are appropriate. In other words, we have no basis for deciding how to improve a situation until we know what that situation is.

Second, the major purpose of this stage of the analysis is to investigate the current and potential problems involved in the case. By sequentially analyzing all elements of the current situation, the analyst clarifies those problems and amasses evidence that they are the central issues.

Third, this stage is useful for delineating the level of analysis for a specific case. By "level of analysis" we mean the overall scope of the problem. For example, some cases emphasize issues arising at the industry level, whereas others focus on particular organizations, certain departments, individual executives, or particular strategic decisions. Clearly, determining the appropriate level of analysis is a very important aspect of case analysis.

In an effort to pinpoint case problems, it is useful to analyze sequentially each component or aspect of the general, operating, and internal environments. Table 12.1 provides a list of these elements and the types of questions that should be asked in the process of analyzing them.

In very few cases are all of these components or aspects crucial for the analysis. However, until each component or aspect is considered, there is no way to judge its relative importance. The analyst who considers each component and aspect in detail avoids missing critical issues. In other words, the key task at this stage of the analysis is to consider every possible environmental element in order to assess problems and opportunities in the case situation.

An analysis of any of the components or aspects of the environment may have important implications for defining case problems and for supporting appropriate solutions to the problems. Thus, keeping a detailed record of all of the relevant information uncovered in the environmental analysis is crucial. Table 12.2 presents a worksheet for recording this information and for further investigating its impact on the case.

In completing an environmental analysis, the analyst should keep six major points in mind:

1. Careful analysis is often required to separate relevant from superfluous information. Just like the situations facing a practicing manager, cases often include information that is irrelevant to the major issues. In order to get a clear understanding of the case problems, the analyst must decide what information is important and what should be ignored.

TABLE 12.1 Study Areas in Environmental Analysis

GENERAL ENVIRONMENT

1. *Economic component:* What is the state of such economic variables as inflation, unemployment, and interest rates? What are the trends in these variables, and how are they relevant to the case?
2. *Social component:* What is the state of such social variables as educational levels, customs, beliefs, and values? What are the trends in these variables, and how are they relevant to the case?
3. *Political component:* What is the state of such political variables as lobbying activities and government attitudes toward business? What are the trends in these variables and how are they relevant to the case?
4. *Legal component:* What is the level of such legal variables as federal, state, and local legislation? What are the trends in these variables and how are they relevant to the case?
5. *Technological component:* What is the level of technology in the industry? What technological trends are relevant to the case?

OPERATING ENVIRONMENT

1. *Customer component:* What are the target markets and customer profiles, and how are they relevant to the case?
2. *Competition component:* What are the major barriers to entry in this industry? What are the strengths, weaknesses, strategies, and market shares of major competitors, and how are they relevant to the case?
3. *Labor component:* What factors influence the supply of labor, and how are they relevant to the case?
4. *Supplier component:* What factors influence relationships between suppliers of resources and the firm, and how are they relevant to the case?
5. *International component:* What is the state of international factors? What international trends are relevant to the case?

INTERNAL ENVIRONMENT

1. *Organizational aspects:* What organizational or managerial issues, concepts, and analyses are relevant to the case?
2. *Marketing aspects:* What marketing issues, concepts, and analyses are relevant to the case?
3. *Financial aspects:* What financial issues, concepts, and analyses are relevant to the case?
4. *Personnel aspects:* What personnel issues, concepts, and analyses are relevant to the case?
5. *Production aspects:* What production issues, concepts, and analyses are relevant to the case?

2. It is important to determine the difference between symptoms of problems and current and potential problems themselves. Symptoms of problems are indicators of a problem but are not problems per se. For example, a decline in sales in a particular sales territory is a symptom

TABLE 12.2 General Worksheet for Analyzing the Current Situation

ENVIRONMENT	RELEVANT ISSUES (SPECIFIC TO CASE)	CASE IMPACT (FAVORABLE/ UNFAVORABLE)	CASE IMPORTANCE (IMPORTANT/ UNIMPORTANT)
General Environment			
Economic			
Social			
Political			
Legal			
Technological			
Operating Environment			
Customers			
Competition			
Labor			
Suppliers			
International			
Internal Environment			
Organizational aspects			
Marketing aspects			
Financial aspects			
Personnel aspects			
Production aspects			

of a problem. The problem is the root cause of the decline in sales—perhaps the field representative stopped making sales calls on minor accounts because she or he is dissatisfied with the firm's compensation plan.

3. In recording the current situation, the analyst must be mindful of the difference between facts and opinions. Facts are objective statements or accounts of information such as financial data reported in a balance sheet or income statement. Opinions are subjective interpretations of facts or situations. For example, when a particular executive says she believes sales will increase by 20 percent next year, she is expressing an opinion. The analyst must not place too much emphasis on unsupported opinions and must carefully consider any factors that may bias people's opinions.
4. It is often useful to collect additional information from outside the case when performing a situational analysis. The Appendix to this book offers a summary of sources of secondary data from which additional information can be obtained. This information can be very useful for putting the problem in context and for supporting an analysis. Remember, though, that the major problems are contained in the case, and the analyst should not need outside information to recognize them.

5. Regardless of how much information is contained in the case and how much additional information is collected, the analyst usually finds it impossible to characterize the current situation completely. At this point assumptions must be made. Clearly, because different analysts might make widely differing assumptions, assumptions must be stated explicitly. Doing so avoids confusion about how the analyst perceives the current situation and enables other analysts to evaluate the reasonableness and necessity of the assumptions.
6. When an analyst concludes that a certain aspect of an environmental analysis has no bearing on the case, he or she should say so explicitly. Moreover, analysts should avoid trying to force or stretch information to fit into each of the environmental components. Indeed some aspects are likely to be irrelevant to any specific case, although each must be evaluated to determine whether it is relevant.

Analyze and Record Problems and Their Core Elements

The environmental analysis just described is useful for developing a general understanding of the current situation. However, its primary purpose is to help the analyst recognize the major problems or issues. In other words, comparing the case situation with an optimal situation should highlight the inconsistencies between them. By an optimal situation we mean a situation in which activities are performed in a manner consistent with sound managerial principles and logic.

For example, suppose analysis of a particular case revealed that although an organization had done an excellent job of setting objectives, its current strategy was not designed appropriately for accomplishing these objectives. Because management principles strongly recommend that strategies flow from objectives, this inconsistency and the reasons for it should be carefully considered. The deviation in strategy is probably symptomatic of a deeper managerial problem.

Recognizing and recording problems and their core elements is crucial to a meaningful case analysis. Obviously, if the root problems are not determined and explicitly stated and understood, the remainder of the case analysis has little merit because it does not focus on the key issues.

Table 12.3 presents a worksheet to help analysts recognize and record problems. This table emphasizes the importance of providing evidence that a particular problem is a critical one. Simply stating that a particular issue is the major problem is not sufficient; analysts must also provide the reasoning by which they reached this conclusion.

Formulate, Evaluate, and Record Alternative Courses of Action

At this stage, the analyst addresses the question of what can be done to resolve the problems defined in the previous part of the analysis. Generally, several alternative courses of action that might help alleviate the problem are available. One approach to developing alternatives is to brainstorm as many as possible and then reduce the list to a workable number of the most feasible. Another

TABLE 12.3 General Worksheet for Defining Problems and Their Core Elements

MAJOR PROBLEM OR ISSUE

Description of problem or issue: __________

Evidence that this is a major problem or issue:

1. Facts __________
2. Symptoms or other effects of the problem __________
3. Opinions __________
4. Assumptions __________

(Repeat as necessary for cases involving several problems or issues.)

approach is to screen each alternative as it is developed, saving for further evaluation and comparison only those that meet predetermined feasibility criteria. Regardless of the method used to develop alternatives, the final list should usually include only three or four of the better solutions.

After listing a number of feasible alternatives, the analyst evaluates them in terms of their strengths and weaknesses. Strengths include anything favorable about the alternative (such as increased efficiency, increased productivity, cost savings, or increased sales and profits). Weaknesses include anything unfavorable about the alternative (such as its costs in time, money, and other resources or its relative ineffectiveness at solving the problem). Table 12.4 offers a worksheet for evaluating alternative courses of action.

Sound logic and the application of managerial principles are particularly important at this stage. It is essential to avoid alternatives that might alleviate the problem but could at the same time spawn a new, more serious problem or require a greater investment of resources than solving the problem warrants. Similarly, analysts must be as objective as possible in their evaluation of alternatives. For example, it is not uncommon for analysts to ignore important weaknesses of an alternative that they favor.

Select, Justify, and Record the Chosen Course of Action and Implementation

It is now time to select the alternative that best solves the problem, while creating a minimum of new problems. This alternative is selected via careful analysis of the strengths and weaknesses of each alternative scrutinized in the previous stage. Recording the logic and reasoning that precipitated the selection

TABLE 12.4 General Worksheet for Evaluating Alternative Courses of Action

ALTERNATIVE 1

Description of alternative: ______________________________

Strengths of alternative: ______________________________

Weaknesses of alternative: ______________________________

Overall evaluation of alternative: ______________________________

ALTERNATIVE 2

Description of alternative: ______________________________

Strengths of alternative: ______________________________

Weaknesses of alternative: ______________________________

Overall evaluation of alternative: ______________________________

(Repeat as necessary for each feasible alternative.)

of a particular alternative is very important. Regardless of what alternative is selected, the analyst must justify the choice.

At this stage in the analysis, an alternative has been selected and the analyst has explained why she or he feels it is the appropriate course of action. The final phase in case analysis is the devising of an action-oriented implementation plan. Analysts should describe their proposed implementation plan in as much detail as possible.

Table 12.5 offers a worksheet to use in considering implementation issues. Although cases do not always contain enough information for the analyst to answer all of these questions in detail, reasonable recommendations for implementation should be formulated. In doing so, the analyst may have to make certain assumptions about commonly used and effective methods of implementing strategic alternatives.

TABLE 12.5 General Worksheet for Implementing the Chosen Alternative

1. What should be done to implement the chosen alternative effectively?
Specific recommendation: ____

____

Justification: ____

____

2. Who should be responsible for implementing the chosen alternative?
Specific recommendation: ____

____

Justification: ____

____

3. When and where should the chosen alternative be implemented?
Specific recommendation: ____

____

Justification: ____

____

4. How should the chosen alternative be evaluated for success or failure?
Specific recommendation: ____

____

Justification: ____

____

PITFALLS TO AVOID IN CASE ANALYSIS

Analysts commonly make a variety of errors in the process of case study. Below we discuss some of the mistakes analysts make most frequently. When evaluating your analyses or those of others, use this list as a guide to spotting potential shortcomings.

Inadequately Defining the Problem

Analysts often recommend courses of action without adequately understanding or defining the problems that characterize the case. This sometimes occurs because analysts jump to premature conclusions upon first reading a case and then proceed to interpret everything in the case as justifying those conclusions—even factors that they should realize argue against them. Closely related is the error of analyzing symptoms without determining the root problems. Sound case analyses absolutely depend on a clear understanding of major case problems.

Searching for "The Answer"

Analysts sometimes spend a great deal of time searching through secondary sources to find out what an organization actually did in a particular case and then present this alternative as though it were "the answer." However, this approach ignores the fact that the objective of undertaking a case study is to learn through exploration and discussion. There is no one "official" or "correct" answer to a case. Rather, many good analyses and solutions, as well as many poor ones, usually exist.

Assuming the Case Away

Analysts sometimes make such sweeping assumptions that the case problem is essentially assumed away. For example, suppose a case concerns a firm that has lost a major share of its market. Simply concluding that the firm will increase its market share by 10 percent per year for the next five years is an example of assuming the case away.

Not Having Enough Information

Analysts often complain that not enough information is given in the case for them to make a good decision. However, there is good reason for not presenting "all" of the information in a case. In real business situations, managers and consultants seldom have all the information they would need to make an optimal decision. Reasonable assumptions and predictions have to be made, and the challenge is to arrive at intelligent solutions in spite of uncertainty and limited information.

Relying on Generalizations

Analysts sometimes discuss case problems and recommendations at such a general level that their work has little value. Case analysis calls for specific problems and recommendations, not sweeping generalizations. For example, to recommend that the structure of the firm be changed is to generalize. However, to provide a detailed plan for changing the organizational structure, to explain just what the structure should be, and to give one's reasons for this solution is to make a specific recommendation.

Postulating a Different Situation

Analysts sometimes exert considerable time and effort contending that "if the situation were different, I'd know what course of action to take" or "if the manager hadn't already fouled things up so badly, the firm wouldn't have any problems." Such reasoning ignores the fact that the events in the case have already happened and cannot be changed. Even though analysis or criticism of past events may be necessary in diagnosing problems, the situation as it exists must be addressed in the end, and decisions must be based on it.

Focusing Too Narrowly

Too often, analysts ignore the effects that a change in one area has on the rest of the situation. Although cases are sometimes labeled as concerning specific types of issues, this does not mean that other variables can be ignored. For example, changing the price of a product may well influence the appropriate methods of promotion and distribution.

Abandoning Realism

In many cases, analysts get so obsessed with solving a particular problem that their solutions become totally unrealistic. For example, designing and recommending a sound $1 million advertising program for a firm with a capital structure of $50,000 is totally unrealistic, even though, if it were possible to implement, it might solve the given problem.

Setting Up "Straw Man" Alternatives

Analysts sometimes offer a single viable alternative and several others that are extremely weak and untenable. The analysts then proceed with the evaluation and selection of an alternative (predictably enough) by discrediting the "straw man" alternatives and accepting the single viable solution. Such an approach to case analysis is inappropriate, because what is desired is a *set* of alternatives that it is worthwhile to evaluate. Case analysis can enhance the development of decision-making skills only when each alternative has some important strengths and analysts must make an informed choice.

Recommending Research or Consultants

Analysts sometimes offer unsatisfactory solutions to case problems by recommending either that some research be conducted to uncover problems or that a consultant be hired to do so. Although engaging in further research and hiring consultants may occasionally be useful recommendations as auxiliary steps in an analysis, it is still the analyst's job to identify the problems and decide how to solve them. When research or consultants are recommended in a case analysis, the rationale, costs, and potential benefits should be fully specified in the case report.

Rehashing Case Material

Analysts sometimes go to great lengths rewriting a history of an organization as presented in the case. This is unnecessary and wasteful: the instructor and other analysts are already familiar with this information. Similarly, student analysts sometimes copy case tables and figures and include them in a written report. This too is unnecessary. However, developing original graphs, pie charts, or other visual aids based on the case material is often a useful way to make a particular point.

Highlight 12.2 offers some further guidelines on approaching cases and gives an example of an effective student analysis.

Not Thinking!

By far the worst mistake analysts make is not thinking. Often analysts mistakenly assume that, having simply organized the case material in a logical format,

HIGHLIGHT 12.2

ILLUSTRATIVE EXAMPLE ■ **What Does Case "Analysis" Mean?**

A common criticism of prepared cases goes something like this: "You repeated an awful lot of case material, but you really didn't analyze the case." And at the same time, it is difficult to verbalize exactly what "analysis" means: "I can't explain exactly what it is, but I know it when I see it!"

It is not surprising that confusion arises, because the term *analysis* has many definitions and means different things in different contexts. In terms of case analysis, analysis means going beyond simply describing the case information. It includes determining the implications of the case information for developing strategy. This may involve careful mathematical analysis of sales and profit data or thoughtful interpretation of the text of the case.

One way of approaching analysis involves taking a series of three steps: synthesis, generalizations, and implications. A brief example of this process follows.

> The high growth rate of frozen pizza sales has attracted a number of large food processors, including Pillsbury (Totino's), Quaker Oats (Celeste), American Home Products (Chef Boy-ar-dee), Nestlé (Stouffer's), General Mills (Saluto), and H. J. Heinz (La Pizzeria). The major independents are Jeno's, Tony's, and

(*Continues*)

they have done a case analysis! And similarly, although analysts usually have some general knowledge of a firm or situation, they often ignore it when working on a case. For example, suppose a case involves a major automobile manufacturer. Although the case may say nothing about foreign imports, they may well have an important impact on the firm and should be considered. Analyzing cases *requires* that knowledge of management principles and sound logic from outside the case be applied.

After attempting unsuccessfully to analyze the first case or two, analysts sometimes give up and assure themselves that they cannot do case analyses. Such a conclusion is almost always unwarranted and ignores the fact that performing case analyses is a *learned* skill. To be sure, some students master

John's. Jeno's and Totino's are the market leaders, with market shares of about 19 percent each. Celeste and Tony's have about 8–9 percent each, and the others have about 5 percent or less. (Excerpted from "The Pillsbury Company—Totino's Pizza," in Philip Kotler, *Principles of Marketing* [Englewood Cliffs, N.J.: Prentice-Hall, Inc., 1980], pp. 192–195.)

The frozen pizza market is a highly competitive and highly fragmented market.

In markets such as this, attempts to gain market share through lower consumer prices or heavy advertising are likely to be quickly copied by competitors and thus not be very effective.

Lowering consumer prices and spending more on advertising are likely to be poor strategies. Perhaps increasing freezer space in retail outlets could be effective; this objective might be obtained through trade discounts. Developing a superior product (such as better tasting pizza or microwave pizza) or increasing geographic coverage of the market might be better strategies for obtaining market share.

Note that none of these three steps includes any repetition of the case material. Rather, they all involve extracting the meaning of the information and, by pairing it with strategic management principles, coming up with its strategic implications.

case analysis much more quickly than others. Yet most students can become skillful analysts of cases and problems if they continue working hard on the cases and learning from class discussions.

Highlight 12.3 is a handy summary of the steps to take in case analysis and of the use of the worksheets included in this chapter.

COMMUNICATION OF THE CASE ANALYSIS

The final task in case analysis that we will consider here is to communicate the results of the analysis. The most comprehensive and insightful analysis has little value if it is not communicated effectively. Communication includes not only organizing the information in a logical manner but also using proper

HIGHLIGHT 12.3

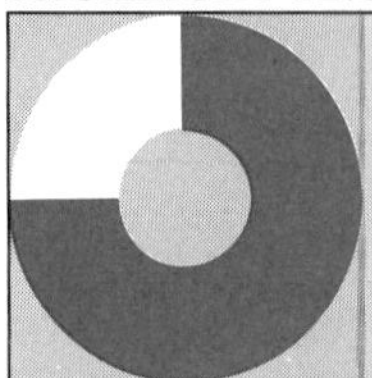

CHECKLIST ■ An Operational Approach to Case and Problem Analysis

- ☐ 1. Read the case quickly to get an overview of the situation.
- ☐ 2. Read the case again thoroughly, underlining relevant information and taking notes on potential areas of concern.
- ☐ 3. Reread and study the case until it is well understood.
- ☐ 4. Review outside sources of information that are relevant to the case, and record important information.
- ☐ 5. Complete the General Worksheet for Analyzing the Current Situation.
- ☐ 6. Review this worksheet in search of potential problems.
- ☐ 7. List all potential problems on the General Worksheet for Defining Problems and Their Core Elements.
- ☐ 8. Review this worksheet and list the major problems in order of priority.
- ☐ 9. Complete the Worksheet for Defining Problems and Their Core Elements.
- ☐ 10. Develop several feasible solutions for dealing with the major problems.
- ☐ 11. Complete the General Worksheet for Evaluating Alternative Courses of Action.
- ☐ 12. Review this worksheet and ensure that all relevant strengths and weaknesses have been considered.
- ☐ 13. Decide which alternative solves the problems most effectively.
- ☐ 14. Complete the General Worksheet for Implementing the Chosen Alternative.
- ☐ 15. Prepare a written or oral report based on the worksheets.

grammar and spelling. In addition, the overall appearance of a written report and that of the presenters and visual aids in an oral report are often used by evaluators as an indication of the effort put into a project and of its overall quality.

The Written Report

Good written reports usually start with an outline. We offer the framework given in Table 12.6 as one useful format. This outline is fully consistent with the approach suggested in this chapter and, with a few exceptions, involves writing out in prose form the information contained on the various worksheets.

TABLE 12.6 An Outline for Written Case Reports

1. Title page
2. Table of contents
3. Introduction
4. Environmental analysis
   A. General environment
   B. Operating environment
   C. Internal environment
   D. Assumptions
5. Problem definition
   A. Major problem 1 and evidence
   B. Major problem 2 (if applicable) and evidence
   C. Major problem 3 (if applicable) and evidence
6. Alternative courses of action
   A. Description of alternative 1
      a. Strengths
      b. Weaknesses
   B. Description of alternative 2
      a. Strengths
      b. Weaknesses
   C. Description of alternative 3
      a. Strengths
      b. Weaknesses
7. Chosen alternative and implementation
   A. Justification for alternative chosen
   B. Implementation specifics and justification
8. Summary of analysis
9. References
10. Technical appendices
   A. Financial analyses
   B. Other technical information

Elements of a Written Report

TITLE PAGE. The title page includes the title of the case and the names of all persons who were involved in preparing the report. It is also useful to include the name and number of the course for which the case was prepared and the date the project was submitted.

TABLE OF CONTENTS. The Table of Contents lists every heading in the report and the number of the page on which that particular section begins. If a variety of exhibits are included in a case report, it may be useful to include a Table of Exhibits listing every exhibit and the page number on which it is located.

INTRODUCTION. The introduction of a case analysis is not a summary of the case. It is a statement of the purpose of the report and a brief description of each of its major sections.

ENVIRONMENTAL ANALYSIS. In this section, the results of the analysis of each environmental component are reported. Subheadings should be used for each of the three major environments and for each relevant component or aspect listed in Table 12.2. Again, if any of the environments or categories has no relevance to a particular case, simply report that the analysis revealed nothing crucial for this particular situational element. Any assumptions made concerning the current situation should also be reported in this section.

PROBLEM DEFINITION. This section offers a concise statement of the major problems in the case and reviews the evidence that led to the conclusion that these are the major issues. Problems should be listed in order of their importance and should be accompanied by an account of the evidence.

ALTERNATIVE COURSES OF ACTION. This section describes each of the alternatives devised for solving the major problems in the case. The strengths and weaknesses of each alternative should be clearly delineated.

CHOSEN ALTERNATIVE AND IMPLEMENTATION. This section reveals which alternative has been selected and explains why it is the appropriate course of action. In addition, it should include a detailed description of how the alternative will be implemented and why this method of implementation is best.

SUMMARY OF ANALYSIS. This brief section simply restates what the report has been about. It describes what was done in preparing the report, the basic problems, and the alternative selected for solving them. It is also useful in this section to offer any additional information that supports the quality of the analysis and the value of the alternative chosen.

REFERENCES. Any outside materials used in the report should be listed alphabetically in an acceptable reference style, such as that used in articles in *The Academy of Management Journal.* (Such information should also be appropriately cited in footnotes throughout the report.)

TECHNICAL APPENDICES. Some cases require considerable financial analysis. Typically, key financial analysis is reported in the text of the report, but detailed analysis and calculations are placed here. Any other types of analysis that are too long or too detailed for the body of the report can also be placed here.

The Oral Presentation

Case analyses are often presented orally in class by individuals or teams of analysts. As is true for the written report, a good outline is critical, and it is often a good idea to provide each class member with a copy of the outline and a list of any assumptions that are made. Although there is no single best way to present a case or to divide responsibility among team members, simply reading a written report is unacceptable. (It encourages boredom and interferes with all-important class discussion.) It is important to emphasize the major points of the analysis and not get bogged down in unnecessary detail. If the instructor or a class member asks for more details on a specific point, of course, the presenter must supply them.

The use of visual aids can be very helpful in presenting case analyses in class. However, simply presenting financial statements or other detailed data contained in the case is a poor use of visual media. On the other hand, taking these statements or figures and recasting them in easy-to-understand pie charts or graphs can be very effective in making specific points. Remember that any type of visual aid should be large enough so that even people sitting in the rear of the classroom can see the information clearly.

Oral presentation of case analyses is particularly helpful to students who are learning the skill of speaking to a group, a common activity in many managerial positions. In particular, the ability to handle objections and disagreements without antagonizing others is a skill well worth developing.

SUMMARY

This chapter presented a framework for case analysis and offered some suggestions for developing and communicating high-quality case reports. Case analysis begins with analysis and recording of the current situation, including all relevant aspects of the environment, followed by analysis and recording of the problems or issues on which the case hinges. The next step is to formulate, evaluate, and record alternative courses of action in order to "narrow the field" to the best feasible alternatives. Then it is necessary to select one of the proposed courses of action, explain this choice, and describe how it is to be implemented.

We cautioned against several pitfalls that can plague the student (or the ill-prepared manager) engaged in case analysis, and we offered some guidelines for communicating case analyses in a written report and in an oral presentation.

Performing good case analyses takes a lot of time and effort. Analysts must be highly motivated and willing to get involved in the case and in class discussion if they expect to learn effectively and succeed in a course where cases are utilized. Analysts with only passive interest who perform "night before" analyses cheat themselves of valuable learning experiences that are critical in preparing for a successful management career.

APPENDIX[1]

Selected Sources of Secondary Information

Secondary sources of data are often useful in case analysis. They provide more thorough environmental analyses and can be used to support one's recommendations and conclusions. Many of the data sources listed below can be found in business libraries. Here they are grouped under five headings: General Business and Industry Sources, Basic U.S. Statistical Sources, Financial Information Sources, Marketing Information Sources, and Indexes and Abstracts.

GENERAL BUSINESS AND INDUSTRY SOURCES

Aerospace Facts and Figures. Aerospace Industries Association of America.

Annual Statistical Report. American Iron and Steel Institute.

Chemical Marketing Reporter. Schnell Publishing. Includes lengthy, continuing list of "Current Prices of Chemicals and Related Materials."

[1] Adapted from J. Paul Peter and James H. Donnelly, Jr., *Marketing Management: Knowledge and Skills,* 2nd ed. (Homewood, Ill.: BPI/Irwin, 1989), pp. 907–919. Reprinted by permission.

Computerworld. Computerworld, Inc. Last December issue includes "Review and Forecast," an analysis of computer industry's past year and the outlook for the next year.

Construction Review. Department of Commerce. Current statistics on construction put in place, costs, and employment.

Distribution Worldwide. Chilton Co. Special annual issue, *Distribution Guide,* compiles information on transportation methods and wage.

Drugs and Cosmetic Industry. Drug Markets, Inc. Separate publication in July, *Drug and Cosmetic Catalog,* provides list of manufacturers of drugs and cosmetics and their respective products.

Electrical World. January and February issues include two-part statistical report on expenditures, construction, and other categories by region; capacity; sales; and financial statistics for the electrical industry.

Encyclopedia of Business Information Sources. Paul Wasserman et al., eds., Gale Research Company. A detailed listing of primary subjects of interest to managerial personnel, with a record of sourcebooks, periodicals, organizations, directories, handbooks, bibliographies, and other sources of information on each topic. Two vols., nearly 17,000 entries in over 1,600 subject areas.

Forest Industries. Miller Freeman Publications. Inc. The March issue includes "Forest Industries Wood-Based Panel," a review of production and sales figures for selected wood products; extra issue in May includes a statistical review of the lumber industry.

Implement and Tractor. Intertec Publishing Corporation. January issue includes equipment specifications and operating data for farm and industrial equipment. November issue includes statistics and information on the farm industry.

Industry Surveys. Standard & Poor's Corp. Continuously revised analysis of leading industries (40 industries made up of 1,300 companies). Basic analysis features company ratio comparisons and balance sheet statistics.

Middle Market Directory. Dun & Bradstreet. Inventories approximately 18,000 U.S. companies with an indicated worth of $500,000 to $999,999, giving officers, products, standard industrial classification, approximate sales, and number of employees.

Million Dollar Directory. Dun & Bradstreet. Lists U.S. companies with an indicated worth of $1 million or more, giving officers and directors, products, standard industrial classification, sales, and number of employees.

Milutinovich, J. S. "Business Facts for Decision Makers: Where to Find Them." *Business Horizons,* March–April 1985, pp. 63–80.

Modern Brewery Age. Business Journals, Inc. February issue includes a review of sales and production figures for the brewery industry. A separate publication, *The Blue Book,* issued in May, compiles sales and consumption figures by state for the brewery industry.

National Petroleum News. McGraw-Hill, Inc. May issue includes statistics on sales and consumption of fuel oils, gasoline, and related products. Some figures are for 10 years, along with 10-year projections.

Operating Results of Department and Specialty Stores. National Retail Merchants Association.

Petroleum Facts and Figures. American Petroleum Institute.

Poor's Register of Corporations, Directors, and Executives of the United States and Canada. Standard & Poor's Corp. Divided into two sections. The first gives officers, products, sales range, and number of employees for about 30,000 corporations. The second gives brief information on executives and directors.

Quick-Frozen Foods. Harcourt Brace Jovanovich Publications. October issue includes "Frozen Food Almanac," providing statistics on the frozen food industry by product.

Statistical Sources. Paul Wasserman et al., eds. Gale Research Corp., 4th ed., 1974. A subject guide to industrial, business, social, educational, and financial data, and other related topics.

BASIC U.S. STATISTICAL SOURCES

Business Service Checklist. Department of Commerce. Weekly guide to Department of Commerce publications, plus key business indicators.

Business Statistics. Department of Commerce. (Supplement to *Survey of Current Business.*) History of the statistical series appearing in the *Survey.* Also included are source references and useful explanatory notes.

Census of Agriculture. Department of Commerce. Data by states and counties on livestock, farm characteristics, values.

Census of Manufacturers. Department of Commerce. Industry statistics, area statistics, subjects reports, location of plants, industry descriptions arranged in Standard Industrial Classification, and a variety of ratios.

Census of Mineral Industries. Department of Commerce. Similar to *Census of Manufacturers.* Also includes capital expenditures and employment and payrolls.

Census of Retail Trade. Department of Commerce. Compiles data for states, SMSAs, counties, and cities with populations of 2,500 or more by kind of business. Data include number of establishments, sales, payroll, and personnel.

Census of Selected Services. Department of Commerce. Includes data on hotels, motels, beauty parlors, barber shops, and other retail service organizations.

Census of Transportation. Passenger Transportation Survey, Commodity Transportation Survey, Travel Inventory and Use Survey, Bus and Truck Carrier Survey.

Census Tract Reports. Department of Commerce, Bureau of Census. Detailed information on both population and housing subjects.

Census of Wholesale Trade. Department of Commerce. Similar to *Census of Retail Trade*—except information is for wholesale establishment.

County and City Data Book. Department of Commerce. Summary statistics for small geographical areas.

Current Business Reports. Department of Commerce. Reports monthly department store sales of selected items.

Economic Report of the President. Transmitted to the Congress, January (each year), together with the *Annual Report* of the Council of Economic Advisers. Statistical tables relating to income, employment, and production.

Handbook of Basic Economic Statistics. Economic Statistics Bureau of Washington, D.C. Current and historical statistics on industry, commerce, labor, and agriculture.

Statistical Abstract of the United States. Department of Commerce. Summary statistics in industrial, social, political, and economic fields in the United States. It is augmented by the *Cities Supplement, The County Data Book,* and *Historical Statistics of the United States.*

Statistics of Income: Corporation Income Tax Returns. Internal Revenue Service. Balance sheet and income statement statistics derived from corporate tax returns.

Statistics of Income: U.S. Business Tax Returns. Internal Revenue Service. Summarizes financial and economic data for proprietorships, partnerships, and small business corporations.

Survey of Current Business. Department of Commerce. Facts on industrial and business activity in the United States and statistical summary of national income and product accounts. A weekly supplement provides an up to date summary of business.

FINANCIAL INFORMATION SOURCES

Blue Line Investment Survey. Quarterly ratings and reports on 1,000 stocks; analysis of 60 industries and special situations analysis (monthly); supplements on new developments and editorials on conditions affecting price trends.

Commercial and Financial Chronicle. Variety of articles and news reports on business, government, and finance. Monday's issue lists new securities, dividends, and called bonds. Thursday's issue is devoted to business articles.

Dun's Review. Dun & Bradstreet. This monthly includes very useful annual financial ratios for about 125 lines of business.

Fairchild's Financial Manual of Retail Stores. Information about officers and directors, products, subsidiaries, sales, and earnings for apparel stores, mail order firms, variety chains, and supermarkets.

Federal Reserve Bulletin. Board of Governors of the Federal Reserve System. The "Financial and Business Statistics" section of each issue of this monthly bulletin is the best single source for current U.S. banking and monetary statistics.

Financial World. Articles on business activities of interest to investors, including investment opportunities and pertinent data on firms, such as earnings and dividend records.

Moody's Bank and Finance Manual; Moody's Industrial Manual; Moody's Municipal & Government Manual; Moody's Public Utility Manual; Moody's Transportation Manual; Moody's Directors Service. Brief histories of companies and their operations, subsidiaries, officers and directors, products, and balance sheet and income statements over several years.

Moody's Bond Survey. Moody's Investors Service. Weekly data on stocks and bonds, including recommendations for purchases or sale and discussions of industry trends and developments.

Moody's Handbook of Widely Held Common Stocks. Moody's Investors Service. Weekly data on stocks and bonds, including recommendations for purchases or sale and discussions of industry trends and developments.

Security Owner's Stock Guide. Standard & Poor's Corp. Standard & Poor's rating, stock price range, and other helpful information for about 4,200 common and preferred stocks.

Security Price Index. Standard & Poor's Corp. Price indexes, bond prices, sales, yields, Dow Jones averages, etc.

Standard Corporation Records. Standard & Poor's Corp. Published in looseleaf form, offers information similar to Moody's manuals. Use of this extensive service facilitates buying securities for both the individual and the institutional investor.

MARKETING INFORMATION SOURCES[2]

Advertising Age. This important advertising weekly publishes a number of annual surveys or features of special interest related to U.S. national advertising statistics.

[2] Based in part on Gilbert A. Churchill, Jr., *Marketing Research: Methodological Foundations* (Hinsdale, Ill.: Dryden Press, 1987), pp. 188–201.

Audits and Surveys National Total-Market Index. Contains information on various product types including total market size, brand market shares, retail inventory, distribution coverage, and out of stock.

Commercial Atlas and Marketing Guide. Skokie, Ill.: Rand-McNally & Co. Statistics on population, principal cities, business centers, trading areas, sales and manufacturing units, transportation data, and so forth.

Current Sources of Marketing Information. Gunther, Edgar, and F. A. Goldstein. This is a bibliography of primary marketing. Subjects include basic sources of information, the national market, regional data on the economy, and advertising and promotion.

Dun & Bradstreet Market Identifiers. Relevant marketing information on over 4.3 million establishments for constructing sales prospect files, sales territories, and sales territory potentials and isolating potential new customers with particular characteristics.

Editor and Publisher "Market Guide." Market information for 1,500 American and Canadian cities. Data include population, household, gas meters, climate, retailing, and newspaper information.

Guide to Consumer Markets. New York: The Conference Board. This useful annual compilation of U.S. statistics on the consumer marketplace covers population, employment, income, expenditures, production, and prices.

Industrial Marketing. "Guide to Special Issues." This directory is included in each issue. Publications are listed within primary market classifications and are listed for up to three months prior to advertising closing date.

Marketing Communications (January 1968 to January 1972, formerly *Printer's Ink,* 1914–1967). Pertinent market information on regional and local consumer markets as well as international markets to January 1972.

Marketing Information Guide. Washington D.C.: Department of Commerce. Annotations of selected current publications and reports, with basic information and statistics on marketing and distribution.

National Purchase Diary Panel (NPD). Monthly purchase information based on the largest panel diary in the United States with detailed brand, frequency of purchase, characteristics of heavy buyers, and other market data.

Nielson Retail Index. Contains basic product turnover data, retail prices, store displays, promotional activity, and local advertising based on a national sample of supermarkets, drugstores, and mass merchandisers.

Nielson Television Index. Well-known index which provides estimates of the size and nature of the audience for individual television programs.

Population and Its Distribution: The United States Markets. J. Walter Thompson Co. New York: McGraw-Hill Book Co. A handbook of marketing facts selected from the U.S. *Census of Population* and the most recent census data on retail trade.

Sales and Marketing Management. (Formerly *Sales Management,* to October 1975.) This valuable semimonthly journal includes four useful annual statistical issues: *Survey of Buying Power* (July); *Survey of Buying Power, Part II* (October); *Survey of Industrial Purchasing Power* (April); *Survey of Selling Costs* (January). These are excellent references for buying income, buying power index, cash income, merchandise line, manufacturing line, and retail sales.

Selling Areas Marketing Inc. Reports on warehouse withdrawals of various food products in each of 42 major markets covering 80 percent of national food sales.

Simmons Media/Marketing Service. Provides cross referencing of product usage and media exposure for magazine, television, newspaper, and radio based on a strict national probability sample.

Standard Rate and Data. Nine volumes on major media which include a variety of information in addition to prices for media in selected markets.

Starch Advertising Readership Service. Measures the reading of advertisements in magazines and newspapers and provides information on overall readership percentages, readers per dollar, and rank when grouped by product category.

INDEXES AND ABSTRACTS

Accountants Digest. L. L. Briggs. A digest of articles appearing currently in accounting periodicals.

Accountants Index. American Institute of Certified Public Accountants. An index to books, pamphlets, and articles on accounting and finance.

Accounting Articles. Commerce Clearing House. Loose-leaf index to articles in accounting and business periodicals.

Advertising Age Editorial Index. Crain Communications, Inc. Index to articles in *Advertising Age.*

American Statistical Index. Congressional Information Service. A comprehensive two-part annual index to the statistical publications of the U.S. government.

Applied Science & Technology Index. H. W. Wilson Co. Reviews over 200 periodicals relevant to the applied sciences, many of which pertain to business.

Battelle Library Review. (Formerly *Battelle Technical Review* to 1962.) Battelle Memorial Institute. Annotated bibliography of books, reports, and articles on automation and automatic processes.

Bulletin of Public Affairs Information Service. Public Affairs Information Service, Inc. (Since 1915—annual index.) A selective list of the latest books, pamphlets, government publications, reports of public and private agencies, and periodicals related to economic conditions, public administration, and international relations.

Business Education Index. McGraw-Hill Book Co. (Since 1940—annual index.) Annual author and subject index of books, articles, and theses on business education.

Business Periodicals Index. H. W. Wilson Co. A subject index to the disciplines of accounting, advertising, banking, general business, insurance, labor, management, and marketing.

Catalog of United States Census Publication. Washington, D.C.: Dept. of Commerce, Bureau of Census. Indexes all available at Census Bureau Data. Main divisions are agriculture, business, construction, foreign trade, government, guide to locating U.S. census information.

Computer and Information Systems. (Formerly *Information Processing Journal* to 1969.) Cambridge Communications Corporation.

Cumulative Index of NICB Publications. The National Industrial Conferences Board. Annual index of NICB books, pamphlets, and articles in the area of management of personnel.

Funk and Scott Index International. Investment Index Company. Indexes articles on foreign companies and industries from over 1,000 foreign and domestic periodicals and documents.

Guide to U.S. Government Publications. McLean, Va., Documents Index. Annotated guide to publications of various U.S. government agencies.

International Abstracts in Operations Research. Operations Research Society of America.

International Journal of Abstracts of Statistical Methods in Industry. The Hague, Netherlands: International Statistical Institute.

Management Information Guides. Gale Research Company. Bibliographical references to information sources for various business subjects.

Management Review. American Management Association.

Monthly Catalog of U.S. Government Publications. U.S. Government Printing Office. Continuing list of federal government publications.

Monthly Checklist of State Publications. U.S. Library of Congress, Exchange and Gift Division. Record of state documents received by Library of Congress.

New York Times Index. New York. Very detailed index of all articles in the *Times,* arranged alphabetically with many cross-references.

Psychological Abstracts. American Psychological Association.

Public Affairs Information Service. Public Affairs Information Service, Inc. A selective subject list of books, pamphlets, and government publications covering business, banking, and economics as well as subjects in the area of public affairs.

Reader's Guide to Periodical Literature. H. W. Wilson Co. Index by author and subject to selected U.S. general and nontechnical periodicals.

Sociological Abstracts. American Sociological Association.

The Wall Street Journal Index. Dow Jones & Company, Inc. An index of all articles in *The WSJ* grouped in two sections: corporate news and general news.

NAME INDEX

SUBJECT INDEX